CASES AND MATERIALS ON FEDERAL CONSTITUTIONAL LAW

Volume III
Introduction to the Federal Legislative Power

CASES AND MATERIALS ON FEDERAL CONSTITUTIONAL LAW

Volume III
Introduction to the Federal Legislative Power

Thomas H. Odom

VOLUME 3 ISBN: 978-1-4224-2207-6

Odom, Thomas H.
Introduction to interpretive methods & introduction to the federal judicial power / Thomas H. Odom.
p. cm. -- (Cases and materials on federal constitutional law ; v. 1)
Includes index.
ISBN 978-1-4224-2205-2 (soft cover)
1. Courts--United States. I. Title.
KF8718.O36 2008
347.73'1--dc22 2008036946

NOTE TO USERS

To ensure that you are using the latest materials available in this area, please be sure to periodically check the LexisNexis Law School web site for downloadable updates and supplements at www.lexisnexis.com/lawschool.

Editorial Offices
744 Broad Street, Newark, NJ 07102 (973) 820-2000
201 Mission St., San Francisco, CA 94105-1831 (415) 908-3200
www.lexisnexis.com

MATTHEW◆BENDER

INTRODUCTION TO THE MODULAR CASEBOOK SERIES

By now you have realized that the course materials assigned by your instructor have a very different form than "traditional" casebooks. The *Modular Casebook Series* is intentionally designed to break the mold. Course materials consist of one or more separate volumes selected from among a larger and growing set of volumes. Each of those volumes is only about 225 to 250 pages in length so that an instructor may "mix and match" a suitable number of volumes for a course of varying length and focus. Each volume is designed to serve an instructional purpose rather than as a treatise. As a result, the volumes are published in soft cover. Publication of the separate volumes in soft cover also permits course materials to be revised more easily so that they will incorporate recent developments. Moreover, by purchasing only the assigned volumes for a given course students are likely to recognize significant savings over the cost of a traditional casebook.

Traditional casebooks are often massive tomes, sometimes exceeding 1000 or even 1500 pages. Traditional casebooks are lengthy because they attempt to cover the entire breadth of material that might be useful to an instructor for a two-semester course of five or six credits. Even with six credits, different instructors may choose which portions of a traditional casebook do not fit within the time available. As a consequence, traditional casebooks may include a range of materials that would leave hundreds of pages unexplored in any particular six-credit class. For a student in a three or four credit course, such a book is hardly an efficient means for delivering the needed materials. Students purchase much more book than they need, at great expense. And students carry large, heavy books for months at a time.

Traditional casebooks are usually hard cover publications. It seems as though they are constructed so as to last as a reference work throughout decades of practice. In fact, as the presence of annual supplements to most casebooks makes clear, many are obsolete very shortly after publication. Treatises and hornbooks are designed to serve as reference works; casebooks serve a different purpose. Once again, the traditional format of casebooks seems to impose significant added costs on students without much reason.

The form of traditional casebooks increases the probability that the contents will become obsolete shortly after publication. The publication of lengthy texts in hardcover produces substantial delay between the time the author completes the final draft and the time the book reaches the hands of students. In addition, the broader scope of material addressed in a 1,000 or 1,500 page text means that portions of the text are more likely to be superceded by later developments than any particular narrowly-tailored volume in the *Modular Casebook Series*. Because individual volumes in the *Modular Casebook Series* may be revised without requiring revision of other volumes, the materials for any particular course will be less likely to require supplementation.

We hope you enjoy this innovative approach to course materials.

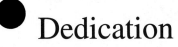

Dedication

For EBM & LAL

Acknowledgments

I would like to thank Dickinson School of Law and Pennsylvania State University for their financial support. I am indebted to my students whose daily interaction with me and the materials provide the impetus for constant improvement.

The hard work of numerous research assistants is reflected in this collection, notably: Michael Lynch, Justin Pickens, Chris VanLandingham and Brian McMorrow.

All remaining errors and omissions are my own.

Preface to the First Edition

Technological improvements permit the compilation of resources in a manner unthinkable when I was a law student. Materials that permit further examination of assigned reading can be delivered in a cost-effective manner and in a format more likely to be useful in practice than reams of photocopies. The associated DVD-ROM contains full, searchable text of several of the most important resources for interpreting the Constitution, lowering the wall between doctrinal courses and research courses.

With regard to assigned reading, there is no good reason to burden students with stacks of hand-outs or expensive annual supplements. Publication through the *Modular Casebook Series* virtually ensures that even very recent developments may be incorporated prior to publication. Moreover, if important cases are decided after publication of the latest edition of the volume, they will be included on the DVD-ROM. Cases and materials that shed additional light on matter in the hard copy casebook are also included.

I welcome comments from readers so that I may make further improvements in the next edition of this publication.

THO

TECHNICAL NOTE FROM THE EDITOR

The cases and other materials excerpted in this volume have been edited in an effort to enhance readability. Case citation forms have been revised to include the year of decision and reference to the volume number of the United States Reports. Many citations to secondary sources have been expanded to include the full names of authors or editors, and to reference the date of publication. Citations of multiple cases for a single proposition have been shortened in many places to reference only one or two prominent authorities.

In some places archaic language or spelling has been revised.

Headings were added to some of the longer decisions to permit ease of reference to various parts of the opinion. Such headings may also assist the reader in identifying a transition from one point to another.

None of these changes were intended to substantively alter the original materials.

With the exception of one or two cases per Volume, cases have been edited to a length suitable for reading as a single assignment. In order to achieve that result, many interesting but tangential points have been omitted. The length of some opinions also hindered the inclusion of excerpts from concurring or dissenting opinions. Where such opinions have been omitted, it is noted in the text. These omissions are not intended to present a biased view of the doctrine under review. In most instances, a subsequent case will present significant points raised by the omitted concurring and dissenting opinions. Any remaining unintentional bias is solely the responsibility of the editor.

THO

TABLE OF CONTENTS

TABLE OF CONTENTS

TABLE OF CONTENTS

CHAPTER 1

RAISING AND SPENDING REVENUE

The Constitution of the United States

We the People of the United States, in Order to form a more perfect Union, establish Justice, insure domestic Tranquility, provide for the common defence, promote the general Welfare, and secure the Blessings of Liberty to ourselves and our Posterity, do ordain and establish this Constitution for the United States of America.

Article I

Section 1. All legislative Powers herein granted shall be vested in a Congress of the United States, which shall consist of a Senate and House of Representatives.

Section 2. The House of Representatives shall be composed of Members chosen every second Year by the People of the several States, and the Electors in each State shall have the Qualifications requisite for Electors of the most numerous Branch of the State Legislature.

No person shall be a Representative who shall not have attained to the Age of twenty five Years, and been seven Years a Citizen of the United States, and who shall not, when elected, be an Inhabitant of that State in which he shall be chosen.

Representatives and direct Taxes shall be apportioned among the several States which may be included within this Union, according to their respective Numbers, which shall be determined by adding to the whole Number of free Persons, including those bound to Service for a Term of Years, and excluding Indians not taxed, three fifths of all other Persons. The actual Enumeration shall be made within three Years after the first Meeting of the Congress of the United States, and within every subsequent Term of ten Years, in such Manner as they shall by Law direct. The Number of Representatives shall not exceed one for every thirty Thousand, but each State shall have at Least one Representative; and until such enumeration shall be made, the State of New Hampshire shall be entitled to chuse three, Massachusetts eight, Rhode-Island and Providence Plantations one, Connecticut five, New-York six, New Jersey four, Pennsylvania eight, Delaware one, Maryland six, Virginia ten, North Carolina five, South Carolina five, and Georgia three.

When vacancies happen in the Representation from any State, the Executive Authority thereof shall issue Writs of Election to fill such Vacancies.

The House of Representatives shall chuse their Speaker and other Officers; and shall have the sole Power of Impeachment.

Section 3. The Senate of the United States shall be composed of two Senators from each State, chosen by the Legislature thereof, for six Years; and each Senator shall have one Vote.

Immediately after they shall be assembled in Consequence of the first Election, they shall be divided as equally as may be into three Classes. The Seats of the Senators of the first Class shall be vacated at the Expiration of the second Year, of the second Class at the Expiration of the fourth Year, and of the third Class at the Expiration of the sixth Year, so that one third may be chosen every second Year; and if Vacancies happen by Resignation, or otherwise, during the Recess of the Legislature of any State, the Executive thereof may make temporary Appointments until the next Meeting of the Legislature, which shall then fill such Vacancies.

No Person shall be a Senator who shall not have attained to the Age of thirty Years, and been nine Years a Citizen of the United States, and who shall not, when elected, be an Inhabitant of that State for which he shall be chosen.

The Vice President of the United States shall be President of the Senate, but shall have no Vote, unless they be equally divided.

The Senate shall chuse their other Officers, and also a President pro tempore, in the Absence of the Vice President, or when he shall exercise the Office of President of the United States.

The Senate shall have the sole Power to try all Impeachments. When sitting for that Purpose, they shall be on Oath or Affirmation. When the President of the United States is tried, the Chief Justice shall preside: and no Person shall be convicted without the Concurrence of two thirds of the Members present.

Judgment in Cases of Impeachment shall not extend further than to removal from Office, and disqualification to hold and enjoy any Office of honor, Trust or Profit under the United States: but the Party convicted shall nevertheless be liable and subject to Indictment, Trial, Judgment and Punishment, according to Law.

Section 4. The Times, Places and Manner of holding Elections for Senators and Representatives, shall be prescribed in each State by the Legislature thereof; but the Congress may at any time by Law make or alter such Regulations, except as to the Places of chusing Senators.

The Congress shall assemble at least once in every Year, and such Meeting shall be on the first Monday in December, unless they shall by Law appoint a different Day.

Section 5. Each House shall be the Judge of the Elections, Returns and Qualifications of its own Members, and a Majority of each shall constitute a Quorum to do Business; but a smaller Number may adjourn from day to day, and may be authorized to compel the Attendance of absent Members, in such Manner, and under such Penalties as each House may provide.

Each House may determine the Rules of its Proceedings, punish its Members for disorderly Behaviour, and, with the Concurrence of two thirds, expel a Member.

Each House shall keep a Journal of its Proceedings, and from time to time publish the same, excepting such Parts as may in their Judgment require Secrecy; and the Yeas and Nays of the Members of either House on any question shall, at the Desire of one fifth of those Present, be entered on the Journal.

Section 6. The Senators and Representatives shall receive a Compensation for their Services, to be ascertained by Law, and paid out of the Treasury of the United States. They shall in all Cases, except Treason, Felony and Breach of the Peace, be privileged from Arrest during their Attendance at the Session of their respective Houses, and in going to and returning from the same; and for any Speech or Debate in either House, they shall not be questioned in any other Place.

No Senator or Representative shall, during the Time for which he was elected, be appointed to any civil Office under the Authority of the United States, which shall have been created, or the Emoluments whereof shall have been encreased during such time; and no Person holding any Office under the United States, shall be a Member of either House during his Continuance in Office.

Section 7. All Bills for raising Revenue shall originate in the House of Representatives; but the Senate may propose or concur with Amendments as on other Bills.

Every Bill which shall have passed the House of Representatives and the Senate, shall, before it become a Law, be presented to the President of the United States; If he approve he shall sign it, but if not he shall return it, with his Objections to that House in which it shall have originated, who shall enter the Objections at large on their Journal, and proceed to reconsider it. If after such Reconsideration two thirds of that House shall agree to pass the Bill, it shall be sent, together with the Objections, to the other House, by which it shall likewise be reconsidered, and if approved by two thirds of that House, it shall become a Law. But in all such Cases the Votes of both Houses shall be determined by yeas and Nays, and the Names of the Persons voting for and against the Bill shall be entered on the Journal of each House respectively. If any Bill shall not be returned by the President within ten days (Sundays excepted) after it shall have been presented to him, the Same shall be a Law, in like Manner as if he had signed it, unless the Congress by their Adjournment prevent its Return in which Case it shall not be a Law.

Every Order, Resolution, or Vote to which the Concurrence of the Senate and House of Representatives may be necessary (except on a question of Adjournment) shall be presented to the President of the United States; and before the Same shall take Effect, shall be approved by him, or being disapproved by him, shall be repassed by two thirds of the Senate and House of Representatives, according to the Rules and Limitations prescribed in the Case of a Bill.

Section 8.   The Congress shall have Power To lay and collect Taxes, Duties, Imposts and Excises, to pay the Debts and provide for the common Defence and general Welfare of the United States; but all Duties, Imposts and Excises shall be uniform throughout the United States;

To borrow Money on the credit of the United States;

To regulate Commerce with foreign Nations, and among the several States, and with the Indian Tribes;

To establish an uniform Rule of Naturalization, and uniform Laws on the subject of Bankruptcies throughout the United States;

To coin Money, regulate the Value thereof, and foreign Coin, and fix the Standard of Weights and Measures;

To provide for the Punishment of counterfeiting the Securities and current Coin of the United States;

To establish Post Offices and post Roads;

To promote the Progress of Science and useful Arts, by securing for limited Times to Authors and Inventors the exclusive Right to their respective Writings and Discoveries;

To constitute Tribunals inferior to the supreme Court;

To define and punish Piracies and Felonies committed on the high Seas, and Offences against the Law of Nations;

To declare War, grant Letters of Marque and Reprisal, and make Rules concerning Captures on Land and Water;

To raise and support Armies, but no Appropriation of Money to that Use shall be for a longer Term than two Years;

To provide and maintain a Navy;

To make Rules for the Government and Regulation of the land and naval Forces;

To provide for calling forth the Militia to execute the Laws of the Union, suppress Insurrections and repel Invasions;

To provide for organizing, arming, and disciplining, the Militia, and for governing such Part of them as may be employed in the Service of the United States, reserving to the States respectively, the Appointment of the Officers, and the Authority of training the Militia according to the discipline prescribed by Congress;

To exercise exclusive Legislation in all Cases whatsoever, over such District (not exceeding ten Miles square) as may, by Cession of particular States, and the Acceptance of Congress, become the Seat of the Government of the United States, and to exercise like Authority over all Places purchased by the Consent of the Legislature of the State in which the Same shall be, for the Erection of Forts, Magazines, Arsenals, dock-Yards, and other needful Buildings; — And

To make all Laws which shall be necessary and proper for carrying into Execution the foregoing Powers, and all other Powers vested by this Constitution in the Government of the United States, or in any Department or Officer thereof.

Section 9.   The Migration or Importation of such Persons as any of the States now existing shall think proper to admit, shall not be prohibited by the Congress prior to the Year one thousand eight hundred and eight, but a Tax or duty may be imposed on such Importation, not exceeding ten dollars for each Person.

The Privilege of the Writ of Habeas Corpus shall not be suspended, unless when in Cases of Rebellion or Invasion the public Safety may require it.

No Bill of Attainder or ex post facto Law shall be passed.

No Capitation, or other direct, Tax shall be laid, unless in Proportion to the Census or Enumeration herein before directed to be taken.

No Tax or Duty shall be laid on Articles exported from any State.

No Preference shall be given by any Regulation of Commerce or Revenue to the Ports of one State over those of another; nor shall Vessels bound to, or from, one State, be obliged to enter, clear, or pay Duties in another.

No Money shall be drawn from the Treasury, but in Consequence of Appropriations made by Law; and a regular Statement and Account of the Receipts and Expenditures of all public Money shall be published from time to time.

No Title of Nobility shall be granted by the United States: And no Person holding any Office of Profit or Trust under them, shall, without the Consent of the Congress, accept of any present, Emolument, Office, or Title, of any kind whatever, from any King, Prince, or foreign State.

Section 10.   No State shall enter into any Treaty, Alliance, or Confederation; grant Letters of Marque and Reprisal; coin Money; emit Bills of Credit; make any Thing but gold and silver Coin a Tender in Payment of Debts; pass any Bill of Attainder, ex post facto Law, or Law impairing the Obligation of Contracts, or grant any Title of Nobility.

No State shall, without the Consent of the Congress, lay any Imposts or Duties on Imports or Exports, except what may be absolutely necessary for executing it's inspection Laws: and the net Produce of all Duties and Imposts, laid by any State on Imports or Exports, shall be for the Use of the Treasury of the United States; and all such Laws shall be subject to the Revision and Controul of the Congress.

No State shall, without the Consent of Congress, lay any Duty of Tonnage, keep Troops, or Ships of War in time of Peace, enter into any Agreement or Compact with another State, or with a foreign Power, or engage in War, unless actually invaded, or in such imminent Danger as will not admit of delay.

Article II

Section 1.   The executive Power shall be vested in a President of the United States of America. He shall hold his Office during the Term of four Years, and, together with the Vice President, chosen for the same Term, be elected as follows

Each State shall appoint, in such Manner as the Legislature thereof may direct, a Number of Electors, equal to the whole Number of Senators and Representatives to which the State may be entitled in the Congress: but no Senator or Representative, or Person holding an Office of Trust or Profit under the United States, shall be appointed an Elector.

The Electors shall meet in their respective States, and vote by Ballot for two Persons, of whom one at least shall not be an Inhabitant of the same State with themselves. And they shall make a List of all the Persons voted for, and of the Number of Votes for each; which List they shall sign and certify, and transmit sealed to the Seat of the Government of the United States, directed to the President of the Senate. The President of the Senate shall, in the Presence of the Senate and House of Representatives, open all the Certificates, and the Votes shall then be counted. The Person having the greatest Number of Votes shall be the President, if such Number be a Majority of the whole Number of Electors appointed; and if there be more than one who have such Majority, and have an equal Number of Votes, then the House of Representatives shall immediately chuse by Ballot one of them for President; and if no Person have a Majority, then from the five highest on the List the said House shall in like Manner chuse the President. But in chusing the President, the Votes shall be taken by States, the Representation from each State having one Vote; A quorum for this Purpose shall consist of a Member or Members from two thirds of the States, and a Majority of all the States shall be necessary to a Choice. In every Case, after the Choice of the President, the Person having the greatest Number of Votes of the Electors shall be the Vice President. But if there should remain two or more who have equal Votes, the Senate shall chuse from them by Ballot the Vice President.

The Congress may determine the Time of chusing the Electors, and the Day on which they shall give their Votes; which Day shall be the same throughout the United States.

No Person except a natural born Citizen, or a Citizen of the United States, at the time of the Adoption of this Constitution, shall be eligible to the Office of President; neither shall any Person be eligible to that Office who shall not have attained to the Age of thirty five Years, and been fourteen Years a Resident within the United States.

In the Case of the Removal of the President from Office, or of his Death, Resignation, or Inability to discharge the Powers and Duties of the said Office, the Same shall devolve on the Vice President, and the Congress may by Law provide for the Case of Removal, Death, Resignation or Inability, both of the President and Vice President, declaring what Officer shall then act as President, and such Officer shall act accordingly, until the Disability be removed, or a President shall be elected.

The President shall, at stated Times, receive for his Services, a Compensation, which shall neither be encreased nor diminished during the Period for which he shall have been elected, and he shall not receive within that Period any other Emolument from the United States, or any of them.

Before he enter on the Execution of his Office, he shall take the following Oath or Affirmation: — "I do solemnly swear (or affirm) that I will faithfully execute the Office of the President of the United States, and will to the best of my Ability, preserve, protect and defend the Constitution of the United States."

Section 2. The President shall be the Commander in Chief of the Army and Navy of the United States, and of the Militia of the several States, when called into the actual service of the United States; he may require the Opinion, in writing, of the principal Officer in each of the executive Departments, upon any Subject relating to the Duties of their respective Offices, and he shall have Power to grant Reprieves and Pardons for Offenses against the United States, except in Cases of Impeachment.

He shall have Power, by and with the Advice and Consent of the Senate, to make Treaties, provided two thirds of the Senators present concur; and he shall nominate, and by and with the Advice and Consent of the Senate, shall appoint Ambassadors, other public Ministers and Consuls, Judges of the supreme Court, and all other Officers of the United States, whose Appointments are not herein otherwise provided for, and which shall be established by Law but the Congress may by Law vest the Appointment of such inferior Officers, as they think proper, in the President alone, in the Courts of Law, or in the Heads of Departments.

The President shall have Power to fill up all Vacancies that may happen during the Recess of the Senate, by granting Commissions which shall expire at the End of their next Session.

Section 3. He shall from time to time give to the Congress Information of the State of the Union, and recommend to their Consideration such Measures as he shall judge necessary and expedient; he may, on extraordinary Occasions, convene both Houses, or either of them, and in Case of Disagreement between them, with Respect to the Time of Adjournment, he may adjourn them to such Time as he shall think proper; he shall receive Ambassadors and other public Ministers; he shall take Care that the Laws be faithfully executed, and shall Commission all the Officers of the United States.

Section 4. The President, Vice President and all civil Officers of the United States, shall be removed from Office on Impeachment for, and Conviction of, Treason, Bribery, or other high Crimes and Misdemeanors.

Article III

Section 1. The judicial Power of the United States, shall be vested in one supreme Court, and in such inferior Courts as the Congress may from time to time ordain and establish. The Judges, both of the supreme and inferior Courts, shall hold their Offices during good Behaviour, and shall, at stated Times, receive for their Services, a Compensation, which shall not be diminished during their Continuance in Office.

Section 2. The judicial Power shall extend to all Cases, in Law and Equity, arising under this Constitution, the Laws of the United States, and Treaties made, or which shall be made, under their Authority; — to all Cases affecting Ambassadors, other public Ministers and Consuls; — to all Cases of admiralty and maritime Jurisdiction; — to Controversies to which the United States shall be a Party; — to Controversies between two or more States; — between a State and Citizens of another State; — between Citizens of different States; — between Citizens of the same State claiming Lands under Grants of different States, and between a State, or the Citizens thereof, and foreign States, Citizens or Subjects.

In all cases affecting Ambassadors, other public Ministers and Consuls, and those in which a State shall be a Party, the supreme Court shall have original Jurisdiction. In all the other Cases before mentioned, the supreme Court shall have appellate Jurisdiction, both as to Law and Fact, with such Exceptions, and under such Regulations as the Congress shall make.

The Trial of all Crimes, except in Cases of Impeachment, shall be by Jury; and such Trial shall be held in the State where the said Crimes shall have been committed; but when not committed within any State, the Trial shall be at such Place or Places as the Congress may by Law have directed.

Section 3. Treason against the United States, shall consist only in levying War against them, or in adhering to their Enemies, giving them Aid or Comfort. No Person shall be convicted of Treason unless on the Testimony of two Witnesses to the same overt Act, or on Confession in open Court.

The Congress shall have Power to declare the Punishment of Treason, but no Attainder of Treason shall work Corruption of Blood, or Forfeiture except during the Life of the Person attainted.

Article IV

Section 1. Full Faith and Credit shall be given in each State to the public Acts, Records, and judicial Proceedings of every other State. And the Congress may by general Laws prescribe the Manner in which such Acts, Records and Proceedings shall be proved, and the Effect thereof.

Section 2. The Citizens of each State shall be entitled to all Privileges and Immunities of Citizens in the several States.

A Person charged in any State with Treason, Felony, or other Crime, who shall flee from Justice, and be found in another State, shall on Demand of the executive Authority of the State from which he fled, be delivered up, to be removed to the State having Jurisdiction of the Crime.

No Person held to Service or Labour in one State, under the Laws thereof, escaping into another, shall, in Consequence of any Law or Regulation therein, be discharged from such Service or Labour, but shall be delivered up on Claim of the Party to whom such Service or Labour may be due.

Section 3. New States may be admitted by the Congress into this Union; but no new State shall be formed or erected within the Jurisdiction of any other State; nor any State be formed by the Junction of two or more States, or Parts of States, without the Consent of the Legislatures of the States concerned as well as of the Congress.

The Congress shall have Power to dispose of and make all needful Rules and Regulations respecting the Territory or other Property belonging to the United States; and nothing in this Constitution shall be so construed to Prejudice any Claims of the United States, or of any particular State.

Section 4. The United States shall guarantee to every State in this Union a Republican Form of Government, and shall protect each of them against Invasion; and on Application of the Legislature, or of the Executive (when the Legislature cannot be convened) against domestic Violence.

Article V

The Congress, whenever two thirds of both Houses shall deem it necessary, shall propose Amendments to this Constitution, or, on the Application of the Legislatures of two thirds of the several States, shall call a Convention for proposing Amendments, which, in either Case, shall be valid to all Intents and Purposes, as Part of this Constitution, when ratified by the Legislatures of three fourths of the several States, or by Conventions in three fourths thereof, as the one or the other Mode of Ratification may be proposed by the Congress; provided that no Amendment which may be made prior to the Year One thousand eight hundred and eight shall in any Manner affect the first and fourth Clauses in the Ninth Section of the first Article; and that no State, without its Consent, shall be deprived of it's equal Suffrage in the Senate.

Article VI

All Debts contracted and Engagements entered into, before the adoption of this Constitution, shall be as valid against the United States under this Constitution, as under the Confederation.

This Constitution, and the Laws of the United States which shall be made in Pursuance thereof; and all Treaties made, or which shall be made, under the Authority of the United States, shall be the supreme Law of the Land; and the Judges in every State shall be bound thereby, any Thing in the Constitution or Laws of any State to the Contrary notwithstanding.

The Senators and Representatives before mentioned, and the members of the several State Legislatures, and all executive and judicial Officers, both of the United States and of the several States, shall be bound by Oath or Affirmation, to support this Constitution; but no religious Test shall ever be required as a Qualification to any Office or public Trust under the United States.

Article VII

The Ratification of the Conventions of nine States, shall be sufficient for the Establishment of this Constitution between the States so ratifying the Same.

Go. Washington — Presidt.
And deputy from Virginia

New Hampshire
John Langdon
Nicholas Gilman

New Jersey
Wil: Livingston
David Brearley
Wm. Paterson
Jona: Dayton

Massachusetts
Nathaniel Gorham
Rufus King
Connecticut
Wm. Saml. Johnson
Roger Sherman
New York
Alexander Hamilton

Pennsylvania
B Franklin
Thomas Mifflin
Robt. Morris
Geo. Clymer
Thos. Fitzsimons
Jared Ingersoll
James Wilson
Gouv Morris

Delaware
Geo: Read
Cunning Bedford jun
John Dickinson
Richard Bassett
Jaco: Broom

North Carolina
Wm: Blount
Richd. Dobbs Spaight.
Hu Williamson

Maryland
James McHenry
Dan of St. Thos. Jenifer
Danl. Carroll

South Carolina
J. Rutledge
Charles Cotesworth Pinckney
Pierce Butler.

Virginia
John Blair —
James Madison Jr.

Georgia
William Few
Abr Baldwin

The Bill of Rights
(1791)

Amendment I

Congress shall make no law respecting an establishment of religion, or prohibiting the free exercise thereof; or abridging the freedom of speech, or of the press; or the right of the people peaceably to assemble, and to petition the government for a redress of grievances.

Amendment II

A well regulated militia, being necessary to the security of a free state, the right of the people to keep and bear arms, shall not be infringed.

Amendment III

No soldier shall, in time of peace be quartered in any house, without the consent of the owner, nor in time of war, but in a manner to be prescribed by law.

Amendment IV

The right of the people to be secure in their persons, houses, papers, and effects, against unreasonable searches and seizures, shall not be violated, and no warrants shall issue, but upon probable cause, supported by oath or affirmation, and particularly describing the place to be searched, and the persons or things to be seized.

Amendment V

No person shall be held to answer for a capital, or otherwise infamous crime, unless on a presentment or indictment of a grand jury, except in cases arising in the land or naval forces, or in the militia, when in actual service in time of war or public danger; nor shall any person be subject for the same offense to be twice put in jeopardy of life or limb; nor shall be compelled in any criminal case to be a witness against himself, nor be deprived of life, liberty, or property, without due process of law; nor shall private property be taken for public use, without just compensation.

Amendment VI

In all criminal prosecutions, the accused shall enjoy the right to a speedy and public trial, by an impartial jury of the state and district wherein the crime shall have been committed, which district shall have been previously ascertained by law, and to be informed of the nature and cause of the accusation; to be confronted with the witnesses against him; to have compulsory process for obtaining witnesses in his favor, and to have the assistance of counsel for his defense.

Amendment VII

In suits at common law, where the value in controversy shall exceed twenty dollars, the right of trial by jury shall be preserved, and no fact tried by a jury, shall be otherwise reexamined in any court of the United States, then according to the rules of the common law.

Amendment VIII

Excessive bail shall not be required, nor excessive fines imposed, nor cruel and unusual punishments inflicted.

Amendment IX

The enumeration in the Constitution, of certain rights, shall not be construed to deny or disparage others retained by the people.

Amendment X

The powers not delegated to the United States by the Constitution, nor prohibited by it to the states, are reserved to the states respectively, or to the people.

Later Amendments

Amendment XI

(1798)

The judicial power of the United States shall not be construed to extend to any suit in law or equity, commenced or prosecuted against one of the United States by Citizens of another State, or by Citizens or Subjects of any Foreign State.

Amendment XII

(1804)

The Electors shall meet in their respective states and vote by ballot for President and Vice-President, one of whom, at least, shall not be an inhabitant of the same state with themselves; they shall name in their ballots the person voted for as President, and in distinct ballots the person voted for as Vice-President, and they shall make distinct lists of all persons voted for as President, and of all persons voted for as Vice-President, and of the number of votes for each, which lists they shall sign and certify, and transmit sealed to the seat of the government of the United States, directed to the President of the Senate; — The President of the Senate shall, in the presence of the Senate and House of Representatives, open all the certificates and the votes shall then be counted; — the person having the greatest number of votes for President, shall be the President, if such number be a majority of the whole number of Electors appointed; and if no person have such majority, then from the persons having the highest numbers not exceeding three on the list of those voted for as President, the House of Representatives shall choose immediately, by ballot, the President. But in choosing the President, the votes shall be taken by states, the representation from each state having one vote; a quorum for this purpose shall consist of a member or members from two-thirds of the states, and a majority of all the states shall be necessary to a choice. And if the House of Representatives shall not choose a President whenever the right of choice shall devolve upon them, before the fourth day of March next following, then the Vice-President shall act as President, as in the case of the death or other constitutional disability of the President. The person having the greatest number of votes as Vice-President, shall be the Vice-President, if such number be a majority of the whole number of Electors appointed, and if no person have a majority, then from the two highest numbers on the list, the Senate shall choose the Vice-President; a quorum for the purpose shall consist of two-thirds of the whole number of Senators, and a majority of the whole number shall be necessary to a choice. But no person constitutionally ineligible to the office of President shall be eligible to that of Vice-President of the United States.

Amendment XIII

(1865)

Section 1.   Neither slavery nor involuntary servitude, except as a punishment for crime whereof the party shall have been duly convicted, shall exist within the United States, or any place subject to their jurisdiction.

Section 2.   Congress shall have power to enforce this article by appropriate legislation.

Amendment XIV

(1868)

Section 1.   All persons born or naturalized in the United States, and subject to the jurisdiction thereof, are citizens of the United States and of the State wherein they reside. No State shall make or enforce any law which shall abridge the privileges or immunities of citizens of the United States; nor shall any State deprive any person of life, liberty, or property, without due process of law; nor deny to any person within its jurisdiction the equal protection of the laws.

Section 2. Representatives shall be apportioned among the several States according to their respective numbers, counting the whole number of persons in each State, excluding Indians not taxed. But when the right to vote at any election for the choice of electors for President and Vice President of the United States, Representatives in Congress, the Executive and Judicial officers of a State, or the members of the Legislature thereof, is denied to any of the male inhabitants of such State, being twenty-one years of age, and citizens of the United States, or in any way abridged, except for participation in rebellion, or other crime, the basis of representation therein shall be reduced in the proportion which the number of such male citizens shall bear to the whole number of male citizens twenty-one years of age in such State.

Section 3. No person shall be a Senator or Representative in Congress, or elector of President and Vice President, or hold any office, civil or military, under the United States, or under any State, who, having previously taken an oath, as a member of Congress, or as an officer of the United States, or as a member of any State legislature, or as an executive or judicial officer of any State, to support the Constitution of the United States, shall have engaged in insurrection or rebellion against the same, or given aid or comfort to the enemies thereof. But Congress may by a vote of two-thirds of each House, remove such disability.

Section 4. The validity of the public debt of the United States, authorized by law, including debts incurred for payment of pensions and bounties for services in suppressing insurrection or rebellion, shall not be questioned. But neither the United States nor any State shall assume or pay any debt or obligation incurred in aid of insurrection or rebellion against the United States, or any claim for the loss or emancipation of any slave; but all such debts, obligations and claims shall be held illegal and void.

Section 5. The Congress shall have power to enforce, by appropriate legislation, the provisions of this article.

Amendment XV

(1870)

Section 1. The right of citizens of the United States to vote shall not be denied or abridged by the United States or by any State on account of race, color, or previous condition of servitude.

Section 2. The Congress shall have power to enforce this article by appropriate legislation.

Amendment XVI

(1913)

The Congress shall have power to lay and collect taxes on incomes, from whatever source derived, without apportionment among the several States, and without regard to any census or enumeration.

Amendment XVII

(1913)

The Senate of the United States shall be composed of two Senators from each State, elected by the people thereof, for six years; and each Senator shall have one vote. The electors in each State shall have the qualifications requisite for electors of the most numerous branch of the State legislature.

When vacancies happen in the representation of any State in the Senate, the executive authority of such State shall issue writs of election to fill such vacancies: *Provided,* That the legislature of any State may empower the executive thereof to make temporary appointments until the people fill the vacancies by election as the legislature may direct.

This amendment shall not be so construed as to effect the election or term of any Senator chosen before it becomes valid as part of the Constitution.

Amendment XVIII
(1919)

Section 1. After one year from the ratification of this article the manufacture, sale, or transportation of intoxicating liquors within, the importation thereof into, or the exportation thereof from the United States and all territory subject to the jurisdiction thereof for beverage purposes is hereby prohibited.

Section 2. The Congress and the several States shall have concurrent power to enforce this article by appropriate legislation.

Section 3. This article shall be inoperative unless it shall have been ratified as an amendment to the Constitution by the legislatures of the several States, as provided in the Constitution, within seven years from the date of the submission hereof to the States by the Congress.

Amendment XIX
(1920)

The right of citizens of the United States to vote shall not be denied or abridged by the United States or by any State on account of sex.

Congress shall have power to enforce this article by appropriate legislation.

Amendment XX
(1933)

Section 1. The terms of the President and Vice President shall end at noon on the 20th day of January, and the terms of Senators and Representatives at noon on the 3d day of January, of the years in which such terms would have ended if this article had not been ratified; and the terms of their successors shall then begin.

Section 2. The Congress shall assemble at least once in every year, and such meeting shall begin at noon on the 3d day of January, unless they shall by law appoint a different day.

Section 3. If, at the time fixed for the beginning of the term of the President, the President elect shall have died, the Vice President elect shall become President. If a President shall not have been chosen before the time fixed for the beginning of his term, or if the President elect shall have failed to qualify, then the Vice President elect shall act as President until a President shall have qualified; and the Congress may by law provide for the case wherein neither a President elect nor a Vice President elect shall have qualified, declaring who shall then act as President, or the manner in which one who is to act shall be selected, and such person shall act accordingly until a President or Vice President shall have qualified.

Section 4. The Congress may by law provide for the case of the death of any of the persons from whom the House of Representatives may choose a President whenever the right of choice shall have devolved upon them, and for the case of the death of any of the persons from whom the Senate may choose a Vice President whenever the right of choice shall have devolved upon them.

Section 5. Sections 1 and 2 shall take effect on the 15th day of October following the ratification of this article.

Section 6. This article shall be inoperative unless it shall have been ratified as an amendment to the Constitution by the legislatures of three-fourths of the several States within seven years from the date of its submission.

Amendment XXI

(1933)

Section 1.   The eighteenth article of amendment to the Constitution of the United States is hereby repealed.

Section 2.   The transportation or importation into any State, territory, or possession of the United States for delivery or use therein of intoxicating liquors, in violation of the laws thereof, is hereby prohibited.

Section 3.   This article shall be inoperative unless it shall have been ratified as an amendment to the Constitution by conventions in the several States, as provided in the Constitution, within seven years from the date of the submission hereof to the States by the Congress.

Amendment XXII

(1951)

Section 1.   No person shall be elected to the office of the President more than twice, and no person who has held the office of President, or acted as President, for more than two years of a term to which some other person was elected President shall be elected to the office of the President more than once. But this article shall not apply to any person holding the office of President when this article was proposed by the Congress, and shall not prevent any person who may be holding the office of President, or acting as President, during the term within which this article becomes operative from holding the office of President or acting as President during the remainder of such term.

Section 2.   This article shall be inoperative unless it shall have been ratified as an amendment to the Constitution by the legislatures of three-fourths of the several States within seven years from the date of its submission to the States by the Congress.

Amendment XXIII

(1961)

Section 1.   The District constituting the seat of government of the United States shall appoint in such manner as the Congress may direct:

A number of electors of President and Vice President equal to the whole number of Senators and Representatives in Congress to which the District would be entitled if it were a State, but in no event more than the least populous State; they shall be in addition to those appointed by the States, but they shall be considered, for the purposes of the election of the President and Vice President, to be electors appointed by a State; and they shall meet in the District and perform such duties as provided by the twelfth article of amendment.

Section 2.   The Congress shall have power to enforce this article by appropriate legislation.

Amendment XXIV

(1964)

Section 1.   The right of citizens of the United States to vote in any primary or other election for President or Vice President, for electors for President or Vice President, or for Senator or Representative in Congress, shall not be denied or abridged by the United States or any State by reason of failure to pay any poll tax or other tax.

Section 2.   The Congress shall have the power to enforce this article by appropriate legislation.

Amendment XXV

(1967)

Section 1. In case of the removal of the President from office or his death or resignation, the Vice President shall become President.

Section 2. Whenever there is a vacancy in the office of the Vice President, the President shall nominate a Vice President who shall take office upon confirmation by a majority vote of both Houses of Congress.

Section 3. Whenever the President transmits to the President pro tempore of the Senate and the Speaker of the House of Representatives his written declaration that he is unable to discharge the powers and duties of his office, and until he transmits to them a written declaration to the contrary, such powers and duties shall be discharged by the Vice President as Acting President.

Section 4. Whenever the Vice President and a majority of either the principal officers of the executive departments or such other body as Congress may by law provide, transmit to the President pro tempore of the Senate and the Speaker of the House of Representatives their written declaration that the President is unable to discharge the powers and duties of his office, the Vice President shall immediately assume the powers and duties of the office as Acting President.

Thereafter, when the President transmits to the President pro tempore of the Senate and the Speaker of the House of Representatives his written declaration that no inability exists, he shall resume the powers and duties of his office unless the Vice President and a majority of either the principal officers of the executive department or of such other body as Congress may by law provide, transmit within four days to the President pro tempore of the Senate and the Speaker of the House of Representatives their written declaration that the President is unable to discharge the powers and duties of his office. Thereupon Congress shall decide the issue, assembling within forty-eight hours for that purpose if not in session. If the Congress, within twenty-one days after receipt of the latter written declaration, or, if Congress is not in session, within twenty-one days after Congress is required to assemble, determine by two-thirds vote of both Houses that the President is unable to discharge the powers and duties of his office, the Vice President shall continue to discharge the same as Acting President; otherwise, the President shall resume the powers and duties of his office.

Amendment XXVI

(1971)

Section 1. The right of citizens of the United States, who are 18 years of age or older, to vote, shall not be denied or abridged by the United States or any State on account of age.

Section 2. The Congress shall have the power to enforce this article by appropriate legislation.

Amendment XXVII

(1992)

No law varying the compensation for the services of the Senators and Representatives shall take effect until an election of Representatives shall have intervened.

If your instructor assigned *Volume 2*, you previously encountered limitations on the manner in which Congress may enact legislation. The procedural requirements of bicameralism, presentment, and the non-delegation doctrine apply without regard to the substantive policy Congress seeks to pursue.

Even when Congress complies with the applicable process in enacting legislation, the Constitution imposes substantive limits on the exercise of enumerated powers. Two of the most important powers of any government are the ability to raise revenue and to spend those revenues to accomplish its ends.

Volume I in this series introduced five commonly-accepted forms of argument in problems involving interpretation of the Constitution: (1) the broad *structure* of government established by the Constitution, (2) the *historical setting* from which the Constitution emerged, (3) the *text* of the Constitution itself, (4) the *tradition* or historical precedent of understanding the Constitution in a particular matter, and (5) the weight of *judicial precedent* in light of the doctrine of *stare decisis*. Those forms of argument were introduced through materials primarily directed to the structure and power of the federal judiciary.

Each of the five forms of argument were introduced in *Volume I* with materials selected to support the different forms of argument, including ratification debates, legislation from the First Congress, letters illustrating early interpretations of the Constitution, and early judicial precedents. The next step beyond understanding the various forms of argument is the identification and use of source material to support one or more arguments.

Exercise 1:

Apply the first four forms of argument to questions regarding the scope of the congressional power, particularly with respect to the power to raise and spend revenue.

(1)   If *Volume I* was assigned prior to this Volume, re-read the description of government prepared in *Volume I, Exercise 1*. Regardless of whether you previously performed that exercise, consider what the *structure* of government suggests is the scope of Congress' power to raise and spend revenue. Conversely, what does the structure of government suggest about the power of Congress to limit the States' ability to raise and spend revenue? What does the structure of government suggest about the power of the States to limit congressional power to raise and spend revenue?

(2)   (Re)read the U.S. Constitution of 1789 and the Bill of Rights. What does the *text* of the Constitution provide as to the power of Congress to raise and spend revenue?

- What form(s) of revenue-raising measures, if any, are *expressly* authorized?

- What additional form(s) of revenue-raising measures, if any, are *implicitly* authorized?

- What form(s) of revenue-raising measures, if any, are *expressly* prohibited?

- What additional form(s) of revenue-raising measures, if any, are *implicitly* prohibited?

In summary, does the *text* indicate that the Constitution grants Congress a virtually-unlimited range of measures to raise revenue or does the Constitution grant only a few specifically-identified options? That is, which of the diagrams below better illustrates the scope of the federal power to raise revenue:

Article I, Section 8

(outer circle represents all forms of revenue measures)

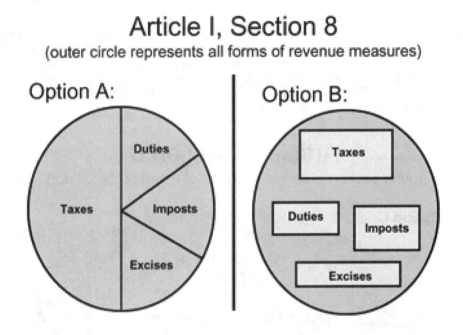

Option A:

Duties

Taxes

Imposts

Excises

Option B:

Taxes

Duties

Imposts

Excises

Does the Constitution limit the *purposes* for which Congress may either raise or spend revenue? Or, does the *text* of the Constitution grant Congress virtually-unlimited discretion as to reasons for raising revenue and the ways in which it may be spent?

(3) Consider both the *structure* of government established by the Constitution and the *text* of the Constitution in answering the following questions:

(a) Are there any limitations on the manner in which some, or all, revenue-raising measures must be structured?

(b) If enacted by Congress in 1791, what constitutional objections, if any, could be raised against each of the following revenue-raising measures:

- a levy of $10 per year on every inhabitant, over the age of 21, within the United States for more than three of the preceding twelve months;

- a levy of $10 on every horse imported into the United States to be paid at the time of importation;

- a levy of $10 on every horse exported from the United States to be paid at the time of export;

- a levy of $10 on every horse imported into the United States via an Atlantic-coast port and $5 on every horse imported into the United States via a Gulf-coast port or via a Mississippi River port, with the respective levy to be paid at the time of importation;

- a levy of 1% of the annual net income of all inns and other houses of public lodging that serve travelers from outside the State in which the establishment is located.

(c) What forms of revenue-raising measures are "direct" that must be apportioned in accordance with the census?

(d)   What forms of revenue-raising measures must be "uniform throughout the United States"?

(e)   Is it possible for a revenue-raising measure to be levied in a manner so as both to be apportioned and to be uniform? How so? If not, are all revenue-raising measures subject to one or the other of those requirements (Option C) or are some permissible revenue-raising measures not subject to either requirement (Option D)? That is, which of the diagrams below better illustrates the scope of the federal power to raise revenue:

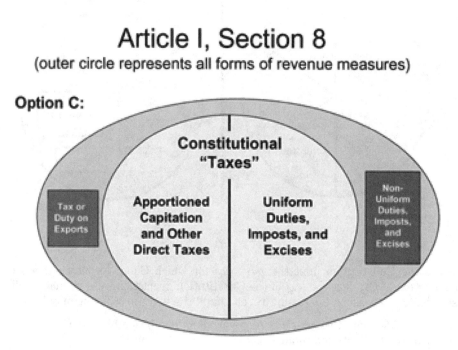

Article I, Section 8

(outer circle represents all forms of revenue measures)

Option C:

Constitutional "Taxes"

Tax or Duty on Exports

Apportioned Capitation and Other Direct Taxes

Uniform Duties, Imposts, and Excises

Non-Uniform Duties, Imposts, and Excises

Article I, Section 8

(outer circle represents all forms of revenue measures)

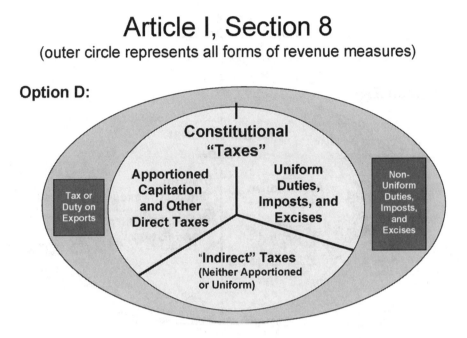

Option D:

If all revenue-raising measures are subject to *either* the requirement of apportionment *or* the requirement of uniformity, are there indirect taxes subject to the uniformity requirement that are not "duties, imposts, and excises" as illustrated in the following Diagram?

Article I, Section 8

(outer circle represents all forms of revenue measures)

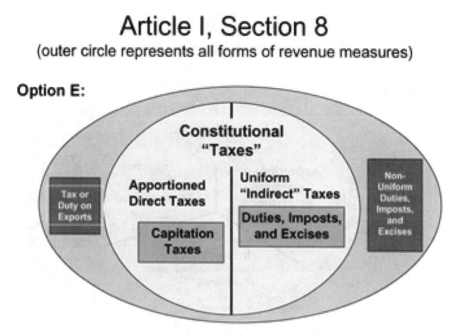

Option E:

(f) Provided it follows the proper limitation(s) of apportionment and/or uniformity, is there any form of revenue-raising measure beyond the power of Congress? If so and/or if you determined that at least some revenue-raising measures must be apportioned and at least some other measures must be uniform, could Congress overcome those boundaries by legislating pursuant to its authority to regulate commerce? Why or why not?

(g) Could Congress levy a tax on the income collected by a State? Could Congress tax the land on which state capitols are situated? Why or why not?

(h) Could a State levy a tax on the salary the U.S. Treasury paid federal officers who reside within the State? Could a State tax the land on which a U.S. Post Office is situated? Why or why not?

(i) Are there any limits to the power of Congress to require recipients of funds from the U.S. Treasury to comply with specified obligations?

(4) The DVD-ROM associated with these printed materials contains additional "Tools for Textualists" that may permit you to frame additional textual arguments. You may want to examine the partial concordance or a dictionary that defines terms that may have been more-familiar to those who drafted and ratified the Constitution. If you do so, does the additional information change your answer to Question 2 or Question 3?

(5) The DVD-ROM contains additional "Tools for Originalists" including the text of many essays written to influence the decision of whether to ratify the Constitution. You may want to examine those materials to support an argument regarding the shared public understanding of the Constitution. If you do so, does the additional information change your answer to Question 2 or Question 3?

(6) The DVD-ROM contains additional "Tools for Originalists & Traditionalists — early Legislation" including the full text of a selection of "Early Revenue Measures." You may want to examine those materials, particularly the statutes enacted by the First

Congress. What does the text of these post-ratification *historical* sources reveal regarding the scope of congressional power to raise revenue?

A.   Early Understandings and the Apportionment Requirement

THE ORIGINS OF THE FEDERAL TAXING POWER

1. Historical Context

The first Continental Congress confronted two threshold issues to the formation of any confederation government. *First,* upon what basis would the several States be represented in the Congress; that is, how would the relative voting power of the States be settled? *Second,* upon what basis would the several States contribute to the support of the central government; that is, how would the tax burden be allocated among the States? The two issues quickly became intertwined.

As an initial matter, the first Continental Congress determined that States would have equal representation of one vote each simply as a practical matter that insufficient data was available regarding the population, extent of property, and value of property. The resolution for equal representation specifically cited the lack of data as the basis for the decision so as to simply postpone a permanent resolution of the issue.[1]

In the first measure to raise revenue to support the war, the Continental Congress apportioned the sum to be raised from each of the colonies according to their respective populations but left it to each colony to determine how best to raise the funds.[2] Once again, data was unavailable to permit the actual apportionment so the Continental Congress specified sums for each colony in anticipation of later adjustments.

The same month that the Continental Congress voted to declare independence, it considered a plan of confederation. The first draft of the terms of confederation that were presented to the whole Continental Congress by its committee would have formally perpetuated one vote per State but requisitions proportionate to the population of each State.[3] The proposal prompted heated debate. Eventually, equal representation of each State prevailed in the plan submitted to the States for adoption.[4] After debating various bases on which the tax burden was to be allocated, the proposed Articles of Confederation apportioned the burden among the several States on the basis of the value of real property.[5]

It was March 1, 1781, before the last State ratified the Articles of Confederation and they became operative. Even before the Articles of Confederation became operative, it was apparent that the central government required some other (or additional) means of raising revenue. On February 3, 1781, Congress requested authority to levy a duty on imported merchandise[6] but Rhode Island (and later Virginia) refused.[7]

---

[1] 1 JOURNALS OF THE CONTINENTAL CONGRESS 25 (1904 ed.) (Sept. 6, 1774) ("Resolved, That in determining questions in this Congress, each Colony or Province shall have one Vote. — The Congress not being possessed of, or at present able to procure proper materials for ascertaining the importance of each Colony."). The 1904 edition of the Journals, in 34 volumes, is available at *http://memory.loc.gov/ammem/amlaw/lwjc.html.*

[2] 2 JOURNALS OF THE CONTINENTAL CONGRESS 221 (1904 ed.) (July 29, 1775) ("That the proportion or quota of each colony be determined according to the number of Inhabitants, of all ages, including negroes and mulattoes in each colony."); *id.* (providing that revenue may be raised "in such manner as may be most effectual and best adapted to the conditions, circumstances, and usual mode of levying taxes in such colony").

[3] 5 JOURNALS OF THE CONTINENTAL CONGRESS 548, 550 (1904 ed.) (July 12, 1776).

[4] 9 JOURNALS OF THE CONTINENTAL CONGRESS 779–782 (1904 ed.) (Oct. 7, 1777).

[5] 9 JOURNALS OF THE CONTINENTAL CONGRESS 801–802 (1904 ed.) (Oct. 13, 1777).

[6] 19 JOURNALS OF THE CONTINENTAL CONGRESS 110 (1912 ed.) (Feb. 3, 1781). The proposal included other

Congress still had not attempted any valuation of property in the several States when James Madison, on January 27, 1783, unsuccessfully renewed the proposal to grant authority "to levy a duty on certain goods and merchandises, and also all prizes."[8] On March 7, 1783, Congress received a committee proposal to amend the Articles of Confederation to change the basis for apportionment of taxation from land valuation to the number of inhabitants. When Congress took up that report it raised again the question of how slaves should be counted in any such allocation. On March 25, 1783, Congress agreed to count five slaves as the equivalent of three freemen for purposes of allocating the expense of the central government among the States. On April 26, 1783, Congress forwarded the proposed amendment to the States for ratification. The proposal was still awaiting ratification when the Philadelphia Convention met in the summer of 1787.

Under this system, States freely disregarded requisitions from the central government.[9] No effort to value property for apportionment was ever even started. And the proposals to permit imposition of a duty on imported articles or change the basis of allocation from the value of land to the number of inhabitants both stalled.

2. Drafting History

At the outset of the Constitutional Convention, the Virginia Resolutions proposed to link the issues of representation in Congress and the tax burden to be allocated to each State.[10]

> Mr. Dickinson contended for the *actual* contributions of the States as the rule of their representation & suffrage in [the first branch]. By thus connecting the interest of the States with their duty, the latter would be sure to be performed.

> Mr. King remarked that it was uncertain what mode might be used in levying a national revenue; but that it was probable, imports would be one source of it. If the *actual* contributions were to be the rule the non-importing States, as Con[necticut] & N[ew] Jersey, w[oul]d be in a bad situation indeed. It might so happen that they w[oul]d have no representation. This situation of particular States had always been one powerful argument in favor of the 5 Per C[en]t impost.[11]

---

powers in addition to the revenue authority. With respect to revenue, the proposal was that Congress "should be vested with the exclusive right of laying duties upon all imported articles, . . . no such duty to be laid, but with the consent of nine states." *Id.* The proposal included limits on the imposition of any such duties. "Provided, that all duties and imposts laid by the United States in Congress assembled, shall always be a certain proportion of the value of the article or articles on which the same shall be laid; and the same article shall bear the same duty and impost throughout the said states without exemption: and provided that all such duties and imposts shall be for the perfecting of certain specified purposes, which purposes being perfected, the said duties and imposts so appropriated, shall cease . . . ." *Id.*

[7] *See* 24 Journals of the Continental Congress 101–102 (Jan. 30, 1783).

[8] 24 Journals of the Continental Congress 96 (Jan. 27, 1783); *see also id.* at 188 (Mar. 18, 1783) (proposing to levy "duties upon goods imported into the said states from any foreign port, island, or plantation" of specified percentages for various goods and on all other goods "a duty of five per cent. ad valorem").

[9] For example, of the $8,000,000 requisition for year 1782 (established in 1781), Congress received only $420,031 a month after the conclusion of 1782. *See* 24 Journals of the Continental Congress 102 (Jan. 30, 1783).

[10] 1 Max Farrand, Records of the Federal Convention of 1787, p. 20 (1966) (May 29, 1787) (Madison's notes).

[11] *Id.* at 196–97 (June 11, 1787) (Madison's notes). For further discussion of the reference to revenue or property as the basis for apportionment, see *id.* at 525 (July 5, 1787) (Journal); *id.* at 534 (Madison's notes); *id.* at 536–37 (King's notes); *id.* at 542 (July 6, 1787) (Madison's notes); *id.* at 559–62 (July 9, 1787) (Madison's notes).

On July 12, Gouverneur Morris suggested a provision to assist the compromise with respect to adjustments to representation in Congress. He moved to add the requirement that "taxation shall be in proportion to Representation."[12] He explained that such a provision, however, would not apply "with regard to indirect taxes on exports & imports & on consumption."[13] To achieve that end, he amended his proposal to state: "provided always that direct taxation ought to be proportioned to representation."[14] The proposal passed in that form.[15]

The Convention considered the problem of apportioning direct taxes during the period from the establishment of the new government until the completion of the first census. Elbridge Gerry proposed:

> That from the first meeting of the Legislature [of the United States] till a census shall be taken all monies to be raised [for supplying the public Treasury] by direct taxation, shall be assessed on the inhabitants of the [several] States, according to the [number of their] Representatives [respectively] in the [first] branch.[16]

After that proposal was defeated, Gerry suggested an alternative that was adopted by the Convention:

> Mr. Gerry finding that the loss of the question had proceeded from an objection with some, to the proposed assessment of direct taxes on the *inhabitants* of the States, which might restrain the legislature to a poll tax, moved his proposition again, but so varied as to authorize the assessment on the States, which w[oul]d leave the mode to the Legislature. [The revised language was] "that from the [first] meeting of the Legislature of the U.S. until a census shall be taken, all monies for supplying the public Treasury by direct taxation shall be raised from the several States according to the number of their representatives respectively in the [first] branch."[17]

Just before the Committee of the Whole selected the Committee of Detail to prepare a draft, Daniel Carroll suggested abandoning the apportionment requirement for direct taxation prior to the first census.[18] Gouverneur Morris then advocated omitting the requirement of apportionment altogether.[19] Neither suggestion was presented as a motion and there is no recorded debate on either matter.[20]

In pertinent part, the draft prepared by the Committee of Detail provided as follows:

> Sect. 1. The Legislature of the United States shall have the power to lay and collect taxes, duties, imposts and excises . . . .
>
> . . . .

---

[12] *Id.* at 591–92 (Madison's notes).

[13] *Id.* at 592; *see also id.* (James Wilson "approved the principle, but could not see how it could be carried into execution; unless restrained to direct taxation").

[14] *Id.* at 592–93.

[15] *Id.; see also id.* at 589 (Journal).

[16] *Id.* at 600–01 (July 13, 1787) (Madison's notes).

[17] *Id.* at 603.

[18] 2 Max Farrand, Records of the Federal Convention of 1787, p. 106 (July 24, 1787) (Madison's notes).

[19] *Id.*

[20] *Id.* at 131 (papers of James Wilson) (including the apportionment of direct taxes among the matters referred to the Committee of Detail), 168–69 (Committee of Detail draft relating to apportionment of direct taxes and capitation taxes).

Sect. 3. The proportions of direct taxation shall be regulated by the whole number of white and other free citizens and inhabitants, of every age, sex and condition, including those bound to servitude for a term of years, and three fifths of all other persons not comprehended in the foregoing description, (except Indians not paying taxes) which number shall, within six years after the first meeting of the Legislature, and within the term of every ten years afterwards, be taken in such manner as the said Legislature shall direct.

Sect. 4. No tax or duty shall be laid by the Legislature on articles exported from any State; nor on the migration or importation of such persons as the several States shall think proper to admit; nor shall such migration or importation be prohibited.

Sect. 5. No capitation tax shall be laid, unless in proportion to the Census hereinbefore directed to be taken.[21]

When the Committee of Detail reported its draft, Luther Martin questioned the phrasing of section 1. He asked what the Committee meant by the terms "duties" and "imposts," pointing out that the terms were either redundant or unclear as to any distinction.[22] In response, James Wilson explained that "imposts" are a subset of the broader class of "duties"; the broader class would include, for example, "stamp duties," but the term "imposts" relates "to commerce."[23] There was considerable debate over the provision prohibiting the raising of revenue on exports. Gouverneur Morris argued: "Taxes on exports are a necessary source of revenue. For a long time the people of America will not have money to pay direct taxes. Seize and sell their effects and you push them into Revolts —."[24]

With respect to section 2 of the draft, "Mr. [Rufus] King asked what was the precise meaning of *direct* taxation? No one answ[ere]d."[25] Elbridge Gerry then moved to insert a provision into section 3 of the draft requiring that direct taxes levied in advance of the first census must be apportioned on the basis of representation.[26] Debate followed into the following day before the proposal was rejected.[27]

Another effort was made to amend section 3 of the draft to add the language:

and whenever the Legislature of the United States shall find it necessary that revenue should be raised by direct taxation, having apportioned the same, according to the above rule, on the several States, requisitions shall be made of the respective States to pay into the Continental Treasury their respective quotas within a time in the said requisition specified, and in case of any of the States failing to comply with such requisitions, then and only then to devise and pass acts directing the mode and authorising the collection of the same.[28]

---

[21] *Id.* at 181–83 (Aug. 6, 1787) (Madison's notes).

[22] *Id.* at 305 (Aug. 16, 1787) (Madison's notes).

[23] *Id.*

[24] *Id.* at 307. Earlier, in the context of a broader argument against condoning slavery, he had asserted: "Let it not be said that direct taxation is to be proportioned to representation. It is idle to suppose that the Gen[eral] Gov[ervnmen]t can stretch its hand directly into the pockets of the people scattered over so vast a Country. They can only do it through the medium of exports imports & excises." *Id.* at 223 (Madison's notes) (Aug. 8, 1787).

[25] *Id.* at 350 (Madison's notes) (Aug. 20, 1787).

[26] *Id.*

[27] *Id.* at 353 (Journal) (Aug. 21, 1787).

[28] *Id.* at 353–54; *see also id.* at 359 (Madison's notes).

That proposed amendment was also rejected. A proposal to add the clause "for the purpose of revenue" after the word "duty" in section 4 was defeated.[29] And a proposal to replace the prohibition on taxation of exports in section 4 with a requirement of a two-thirds majority of each house of Congress also failed.[30]

Weeks later, the Convention approved the provision that "all tonnage, duties, imposts, and excises, laid by the Legislature shall be uniform throughout the United States."[31] Subsequently, it was agreed to strike out the word "tonnage" and reaffirm the remainder of the provision.[32] Madison recorded that the word "tonnage" was omitted as redundant in light of the term "duties."[33]

When the Committee of Eleven reported to the Convention, it recommended a revision to the wording regarding the powers of Congress to raise and spend revenue. The proposal was adopted so as to provide: "The Legislature shall have the power to lay and collect taxes, duties, imposts, and excises, to pay the debts and provide for the common defence and general welfare of the United States."[34]

In the waning days of the Convention, the Committee of Style reported its draft. That draft reflected the final language of the Constitution with respect to many of the provisions relating to the raising of revenue. The apportionment provision in Article I, Section 2, Paragraph 3 was in the form finally adopted.[35] The provision in Article I, Section 9, Paragraph 1 authorizing a limited tax on persons admitted to the United States was in the form finally adopted.[36] The provision in Article I, Section 9, Paragraph 5 prohibiting the taxation of exports was in the form finally adopted.[37]

Three pertinent provisions had not yet taken final form. *First,* the general provision in Article I, Section 8, Clause 1 omitted at that time the language requiring that "all duties, imposts, and excises shall be uniform."[38] By unanimous consent, the omitted text was added September 14, 1787.[39] *Second,* the provision in Article I, Section 9, Paragraph 4 regarding the apportionment of taxes referred only to "capitation taxes" and did not then expressly reference "other direct" taxes.[40] On September 14, 1787, the motion of George Read to insert the words "or other direct taxes" passed.[41] Madison recorded that Read "was afraid that some liberty might otherwise be taken to saddle the States with a readjustment by this rule, of past Requisitions of Cong[ress] — and that his amendment by giving another cast to the meaning would take away the pretext."[42] *Third,* the provision in Article I, Section 10, Paragraph 2 regarding the limited power of States to "lay any Imposts or Duties on Imports or Exports" was phrased as follows: "No state shall, without the consent of Congress, lay imposts or duties on imports or

---

[29] *Id.* at 354 (Journal); *see also id.* at 363 (Madison's notes).

[30] *Id.* at 354 (Journal); *see also id.* at 363 (Madison's notes).

[31] *Id.* at 434 (Journal) (Aug. 28, 1787); *see also id.* at 437 (Madison's notes).

[32] *Id.* at 473 (Journal) (Aug. 31, 1787).

[33] *Id.* at 481 (Madison's notes) (Aug. 31, 1787).

[34] *Id.* at 493, 496 (Journal) (Sept. 4, 1787); *see also id.* at 497 (Madison's notes).

[35] *Id.* at 590 (report of Committee on Style).

[36] *Id.* at 596.

[37] *Id.*

[38] *Id.* at 594.

[39] *Id.* at 614 (Madison's notes); *id.* at 610 n.2 (Journal).

[40] *Id.* at 594 (report of Committee on Style).

[41] *Id.* at 618 (Madison's notes).

[42] *Id.*

exports, nor with such consent, but to the use of the treasury of the United States."[43] On September 13, 1787, George Mason suggested additional language to permit States to charge fees for inspection laws together with congressional power to control such laws. His proposal was adopted without debate.[44] On the final day of debate — September 15, 1787 — Mason successfully suggested alternative language which, for the first time, included the phrase "absolutely necessary" and which became the final text of this provision.[45] There is no recorded debate on the change in phrasing.

3. Ratification Debates

The proposed powers of the central government to raise and spend revenue drew considerable attention during the ratification debates. As an initial matter, supporters and opponents alike acknowledged that the proposed constitution set no ceiling on the *rate* at which Congress could tax and that the combined scope of the revenue-raising powers was quite broad.

> To detail the particulars comprehended in the general terms, taxes, duties, imposts, and excises, would require a volume, instead of a single piece in a news-paper. Indeed, it would be a task far beyond my ability, and to which no one can be competent, unless possessed of a mind capable of comprehending every possible source of revenue; for they extend to every possible way of raising money, whether by direct or indirect taxation. Under this clause may be imposed a poll-tax, a land-tax, a tax on houses and buildings, on windows and fire places, on cattle and all kinds of personal property: — It extends to duties on all kinds of goods *to any amount*, to tonnage and poundage on vessels, to duties on written instruments, news-papers, almanacs, and books: — It comprehends an excise on all kinds of liquors, spirits, wines, cider, beer, etc. and indeed takes in duty or excise on every necess[ity] or convenienc[e] of life; whether of foreign or home growth or manufactory. In short, we can have no conception of any way in which a government can raise money from the people, but what is included in one or other of these general terms.[46]

The breadth of that power was asserted to amount to a general power to legislate on any matter.[47]

Supporters of ratification denied that the taxing power in the proposed constitution could be applied to achieve unlimited *ends*.

> He tells you that, under pretense of providing for the general welfare, they may lay the most enormous taxes. There is nothing in the clause which warrants this suggestion.
>
> It provides "that Congress shall have the power to lay and collect taxes, duties, imposts, and excises; to pay the debts, and provide for the common defence and general welfare of the United States." . . . The amounts to be raised are confined to these purposes solely. Will oppressive burdens be warranted by this clause? They are not to raise money for any other purpose.

---

[43] *Id.* at 597 (report of Committee on Style).

[44] *Id.* at 607 (Madison's notes) (Sept. 13, 1787).

[45] *Id.* at 624 (Madison's notes). For a discussion of the later significance of Mason's last-minute change in the wording of this provision, see Randy E. Barnett, *The Original Meaning of the Necessary and Proper Clause*, 6 U. PA. J. CONST. L. 183, 200–09 (2003).

[46] Brutus V, reprinted in 19 DOCUMENTARY HISTORY OF THE RATIFICATION OF THE CONSTITUTION 412–13 (John P. Kaminski et al. eds. 2003) (emphasis added).

[47] *See id.* at 413 ("the legislature having every source from which money can be drawn under their direction, with a right to make all laws necessary and proper for drawing forth all the resource[s] of the country, would have, in fact, all power").

It is a power drawn from [Article VIII of the Articles of Confederation]. . . .

. . . The same power is intended by the Constitution. The only difference between them is, that Congress is, by this plan, to impose taxes on the people, whereas, by the Confederation, they are laid by the states. The mode of raising only is different . . . .[48]

Opponents of ratification suggested four additional ways to limit this power.

a. *Distinguishing Exclusive Objects of Taxation*

Some Antifedcralists argued that the power to raise revenue should be divided between the central government and the States rather than operating concurrently on the same *objects*. In that manner States as well as the central government would be assured independent sources of revenue to support operations contemplated by the Constitution.[49]

b. *Distinguishing External from Internal Taxation*

Certain Antifederalists argued that it would be expensive and oppressive to have federal tax collectors operating throughout the States. In contrast, taxes on imported goods would be conveniently collected at ports of entry by relatively few federal officers. Consequently, these Antifederalists were willing to cede to Congress the power to tax all objects provided that the taxes were on imported goods, with all forms of *internal taxes* reserved to the States.[50] Proponents of ratification argued that because the central government might be subject to unlimited expense in the event of war, the division between internal and external taxes was inadequate.[51]

c. *Denying Congress Power to Levy Direct Taxes*

Some Antifederalists objected to the power to levy *direct taxes*. Such taxes had the potential to operate oppressively due to ignorance of the local conditions such that the object of the tax that was common in one place was rare in another. In the Virginia ratification convention, several prominent individuals opposed the constitution on this basis.[52] This group was willing to cede slightly more power, by limiting Congress to

---

[48] 3 Debates in the Several State Conventions on the Adoption of the Federal Constitution 244 (Jonathan Elliot ed. 1836) (George Nicholas) [hereafter Elliott's Debates].

[49] *See, e.g.*, Brutus VII, reprinted in 20 Documentary History of the Ratification of the Constitution 566 (John P. Kaminski et al. eds. 2004) ("No such allotment is made in this constitution,. . . every source of revenue is under the control of Congress; it therefore follows, that if this system is intended to be a complex and not a simple, a confederate and not an entire consolidated government, it contains the sure seeds of its own dissolution").

[50] *See, e.g.*, Brutus V, *supra* note 46, at 415 ("The distinction between external and internal taxes, is not a novel one in this country, it is a plain one, and easily understood. The first includes impost duties on all imported goods . . . ."); Brutus VII, *supra* note 49, at 570 ("There is one source of revenue, which it is agreed, the general government ought to have the sole control of. This is an impost upon all goods imported from foreign countries. This would, of itself, be very productive, and would be collected with ease and certainty.").

[51] *See, e.g.*, Federalist No. 30 (Hamilton) ("future necessities admit not of calculation or limitation"); Federalist No. 31 (Hamilton) ("[T]here ought to be no limitation of a power destined to effect a purpose, which is itself incapable of limitation."); *id.* ("As the duties of superintending the national defense and of securing public peace against foreign or domestic violence, involve a provision for casualties and dangers, to which no possible limits can be assigned, the power of making that provision ought to know no other bounds than the exigencies of the nation of the resources of the community.").

[52] *See, e.g.*, 3 Elliott's Debates, *supra* note 48, at 29, 31 (George Mason); *id.* at 56–57 (Patrick Henry); *id.*

duties, imposts, and excises. That position would have permitted Congress to levy internal taxes as long as they were not *direct taxes*. Direct taxes — like a capitation tax — would be reserved as a source of revenue for the States.

Proponents of ratification explained that direct taxes would rarely be imposed and then only to a small extent.[53] At the Virginia convention, James Madison explained that the power to levy direct taxes would rarely be resorted to but needed in time of war.[54]

Supporters and opponents of ratification alike recognized potential difficulties in levying direct taxes and their exchanges illustrated different views of the operation of such taxes. Governor Edmund Randolph, although supporting ratification, observed: "Were the tax laid *on one uniform article* throughout the Union, its operation would be oppressive on a considerable part of the people."[55] James Monroe explained his hostility to the power of direct taxation:

> [I]t appears to me that the exercise of the power of direct taxation is impracticable in this country, under a democracy.
>
> Consider the territory lying between the Atlantic Ocean and the Mississippi. . . . It is larger than any territory that every was under any one free government. . . . Taxes cannot be laid justly and equally in such a territory. What are the objects of direct taxation? Will the taxes be laid on land? One gentleman has said that the United States would select out a particular object, or objects, and leave the rest to the states. Suppose land to be the object selected by Congress: examine its consequences. The landholder alone would suffer by such a selection. A very considerable part of the community would escape. Those who pursue commerce and arts would escape. It could not possibly be estimated equally. Will the taxes be paid on polls only? Would not the landholder escape in that case? How, then will it be laid? On all property? Consider the consequences. Is it possible to make a law that shall operate alike in all the states? . . .
>
> Are there not a thousand circumstances showing clearly that there can be no law that can be uniform in its operation throughout the United States? . . . The tax that may be convenient in one state may be oppressive in another. If they vary the objects of taxation in different states, the operation must be unequal and unjust. If Congress should fix the tax on some mischievous objects, what will be the tendency? . . .[56]

John Marshall replied:

> It is objected, that Congress will not know how to lay taxes so as to be easy and convenient for the people at large. Let us pay strict attention to this

---

at 214 (James Monroe) ("To render the system under consideration safe and proper I would take from it one power only — I mean that of direct taxation. I conceive its other powers are sufficient without this.").

[53] *See, e.g.,* FEDERALIST No. 45 (Madison) ("It is true that the Confederacy is to possess, and may exercise, the power of collecting internal as well as external taxes throughout the States: but it is probable that this power will not be resorted to, except for supplemental purposes of revenue"); 3 ELLIOTT'S DEBATES, *supra* note 48, at 109 (Francis Corbin) ("the probable amount of duties on imported articles throughout the continent . . . would exceed the annual expenses of the administration of the general government, including the civil list, contingent charges, and the interest of the foreign and domestic debts" so that "no danger was to be apprehended from the power of direct taxation, since there was every reason to believe it would be very seldom used.").

[54] *See* 3 ELLIOTT'S DEBATES, *supra* note 48, at 95–96 ("Direct taxes will only be recurred to for great purposes. . . . [I]t is necessary to establish funds for extraordinary exigencies, and to give this power to the general government").

[55] *Id.* at 122 (emphasis added).

[56] *Id.* at 215–16.

objection. If it appears to be totally without foundation, the necessity of levying direct taxes will obviate what the gentleman says; nor will there be any color for refusing the power.

The objects of direct taxes are well understood: they are but few: what are they? Lands, slaves, stock of all kinds, and a few other articles of domestic property. Can you believe that ten men selected from all parts of the state, chosen because they know the situation of the people, will be unable to determine so as to make the tax equal on, and convenient for, the people?

. . . .

[James Monroe] then spoke of a selection of particular objects by Congress, which he says must necessarily be oppressive; that Congress, for instance, might select taxes, and that all but landholders would escape. Cannot Congress regulate the taxes so as to be equal on all parts of the community? Where is the absurdity of having thirteen revenues? Will they clash with, or injure, each other? If not, why cannot Congress make thirteen distinct laws, and impose the taxes on the general objects of taxation in each state, so that all persons of the society shall pay equally, as they ought?[57]

d. *Direct Taxation Only Upon Failure of Requisitions*

As a fallback position, some Antifederalists were willing to grant Congress the full measure of taxing power specified in the Constitution provided that States were first allowed the opportunity to raise their proportionate share of any direct taxes through their own measures. Thus, Congress would have access to funds from direct taxes in the event of war or other emergency but States would have the opportunity to collect the funds in a manner calculated to distribute the burden and ease payment. Prominent proponents of the Constitution assured that the imposition of direct taxes would follow that approach.[58]

This limitation upon the power to levy direct taxes drew considerable formal support during the ratification process. After conventions in the first five States ratified the Constitution — Delaware, Pennsylvania, New Jersey, Georgia, and Connecticut — Massachusetts adopted a middle course between outright rejection or acceptance of the proposed Constitution. The Massachusetts convention ratified the Constitution with "recommend[ed]" amendments designed to "remove the fears, and quiet the apprehensions, of many of the good people of this commonwealth, and more effectually guard against an undue administration of the federal government."[59] Among the recommendations was the following measure:

That Congress do not lay direct taxes but when the money arising from the impost and excise are insufficient for the public exigencies, not then until Congress shall have first made a requisition upon the states to assess, levy, and pay their respective proportions of such requisition, agreeable to census fixed in the said Constitution, in such a way and manner as the legislatures of the states shall think best; and in such case, if any state shall neglect or refuse to pay its proportion, pursuant to such requisition, then Congress may assess and levy such state's proportion, together with interest thereon at the rate of six per cent per annum, from the time of payment prescribed in such requisition.

---

[57] *Id.* at 229–30, 235.

[58] *See, e.g.,* FEDERALIST No. 45 (Madison) ("an option will then be given to the States to supply their quotas by previous collections of their own").

[59] 1 ELLIOT'S DEBATES, *supra* note 48, at 319–22.

The Massachusetts convention further required the State's representatives in Congress pursue such an amendment.[60] Thereafter the conventions in South Carolina and New Hampshire adopted almost identical provisions.[61] In the meantime, the Maryland convention had also ratified the Constitution and a minority of its members proposed a limitation upon direct taxes similar to that of Massachusetts.[62] After the Massachusetts precedent, a meeting in Harrisburg, Pennsylvania, proposed a set of amendments that also included a limit on direct taxation.[63] Thus, a majority in the conventions of three of the first nine States to act identified the unconditional power to levy direct taxes as particularly problematic and those States were joined in that view by minority reports from two additional States.

Although the Virginia convention withheld the call for amendments prior to the meeting of the First Congress,[64] it did prepare a list of proposals.[65] Among the Virginia proposals was a limitation on the imposition of direct taxes that would have required Congress to first permit States to raise their apportioned sum.[66] "Virginia Federalists had to accept these recommendations in return for unconditional ratification."[67]

The New York convention followed the approach of Massachusetts, South Carolina, and New Hampshire with respect to limiting the imposition of direct taxes.[68] New York further proposed that Congress "not impose any excise on any article (ardent spirits excepted) of the growth, production, or manufacture of the United States, or any of them" and that "no capitation tax shall ever be laid by Congress."[69] No other State ratified the Constitution prior to the meeting of the First Congress in 1789.

North Carolina insisted upon amendments as a precondition to ratification. Among the amendments it required were those proposed by Virginia, including the limitation on direct taxes.[70] The Rhode Island electorate rejected the proposed Constitution outright.[71] Of the eleven States that had ratified the Constitution, five — including both Virginia and New York — had called for amendments to limit the federal taxing power, the so-called "minority report" from Pennsylvania and Maryland did so as well, and North Carolina declined to ratify in the absence of such an amendment.

Even in Virginia, where Madison himself led the efforts for ratification, he "later conceded that the Constitution would have been defeated without a pledge from its supporters to back subsequent amendments."[72] Indeed, he "gave tacit support to the convention's amendments even though he found many highly objectionable."[73]

---

[60] *Id.* at 323.

[61] *Id.* at 325, 326.

[62] *See* 2 ELLIOTT'S DEBATES, *supra* note 48, at 552–53.

[63] *See id.* at 542, 545.

[64] *See* 1 ELLIOTT'S DEBATES, *supra* note 48, at 327.

[65] *See* LEONARD W. LEVY, ORIGINS OF THE BILL OF RIGHTS 275–80 (1999).

[66] *Id.* at 278.

[67] HELEN E. VEIT ET AL., CREATING THE BILL OF RIGHTS x (1991).

[68] 1 ELLIOTT'S DEBATES, *supra* note 48, at 329.

[69] *Id.* at 329, 330.

[70] *See* HELEN E. VEIT ET AL., *supra* note 67, at xi.

[71] *Id.*

[72] LEONARD W. LEVY, *supra* note 65, at 32.

[73] HELEN E. VEIT ET AL., *supra* note 67, at xiii.

Several States had already called for a second constitutional convention.[74] In the absence of a preemptive move to ameliorate the concerns of the Antifederalists through amendments, Madison feared such a convention might well follow. One of his chief concerns with a second convention was that it would limit the taxing power of Congress.[75]

Despite the number of States expressing concern with the imposition of direct taxes, when Madison proposed a list of nineteen amendments to the First Congress, his list omitted any provision that would limit federal taxing power.[76] Thereafter, no provision addressing taxation appeared in the draft of the Select Committee in the House of Representatives, the proposals passed by the House of Representatives, the proposals passed by the Senate, or the proposed amendments agreed to by the House and Senate after conference.

Exercise 2(A):

Consider the scope of the power of the central government to raise revenue and to spend it.

(1)   Under the Articles of Confederation, what power did the central government have to raise revenue? What power did the central government have to spend such revenue?

(2)   Does the Constitution provide powers in addition to those under the Articles of Confederation or in lieu of those powers?

(3)   Do the historical materials suggest a different answer to any of the questions posed in *Exercise 1*?

THE FIRST CONGRESS

The DVD-ROM contains the full text of the revenue-raising measures enacted by the First Congress. *See* An Act for Laying a Duty on Goods, Wares, and Merchandises Imported into the United States, 1 Stat. 24 (July 4, 1789), and An Act Imposing Duties on Tonnage, 1 Stat. 27 (July 20, 1789).

On the final day of the First Congress, it enacted another revenue-raising measure. *See* Act of March 3, 1791, 1 Stat. 199.

Exercise 2(B):

What do the enactments of the First Congress indicate was its understanding of its revenue-raising authority? Consider specifically:

(1)   Were these measures required to be apportioned? If so, were they apportioned properly?

(2)   Were these measures required to be "uniform"? If so, are they uniform in some way? What is the implicit meaning of the uniformity requirement? Or, are these measures improperly lacking any uniformity?

(3)   Are these early revenue-raising measures consistent with the text, structure, and shared public understanding of the Constitution?

---

[74]   *See id.* at xi.

[75]   *See* LEONARD W. LEVY, *supra*, note 65, at 34.

[76]   *See id.* at 281–83.

THE FIRST ADMINISTRATION:
REPORT ON THE SUBJECT OF MANUFACTURES

The Secretary of the Treasury in obedience to the order of the House of Representatives, of [January 15, 1790], has applied his attention, at as early a period as his other duties would permit, to the subject of Manufactures; and particularly to the means of promoting such as will render the United States, independent of foreign nations, for military and other essential supplies. And he there upon respectfully submits the following Report.

[1. Preliminary, General Observations]

The expediency of encouraging manufactures in the United States, which was not long since deemed very questionable, appears at this time to be pretty generally admitted. The embarrassments, which have obstructed the progress of our external trade, have led to serious reflections on the necessity of enlarging the sphere of our domestic commerce . . . .

  . . . .

It ought readily to be conceded, that the cultivation of the earth — as the primary and most certain source of national supply — as the immediate and chief source of subsistence to a man — as the principal source of those materials which constitute the nutriment of other kinds of labor — as including a state most favorable to the freedom and independence of the human mind — one, perhaps, most conducive to the multiplication of the human species, has *intrinsically a strong claim to pre-eminence over every other kind of industry.*

But, that it has a title to any thing like an exclusive predilection, in any country, ought to be admitted with great caution. That it is even more productive than every other branch of Industry requires more evidence, than has yet been given in support of the position. That its real interests, precious and important as . . . they truly are, will be advanced, rather than injured by the due encouragement of manufactures, may, it is believed, be satisfactorily demonstrated. And it is also believed that the expediency of such encouragement in a general view may be shewn to be recommended by the most cogent and persuasive motives of national policy.

  . . . .

[A. There Are Advantages to an Economy that Includes Manufacture and Not Only Agriculture]

[1]. *As to the Division of Labour.*

It has justly been observed, that there is scarcely any thing of greater moment in the economy of a nation, than the proper division of labour. The separation of occupations causes each to be carried to a much greater perfection, than it could possibly acquire, if they were blended. . . .

  . . . .

And from these causes united, the mere separation of the occupation of the cultivator from that of the Artificer, has the effect of augmenting the *productive powers* of labour, and with them, the total mass of the produce or revenue of a Country. In this single view of the subject, therefore, the utility of Artificers or Manufacturers, toward producing an increase of productive industry, is apparent.

[2]. *As to an extension of the use of Machinery a point which though partly anticipated, requires to be placed in one or two additional lights.*

The employment of Machinery forms an item of great importance in the general mass of national industry. . . . May it not . . . be fairly inferred, that those occupations, which give greatest scope to the use of this auxiliary, contribute most to the general Stock of industrious effort, and, in consequence, to the general product of industry?

It shall be taken for granted . . . that manufacturing pursuits are susceptible in a greater degree of the application of machinery, than those of Agriculture. . . .

. . . .

[3]. *As to the additional employment of classes of the community, not originally engaged in the particular business.*

This is not among the least valuable of the means, by which manufacturing institutions contribute to augment the general stock of industry and production. In places where those institutions prevail, besides the persons regularly engaged in them, they afford occasional and extra employment to industrious individuals and families, who are willing to devote the leisure resulting from the intermissions of their ordinary pursuits to collateral labours, as a resource for multiplying their acquisitions or their enjoyments. . . .

Besides this advantage of occasional employment to classes having different occupations, there is another . . . . This is — the employment of persons who would other wise be idle (and in many cases a burthen on the community). . . . It is worthy of particular remark, that, in general, women and Children are rendered more useful and the latter more early useful by manufacturing establishments, than they would otherwise be. . . .

. . . .

[4]. *As to the promoting of emigration from foreign Countries.*

Men reluctantly quit one course of occupation and livelihood for another, unless invited to it by very apparent and proximate advantages. . . . Manufacturers, who listening to the powerful invitations of a better price for their fabrics, or their labour, of greater cheapness of provisions and raw materials, of an exemption from the chief part of the taxes burthens and restraints, which they endure in the old world, of greater independence and consequence, under the operation of a more equal government, and of what is far more precious than mere religious toleration — a perfect equality of religious privileges; would probably flock from Europe to the United States to pursue their own trades or professions, if they were once made sensible of the advantages they would enjoy, and were inspired with an assurance of encouragement and employment, will, with difficulty, be induced to transplant themselves, with a view to becoming Cultivators of Land.

. . . .

[5]. *As to the furnishing greater scope for the diversity of talents and dispositions, which discriminate men from each other.*

. . . When all the different kinds of industry obtain in a community, each individual can find his proper element, and call into activity the whole vigour of his nature. And the community is benefitted by the services of its respective members, in the manner, in which each can serve it with most effect.

. . . .

[6]. *As to the affording a more ample and various field for enterprise.*

. . . To cherish and stimulate the activity of the human mind, by multiplying the objects of enterprise, is not among the least considerable of the expedients, by which the wealth of a nation may be promoted. . . .

The spirit of enterprise, useful and prolific as it is, must necessarily be contracted or expanded, in proportion to the simplicity or variety of the occupations and productions, which are to be found in a Society. It must be less in a nation of mere cultivators, than in a nation of cultivators and merchants; less in a nation of cultivators and merchants, than in a nation of cultivators, artificers, and merchants.

[7]. *As to the creating, in some instances, a new, and securing, in all, a more certain and steady demand for the surplus of the soil.*

. . . .

It is evident, that the exertions of the husbandman will be steady or fluctuating, vigorous or feeble, in proportion to the steadiness of fluctuation, adequateness, or inadequateness of the markets on which he must depend, for the vent of the surplus, which may be produced by his labour; and that such surplus in the ordinary course of things will be greater or less in the same proportion.

For the purpose of this vent, a domestic market is greatly to be preferred to a foreign one; because it is in the nature of things, far more to be relied upon.

. . . .

This idea of an extensive domestic market for the surplus produce of the soil is of the first consequence. It is of all things, that which most effectually conduces to a flourishing state of Agriculture. . . .

It merits particular observation, that the multiplication of manufactories not only furnishes a Market for those articles, which have been accustomed to be produced in abundance, in a country; but it likewise creates a demand for such as were either unknown or produced in inconsiderable quantities. The bowels as well as the surface of the earth are ransacked for articles which were before neglected. Animals, Plants and Minerals acquire an utility and value, which were before unexplored.

. . . .

[B. The Development of Manufactures Requires Affirmative Measures]

The remaining objections to a particular encouragement of manufactures in the United States now require to be examined.

One of these turns on the proposition, that Industry, if left to itself, will naturally find its way to the most useful and profitable employment: whence it is inferred, that manufactures without the aid of government will grow up as soon and as fast as the natural state of things and the interest of the community may require . . . .

. . . .

Experience teaches, that men are often so much governed by what they are accustomed to see and practice, that the simplest and most obvious improvements, in the most ordinary occupations, are adopted with hesitation, reluctance and by slow gradations. The spontaneous transition to new pursuits, in a community long habituated to different ones, may be expected to be attended with proportionably greater difficulty. When former occupations ceased to yield a profit adequate to the subsistence of their followers, or when there was an absolute deficiency of employment in them, owing to the superabundance of hands, changes would ensue; but these changes would be likely to be more tardy than might consist with the interest either of individuals or of the Society. In many cases they would not happen, while a bare support could be ensured by an adherence to ancient courses; though a resort to a more profitable employment might be practicable. To produce the desirable changes, as early as may be expedient, may therefore require the incitement and patronage of government.

The apprehension of failing in new attempts is perhaps a more serious impediment. . . .

The superiority antecedently enjoyed by nations, who have preoccupied and perfected a branch of industry, constitutes a more formidable obstacle . . . .

But the greatest obstacle of all to the successful prosecution of a new branch of industry in a country, in which it was before unknown, consists, as far as the instances apply, in the bounties premiums and other aids which are granted, in a variety of cases, by the nations, in which the establishments to be imitated are previously introduced. It is well known . . . that certain nations grant bounties on the exportation of particular commodities, to enable their own workmen to under-sell and supplant all competitors, in the countries to which those commodities are sent. Hence the undertakers of a new manufacture have to contend not only with the natural disadvantages of a new undertaking, but with the gratuities and remunerations which other governments bestow. To be enabled to contend with success, it is evident, that the interference and aid of their own government are indispensible.

Combinations by those engaged in a particular branch of business in one country, to frustrate the first efforts to introduce it into another, by temporary sacrifices . . . are believed to have existed . . . .

. . . .

There remains to be noticed an objection to the encouragement of manufactures, of a nature different from those which question the probability of success. This is derived from its supposed tendency to give a monopoly of advantages to particular classes at the expense of the rest of the community, who, it is affirmed, would be able to procure the requisite supplies of manufactured articles on better terms from foreigners . . . and who it is alleged, are reduced to a necessity of paying an enhanced price for whatever they want, by every measure, which obstructs the free competition of foreign commodities.

. . . .

But though it were true, that the immediate and certain effect of regulations controuling the competition of foreign with domestic fabrics was an increase of price, it is universally true, that the contrary is the ultimate effect with every successful manufacture. When a domestic manufacture has attained to perfection, and has engaged in the prosecution of it a competent number of Persons, it invariably becomes cheaper. . . .

. . . .

. . . The extreme embarrassments of the United States during the late War, from an incapacity of supplying themselves, are still a matter of keen recollection: A future war might be expected again to exemplify the mischiefs and dangers of a situation, to which that incapacity is still in too great a degree applicable, unless changed by timely and vigorous exertion. To effect this change as fast as shall be prudent, merits all the attention and all the Zeal of our Public Councils; 'tis the next great work to be accomplished.

The want of a Navy to protect our external commerce, as long as it shall Continue, must render it a peculiarly precarious reliance, for the supply of essential articles, and must serve to strengthen prodigiously the arguments in favour of manufactures.

. . . .

It is not uncommon to meet with an opinion that though the promoting of manufactures may be the interest of a part of the Union, it is contrary to that of another part. The northern & southern regions are sometimes represented as having adverse interests in this respect. . . .

. . . [T]he *aggregate* prosperity of manufactures, and the *aggregate* prosperity of Agriculture are intimately connected. . . . Perhaps the superior steadiness of the demand of a domestic market for the surplus produce of the soil, is alone a convincing argument of its truth.

. . . .

But there are particular considerations which serve to fortify the idea, that the encouragement of manufactures is the interest of all parts of the Union. If the northern and middle states should be the principal scenes of such establishments, they would immediately benefit the more southern, by creating a demand for productions . . . .

If then, it satisfactorily appears, that it is in the Interest of the United States, generally, to encourage manufactures, it merits particular attention, that there are circumstances, which Render the present a critical moment for entering with Zeal upon the important business. . . .

. . . .

There is at the present juncture a certain fermentation of mind, a certain activity of speculation and enterprise which if properly directed, may be made subservient to useful purposes; but which if left entirely to itself, may be attended with pernicious effects.

The disturbed state of Europe, inclining its citizens to emigration, the requisite workmen, will be more easily acquired, than at another time; and the effect of multiplying the opportunities of employment to those who emigrate, may be an increase of the number and extent of valuable acquisitions to the population arts and industry of the Country. . . .

. . . .

[C. The Means for Promotion of Manufactures]

In order to a better judgment of the Means proper to be resorted to by the United States, it will be of use to Advert to those which have been employed with success in other Countries. The principal of these are.

[1]. *Protecting duties — or duties on those foreign articles which are the rivals of the domestic ones, intended to be encouraged.*

. . . The propriety of this species of encouragement need not be dwelt upon; as it is not only a clear result from the numerous topics which have been suggested, but is sanctioned by the laws of the United States in a variety of instances; it has the additional recommendation of being a resource of revenue. . . .

[2]. *Prohibitions of rival articles or duties equivalent to prohibitions.*

. . . Of duties equivalent to prohibitions, there are examples in the Laws of the United States, and there are other Cases to which the principle may be advantageously extended, but they are not numerous.

. . . .

[3]. *Prohibitions of the exportation of the materials of manufactures.*

. . . [T]he expedient in question, ought to be indulged with a sparing hand.

[4]. *Pecuniary bounties.*

This has been found one of the most efficacious means of encouraging manufactures, and it is in some views, the best. Though it has not yet been practiced upon by the Government of the United States . . . and though it is less favored by public opinion than some other modes.

. . . .

The true way . . . is to lay a duty on foreign *manufactures* of the material, the growth of which is desired to be encouraged, and to apply the produce of that duty by way of bounty, either upon the production of the material itself or upon its manufacture at home or upon both. In this disposition of the thing, the Manufacturer commences his enterprise under every advantage, which is attainable, as to quantity or price, of the raw material: And the Farmer if the bounty be immediately to him, is enabled by it to enter into a successful competition with the foreign material . . . .

Except for the simple and ordinary kinds of household Manufactures, or those for which there are very commanding local advantages, pecuniary bounties are, in most cases indispensable to the introduction of a new branch. A stimulus and a support not less powerful and direct is generally speaking essential to the overcoming of the obstacles which arise from the Competitions of superior skill and maturity elsewhere. Bounties are especially essential, in regard to articles, upon which those foreigners, who have been accustomed to supply a Country, are in the practice of granting them.

The continuance of bounties on manufactures long established must almost always be of questionable policy: Because a presumption would arise, in every such Case, that there were natural and inherent impediments to success. But in new undertakings, they are as justifiable, as they are oftentimes necessary.

There is a degree of prejudice against bounties from an appearance of giving away the public money, without an immediate consideration, and from a supposition, that they serve to enrich particular classes, at the expense of the Community.

But neither of these sources of dislike will bear a serious examination. There is no purpose, to which public money can be more beneficially applied, than to the acquisition of a new and useful branch of industry; no Consideration more valuable than a permanent addition to the general stock of productive labour.

. . . .

A Question has been made concerning the Constitutional right of the Government of the United States to apply this species of encouragement, but there is certainly no good foundation for such a question. The National Legislature has express authority "To lay and Collect taxes, duties, imposts, and excises, to pay the debts and to provide for the *Common defence* and *general welfare*" with no other qualifications than that "all duties, imposts, and excises, shall be *uniform* throughout the United States," "that no capitation or other direct tax shall be laid unless in proportion to numbers ascertained by a census or enumeration" taken on the principles prescribed in the Constitution, and that "no tax or duty shall be laid on articles exported from any state." These three qualifications excepted, the power to *raise money* is *plenary,* and *indefinite;* and the objects to which it may be *appropriated* are no less comprehensive, than the payment of the public debts and the providing for the common defense and " *general Welfare.*" The terms " *general Welfare*" were doubtless intended to signify more than was expressed or imported in those which Preceded; otherwise numerous exigencies incident to the affairs of a Nation would have been left without a provision. The phrase is as comprehensive as any that could have been used; because it was not fit that the constitutional authority of the Union, to appropriate its revenues should have been restricted within narrower limits than the "General Welfare" and because this necessarily embraces a vast variety of particulars, which are susceptible neither of specification nor of definition.

It is therefore of necessity, left to the discretion of the National Legislature, to pronounce, upon the objects, which concern the general Welfare, and for which under that description, an appropriation of money is requisite and proper. And there seems to be no room for a doubt that whatever concerns the general Interests of *learning* of *Agriculture* of *Manufactures* and of *Commerce* are within the sphere of the national Councils *as far as regards an application of Money.*

The only qualification of the generality of the Phrase in question, which seems to be admissible, is this — That the object to which an appropriation of money is to be made be *General* and not *local;* its operation extending in fact, or by possibility, throughout the Union, and not being confined to a particular spot.

No objection ought to arise to this construction from a supposition that it would imply a power to do whatever else should appear to Congress conducive to the General Welfare. A power to appropriate money with this latitude which is granted too in *express terms* would not carry a power to do any other thing, not authorised in the constitution, either expressly or by fair implication.

[5]. *Premiums.*

. . . .

Bounties are applicable to the whole quantity of an article produced, or manufactured, or exported, and involve a correspondent expense. Premiums serve to reward some particular excellence or superiority . . . and are dispensed only in a small number of cases. . . .

There are various Societies in different countries, whose object is the dispensation of Premiums for the encouragement of *Agriculture Arts manufactures* and *Commerce* . . . . From a similar establishment in the United States, supplied and supported by the Government of the Union, vast benefits might reasonably be expected. . . .

[6]. *The Exemption of the Materials of manufactures from duty.*

. . . .

The Laws of the Union afford instances of the observance of the policy here recommended, but it will probably be found advisable to extend it to some other Cases. . . .

[7]. *Drawbacks of the duties which are imposed on the Materials of Manufactures.*

. . . .

Where duties on the materials of manufactures are not laid for the purpose of preventing a competition with some domestic production, the same reasons which recommend, as a general rule, the exemption of those materials from duties, would recommend as a like General rule, the allowance of draw backs, in favor of the manufacturer. . . . [T]he Idea has been adopted by the laws of the Union in the instances of salt and Molasses. . . .

[8]. *The encouragement of new inventions and discoveries, at home, and of the introduction into the United States of such as may have been made in other countries; particularly those, which relate to machinery.*

This is among the most useful and unexceptional of the aids, which can be given to manufactures. The usual means of that encouragement are pecuniary rewards, and, for a time, exclusive privileges. . . . [S]o far as respects "authors and inventors" provision has been made by Law. But it is desirable in regard to improvements and secrets of extraordinary value, to be able to extend the same benefit to Introducers, as well as Authors and Inventors; a policy which has been practiced with advantage in other countries. Here, however, as in some other cases, there is cause to regret, that the competency of the authority of the National Government to the *good,* which might be done, is not without a question. Many aids might be given to industry; many internal improvements of primary magnitude might be promoted, by an authority operating throughout the Union, which cannot be effected, as well, if at all, by an authority confined within the limits of a single state.

But if the legislature of the Union cannot do all the good, that might be wished, it is at least desirable, that all may be done, which is practicable. Means for promoting the introduction of foreign improvements, though less efficaciously than might be accomplished with more adequate authority, will form a part of the plan intended to be submitted in the close of this report.

. . . .

[9]. *Judicious regulations for the inspection of manufactured commodities.*

. . . Contributing to the prevention of frauds upon consumers at home and exporters to foreign countries — to improve the quality & preserve the character of the national manufactures, it cannot fail to aid the expeditious and advantageous Sale of them, and to serve as a guard against competition from other quarters. . . .

[10]. The facilitating of pecuniary remittances from place to place is a point of considerable moment to trade in general, and to manufactures in particular; by rendering more easy the purchase of raw materials and provisions and the payment for manufactured supplies. . . .

[11]. *The facilitating the transportation of commodities.*

Improvements favoring this object intimately concern all the domestic interests of a community; but they may without impropriety be mentioned as having an important relation to manufactures. . . .

The symptoms of attention to the improvement of inland Navigation, which have lately appeared in some quarters, must fill with pleasure every breast warmed with a true Zeal for the prosperity of the Country. These examples, it is to be hoped, will stimulate the exertions of the Government and the Citizens of every state. There can certainly be no object, more worthy of the cares of the local administrations; and it were to be wished, that there was no doubt of the power of the national Government to lend its direct aid, on a comprehensive plan. This is one of those improvements, which could be prosecuted with more efficacy by the whole, than by any part or parts of the Union. . . .

. . . .

The foregoing are the principal of the means, by which the growth of manufactures is ordinarily promoted. . . .

There are certain species of taxes, which are apt to be oppressive to different parts of the community; and among other ill effects have a very unfriendly aspect toward manufactures. All Poll or Capitation taxes are of this nature. They either proceed, according to a fixed rate, which operates unequally, and injuriously to the industrious poor; or they vest a discretion in certain officers, to make estimates and assessments which are necessarily vague, conjectural and liable to abuse. They ought therefore to be abstained from, in all but cases of distressing emergency.

All such taxes (including all taxes on occupations) which proceed according to the amount of capital *supposed* to be employed in a business, or of profits *supposed* to be made in it are unavoidably hurtful to industry. . . .

. . . .

[II. Specific Proposals]

[A.] Iron

. . . .

The only further encouragement of manufactories of this article, the propriety of which may be considered as unquestionable, seems to be an increase of the duties on foreign rival commodities.

. . . .

To ensure the end [*i.e.*, the development of iron castings], it seems equally safe and prudent to extend the duty ad valorem upon all manufactures of Iron, or of which iron is the article of chief value, to ten per Cent.

. . . .

[G.] Grain

. . . .

[1. *Flour*]

Though flour may with propriety be noticed as a manufacture of Grain, it were useless to do it, but for the purpose of submitting the expediency of a general system of inspection, throughout the ports of the United States; which, if established upon proper principles, would be likely to improve the quality of our flour every where, and to raise its reputation in foreign markets. There are however considerations which stand in the way of such an arrangement.

[2. *Spirits and Malt Liquors — General*]

Ardent spirits and malt liquors are, next to flour, the two principle manufactures of Grain. The first has made a very extensive, the last a considerable progress in the United States. In respect to both, an exclusive possession of the home market ought to be secured to the domestic manufacturers; as fast as circumstances will admit. Nothing is more practicable & nothing more desirable.

The existing laws of the United States have done much towards attaining this valuable object; but some additions to the present duties, on foreign distilled spirits, and foreign malt liquors, and perhaps an abatement of those on home made spirits, would more effectually secure it; and there does not occur any very weighty objection to either.

An augmentation of the duties on imported spirits would favour, as well the distillation of Spirits from molasses, as that from Grain. And to secure to the nation the benefit of the manufacture, even of foreign materials, is always of great, though perhaps secondary importance.

A strong impression prevails in the minds of those concerned in distilleries (including too the most candid and enlightened) that greater differences in the rates of duty on foreign and domestic spirits are necessary, completely to secure the successful manufacture of the latter; and there are facts which entitle this impression to attention.

[3. *Molasses & Rum*]

It is known, that the price of molasses for some years past, has been successively rising in the West India Markets . . . . [T]he duty of three cents per Gallon on molasses, may render it difficult for the distillers of that material to maintain with adequate profit a competition, with the rum brought from the West Indies, the quality of which is so considerably superior.

[4. *Gin and Whiskey*]

. . . .

It is therefore submitted, that an addition of two cents per Gallon be made to the duty on imported spirits of the first class of proof, with a proportionable increase on those of higher proof; and that a deduction of one cent per Gallon be made from the duty on spirits distilled within the United States, beginning with the first class of proof, and a proportionable deduction from the duty on those of higher proof.

[5. *Malt Liquors*]

It is ascertained, that by far the greatest part of the malt liquors consumed in the United States are the produce of domestic breweries. . . .

. . . .

To render the encouragement to domestic breweries decisive, it may be adviseable to substitute to the present rates of duty eight cents per gallon generally; and it will deserve to be considered as a guard against evasions, whether there ought not to be a prohibition of their importation, except in casks of considerable capacity. It is to be hoped, that such a duty would banish from the market, foreign malt liquors of inferior quality; and that the best kind only would continue to be imported till it should be supplanted, by the efforts of equal skill or care at home.

Till that period, the importation so qualified would be a useful stimulus to the improvement: And in the mean time, the payment of the increased price, for the enjoyment of a luxury, in order to the encouragement of a most useful branch of domestic industry, could not reasonably be deemed a hardship.

. . . .

[J.] Wool

. . . .

Premiums would probably be found the best means of promoting the domestic, and bounties the foreign supply. The first may be within the compass of the institution hereafter to be submitted — The last would require a specific legislative provision. If any bounties are granted they ought of course to be adjusted with an eye to quality, as well as quantity.

A fund for the purpose may be derived from the addition of 2½ per Cent, to the present rate of duty, on Carpets and Carpeting . . . .

. . . .

[III. Conclusion]

Bounties are in various instances proposed as one species of encouragement.

It is a familiar objection to them, that they are difficult to be managed and liable to frauds. But neither that difficulty nor this danger seems sufficiently great to countervail the advantages of which they are productive, when rightly applied. And it is presumed to have been shewn, that they are in some cases, particularly in the infancy of new enterprises indispensable.

It will however be necessary to guard, with extraordinary circumspection, the manner of dispensing them. . . .

If the principle shall not be deemed inadmissible the means of avoiding abuse of it will not be likely to present insurmountable obstacles. There are useful guides from practice in other quarters.

It shall therefore only be remarked here, in relation to this point, that any bounty, which may be applied to the *manufacture* of an article, cannot with safety extend beyond those manufactories, at which the making of the article is a *regular trade*.

It would be impossible to annex adequate precautions to a benefit of that nature, if extended to every private family, in which the manufacture was incidentally carried on, and its being a merely incidental occupation which engages a portion of time that would otherwise be lost, it can be advantageously carried on, without so special an aid.

The possibility of a diminution of the revenue may also present itself, as an objection to the arrangements, which have been submitted.

But there is no truth, which may be more firmly relied upon, than that the interests of the revenue are promoted, by whatever promotes an increase of National industry and wealth.

. . . .

The measures . . . which have been submitted, taken aggregately, will for a long time to come rather augment than decrease the public revenue.

. . . .

The operation and utility of premiums have been adverted to; together with the advantages which have resulted from their dispensation, under the direction of certain public and private societies. . . .

In countries where there is great private wealth much may be effected by the voluntary contributions of patriotic individuals, but in a community situated like that of the United States, the public purse must supply the deficiency of private resource. In what can it be so useful as in prompting and improving the efforts of industry?

All of which is humbly submitted.

Alexander Hamilton
Secy of the Treasury
December 5, 1791

Exercise 2(C):

Consider the following matters in connection with Hamilton's Report on Manufactures:

(1) In the second excerpted paragraph, Hamilton used the phrase "domestic commerce." In Part I(C)(4), Hamilton made reference to matters "of learning of Agriculture of Manufactures and of Commerce." In Part I(C)(5), Hamilton used the phrase "Agriculture Arts manufactures and Commerce." What is the scope of the word "commerce" as used by Hamilton?

(2) In Part I(B), Hamilton advocated "the incitement and patronage of government" to foster the development of industry. Was he suggesting government intrusion into the free market? Was he advocating central planning of the economy?

(3) Hamilton suggested offering "bounties" to encourage the development of industry. For his plan to work, what did he anticipate would be the source of money for the bounties?

(4) Upon what enumerated powers did Hamilton rely for his proposed legislative program for the promotion of industry? In which clause of the Constitution are those powers located? What is his implicit understanding of the scope of that clause?

(5) What limitations, if any, did Hamilton acknowledge with respect to the legislative powers upon which he relied?

(6) What role, if any, did Hamilton anticipate for judiciary in enforcing any such limits?

(7) Do any of Hamilton's suggestions exceed federal legislative powers?

HYLTON v. UNITED STATES
3 U.S. 171 (1796)

[On June 5, 1794, Congress enacted a tax on carriages. Congress established annual tax rates from two dollars for small carriages to ten dollars on the largest carriages, denominated "chariots." The tax was unsuccessfully opposed in both houses of Congress as exceeding federal taxing authority. It was also opposed on policy, as carriages subject to the tax were much more predominant in southern States.

Several prominent citizens refused to pay the tax. In order to define the scope of federal tax authority, the administration determined to file an enforcement action.

Daniel Hylton owned a chariot and the taxes and penalties due amounted to sixteen dollars. In order to ensure a determination of the issue by the U.S. Supreme Court which, under the Federal Judiciary Act of 1789, had appellate jurisdiction limited to amounts in controversy in excess of $2,000, Hylton waived jury trial and the parties stipulated:

> That the Defendant, on June 5, 1794, and therefrom to the last day of September following, owned, possessed, and kept 125 chariots for the conveyance of persons, and no more: that the chariots were kept exclusively for the Defendant's own private use, and not to let out to hire: and that the Defendant had notice according to the act of Congress, entitled 'An act laying duties upon carriages for the conveyance of persons,' but that he omitted and refused to make an entry of the said chariots, and to pay the duties thereupon, as in and by the said law is required, alleging that the said law was unconstitutional and void. If the court adjudged the Defendant to be liable to pay the tax and fine for not doing so, and for not entering the carriages, then judgment shall be entered for the Plaintiff for 2000 dollars, to be discharged by the payment of 16 dollars, the amount of the duty and penalty; otherwise that judgment be entered for the Defendant.

The Circuit Court for the District of Virginia equally divided on the matter. Hylton's counsel then withdrew from the case and the government hired two attorneys to represent Hylton. Upon agreement of the parties, Hylton then confessed judgment so as to lay a foundation for Supreme Court review.

The Justices who heard the case delivered their opinions seriatim.]

JUSTICE CHASE.

By the case stated, only one question is submitted to the opinion of this court; whether the law of Congress . . . is unconstitutional and void?

. . . .

[Article I, section 2, of the Constitution provides that] direct taxes shall be apportioned among the several States, according to their numbers, to be determined by the rule prescribed.

[Article I, section 9 of the Constitution provides that] no capitation, or other direct tax, shall be laid, unless in proportion to the census, or enumeration, before directed.

[Article I, section 8 of the Constitution declares] that Congress shall have power to lay and collect taxes, duties, imposts, and excises; but all duties, imposts, and excises, shall be uniform throughout the United States.

[Hylton] took great pains to prove, that the tax on carriages was a direct tax; but they did not satisfy my mind. I think, at least, it may be doubted; and if I only doubted, I should affirm the judgment of the Circuit Court. The deliberate decision of the National Legislature (who did not consider a tax on carriages a direct tax, but thought it was within the description of a duty) would determine me, if the case was doubtful, to receive the construction of the Legislature: But I am inclined to think, that a tax on carriages is not a direct tax, within the letter, or meaning of the Constitution.

The great object of the Constitution was, to give Congress a power to lay taxes, adequate to the exigencies of government; but they were to observe two rules in imposing them, namely, the rule of uniformity, when they laid duties, imposts, or excises; and the rule of apportionment, according to the census, when they laid any direct tax.

. . . If the framers of the Constitution did not contemplate other taxes than direct taxes, and duties, imposts, and excises, there is great inaccuracy in their language. If these four species of taxes were all that were mediated, the general power to lay taxes was unnecessary. If it was intended, that Congress should have authority to lay only one of the four enumerated, to wit, direct taxes, by the rule of apportionment, and the other three by the rule of uniformity, the expressions would have run thus: 'Congress shall have power to lay and collect direct taxes, and duties, imposts, and excises; the first shall be laid according to the census; and the three last shall be uniform throughout the United States.' The power, in [Article I, section 8], to lay direct taxes, included a power to lay direct taxes (whether capitation, or any other) and also duties, imposts, and excises; and every other species of kind of tax whatsoever, and called by any other name. Duties, imposts, and excises, were enumerated, after the general term taxes, only for the purpose of declaring, that they were to be laid by the rule of uniformity. I consider the Constitution to stand in this manner. A general power is given to Congress, to lay and collect taxes, of every kind or nature, without any restraint, except only on exports; but two rules are prescribed for their government, namely, uniformity and apportionment: Three kinds of taxes, to wit, duties, imposts, and excises by the first rule, and capitation, or other direct taxes, by the second rule.

I believe some taxes may be both direct and indirect at the same time. If so, would Congress be prohibited from laying such a tax, because it is partly a direct tax?

The Constitution evidently contemplates no taxes as direct taxes, but only such as Congress could lay in proportion to the census. The rule of apportionment is only to be adopted in such cases where it can reasonably apply; and the subject taxed, must ever determine the application of the rule.

If it is proposed to tax any specific article by the rule of apportionment, and it would evidently create great inequality and injustice, it is unreasonable to say, that the Constitution intended such tax should be laid by that rule.

It appears to me, that a tax on carriages cannot be laid by the rule of apportionment, without very great inequality and injustice. For example: Suppose two States, equal in census, to pay 80,000 dollars each, by a tax on carriages, of 8 dollars on every carriage; and in one State there are 100 carriages, and in the other 1000. The owners of carriages in one State, would pay ten times the tax of owners in the other. *A* in one State, would pay for his carriage 8 dollars, but *B* in the other state, would pay for his carriage, 80 dollars.

It was argued, that a tax on carriages was a direct tax, and might be laid according to the rule of apportionment, and (as I understood) in this manner: Congress, after determining on the gross sum to be raised was to apportion it, according to the census, and then lay it in one State on carriages, in another on horses, in a third on tobacco, in a fourth on rice; and so on. I admit that this mode might be adopted, to raise a certain sum in each State, according to the census, but it would not be a tax on carriages, but on a number of specific articles; and it seems to me, that it would be liable to the same objection of abuse and oppression, as a selection of any one article in all the States.

I think, an annual tax on carriages for the conveyance of persons, may be considered as within the power granted to Congress to lay duties. The term duty, is the most comprehensive next to the generical term tax; and practically in Great Britain (whence we take our general ideas of taxes, duties, imposts, excises, customs, etc.) embraces taxes on stamps, tolls for passage, etc. etc. and is not confined to taxes on importation only.

It seems to me, that a tax on expense is an indirect tax; and I think, an annual tax on a carriage for the conveyance of persons, is of that kind; because a carriage is a consumeable commodity; and such annual tax on it, is on the expense of the owner.

I am inclined to think, but of this I do not give a judicial opinion, that the direct taxes contemplated by the Constitution, are only two, to wit, a capitation, or poll tax, simply, without regard to property, profession, or any other circumstance; and a tax on LAND. I doubt whether a tax, by a general assessment of personal property, within the United States, is included within the term direct tax.

As I do not think the tax on carriages is a direct tax, it is unnecessary, at this time, for me to determine, whether this court, constitutionally possesses the power to declare an act of Congress void, on the ground of its being made contrary to, and in violation of, the Constitution; but if the court have such power, I am free to declare, that I will never exercise it, but in a very clear case.

I am for affirming the judgment of the Circuit Court.

JUSTICE PATERSON.

. . . .

The question is whether a tax upon carriages be a direct tax? If it be a direct tax, it is unconstitutional because it has been laid pursuant to the rule of uniformity, and not to the rule of apportionment. [Hylton argued] that a tax on carriages does not come within the description of a duty, impost, or excise, and therefore is a direct tax. It has, on the other hand, been contended, that as a tax on carriages is not a direct tax; it must fall within one of the classifications just enumerated, and particularly must be a duty or excise. The argument on both sides turns in a circle; it is not a duty, impost, or excise, and therefore must be a direct tax; it is not [a direct] tax, and therefore must be a duty or excise. What is the natural and common, or technical and appropriate, meaning of the words, duty and excise, it is not easy to ascertain. . . . It was, however, obviously the intention of the framers of the Constitution, that Congress should possess full power over every species of taxable property, except exports. The term taxes, is generical, and was made use of to vest in Congress plenary authority in all cases of taxation. The general division of taxes is into direct and indirect. . . . There may, perhaps, be an indirect tax on a particular article, that cannot be comprehended within the description of duties, or imposts, or excises; in such case it will be comprised under the general denomination of taxes. For the term tax is the genus, and includes,

(1) Direct taxes.

(2) Duties, imposts, and excises.

(3) All other classes of an indirect kind, and not within any of the classifications enumerated under the preceding heads.

The question occurs, how is such tax to be laid, uniformly or apportionately? The rule of uniformity will apply, because it is an indirect tax, and direct taxes only are to be apportioned. What are direct taxes within the meaning of the Constitution? The Constitution declares, that a capitation tax is a direct tax; and, both in theory and practice, a tax on land is deemed to be a direct tax. . . . It is not necessary to determine, whether a tax on the product of land be a direct or indirect tax. . . . Whether direct taxes, in the sense of the Constitution, comprehended any other tax than a capitation tax, and tax on land, is a questionable point. If Congress, for instance, should tax, in the aggregate or mass, things that generally pervade all the states in Union, then, perhaps, the rule of apportionment would be the most proper, especially if an assessment was to intervene. This appears by the practice of some of the states, to have been considered a direct tax. Whether it be so under the Constitution of the United States, is a matter of some difficulty; but as it is not before the court, it would be improper to give any decisive opinion upon it. I never entertained a doubt, that the principal, I will not say, the only, objects, that the framers of the Constitution contemplated as falling within the rule of apportionment, were a capitation tax and a tax on land. . . .

. . . The Constitution has been considered as an accommodating system; it was the effect of mutual sacrifices and concessions; it was the work of compromise. The rule of apportionment is of this nature; it is radically wrong; it cannot be supported by any solid reasoning. . . .

Again, numbers do not afford a just estimate or rule of wealth. It is, indeed, a very uncertain and incompetent sign of opulence. There is another reason against the extension of the principle laid down in the Constitution.

[Hylton argued] that an equal participation of the expense or burden by the several states in the Union, was the primary object, which the framers of the Constitution had in view; and that this object will be effected by the principle of apportionment, which is an operation upon states, and not on individuals; for, each state will be debited for the amount of its quota of the tax, and credited for its payments. This brings it to the old system of requisitions. An equal rule is doubtless the best. But how is this to be applied to states or individuals? The latter are the objects of taxation, without reference to states, except in the case of direct taxes. The fiscal power is exerted certainly, equally, and effectually on individuals; it cannot be exerted on states. The history . . . of our own country, will evince the truth of this position. . . . Congress could not, under the old confederation, raise money by taxes, be the public exigencies ever so pressing and great. They had no coercive authority — if they had, it must have been exercised against the delinquent states, which would be ineffectual, or terminate in a separation. Requisitions were a dead letter, unless the state legislatures could be brought into action; and when they were, the sums raised were very disproportional. Unequal contributions or payments encouraged discontent, and formed state-jealousy. . . . A tax on carriages, if apportioned, would be oppressive and pernicious. How would it work? In some states there are many carriages, and in others but few. Shall the whole sum fall on one or two individuals in a state, who may happen to own and possess carriages? The thing would be absurd, and inequitable. In answer to this objection, it has been observed, that the sum, and not the tax, is to be apportioned; and that Congress may select in the different states different articles or objects from whence to raise the apportioned sum. The idea is novel. . . . It would not work well, and perhaps is utterly impracticable. . . . If a tax upon land, where the object is simple and uniform throughout the states, is scarcely practicable, what shall we say of a tax attempted to be apportioned among, and raised and collected from, a number of dissimilar objects. The difficulty will increase with the number and variety of the things proposed for taxation. We shall be obliged to resort to intricate and endless valuations and assessments, in which every thing will be arbitrary, and nothing certain. . . . The rule of uniformity, on the contrary, implies certainty, and leaves nothing to the will and pleasure of the assessor. . . . Apportionment is an operation on states, and involves valuations and assessments, which are arbitrary, and should not be resorted to but in case of necessity. Uniformity is an instant operation on individuals, without the intervention of assessments, or any regard to states, and is at once easy, certain, and efficacious. All taxes on expenses or consumption are indirect taxes. A tax on carriages is of this kind, and of course is not a direct tax. Indirect taxes are circuitous modes of reaching the revenue of individuals . . . .

. . . .

I am, therefore, of opinion, that the judgment rendered in the Circuit Court of Virginia ought to be affirmed.

JUSTICE IREDELL.

I agree in opinion with my brothers, who have already expressed theirs, that the tax in question, is agreeable to the Constitution . . . .

The Congress possess the power of taxing all taxable objects, without limitation, with the particular exception of a duty on exports.

There are two restrictions only on the exercise of this authority:

(1)   All direct taxes must be apportioned.

(2)   All duties, imposts, and excises must be uniform.

If the carriage tax be a direct tax, within the meaning of the Constitution, it must be apportioned.

If it be a duty, impost, or excise, within the meaning of the Constitution, it must be uniform.

If it can be considered as a tax, neither direct within the meaning of the Constitution, nor comprehended within the term duty, impost, or excise; there is no provision in the Constitution, one way or another, and then it must be left to such an operation of the power, as if the authority to lay taxes had been given generally in all instances, without saying whether they should be apportioned or uniform; and in that case, I should presume, the tax ought to be uniform; because the present Constitution was particularly intended to affect individuals, and not states, except in the particular cases specified: And this is the leading distinction between the articles of Confederation and the present Constitution.

[I]

As all direct taxes must be apportioned, it is evident that the Constitution contemplated none as direct but such as could be apportioned.

If this cannot be apportioned, it is, therefore, not a direct tax in the sense of the Constitution.

That this tax cannot be apportioned is evident. Suppose 10 dollars contemplated as a tax on each chariot, or post chaise, in the United States, and the number of both in all the United States be computed at 105, the number of Representatives in Congress.

This would produce in the whole [$1050 of revenue].

The share of Virginia being 19/105 parts, would be [$190].

The share of Connecticut being 7/105 parts, would be [$70].

Then suppose Virginia had 50 carriages [and] Connecticut [only 2].

The share of Virginia being [$190], this must of course be collected from the owners of carriages, and there would therefore be collected from each carriage [$3.80].

The share of Connecticut being [$70], each carriage would pay [$35.00].

If any state had no carriages, there could be no apportionment at all. This mode is too manifestly absurd to be supported, and has not even been attempted in debate.

[II]

But two expedients have been proposed of a very extraordinary nature, to evade the difficulty.

[A]

[First, to] raise the money a tax on carriages would produce, not by laying a tax on each carriage uniformly, but by selecting different articles in different states, so that the amount paid in each state may be equal to the sum due upon a principle of apportionment. One state might pay by a tax on carriages, another by a tax on slaves, etc.

. . . .

[(1) That proposal] is not an apportionment, of a tax on Carriages, but of the money a tax on carriages might be supposed to produce, which is quite a different thing.

(2) It admits that Congress cannot lay an uniform tax on all carriages in the Union, in any mode, but that they may on carriages in one or more states. They may therefore lay a tax on carriages in 14 states, but not in the 15th.

. . . .

(4) Such an arbitrary method of taxing different states differently, is a suggestion altogether new, and would lead, if practised, to such dangerous consequences, that it will require very powerful arguments to show, that that method of taxing would be in any manner compatible with the Constitution . . . .

[B]

The second expedient proposed, was, that of taxing carriages, among other things, in a general assessment. This amounts to saying, that Congress may lay a tax on carriages, but that they may not do it unless they blend it with other subjects of taxation. For this, no reason or authority has been given . . . .

[III]

There is no necessity, or propriety, in determining what is or is not, a direct, or indirect, tax in all cases.

Some difficulties may occur which we do not at present foresee. Perhaps a direct tax in the sense of the Constitution, can mean nothing but a tax on something inseparably annexed to the soil: Something capable of apportionment under all such circumstances.

A land or poll tax may be considered of this description.

. . . .

Either of these is capable of apportionment.

In regard to other articles, there may possibly be considerable doubt.

It is sufficient, on the present occasion, for the court to be satisfied, that this is not a direct tax contemplated by the Constitution, in order to affirm the present judgment; since, if it cannot be apportioned, it must necessarily be uniform.

I am clearly of opinion, this is not a direct tax in the sense of the Constitution, and, therefore, that the judgment ought to be affirmed.

JUSTICE WILSON.

As there were only four Judges, including myself, who attended the argument of this cause, I should have thought it proper to join in the decision, though I had before expressed judicial opinion on the subject, in the Circuit Court of Virginia, did not the unanimity of the other three Judges, relieve me from the necessity. I shall now, however, only add, that my sentiments, in favor of the constitutionality of the tax in question, have not been changed.

JUSTICE CUSHING.

As I have been prevented, by indisposition, from attending to the argument, it would be improper to give an opinion on the merits of the cause.

Judgment affirmed.

Exercise 3(A):

Consider the following questions in connection with *Hylton v. United States*:

(1)   According to the views expressed in this case, provided Congress follows the proper limitations, is there any form of tax beyond its power other than a tax on exports?

(2)   According to the views expressed in this case, what forms of taxes are "direct" that must be apportioned in accordance with the census?

(3)   According to the views expressed in this case, what forms of taxes must be "uniform throughout the United States"?

(4)   What techniques of textual analysis, if any, does the Court employ to answer these questions? What techniques of historical analysis, if any, does the Court employ to answer the questions?

(5)   If your instructor assigned *Volume 1*, consider what pre-*Marbury* precedent for judicial review, if any, this case establishes beyond the prior decisions regarding the Hayburn and Todd applications for Revolutionary War pensions.

(6)   If your instructor assigned *Volume 1*, consider how the exercise of judicial review in this case compares with the predictions of Brutus and Hamilton regarding the role of the federal judiciary.

EARLY "DIRECT TAXATION"

Although the result in *Hylton* seemed to very narrowly define the revenue-raising measures that would be subject to apportionment, Congress did enact such a direct tax shortly thereafter. *See* An Act to Lay and Collect a Direct Tax within the United States, 1 Stat. 597 (July 14, 1798). The full text of that statute is reproduced on the DVD-ROM in the collection of "Early Revenue Measures." In light of the practical problems the *Hylton* Court identified with treating the carriage tax as one subject to apportionment, examine the manner in which the so-called "House Tax" was calculated.

Exercise 3(B):

(1)   In the very likely event that the value of real estate within the several States was not distributed among them in the same proportion as inhabitants (as counted in the census), how did Congress instruct calculation of the tax? For example, if applying the rates specified in the statute to the value of appraised land in a State generated a greater sum than the State's apportioned share of the tax, would the State pay the greater sum or would the rate be lower in such a State than elsewhere?

(2)   How does that manner of calculation compare with an apportionment of the Carriage Tax at issue in *Hylton*?

(3)   If the only tax imposed by the 1798 statute was the tax on slaves, could it have been apportioned? Would any State that had abolished slavery been exempt from contributing its apportioned share? Alternatively, would such a tax have been considered uniform in light of the great geographical disparity in the incidence of slavery?

(4)   Would the acknowledgment and protection of slavery in the Constitution of 1789 have provided a basis for objecting to the 1798 tax? If not, would Congress in 1798 have had authority to effectively abolish slavery by imposing a tax of $5000 rather than $0.50?

LATER "DIRECT TAXATION"

The central government adopted an income tax to finance the Civil War. The Supreme Court upheld that tax even though it was not apportioned. In reaching that conclusion, the Court reiterated views first expressed in *Hylton*, that "direct taxes, within the meaning of the Constitution, are only capitation taxes, as expressed in that instrument, and taxes on real estate." *Springer v. United States*, 102 U.S. 586, 602 (1880). The Court found that the challenged income tax was instead "within the category of an excise or duty." *Id.*[1]

Only fifteen years later, the Supreme Court reversed course and determined that an income tax was subject to the requirement of apportionment. *See Pollock v. Farmers' Loan & Trust Co.*, 157 U.S. 429 (1894), *aff'd on reh'g*, 158 U.S. 601 (1895). The Sixteenth Amendment, ratified in 1913, superceded *Pollack* by expressly providing that Congress had the power to impose a "tax on incomes, from whatever source derived, without apportionment among the several States, and without regard to any census or enumeration."

In addition to the change produced by ratification of the Sixteenth Amendment, subsequent case law effectively undermines the rationale of *Pollack*. *See New York ex rel. Cohn v. Graves*, 300 U.S. 308 (1937). The class of revenue-raising measures subject to apportionment was further restricted with the ratification of the Twenty-Fourth Amendment which prohibited certain forms of capitation taxes, specifically those imposed as a condition of participation in federal elections.

B.   Taxation as Regulation

UNITED STATES v. SANCHEZ
340 U.S. 42 (1950)

JUSTICE CLARK delivered the opinion of a unanimous Court.

This is a direct appeal . . . from dismissal by the District Court of a suit for recovery of $8,701.65 in taxes and interest alleged to be due under § 7(a)(2) of the Marihuana Tax Act, 50 Stat. 551, now § 2590(a)(2) of the Internal Revenue Code. In their motion to dismiss, which was granted without opinion, defendants attacked the constitutionality of this subsection on the ground that it levied a penalty, not a tax. The validity of this levy is the issue here.

---

[1] At about the same time, a leading scholar suggested distinct meanings for the various revenue-raising measures referenced in the Constitution. "[T]he word *duty* has a meaning nearly synonymous with tax, but in ordinary use it means an indirect tax, imposed on the importation, exportation or consumption of goods. As thus employed it has a broader meaning than *custom*, which is a duty imposed on imports or exports." THOMAS M. COOLEY, A TREATISE ON THE LAW OF TAXATION 3 (1876). "The term *impost* also signifies any tax, tribute or duty, but it is seldom applies to any but the indirect taxes. An *excise* duty is an inland impost, levied upon articles of manufacture or sale, and also upon licenses to pursue certain trades or deal in certain commodities." *Id.*

In enacting the Marihuana Tax Act, the Congress had two objectives: "First, the development of a plan of taxation which will raise revenue and at the same time render extremely difficult the acquisition of marihuana by persons who desire it for illicit uses and, second, the development of an adequate means of publicizing dealings in marihuana in order to tax and control the traffic effectively." S. Rep. No. 900, 75th Cong., 1st Sess. 3. To the same effect, see H.R. Rep. No. 792, 75th Cong., 1st Sess. 2.

Pursuant to these objectives, § 3230 of the Code imposes a special tax ranging from $1 to $24 on "every person who imports, manufactures, produces, compounds, sells, deals in, disperses, prescribes, administers, or gives away marihuana." For purposes of administration, § 3231 requires such persons to register at the time of the payment of the tax with the Collector of the District in which their businesses are located. The Code then makes it unlawful — with certain exceptions not pertinent here — for any person to transfer marihuana except in pursuance of a written order of the transferee on a blank form issued by the Secretary of the Treasury. Section 2590 requires the transferee at the time he applies for the order form to pay a tax on such transfer of $1 per ounce or fraction thereof if he has paid the special tax and registered or $100 per ounce or fraction thereof if he has not paid the special tax and registered. The transferor is also made liable for the tax so imposed, in the event the transfer is made without an order form and without the payment of the tax by the transferee. Defendants in this case are transferors.

It is obvious that § 2590, by imposing a severe burden on transfers to unregistered persons, implements the congressional purpose of restricting traffic in marihuana to accepted industrial and medicinal channels. Hence the attack here rests on the regulatory character and prohibitive burden of the section as well as the penal nature of the imposition. But despite the regulatory effect and the close resemblance to a penalty, it does not follow that the levy is invalid.

First. It is beyond serious question that a tax does not cease to be valid merely because it regulates, discourages, or even definitely deters the activities taxed. *Sonzinsky v. United States,* 300 U.S. 506, 513–14 (1937). The principle applies even though the revenue obtained is obviously negligible, *id.,* or the revenue purpose of the tax may be secondary, *Hampton & Co. v. United States,* 276 U.S. 394, Treas. Dec. 42706 (1928). Nor does a tax statute necessarily fall because it touches on activities which Congress might not otherwise regulate. As was pointed out in *Magnano Co. v. Hamilton,* 292 U.S. 40, 47 (1934):

> From the beginning of our government, the courts have sustained taxes although imposed with the collateral intent of effecting ulterior ends which, considered apart, were beyond the constitutional power of the lawmakers to realize by legislation directly addressed to their accomplishment.

These principles are controlling here. The tax in question is a legitimate exercise of the taxing power despite its collateral regulatory purpose and effect.

Second. The tax levied by § 2590(a)(2) is not conditioned upon the commission of a crime. . . . Since his [the transferor's] tax liability does not in effect rest on criminal conduct, the tax can be properly called a civil rather than a criminal sanction. The fact that Congress provided civil procedure for collection indicates its intention that the tax be treated as such. *Helvering v. Mitchell,* 303 U.S. 391 (1938). Moreover, the Government is seeking to collect the levy by a judicial proceeding with its attendant safeguards. . . .

Nor is the civil character of the tax imposed by § 2590(a)(2) altered by its severity in relation to that assessed by § 2590(a)(1). The difference has a rational foundation. Unregistered persons are not likely to procure the required order form prior to transfer or pay the required tax. Free of sanctions, dealers would be prone to accommodate such persons in their unlawful activity. The imposition of equally severe tax burdens on such transferors is reasonably adapted to secure payment of the tax by transferees or stop transfers to unregistered persons, as well as to provide an additional source from which the expense of unearthing clandestine transfers can be recovered. *Cf. Helvering v. Mitchell,* 303 U.S. 391 (1938).

The judgment below must be reversed and the cause remanded for further proceedings in conformity with this opinion.

A NOTE REGARDING TAX LAWS AS A MEANS OF DRUG REGULATION

In the course of explaining the history of federal regulation of drugs, the Court in *Gonzales v. Raich,* 545 U.S. 1, 10–11 (2005), observed that Congress primarily relied upon its taxing power prior to the 1970 enactment of the Controlled Substances Act (CSA):

> Aside from . . . labeling restrictions, most domestic drug regulations prior to 1970 generally came in the guise of revenue laws, with the Department of the Treasury serving as the Federal Government's primary enforcer. For example, the primary drug control law, before being repealed by the passage of the CSA, was the Harrison Narcotics Act of 1914, 38 Stat. 785 (repealed 1970). The Harrison Act sought to exert control over the possession and sale of narcotics, specifically cocaine and opiates, by requiring producers, distributors, and purchasers to register with the Federal Government, by assessing taxes against parties so registered, and by regulating the issuance of prescriptions.

> Marijuana itself was not significantly regulated by the Federal Government until 1937 . . . [when] Congress pass[ed] the Marihuana Tax Act, 50 Stat. 551 (repealed 1970). Like the Harrison Act, the Marihuana Tax Act did not outlaw the possession or sale of marijuana outright. Rather, it imposed registration and reporting requirements for all individuals importing, producing, selling, or dealing in marijuana, and required the payment of annual taxes in addition to transfer taxes whenever the drug changed hands. . . . Noncompliance exposed traffickers to severe federal penalties, whereas compliance would often subject them to prosecution under state law. Thus, while the Marihuana Tax Act did not declare the drug illegal *per se,* the onerous administrative requirements, the prohibitively expensive taxes, and the risks attendant on compliance practically curtailed the marijuana trade.

But in *Leary v. United States,* 395 U.S. 6 (1969), the Court held that the Constitution's privilege against self-incrimination constituted a defense to a prosecution for failure to register and pay the federal marihuana tax when possession of marihuana was a violation of state law. The Court reached that result on the basis of precedents finding similar problems with other federal taxes directed to matters that were commonly a violation of state law where Congress had required that tax authorities share such information with state and local authorities. *See Marchetti v. United States,* 390 U.S. 39 (1968) (occupational tax on wagering); *Grosso v. United States,* 390 U.S. 62 (1968) (excise tax on wagering); *Haynes v. United States,* 390 U.S. 85 (1968) (possession of an unregistered firearm).

Exercise 4(A):

Aside from general protections afforded by criminal procedure, is there any limit to the power of Congress to deter conduct by imposing a tax?

UNITED STATES v. BUTLER
297 U.S. 1 (1936)

[The Court examined the Agricultural Adjustment Act of 1933, which was intended to encourage farmers to reduce production in order to increase market prices. The Act created a processing tax on farm products and only distributed the tax revenue to those farmers who were in compliance with federal guidelines.]

Justice Roberts delivered the opinion of the Court.

In this case we must determine whether certain provisions of the Agricultural Adjustment Act, 1933, conflict with the Federal Constitution.

. . . .

[I]

. . . The Government in substance and effect asks us to separate the Agricultural Adjustment Act into two statutes, the one levying an excise on processors of certain commodities, the other appropriating the public moneys independently of the first. Passing the novel suggestion that two statutes enacted as parts of a single scheme should be tested as if they were distinct and unrelated, we think the legislation now before us is not susceptible of such separation and treatment.

The tax can only be sustained by ignoring the avowed purpose and operation of the act, and holding it a measure merely laying an excise upon processors to raise revenue for the support of the government. . . .

. . . .

The statute not only avows an aim foreign to the procurement of revenue for the support of government, but by its operation shows the exaction laid upon processors to be the necessary means for the intended control of agricultural production.

In these aspects the tax, so-called, closely resembles that laid by the Act of August 3, 1882, entitled "An Act to Regulate Immigration," which came before this Court in the *Head Money Cases*, 112 U.S. 580 (1884). The statute directed that there should be levied, collected and paid a duty of fifty cents for each alien passenger who should come by vessel from a foreign port to one in the United States. Payment was to be made to the collector of the port by the master, owner, consignee or agent of the ship; the money was to be paid into the Treasury, was to be called the immigrant fund, and to be used by the Secretary of the Treasury to defray the expense of regulating immigration, for the case of immigrants and relieving those in distress, and for the expenses of effectuating the act.

Various objections to the act were presented. In answering them the Court said:

> But the true answer to all these objections is that the power exercised in this instance is not the taxing power. The burden imposed on the ship owner by this statute is the mere incident of the regulation of commerce — of that branch of foreign commerce which is involved in immigration. . . .

> It is true not much is said about protecting the ship owner. But he is the man who reaps the profit from the transaction . . . . The sum demanded of him is not, therefore, strictly speaking, a tax or duty within the meaning of the Constitution. The money thus raised, though paid into the Treasury, is appropriated in advance to the uses of the statute, and does not go to the general support of the government.

112 U.S. at 595.

. . . .

It is inaccurate and misleading to speak of the exaction from processors prescribed by the challenged act as a tax, or to say that as a tax it is subject to no infirmity. A tax, in the general understanding of the term, and as used in the Constitution, signifies an exaction for the support of the Government. The word has never been thought to connote the expropriation of money from one group for the benefit of another. We may concede that the latter sort of imposition is constitutional when imposed to effectuate regulation of a matter in which both groups are interested and in respect of which there is a power of legislative regulation. But manifestly no justification for it can be found unless as an integral part of such regulation. The exaction cannot be wrested out of its setting, denominated an excise for raising revenue and legalized by ignoring its purpose as a mere instrumentality for bringing about a desired end. . . .

. . . .

It does not follow that as the act is not an exertion of the taxing power and the exaction is not a true tax, the statute is void or the exaction uncollectible. For, to paraphrase what was said in the *Head Money Cases*, if this is an expedient regulation by Congress, of a subject within one of its granted powers, "and the end to be attained is one falling within that power, the act is not void, because, within a loose and more extended sense than was used in the Constitution," the exaction is called a tax. 112 U.S. at 596.

[II]

. . . The Government asserts that even if the respondents may question the propriety of the appropriation embodied in the statute their attack must fail because Article I, § 8 of the Constitution authorizes the contemplated expenditure of the funds raised by the tax. This contention presents the great and the controlling question in the case. We approach its decision with a sense of our grave responsibility to render judgment in accordance with the principles established for the governance of all three branches of the Government.

. . . .

The question is not what power the Federal Government ought to have but what powers they in fact have been given by the people. . . . The federal union is a government of delegated powers. It has only such as are expressly conferred upon it and such as are reasonably to be implied from those granted. In this respect we differ radically from nations where all legislative power, without restriction or limitation, is vested in a parliament or other legislative body subject to no restrictions except the discretion of its members.

Article I, § 8, of the Constitution vests sundry powers in the Congress. But two of its clauses have any bearing upon the validity of the statute under review.

[A]

The third clause endows the Congress with power "to regulate Commerce . . . among the several States." . . . [Here, the statute's] stated purpose is the control of agricultural production, a purely local activity, in an effort to raise the prices paid the farmer. Indeed, the Government does not attempt to uphold the validity of the act on the basis of the commerce clause, which, for the purpose of the present case, may be put aside as irrelevant.

[B]

The clause thought to authorize the legislation, — the first, — confers upon the Congress power "to lay and collect Taxes, Duties, Imposts and Excises, to pay the Debts and provide for the common Defence and general Welfare of the United States . . . ." It is not contended that this provision grants power to regulate agricultural production upon the theory that such legislation would promote the general welfare. The Government concedes that the phrase "to provide for the general welfare" qualifies the power "to lay and collect taxes." The view that the clause grants power to provide for the general welfare, independently of the taxing power, has never been authoritatively accepted. Justice Story points out that if it were adopted "it is obvious that under color of the generality of the words, to 'provide for the common defence and general welfare', the government of the United States is, in reality, a government of general and unlimited powers, notwithstanding the subsequent enumeration of specific powers."[11] The true construction undoubtedly is that the only thing granted is the power to tax for the purpose of providing funds for payment of the nation's debts and making provision for the general welfare.

Nevertheless the Government asserts that warrant is found in this clause for the adoption of the Agricultural Adjustment Act. The argument is that Congress may appropriate and authorize the spending of moneys for the "general welfare"; that the phrase should be liberally construed to cover anything conducive to national welfare; that decision as to what will promote such welfare rests with Congress alone, and the courts may not review its determination; and finally that the appropriation under attack was in fact for the general welfare of the United States.

The Congress is expressly empowered to lay taxes to provide for the general welfare. Funds in the Treasury as a result of taxation may be expended only through appropriation. Art. I, § 9, cl. 7. They can never accomplish the objects for which they were collected unless the power to appropriate is as broad as the power to tax. The necessary implication from the terms of the grant is that the public funds may be appropriated "to provide for the general welfare of the United States." These words cannot be meaningless, else they would not have been used. The conclusion must be that they were intended to limit and define the granted power to raise and to expend money. How shall they be construed to effectuate the intent of the instrument?

Since the foundation of the Nation sharp differences of opinion have persisted as to the true interpretation of the phrase. Madison asserted it amounted to no more than a reference to the other powers enumerated in the subsequent clauses of the same section; that, as the United States is a government of limited and enumerated powers, the grant of power to tax and spend for the general national welfare must be confined to the enumerated legislative fields committed to the Congress. In this view the phrase is mere tautology, for taxation and appropriation are or may be necessary incidents of the exercise of any of the enumerated legislative powers. Hamilton, on the other hand, maintained the clause confers a power separate and distinct from those later enumerated, is not restricted in meaning by the grant of them, and Congress consequently has a substantive power to tax and to appropriate, limited only by the requirement that it shall be exercised to provide for the general welfare of the United States. Each contention has had the support of those whose views are entitled to weight. This court has noticed the question, but has never found it necessary to decide which is the true construction. Justice Story, in his Commentaries, espouses the Hamiltonian position. We shall not review the writings of public men and commentators or discuss the legislative practice. Study of all these leads us to conclude that the reading advocated by Justice Story is the correct one. While, therefore, the power to tax is not unlimited, its confines are set in the clause which confers it, and not in those of § 8 which bestow and define the

---

[11] 1 Joseph Story, Commentaries on the Constitution of the United States § 907 (5th ed.).

legislative powers of the Congress. It results that the power of Congress to authorize expenditure of public moneys for public purposes is not limited by the direct grants of legislative power found in the Constitution.

But the adoption of the broader construction leaves the power to spend subject to limitations.

As Story says: "The Constitution was, from its very origin, contemplated to be the frame of a national government, of special and enumerated powers, and not of general and unlimited powers."

Again he says: "A power to lay taxes for the common defence and general welfare of the United States is not in common sense a general power. It is limited to those objects. It cannot constitutionally transcend them."

That the qualifying phrase must be given effect all advocates of broad construction admit. Hamilton, in his well known Report on Manufactures, states that the purpose must be "general, and not local." Monroe, an advocate of Hamilton's doctrine, wrote: "Have Congress a right to raise and appropriate the money to any and to every purpose according to their will and pleasure? They certainly have not." Story says that if the tax be not proposed for the common defence or general welfare, but for other objects wholly extraneous, it would be wholly indefensible upon constitutional principles. And he makes it clear that the powers of taxation and appropriation extend only to matters of national, as distinguished from local welfare.

As elsewhere throughout the Constitution the section in question lays down principles which control the use of the power, and does not attempt meticulous or detailed directions. Every presumption is to be indulged in favor of faithful compliance by Congress with the mandates of the fundamental law. Courts are reluctant to adjudge any statute in contravention of them. But, under our frame of government, no other place is provided where the citizen may be heard to urge that the law fails to conform to the limits set upon the use of a granted power. When such a contention comes here we naturally require a showing that by no reasonable possibility can the challenged legislation fall within the wide range of discretion permitted to the Congress. How great is the extent of that range, when the subject is the promotion of the general welfare of the United States, we need hardly remark. But, despite the breadth of the legislative discretion, our duty to hear and to render judgment remains. If the statute plainly violates the stated principle of the Constitution we must so declare.

[C]

We are not now required to ascertain the scope of the phrase "general welfare of the United States" or to determine whether an appropriation in aid of agriculture falls within it. Wholly apart from that question, another principle embedded in our Constitution prohibits the enforcement of the Agricultural Adjustment Act. The act invades the reserved rights of the states. It is a statutory plan to regulate and control agricultural production, a matter beyond the powers delegated to the federal government. The tax, the appropriation of the funds raised, and the direction for their disbursement, are but parts of the plan. They are but means to an unconstitutional end.

From the accepted doctrine that the United States is a government of delegated powers, it follows that those not expressly granted, or reasonably to be implied from such as are conferred, are reserved to the states or to the people. To forestall any suggestion to the contrary, the Tenth Amendment was adopted. The same proposition, otherwise stated, is that powers not granted are prohibited. None to regulate agricultural production is given, and therefore legislation by Congress for that purpose is forbidden.

It is an established principle that the attainment of a prohibited end may not be accomplished under the pretext of the exertion of powers which are granted.

> Should Congress, in the execution of its powers, adopt measures which are prohibited by the constitution; or should Congress, under the pretext of executing its powers, pass laws for the accomplishment of objects not intrusted to the government; it would become the painful duty of this tribunal, should a case requiring such a decision come before it, to say that such an act was not the law of the land.

McCulloch v. Maryland, 17 U.S. 316, 423 (1819).

> Congress cannot, under the pretext of executing delegated power, pass laws for the accomplishment of objects not intrusted to the Federal Government. And we accept as established doctrine that any provision of an act of Congress ostensibly enacted under power granted by the Constitution, not naturally and reasonably adapted to the effective exercise of such power but solely to the achievement of something plainly within power reserved to the States, is invalid and cannot be enforced.

Linder v. United States, 268 U.S. 5, 17 (1925).

These principles are as applicable to the power to lay taxes as to any other federal power. Said the court, in *McCulloch v. Maryland,* 17 U.S. 316, 421 (1819): "Let the end be legitimate, let it be within the scope of the constitution, and all means which are appropriate, which are plainly adapted to that end, which are not prohibited, but consist with the letter and spirit of the constitution, are constitutional."

The power of taxation, which is expressly granted, may, of course, be adopted as a means to carry into operation another power also expressly granted. But resort to the taxing power to effectuate an end which is not legitimate, not within the scope of the Constitution, is obviously inadmissible.

" 'Congress is not empowered to tax for those purposes which are within the exclusive province of the states." *Gibbons v. Ogden,* 22 U.S. 1, 34 (1824).

"There are, indeed, certain virtual limitations, arising from the principles of the Constitution itself. It would undoubtedly be an abuse of the [taxing] power if so exercised as to impair the separate existence and independent self-government of the States or if exercised for ends inconsistent with the limited grants of power in the Constitution." *Veazie Bank v. Fenno,* 75 U.S. 533, 541 (1869).

In the *Child Labor Tax Case,* 259 U.S. 20 (1922), and in *Hill v. Wallace,* 259 U.S. 44 (1922), this Court had before it statutes which purported to be taxing measures. But their purpose was found to be to regulate the conduct of manufacturing and trading, not in interstate commerce, but in the states, — matters not within any power conferred upon Congress by the Constitution — and the levy of the tax a means to force compliance. The Court held this was not a constitutional use, but an unconstitutional abuse of the power to tax. In *Linder v. United States,* 268 U.S. 5 (1925), we held that the power to tax could not justify the regulation of the practice of a profession, under the pretext of raising revenue. In *United States v. Constantine,* 296 U.S. 287 (1935), we declared that Congress could not, in the guise of a tax, impose sanctions for violation of state law respecting the local sale of liquor. These decisions demonstrate that Congress could not, under the pretext of raising revenue, lay a tax on processors who refuse to pay a certain price for cotton, and exempt those who agree so to do, with the purpose of benefitting producers.

[D]

Third. If the taxing power may not be used as the instrument to enforce a regulation of matters of state concern with respect to which the Congress has no authority to interfere, may it, as in the present case, be employed to raise the money necessary to purchase a compliance which the Congress is powerless to command? The Government asserts that whatever might be said against the validity of the plan if compulsory, it is constitutionally sound because the end is accomplished by voluntary co-operation. There are two sufficient answers to the contention. The regulation is not in fact voluntary. The farmer, of course, may refuse to comply, but the price of such refusal is the loss of benefits. The amount offered is intended to be sufficient to exert pressure on him to agree to the proposed regulation. The power to confer or withhold unlimited benefits is the power to coerce or destroy. If the cotton grower elects not to accept the benefits, he will receive less for his crops; those who receive payments will be able to undersell him. The result may well be financial ruin. The coercive purpose and intent of the statute is not obscured by the fact that it has not been perfectly successful. It is pointed out that, because there still remained a minority whom the rental and benefit payments were insufficient to induce to surrender their independence of action, the Congress has gone further and, in the Bankhead Cotton Act, used the taxing power in a more directly minatory fashion to compel submission. This progression only serves more fully to expose the coercive purpose of the so-called tax imposed by the present Act. It is clear that the Department of Agriculture has properly described the plan as one to keep a non-cooperating minority in line. This is coercion by economic pressure. The asserted power of choice is illusory.

In *Frost Trucking Company v. Railroad Commission,* 271 U.S. 583 (1926), a state act was considered which provided for supervision and regulation of transportation for hire by automobile on the public highways. Certificates of convenience and necessity were to be obtained by persons desiring to use the highways for this purpose. The regulatory commission required that a private contract carrier should secure such a certificate as a condition of its operation. The effect of the commission's action was to transmute the private carrier into a public carrier. In other words, the privilege of using the highways as a private carrier for compensation was conditioned upon his dedicating his property to the quasi-public use of public transportation. While holding that the private carrier was not obliged to submit himself to the condition, the commission denied him the privilege of using the highways if he did not do so. The argument was, as here, that the carrier had a free choice. This Court said, in holding the act as construed unconstitutional:

> If so, constitutional guaranties, so carefully safeguarded against direct assault, are open to destruction by the indirect but no less effective process of requiring a surrender, which, though in form voluntary, in fact lacks none of the elements of compulsion. Having regard to form alone, the act here is an offer to the private carrier of a privilege, which the state may grant or deny, upon a condition, which the carrier is free to accept or reject. In reality, the carrier is given no choice, except a choice between the rock and the whirlpool, — an option to forego a privilege which may be vital to his livelihood or submit to a requirement which may constitute an intolerable burden.

271 U.S. at 593.

But if the plan were one for purely voluntary co-operation it would stand no better so far as federal power is concerned. At best it is a scheme for purchasing with federal funds submission to federal regulation of a subject reserved to the states.

. . . An appropriation to be expended by the United States under contracts calling for violation of a state law clearly would offend the Constitution. Is a statute less objectionable which authorizes expenditure of federal moneys to induce action in a field in which the United States has no power to intermeddle? The Congress cannot invade state jurisdiction to compel individual action; no more can it purchase such action.

We are referred to numerous types of federal appropriation which have been made in the past, and it is asserted no question has been raised as to their validity. . . .

. . . [S]uch expenditures have not been challenged because no remedy was open for testing their constitutionality in the courts.

We are not here concerned with a conditional appropriation of money, nor with a provision that if certain conditions are not complied with the appropriation shall no longer be available. By the Agricultural Adjustment Act the amount of the tax is appropriated to be expended only in payment under contracts whereby the parties bind themselves to regulation by the Federal Government. There is an obvious difference between a statute stating the conditions upon which moneys shall be expended and one effective only upon assumption of a contractual obligation to submit to a regulation which otherwise could not be enforced. . . . An affirmance of the authority of Congress so to condition the expenditure of an appropriation would tend to nullify all constitutional limitations upon legislative power.

But it is said that there is a wide difference in another respect, between compulsory regulation of the local affairs of a state's citizens and the mere making of a contract relating to their conduct; that, if any state objects, it may declare the contract void and thus prevent those under the state's jurisdiction from complying with its terms. The argument is plainly fallacious. The United States can make the contract only if the federal power to tax and to appropriate reaches the subject matter of the contract. If this does reach the subject matter, its exertion cannot be displaced by state action. To say otherwise is to deny the supremacy of the laws of the United States; to make them subordinate to those of a State. This would reverse the cardinal principle embodied in the Constitution and substitute one which declares that Congress may only effectively legislate as to matters within federal competence when the States do not dissent.

Congress has no power to enforce its commands on the farmer to the ends sought by the Agricultural Adjustment Act. It must follow that it may not indirectly accomplish those ends by taxing and spending to purchase compliance. The Constitution and the entire plan of our government negative any such use of the power to tax and to spend as the Act undertakes to authorize. It does not help to declare that local conditions throughout the nation have created a situation of national concern; for this is but to say that whenever there is a widespread similarity of local conditions, Congress may ignore constitutional limitations upon its own powers and usurp those reserved to the states. If, in lieu of compulsory regulation of subjects within the states' reserved jurisdiction, which is prohibited, the Congress could invoke the taxing and spending power as a means to accomplish the same end, [Article I, Section 8, Clause 1] would become the instrument for total subversion of the governmental powers reserved to the individual states.

If the Act before us is a proper exercise of the federal taxing power, evidently the regulation of all industry throughout the United States may be accomplished by similar exercises of the same power. It would be possible to exact money from one branch of an industry and pay it to another branch in every field of activity which lies within the province of the states. The mere threat of such a procedure might well induce the surrender of rights and the compliance with federal regulation as the price of continuance in business. . . .

. . . .

We have held in *Schechter Poultry Corp. v. United States*, 295 U.S. 495 (1935), that Congress has no power to regulate wages and hours of labor in a local business. If the petitioner is right, this very end may be accomplished by appropriating money to be paid to employers from the federal treasury under contracts whereby they agree to comply with certain standards fixed by federal law or by contract.

. . . .

A possible result of sustaining the claimed federal power would be that every business group which thought itself under-privileged might demand that a tax be laid on its vendors or vendees, the proceeds to be appropriated to the redress of its deficiency of income.

. . . .

Until recently no suggestion of the existence of any such power in the Federal Government has been advanced. The expressions of the framers of the Constitution, the decisions of this Court interpreting that instrument, and the writings of great commentators will be searched in vain for any suggestion that there exists in the clause under discussion or elsewhere in the Constitution, the authority whereby every provision and every fair implication from that instrument may be subverted, the independence of the individual states obliterated, and the United States converted into a central government exercising uncontrolled police power in every state of the Union, superseding all local control or regulation of the affairs or concerns of the states.

Hamilton himself, the leading advocate of broad interpretation of the power to tax and to appropriate for the general welfare, never suggested that any power granted by the Constitution could be used for the destruction of local self-government in the states. Story countenances no such doctrine. It seems never to have occurred to them, or to those who have agreed with them, that the general welfare of the United States (which has aptly been termed "an indestructible Union, composed of indestructible States") might be served by obliterating the constituent members of the Union. But to this fatal conclusion the doctrine contended for would inevitably lead. And its sole premise is that, though the makers of the Constitution, in erecting the federal government, intended sedulously to limit and define its powers, so as to reserve to the states and the people sovereign power, to be wielded by the states and their citizens and not to be invaded by the United States, they nevertheless by a single clause gave power to the Congress to tear down the barriers, to invade the states' jurisdiction, and to become a parliament of the whole people, subject to no restrictions save such as are self-imposed. The argument when seen in its true character and in the light of its inevitable results must be rejected.

. . . .

The judgment is affirmed.

Justice Stone, with whom Justices Brandeis and Cardozo join, dissenting.

I think the judgment should be reversed.

. . . .

. . . [W]e should direct our attention to the pivot on which the decision of the Court is made to turn. It is that a levy unquestionably within the taxing power of Congress may be treated as invalid because it is a step in a plan to regulate agricultural production and is thus a forbidden infringement of state power. The levy is not any the less an exercise of taxing power because it is intended to defray an expenditure for the general welfare rather than for some other support of government. Nor is the levy and collection of the tax pointed to as effecting the regulation. While all federal taxes inevitably have some influence on the internal economy of the states, it is not contended that the levy of a processing tax upon manufacturers using agricultural products as raw material has any perceptible regulatory effect upon either their production or manufacture. The tax is unlike the penalties which were held invalid in the *Child Labor Tax Case*, 259 U.S. 20 (1922), in *Hill v. Wallace*, 259 U.S. 44 (1922), in *Linder v. United States*, 268 U.S. 5, 17 (1925), and in *United States v. Constantine*, 296 U.S. 287 (1935), because they were themselves the instruments of regulation by virtue of their coercive effect on matters left to the control of the states. Here regulation, if any there be, is accomplished not by the tax but by the method by which its proceeds are expended, and would equally be accomplished by any like use of public funds, regardless of their source.

The method may be simply stated. Out of the available fund payments are made to such farmers as are willing to curtail their productive acreage, who in fact do so and who in advance have filed their written undertaking to do so with the Secretary of Agriculture. . . . Although the farmer is placed under no legal compulsion to reduce acreage, it is said that the mere offer of compensation for so doing is a species of economic coercion which operates with the same legal force and effect as though the curtailment were made mandatory by Act of Congress. . . .

. . . .

It is significant that in the congressional hearings on the bill that became the Bankhead Act, which imposes a tax of 50% on all cotton produced in excess of limits prescribed by the Secretary of Agriculture, there was abundant testimony that the restriction of cotton production attempted by the Agricultural Adjustment Act could not be secured without the coercive provisions of the Bankhead Act. . . . The presumption of constitutionality of a statute is not to be overturned by an assertion of its coercive effect which rests on nothing more substantial than groundless speculation.

. . . It is insisted that, while the Constitution gives to Congress, in specific and unambiguous terms, the power to tax and spend, the power is subject to limitations which do not find their origin in any express provision of the Constitution and to which other expressly delegated powers are not subject.

The Constitution requires that public funds shall be spent for a defined purpose, the promotion of the general welfare. Their expenditure usually involves payment on terms which will insure use by the selected recipients within the limits of the constitutional purpose. . . . The power of Congress to spend is inseparable from persuasion to action over which Congress has no legislative control. Congress may not command that the science of agriculture be taught in state universities. But if it would aid the teaching of that science by grants to state institutions, it is appropriate, if not necessary, that the grant be on the condition, incorporated in the Morrill Act, 12 Stat. 503, 26 Stat. 417, that it be used for the intended purpose. Similarly it would seem to be compliance with the Constitution, not violation of it, for the government to take and the university to give a contract that the grant would be so used. It makes no difference that there is a promise to do an act which the condition is calculated to induce. Condition and promise are alike valid since both are in furtherance of the national purpose for which the money is appropriated.

. . . .

Such a limitation is contradictory and destructive of the power to appropriate for the public welfare, and is incapable of practical application. The spending power of Congress is in addition to the legislative power and not subordinate to it. This independent grant of the power of the purse, and its very nature, involving in its exercise the duty to insure expenditure within the granted power, presupposes freedom of selection among divers ends and aims, and the capacity to impose such conditions as will render the choice effective. It is a contradiction in terms to say that there is power to spend for the national welfare, while rejecting any power to impose conditions reasonably adapted to the attainment of the end which alone would justify the expenditure.

. . . .

. . . The power to tax and spend is not without constitutional restraints. One restriction is that the purpose must be truly national. Another is that it may not be used to coerce action left to state control. Another is the conscience and patriotism of

Congress and the Executive. "It must be remembered that legislators are the ultimate guardians of the liberties and welfare of the people in quite as great a degree as the courts." *Missouri, K. & T. Ry. v. May*, 194 U.S. 267, 270 (1904) (Holmes, J.).

. . . Courts are not the only agency of government that must be assumed to have capacity to govern. Congress and the courts both unhappily may falter or be mistaken in the performance of their constitutional duty. But interpretation of our great charter of government which proceeds on any assumption that the responsibility for the preservation of our institutions is the exclusive concern of any one of the three branches of government, or that it alone can save them from destruction is far more likely, in the long run, "to obliterate the constituent members" of "an indestructible union of indestructible states" than the frank recognition that language, even of a constitution, may mean what is says: that the power to tax and spend includes the power to relieve a nationwide economic maladjustment by conditional gifts of money.

Exercise 4(B):

Consider the following issues in connection with *United States v. Butler* and the precedents discussed therein:

(1) Would Congress have authority to enact the Agriculture Adjustment Act under Hamilton's view of legislative powers? Why or why not?

(2) Did the majority fairly quote and characterize Hamilton's Report on Manufactures?

(3) The majority stated: "Congress has no power to enforce its commands on the farmer to the ends sought by the Agricultural Adjustment Act." Is that true or would some enumerated power provide Congress such authority?

(4) Did the majority recognize any limit on the power of Congress to impose taxes?

(5) Did the majority reject the power of Congress to impose *any* conditions upon the receipt of federal spending? If not, what types of conditions would be proper?

(6) Was the majority correct that permitting Congress to tax, spend, and impose conditions upon the receipt of federal funds would — if the dissent's position had prevailed — undermine the Court's precedents regarding federal efforts to regulate child labor, the practice of a profession, the local sale of liquor, or wages and hours of labor in a local business?

(7) What limits, if any, did the dissent acknowledge to the scope of the power of Congress to impose taxes and its power to spend funds? If the dissent's position had prevailed, what would be the consequences for the framework of limited and enumerated federal powers?

C. The Uniformity Requirement

UNITED STATES v. PTASYNSKI
462 U.S. 74 (1983)

JUSTICE POWELL delivered the unanimous opinion of the Court.

The issue is whether excluding a geographically defined class of oil from the coverage of the Crude Oil Windfall Profit Tax Act violates the Uniformity Clause.

I.

During the 1970's the Executive Branch regulated the price of domestic crude oil. Depending on its vintage and type, oil was divided into differing classes or tiers and assigned a corresponding ceiling price. . . .

In 1979, President Carter announced a program to remove price controls from domestic oil by September 30, 1981. By eliminating price controls, the President sought to encourage exploration for new oil and increase production of old oil from marginally economic operations. He recognized, however, that deregulating oil prices would produce substantial gains (referred to as "windfalls") for some producers. The price of oil on the world market had risen markedly, and it was anticipated that deregulating the price of oil already in production would allow domestic producers to receive prices far in excess of their initial estimates. Accordingly, the President proposed that Congress place an excise tax on the additional revenue resulting from decontrol.

Congress responded by enacting the Crude Oil Windfall Profit Tax of 1980, 94 Stat. 229 (codified at 26 U.S.C. § 4986 et seq.). The Act divides domestic crude oil into three tiers and establishes an adjusted base price and a tax rate for each tier. The base prices generally reflect the selling price of particular categories of oil under price controls, and the tax rates vary according to the vintages and types of oil included within each tier. . . .

The Act exempts certain classes of oil from the tax, 26 U.S.C. § 4991(b), one of which is "exempt Alaskan oil," § 4991(b)(3). It is defined as:

any crude oil (other than Sadlerochit oil) which is produced —

(1) from a reservoir from which oil has been produced in commercial quantities through a well located north of the Arctic Circle, or

(2) from a well located on the northerly side of the divide of the Alaska-Aleutian Range and at least 75 miles from the nearest point on the Trans-Alaska Pipeline System.

§ 4994(e). Although the Act refers to this class of oil as "exempt Alaskan oil," the reference is not entirely accurate. The Act exempts only certain oil produced in Alaska from the windfall profit tax. Indeed, less than 20% of current Alaskan production is exempt. Nor is the exemption limited to the State of Alaska. Oil produced in certain offshore territorial waters — beyond the limits of any State — is included within the exemption.

The exemption thus is not drawn on state political lines. Rather it reflects Congress' considered judgment that unique climatic and geographical conditions require the oil produced from this exempt area be treated as a separate class of oil. See H.R. Conf. Rep. No. 98-817, p. 103 (1980). . . . These factors combine to make the average cost of drilling a well in Alaska as much as 15 times greater than that of drilling a well elsewhere in the United States. Accordingly, Congress chose to exempt oil produced in the defined region from the windfall profit tax. It determined that imposing such a tax "would discourage exploration and development of reservoirs in areas of extreme climatic conditions." H.R. Conf. Rep. No. 96-817, at 103.

Six months after the Act was passed, independent oil producers and royalty owners filed suit . . . seeking a refund for taxes paid under the Act. On motion for summary judgment, the District Court held that the Act violated the Uniformity Clause, Art. I, § 8, cl. 1. . . .

. . . .

II

. . . [Appellees] contend that the constitutional requirement that taxes be "uniform throughout the United States" prohibits Congress from exempting a specific geographic region from taxation. They concede that Congress may take geographical considerations into account in deciding what oil to tax. But they argue that the Uniformity Clause prevents Congress from framing, as it did here, the resulting tax in terms of geographic boundaries. . . .

A

The Uniformity Clause conditions Congress' power to impose indirect taxes. It provides that "all Duties, Imposts and Excises shall be uniform throughout the United States." Art. I, § 8, cl. 1. The debates in the Constitutional Convention provide little evidence of the Framers' intent, but the concerns giving rise to the Clause identify its purpose more clearly. The Committee of Detail proposed as a remedy for interstate trade barriers that the power to regulate commerce among the States be vested in the National Government, and the Convention agreed. *See* 2 MAX FARRAND, THE RECORDS OF THE CONSTITUTIONAL CONVENTION OF 1787, p. 308 (1911); CHARLES WARREN, THE MAKING OF THE CONSTITUTION 567–70 (1928). Some States, however, remained apprehensive that the regionalism that had marked the Confederation would persist. *Id.* at 586–88. There was concern that the National Government would use its power over commerce to the disadvantage of particular States. The Uniformity Clause was proposed as one of several measures designed to limit the exercise of that power. *See* 2 MAX FARRAND, *supra,* at 417–18; *Knowlton v. Moore,* 178 U.S. 41, 103–06 (1900). As Justice Story explained:

> [The purpose of the Clause] was to cut off all undue preferences of one State over another in the regulation of subjects affecting their common interests. Unless duties, imposts, and excises were uniform, the grossest and most oppressive inequalities, vitally affecting the pursuits and employments of the people of different States, might exist. The agriculture, commerce, or manufactures of one State might be built up on the ruins of those of another; and a combination of a few States in Congress might secure a monopoly of certain branches of trade and business to themselves, to the injury, if not to the destruction, of their less favored neighbors.

1 JOSEPH STORY, COMMENTARIES ON THE CONSTITUTION OF THE UNITED STATES § 957 (T. Cooley ed. 1873); *see also* 3 ANNALS OF CONGRESS 378–79 (1792) (remarks of Hugh Williamson); Address of Luther Martin to the Maryland Legislature (Nov. 29, 1787), *reprinted in* 3 MAX FARRAND, *supra,* at 205.

This general purpose, however, does not define the precise scope of the Clause. The one issue that has been raised repeatedly is whether the requirement of uniformity encompasses some notion of equality. It was settled fairly early that the Clause does not require Congress to devise a tax that falls equally or proportionately on each State. Rather, as the Court stated in the *Head Money Cases,* 112 U.S. 580, 594 (1884), "a tax is uniform when it operates with the same force and effect in every place where the subject of it is found."

Nor does the Clause prevent Congress from defining the subject of a tax by drawing distinctions between similar classes. In the *Head Money Cases,* the Court recognized that in imposing a head tax on persons coming into this country, Congress could choose to tax those persons who immigrated through the ports, but not those who immigrated at inland cities. As the Court explained, "the evil to be remedied by this legislation has no existence on our inland borders, and immigration in that quarter needed no such regulation." *Id.* at 595. The tax applied to all ports alike, and the Court concluded that "there is substantial uniformity within the meaning and purpose of the Constitution." *Id.*

Subsequent cases have confirmed that the Framers did not intend to restrict Congress' ability to define the class of objects to be taxed. They intended only that the tax apply wherever the classification is found. *See Knowlton v. Moore,* 178 U.S. at 106;[11] *Nicol v. Ames,* 173 U.S. 509, 521–22 (1899).

The question that remains, however, is whether the Uniformity Clause prohibits Congress from defining the class of objects to be taxed in geographic terms. The Court has not addressed this issue squarely. We recently held, however, that the uniformity provision of the Bankruptcy Clause did not require invalidation of a geographically defined class of debtors. *See Regional Rail Reorganization Act Cases,* 419 U.S. 102, 161 (1974). In that litigation, creditors of bankrupt railroads challenged a statute that was passed to reorganize eight major railroads in the northeast and midwest regions of the country. They argued that the statute violated the uniformity provision of the Bankruptcy Clause because it operated only in a single statutorily defined region. The Court found that "[t]he uniformity provision does not deny Congress power to take into account differences that exist between different parts of the country, and to fashion legislation to resolve geographically isolated problems." *Id.* at 159. The fact that the Act applied to a geographically defined class did not render it unconstitutional. We noted that the Act in fact had operated uniformly throughout the United States. During the period in which the Act was effective, no railroad reorganization proceedings had been pending outside the statutorily defined region. *Id.* at 160.

In concluding that the uniformity provision had not been violated, we relied in large part on the *Head Money Cases,* where the effect of the statute had been to distinguish between geographic regions. We rejected the argument that "the Rail Act differs from the head tax statute because *by its own terms* the Rail Act applies only to one designated region . . . . The definition of the region does not obscure the reality that the legislation applies to all railroads under reorganization pursuant to § 77 during the time the Act applies." 419 U.S. at 161 (emphasis added).

B

With these principles in mind, we now consider whether Congress's decision to treat Alaskan oil as a separate class of oil violates the Uniformity Clause. We do not think that the language of the Clause or this Court's decisions prohibit all geographically defined classifications. As construed in the *Head Money Cases,* the Uniformity Clause requires that an excise tax apply, at the same rate, in all portions of the United States where the subject of the tax is found. Where Congress defines the subject of a tax in nongeographic terms, the Uniformity Clause is satisfied. *See Knowlton v. Moore,* 178 U.S. at 106. We cannot say that when Congress uses geographic terms to identify the same subject, the classification is invalidated. The Uniformity Clause gives Congress wide latitude in deciding what to tax and does not prohibit it from considering geographically isolated problems. *See Head Money Cases,* 112 U.S. at 595. This is the substance of our decision in the *Regional Rail Reorganization Act Cases,* 419 U.S. at 156–61. But where Congress does choose to frame a tax in geographic terms, we will examine the classification closely to see if there is actual geographical discrimination. *See id.* at 160–61.

---

[11] *Knowlton* represents the Court's most detailed consideration of the Uniformity Clause. *See* 178 U.S. at 83–106. The issue in *Knowlton,* however, only presented a variation on the question addressed in the *Head Money Cases,* 112 U.S. 580 (1884). Rather than distinguishing between port and inland cities, the statute at issue in *Knowlton* imposed a progressive tax on legacies and varied the rate of the tax among classes of legatees. The argument was that Congress could not distinguish among legacies or people receiving them; it was required to tax all legacies at the same rate or none. *See Knowlton,* 178 U.S. at 83–84. In rejecting this argument, the Court reaffirmed its conclusion in the *Head Money Cases* that Congress may distinguish between similar classes in selecting the subject of a tax. 178 U.S. at 106.

Since *Knowlton,* the Court has not had occasion to consider the Uniformity Clause in any detail.

In this case, we hold that the classification is constitutional. . . .

Congress clearly viewed "exempt Alaskan oil" as a unique class of oil that, consistent with the scheme of the Act, merited favorable treatment. It had before it ample evidence of the disproportionate costs and difficulties — the fragile ecology, the harsh environment, and the remote location — associated with extracting oil from this region. We cannot fault its determination, based on neutral factors, that this oil required separate treatment. Nor is there any indication that Congress sought to benefit Alaska for reasons that would offend the purpose of the Clause. Nothing in the Act's legislative history suggests that Congress intended to grant Alaska an undue preference at the expense of other oil-producing States. . . .

III

Had Congress described this class of oil in nongeographic terms, there would be no question as to the Act's constitutionality. We cannot say that identifying the class in terms of its geographic boundaries renders the exemption invalid. Where, as here, Congress has exercised its considered judgment with respect to an enormously complex problem, we are reluctant to disturb its determination. . . .

Exercise 5:

Consider the following issues in connection with *United States v. Ptasynski* and the precedents discussed therein:

(1) For revenue measures subject to the uniformity requirement, is Congress permitted to set different rates for different classifications? For example, could Congress set one rate of import duty on wine from one region of Europe and a different rate for all other imported wine? Is there any judicially-enforceable limit to such classifications?

(2) For revenue measures subject to the uniformity requirement, may Congress set different rates for different quantities of the subject of the tax? For example, could Congress impose a progressive tax structure so that marginal tax rates would be higher for large volumes, such as 1% of the value of a single case of imported wine but 10% per case when ten or more cases are imported?

(3) For revenue measures subject to the uniformity requirement, may Congress select a subject that is not present in all States (and/or not legal in all States)? For example, could Congress impose a levy only on casinos if they were illegal in many States? Or, could Congress impose a levy on "riverboat casinos" but not other gambling sites?

(4) For revenue measures subject to the uniformity requirement, may Congress impose the tax only at certain locations? For example, could Congress impose a levy on "Mississippi riverboat casinos" but not other gambling sites? Or, could it impose a levy on "Las Vegas casinos" but not other gambling sites?

(5) In light of the very few tax measures that would be subject to apportionment, what are the judicially-enforceable limits to the power of Congress to raise revenue?

(6) The Court explains the Uniformity Clause as an intended limit to congressional power to regulate commerce among the States. How does the requirement of uniform taxes limit the power to regulate commerce? What is the implicit understanding of the scope of the power to tax that would produce such a view?

D.   The Spending Power After the New Deal

SOUTH DAKOTA v. DOLE
483 U.S. 203 (1986)

CHIEF JUSTICE REHNQUIST delivered the opinion of the Court.

Petitioner South Dakota permits persons 19 years of age or older to purchase beer containing up to 3.2% alcohol. In 1984 Congress enacted 23 U.S.C. § 158, which directs the Secretary of Transportation to withhold a percentage of federal highway funds otherwise allocable from States "in which the purchase or public possession . . . of any alcoholic beverage by a person who is less than twenty-one years of age is lawful." The State sued . . . seeking a declaratory judgment that § 158 violates the constitutional limitations on congressional exercise of the spending power and violates the Twenty-first amendment to the United States Constitution. The District court rejected the State's claims, and the Court of Appeals . . . affirmed.

In this Court, the parties direct most of their efforts to defining the proper scope of the Twenty-first Amendment. . . .

   . . . .

. . . Despite the extended treatment of the question by the parties, however, we need not decide in this case whether that Amendment would prohibit an attempt by Congress to legislate directly a national minimum drinking age. Here, Congress has acted indirectly under its spending power to encourage uniformity in the States' drinking ages. As we explain below, we find this legislative effort within constitutional bounds even if Congress may not regulate drinking ages directly.

The Constitution empowers Congress to "lay and collect Taxes, Duties, Imposts, and Excises, to pay Debts and provide for the common Defence and general Welfare of the United States." Art. I, § 8, cl. 1. Incident to this power, Congress may attach conditions on the receipt of federal funds, and has repeatedly employed the power "to further broad policy objectives by conditioning receipt of federal moneys upon compliance by the recipient with federal statutory and administrative directives." *Fullilove v. Klutznick*, 448 U.S. 448, 474 (1980) (opinion of Burger, C.J.). . . . The breadth of this power was made clear in *United States v. Butler*, 297 U.S. 1, 66 (1936), where the Court, resolving a longstanding debate over the scope of the Spending Clause, determined that "the power of Congress to authorize expenditure of public moneys for public purposes is not limited by the direct grants of legislative power found in the Constitution." Thus, objectives not thought to be within Article I's "enumerated legislative fields," *id.* at 65, may nevertheless be attained through the use of the spending power and the conditional grant of federal funds.

The spending power is of course not unlimited, *Pennhurst State School and Hospital v. Halderman*, 451 U.S. 1, 17 & n.13 (1981), but is instead subject to several general restrictions articulated in our cases. The first of these limitations is derived from the language of the Constitution itself: the exercise of the spending power must be in pursuit of "the general welfare." *See Helvering v. Davis*, 301 U.S. 619, 640–41 (1937). In considering whether a particular expenditure is intended to serve general public purposes, courts should defer substantially to the judgment of Congress. *Id.* at 640, 645.[2] Second, we have required that if Congress desires to condition the States' receipt of federal funds, it "must do so unambiguously . . ., enable[ing] the States to exercise their choice knowingly, cognizant of the consequences of their participation."

---

[2] The level of deference to the congressional decision is such that the Court has more recently questioned whether "general welfare" is a judicially enforceable restriction at all. *See Buckley v. Valeo*, 424 U.S. 1, 90–91 (1976) (*per curiam*).

Pennhurst State School & Hosp., 451 U.S. at 17. Third, our cases have suggested (without significant elaboration) that conditions on federal grants might be illegitimate if they are unrelated "to the federal interest in particular national projects or programs." *Massachusetts v. United States*, 435 U.S. 444, 461 (1978) (plurality opinion). Finally, we have noted that other constitutional provisions may provide an independent bar to the conditional grant of federal funds. *Lawrence County v. Lead-Deadwood School Dist.*, 469 U.S. 256, 269–70 (1985).

South Dakota does not seriously claim that § 158 is inconsistent with any of the first three restrictions mentioned above. We can readily conclude that the provision is designed to serve the general welfare, especially in light of the fact that "the concept of welfare or the opposite is shaped by Congress." *Helvering v. Davis*, 301 U.S. at 645. Congress found that the differing drinking ages in the States created particular incentives for young persons to combine their desire to drink with their ability to drive, and that this interstate problem required a national solution. The means it chose to address this dangerous situation were reasonably calculated to advance the general welfare. The conditions upon which States receive the funds, moreover, could not be more clearly stated by Congress. And, the State itself, rather than challenging the germaneness of the condition to federal purposes, admits that it "has never contended that the congressional action was . . . unrelated to a national concern in the absence of the Twenty-first Amendment." Indeed, the condition imposed by Congress is directly related to one of the main purposes for which highway funds are expended — safe interstate travel. This goal of the interstate highway system had been frustrated by varying drinking ages among the States. . . . By enacting § 158, Congress conditioned the receipt of federal funds in a way reasonably calculated to address this particular impediment to a purpose for which the funds are expended.

The remaining question about the validity of § 158 — and the basic point of disagreement between the parties — is whether the Twenty-first Amendment constitutes an "independent constitutional bar" to the conditional grant of federal funds. *Lawrence County*, 469 U.S. at 269–70. Petitioner relying on its view that the Twenty-first Amendment prohibits *direct* regulation of drinking ages by Congress, asserts that "Congress may not use the spending power to regulate that which it is prohibited from regulating directly under the Twenty-first Amendment." But our cases show that this "independent constitutional bar" limitation on the spending power is not of the kind petitioner suggests. *United States v. Butler*, 297 U.S. at 66, for example, established that the constitutional limitations on Congress when exercising its spending power are less exacting than those on its authority to regulate directly.

We have also held that a perceived Tenth Amendment limitation on congressional regulation of state affairs did not concomitantly limit the range of conditions legitimately placed on federal grants. In *Oklahoma v. Civil Service Comm'n*, 330 U.S. 127 (1947), the Court considered the validity of the Hatch Act insofar as it was applied to political activities of state officials whose employment was financed in whole or in part with federal funds. The State contended that an order under this provision to withhold certain federal funds unless a state official was removed invaded its sovereignty in violation of the Tenth Amendment. Though finding that "the United States is not concerned with, and has no power to regulate, local political activities as such of state officials," the Court nevertheless held that the Federal Government "does have power to fix the terms upon which its money allotments to states shall be disbursed." *Id.* at 143. The Court found no violation of the State's sovereignty because the State could, and did, adopt "the 'simple expedient' of not yielding to what she urges is federal coercion. The offer of benefits to a state by the United States dependent upon cooperation by the state with federal plans, assumedly for the general welfare, is not unusual." *Id.* at 143–144 (citations omitted). *See also Steward Machine Co. v. Davis*, 301 U.S. 548, 595 (1937) ("There is only a condition which the state is free at pleasure to disregard or fulfill"); *Massachusetts v. Mellon*, 262 U.S. 447, 482 (1923).

These cases establish that the "independent constitutional bar" limitation on the spending power is not, as petitioner suggests, a prohibition on the indirect achievement of objectives which Congress is not empowered to achieve directly. Instead, we think that the language in our earlier opinions stands for the unexceptionable proposition that the power may not be used to induce the States to engage in activities that would themselves be unconstitutional. Thus, for example, a grant of federal funds conditioned on invidiously discriminatory state action or the infliction of cruel and unusual punishment would be an illegitimate exercise of the Congress' broad spending power. . . .

Our decisions have recognized that in some circumstances the financial inducement offered by Congress might be so coercive as to pass the point at which "pressure turns into compulsion." *Steward Machine Co. v. Davis*, 301 U.S. 548, 590 (1937). Here, however, Congress has directed only that a State desiring to establish a minimum drinking age lower than 21 lose a relatively small percentage of certain federal highway funds. We cannot conclude, however, that a conditional grant of federal money of this sort is unconstitutional simply by reason of its success in achieving the congressional objective.

When we consider, for a moment, that all South Dakota would lose if she adheres to her chosen course as to a suitable minimum drinking age is 5% of the federal funds otherwise obtainable under specified highway grant programs, the argument as to coercion is shown to be more rhetoric than fact. . . .

Here Congress has offered relatively mild encouragement to the States to enact higher minimum drinking ages than they would otherwise choose. But the enactment of such laws remains the prerogative of the States not merely in theory but in fact. Even if Congress might lack the power to impose a national minimum drinking age directly, we conclude that encouragement to state action found in § 158 is a valid use of the spending power. Accordingly, the judgment of the Court of Appeals is Affirmed.

[The dissenting opinion of Justice Brennan has been omitted.]

JUSTICE O'CONNOR, dissenting.

. . . .

My disagreement with the Court is relatively narrow on the spending power issue: it is a disagreement about the application of a principle rather than a disagreement on the principle itself. I agree with the Court that Congress may attach conditions on the receipt of federal funds to further "the federal interest in particular national projects or programs." *Massachusetts v. United States*, 435 U.S. 444, 461 (1978). I also subscribe to the established proposition that the reach of the spending power "is not limited by the direct grants of legislative power found in the Constitution." *United States v. Butler*, 297 U.S. 1, 66 (1936). Finally, I agree that there are four separate types of limitations on the spending power: the expenditure must be for the general welfare, *Helvering v. Davis*, 301 U.S. 619, 640–41 (1937), the conditions imposed must be unambiguous, *Pennhurst State School and Hospital v. Halderman*, 451 U.S. 1, 17 (1981), they must be reasonably related to the purpose of the expenditure, *Massachusetts v. United States*, 435 U.S. at 461, and the legislation may not violate any independent constitutional prohibition, *Lawrence County v. Lead-Deadwood School Dist.*, 469 U.S. 256, 269–70 (1985). . . . Establishment of a national minimum drinking age certainly fits within the broad concept of the general welfare and the statute is entirely unambiguous. I am also willing to assume, *arguendo*, that the Twenty-first amendment does not constitute an "independent constitutional bar" to a spending condition.

But the Court's application of the requirement that the condition imposed be reasonably related to the purpose for which the funds are expended is cursory and unconvincing. We have repeatedly said that Congress may condition grants under the spending power only in ways reasonably related to the purpose of the federal program. *Massachusetts v. United States*, 435 U.S. at 461; *Ivanhoe Irrigation Dist. v. McCracken*, 357 U.S. 275, 295 (1958) (the United States may impose "reasonable conditions relevant to federal interest in the project and to the over-all objectives thereof"); *Steward Machine Co. v. Davis*, 301 U.S. 548, 590 (1937) ("We do not say that a tax is valid, when imposed by act of Congress, if it is laid upon the condition that a state may escape its operation through the adoption of a statute unrelated in subject matter to activities fairly within the scope of the national policy and power"). In my view, establishment of a minimum drinking age of 21 is not sufficiently related to interstate highway construction to justify so conditioning funds appropriated for that purpose.

. . . .

Aside from these "concessions" by counsel [that do not support the Court's characterization], the Court asserts the reasonableness of the relationship between the supposed purpose of the expenditure — "safe interstate travel" — and the drinking age condition. The Court reasons that Congress wishes that the roads it builds may be used safely, that drunken drivers threaten highway safety, and that young people are more likely to drive while under the influence of alcohol under existing law than would be the case if there was a uniform national drinking age of 21. It hardly needs saying, however, that if the purpose of § 158 is to deter drunken driving, it is far too over- and under-inclusive. It is over-inclusive because it stops teenagers from drinking even when they are not about to drive on interstate highways. It is under-inclusive because teenagers pose only a small part of the drunken driving problem in this Nation. *See, e.g.*, 130 Cong. Rec. 18,648 (1984) (remarks of Sen. Humphrey) ("Eighty-four percent of all highway fatalities involving alcohol occur among those whose ages exceed 21"); *id.* at 18,651 (remarks of Sen. McClure) ("Certainly, statistically, if you use that one set of statistics, then the mandatory drinking age ought to be raised at least to 30").

When Congress appropriates money to build a highway, it is entitled to insist that the highway be a safe one. But it is not entitled to insist as a condition of the use of highway funds the State impose or change regulations in other areas of the State's social and economic life because of an attenuated or tangential relationship to highway use or safety. Indeed, if the rule were otherwise, the Congress could effectively regulate almost any area of a State's social, political, or economic life on the theory that use of the interstate transportation system is somehow enhanced. If, for example, the United States were to condition highway moneys upon moving the state capital, I suppose it might argue that interstate transportation is facilitated by locating local governments in places easily accessible to interstate highways — or, conversely, that highways might become overburdened if they had to carry traffic to and from the state capital. . . .

There is a clear place at which the Court can draw the line between permissible and impermissible conditions on federal grants. It is the line identified in the Brief for the National Conference of State Legislatures et al. as *Amici Curiae*:

Congress has the power to *spend* for the general welfare, it has the power to *legislate* only for delegated purposes. . . .

The appropriate inquiry, then, is whether the spending requirement or prohibition is a condition on a grant or whether it is regulation. The difference turns on whether the requirement specifies in some way how the money should be spent, so that Congress' intent in making the grant will be effectuated. Congress has no power under the Spending Clause to impose requirements on a grant that go beyond specifying how the money should be spent. A requirement that is not such a specification is not a condition, but a regulation, which is valid only if it falls within one of Congress' delegated regulatory powers.

This approach harks back to *United States v. Butler,* 297 U.S. 1 (1936), the last case in which this Court struck down an Act of Congress as beyond the authority granted by the Spending Clause. There the Court wrote that "[t]here is an obvious difference between a statute stating the conditions upon which moneys shall be expended and one effective only upon assumption of a contractual obligation to submit to a regulation which otherwise could not be enforced." *Id.* at 73. . . .

While *Butler*'s authority is questionable insofar as it assumes that Congress has no regulatory power over farm production, its discussion of the spending power and its description of both the power's breadth and its limitations remain sound. The Court's decision in *Butler* also properly recognizes the gravity of the task of appropriately limiting the spending power. If the spending power is to be limited only by Congress' notion of the general welfare, the reality, given the vast financial resources of the Federal Government, is that the Spending Clause gives "power to the Congress to tear down the barriers, to invade the states' jurisdiction, and to become a parliament of the whole people, subject to no restrictions save such as are self-imposed." *United States v. Butler,* 297 U.S. at 78. This, of course, as *Butler* held, was not the Framers' plan and it is not the meaning of the Spending Clause.

Our later cases are consistent with the notion that, under the spending power, the Congress may only condition grants in ways that can fairly be said to be related to the expenditure of federal funds. For example, in *Oklahoma v. CSC,* 330 U.S. 127 (1947), the Court upheld application of the Hatch Act to a member of the Oklahoma State Highway Commission who was employed in connection with an activity financed in part by loans and grants from a federal agency. This condition is appropriately viewed as a condition relating to how federal moneys were to be expended. Other conditions that have been upheld by the Court may be viewed as independently justified under some regulatory power of the Congress. Thus, in *Fullilove v. Klutznick,* 448 U.S. 448 (1980), the Court upheld a condition on federal grants that 10% of the money be "set aside" for contracts with minority business enterprises. But the Court found that the condition could be justified as a valid regulation [under enumerated powers]. *Id.* at 476, 478. . . .

This case, however, falls into neither class. As discussed above, a condition that a State will raise its drinking age to 21 cannot fairly be said to be reasonably related to the expenditure of funds for highway construction. The only possible connection, highway safety, has nothing to do with how the funds Congress has appropriated are expended. Rather than a condition determining how federal highway money shall be expended, it is a regulation determining who shall be able to drink liquor. As such it is not justified by the spending power.

. . . .

The immense size and power of the Government of the United States ought not to obscure its fundamental character. It remains a Government of enumerated powers. *McCulloch v. Maryland,* 17 U.S. 316, 405 (1819). Because 23 U.S.C. § 158 cannot be justified as an exercise of any power delegated to the Congress, it is not authorized by the Constitution. The Court errs in holding it to be the law of the land, and I respectfully dissent.

Exercise 6(A):

Consider the following matters with respect to *South Dakota v. Dole*:

(1)   The majority asserted that even if Congress lacked authority directly to legislate a nation-wide minimum drinking age, Congress could nonetheless achieve that end indirectly through conditions upon federal spending. Does the constitutional text

authorize Congress to spend funds for purposes other than the enumerated powers? What are the arguments for or against such an interpretation?

(2) Prior to the Court's decision in *United States v. Butler,* it had not upheld any federal spending for a purpose that Congress could not have regulated directly. Did the Court identify any historical understanding or practice for its broader construction of congressional powers? Does the structure of the Constitution or the system of government it establishes provide a basis for the broader construction?

(3) In *Dole,* the majority synthesized its prior cases to suggest five limits to the so-called "spending power" of Congress. What are the five limits? Which of those five limits, if any, pose any judicially-enforceable restraint on the substance of policies Congress may achieve indirectly?

(4) To the extent "Congress found that the differing drinking ages in the States created particular incentives for young persons to combine their desire to drink with their ability to drive, and that this interstate problem required a national solution," did the federal legislation actually provide such a "solution"? Why or why not?

(5) To the extent that the reasoning recited in question 4 was sufficient to justify "a national solution," may Congress address any matter as to which State laws vary from one another? For example, could Congress reason that roads are more congested and more traffic accidents result due to longer commutes to schools because of local variations in the quality of school programs, so that a uniform school curriculum could be imposed as a condition upon acceptance of federal highway funds?

(6) In *Dole,* the majority asserted that even when the Tenth Amendment (or broader principles of federalism reflected in that provision) would prohibit Congress from directly legislating, Congress could nonetheless indirectly achieve its ends through conditions on grants of federal funds. Why are those bases excluded from the "independent constitutional bar" limitation? If the distinction is between constitutional provisions directed to the protection of individual rights and mere structural provisions of the Constitution, can that be harmonized with the view that the structural provisions serve to protect individual liberty? If the "independent constitutional bar" limitation does not include separation of constitutional power between the central government and the States, would it be consistent to apply it to separation of constitutional power among the branches of the central government?

(a) If your instructor assigned *Volume 2,* consider why it is permissible for Congress to authorize the Secretary of Transportation to withhold a percentage of "federal highway funds otherwise allocable from States" but it is not permissible for Congress to authorize the President to withhold appropriated expenditures in order to "reduce the Federal budget deficit" (*see Clinton v. City of New York,* 524 U.S. 417 (1998)), even when the President exercised that authority under the Line Item Veto Act to reduce funds appropriated for preferential treatment of New York City's Medicaid program costs under the Line Item Veto Act.

(b) In that light, may Congress circumvent limitations on its authority in the appointment and/or removal process by imposing conditions on the expenditure of federal funds or a lease of federal property?

(7) Would *Dole* be decided the same way if 90% of the federal highway funds allocated to the State were conditioned on raising the drinking age? Why or why not?

(8) In dissent, Justice O'Connor asserted that she agreed with many of the propositions relied upon by the majority. On what point did she disagree?

(9) Did Justice O'Connor succeed in demonstrating that the five limits identified by the majority (*see* question 3) do not have their ordinary meaning? Did she succeed in

demonstrating that the condition at issue did not satisfy the standard articulated by the majority? Why or why not?

(10)   In dissent, Justice O'Connor suggested that under the majority's approach, Congress could induce States to relocate the capitals (an indirect reference to *Coyle v. Smith*, 221 U.S. 559 (1911), in which the Court held Congress could not require Oklahoma to relocate its capital as a condition of admission to statehood). Assuming Congress may not directly compel a State to relocate its capital, may Congress use the spending power in the manner suggested by Justice O'Connor to induce a State to do so? Why or why not?

METROPOLITAN WASHINGTON AIRPORTS AUTHORITY v. CITIZENS FOR THE ABATEMENT OF AIRCRAFT NOISE, INC.
501 U.S. 252 (1991)

JUSTICE STEVENS delivered the opinion of the Court.

An Act of Congress authorizing the transfer of operating control of two major airports from the Federal Government to the Metropolitan Washington Airports Authority (MWAA) conditioned the transfer on the creation by MWAA of a unique "Board of Review" composed of nine Members of Congress and vested with veto power over decisions made by MWAA's Board of Directors. The principal question presented is whether this unusual statutory condition violates the constitutional principle of separation of powers, as interpreted in *INS v. Chadha*, 462 U.S. 919 (1983), *Bowsher v. Synar*, 478 U.S. 714 (1986), and *Springer v. Philippine Islands*, 277 U.S. 189 (1928). We conclude, as did the Court of Appeals for the District of Columbia Circuit, that the condition is unconstitutional.

I

In 1940, Congress authorized the Executive Branch to acquire a tract of land a few miles from the Capitol and to construct what is now Washington National Airport (National). From the time it opened until 1987, National was owned and operated by the Federal Government. . . .

. . . [W]hen Congress authorized construction of a second major airport to serve the Washington area, it again provided for federal ownership and operation. Dulles International Airport (Dulles) was opened in 1962 under the direct control of the FAA. . . .

National and Dulles are the only two major commercial airports owned by the Federal Government. . . .

. . . .

Despite the FAA's history of profitable operation of National . . . the Secretary of Transportation concluded that necessary capital improvements could not be financed for either National or Dulles unless control of the airports was transferred to a regional authority with power to raise money by selling tax-exempt bonds. In 1984, she therefore appointed an advisory commission to develop a plan for the creation of such a regional authority.

The Commission recommended that the proposed authority be created by congressionally approved compact between Virginia and the District, and that its Board of Directors be composed of 11 members serving staggered 6-year terms, with 5 members to be appointed by the Governor of Virginia, 3 by the Mayor of the District, 2 by the Governor of Maryland, and 1 by the President, with the advice and consent of the Senate. Emphasizing the importance of a "non-political, independent authority," the

Commission recommended that members of the board "should not hold elective or appointive political office." . . .

In 1985, Virginia and the District both passed legislation authorizing the establishment of the recommended regional authority. A bill embodying the advisory committee's recommendations passed the Senate. In the House of Representatives, however, the legislation encountered strong opposition from Members who expressed concern that the surrender of federal control of the airports might result in the transfer of a significant amount of traffic from National to Dulles.

Substitute bills were therefore drafted to provide for the establishment of a review board with veto power over major actions of MWAA's Board of Directors. Under two of the proposals, the board of review would clearly have acted as an agent of the Congress. After Congress received an opinion from the Department of Justice that a veto of MWAA action by such a board of review "would plainly be legislative action that must conform to the requirements of Article I, section 7 of the Constitution," the Senate adopted a version of the review board that required Members of Congress to serve in their individual capacities as representatives of users of the airports. . . .

Subparagraph (1) of § 2456(f) [of the final Transfer Act] specifies that the Board of Review "shall consist" of nine Members of the Congress, eight of whom serve on committees with jurisdiction over transportation issues and none of whom may be a Member from Maryland, Virginia, or the District of Columbia. Subparagraph (4)(B) details the actions that must be submitted to the Board of Review for approval, which include adoption of a budget, authorization of bonds, promulgation of regulations, endorsement of a master plan, and appointment of the chief executive officer of the Authority. Subparagraph (4)(D) explains that disapproval by the Board will prevent submitted actions from taking effect. . . . Other significant provisions of the Act include . . . subsection (h), which contains a provision disabling MWAA's Board of Directors from performing any action subject to the veto power if a court should hold that the Board of Review provisions of the Act are invalid.

On March 2, 1987, the Secretary of Transportation and MWAA entered into a long-term lease complying with all of the conditions specified in the then recently enacted Transfer Act. . . . After the lease was executed, MWAA's Board of Directors adopted bylaws providing for the Board of Review, and Virginia and the District of Columbia amended their legislation to give MWAA power to establish the Board of Review. On September 2, 1987, the directors appointed the nine members of the Board of Review from lists that had been submitted by the Speaker of the House of Representatives and the President *pro tempore* of the Senate.

. . . .

II

In November 1988, Citizens for the Abatement of Aircraft Noise., Inc., and two individuals who reside under flight paths of aircraft departing from, and arriving at, National (collectively CAAN) brought this action. CAAN sought a declaration that the Board of Review's power to veto actions of MWAA's Board of Directors is unconstitutional and an injunction against any action by the Board of Review . . . .

. . . On the merits, the District Court concluded that there was no violation of the doctrine of separation of powers because the members of the Board of Review acted in their individual capacities as representatives of airport users, and therefore the Board was not an agent of Congress. Moreover, the Board's powers were derived from the legislation enacted by Virginia and the District, as implemented by MWAA's bylaws, rather than from the Transfer Act. "In short, because Congress exercises no federal power under the Act, it cannot overstep its constitutionally-designated bounds."

A divided panel of the Court of Appeals for the District of Columbia Circuit reversed. . . . On the merits, the majority concluded that it was "wholly unrealistic to view the Board of Review as solely a creature of state law immune to separation-of-powers scrutiny" because it was federal law that had required the establishment of the Board and defined its powers. It held that the Board was "in essence a congressional agent" with disapproval powers over key operational decisions that were "quintessentially executive" and therefore violated the separation of powers. . . .

. . . [Before this Court,] the United States has again taken the position that the Transfer Act is constitutional.[12]

. . . .

IV

Petitioners argue that this case does not raise any separation-of-powers issue because the Board of Review neither exercises federal power nor acts as an agent of Congress. Examining the origin and structure of the Board, we conclude that petitioners are incorrect.

. . . .

Control over National and Dulles was originally in federal hands, and was transferred to MWAA only subject to the condition that the States create the Board of Review. . . . Most significant, membership on the Board of Review is limited to federal officials, specifically members of congressional committees charged with authority over air transportation.

That the Members of Congress who serve on the Board nominally serve "in their individual capacities, as representatives of users" of the airports does not prevent this group of officials from qualifying as a congressional agent exercising federal authority for separation-of-powers purposes. As we recently held, "separation-of-powers analysis does not turn on the labeling of an activity," *Mistretta v. United States*, 488 U.S. 361, 393 (1989). The Transfer Act imposes no requirement that the Members of Congress who are appointed to the Board actually be users of the airports. Rather, the Act imposes the requirement that the Board members have congressional responsibilities related to the federal regulation of air transportation. These facts belie the *ipse dixit* that the Board members will act "in their individual capacities."

Although the legislative history is not necessary to our conclusion that the Board members act in their official congressional capacities, the floor debates in the House confirm our view. . . .

Congress as a body also exercises substantial power over the appointment and removal of the particular Members of Congress who serve on the Board. The Transfer Act provides that the Board "shall consist" of "two members of the Public Works and Transportation Committee and two members of the Appropriations Committee of the House of Representatives from a list provided by the Speaker of the House," "two members of the Commerce, Science, and Transportation Committee and two members of the Appropriations Committee of the Senate from a list provided by the President

---

[12] . . . .

The United States does not support the position taken by petitioners and the dissent. The United States argues that "[i]f the exercise of state authority were sufficient in itself to validate a statutorily imposed condition like the one in this case, a massive loophole in the separation of powers would be opened." Brief for United States 31. According to the United States, the condition in this case is constitutional only because "there is here a reasonable basis for the appointment of Members of Congress 'in their individual capacities.'" *Id.* at 33.

pro tempore of the Senate," and "one member chosen alternately . . . from a list provided by the Speaker of the House or the President pro tempore of the Senate, respectively." Significantly, appointments *must* be made from the lists, and there is no requirement that the lists contain more recommendations than the number of Board openings. . . . The list system, combined with congressional authority over committee assignments, guarantees Congress effective control over appointments. Control over committee assignments also gives Congress effective removal power over Board members because depriving a Board member of membership in the relevant committees deprives the member of authority to sit on the Board.

We thus confront an entity created at the initiative of Congress, the powers of which Congress has delineated, the purpose of which is to protect an acknowledged federal interest, and membership in which is restricted to congressional officials. Such an entity necessarily exercises sufficient federal power as an agent of Congress to mandate separation-of-powers scrutiny. Any other conclusion would permit Congress to evade the "carefully crafted" constraints of the Constitution, *INS v. Chadha*, 462 U.S. 919, 959 (1983), simply by delegating primary responsibility for execution of national policy to the States, subject to the veto power of Members of Congress acting "in their individual capacities." *Cf. Bowsher v. Synar*, 478 U.S. at 755 (Stevens, J., concurring in judgment).[16]

Petitioners contend that the Board of Review should nevertheless be immune from scrutiny for constitutional defects because it was created in the course of Congress' exercise of its power to dispose of federal property. *See* U.S. Const., Art. IV, § 3, cl. 2. In *South Dakota v. Dole*, 483 U.S. 203 (1987), we held that a grant of highway funds to a State conditioned on the State's prohibition of the possession of alcoholic beverages by persons under the age of 21 was a lawful exercise of Congress' power to spend money for the general welfare. Even assuming that "Congress might lack the power to impose a national drinking age directly," we held that this indirect "encouragement to state action" was a valid use of the spending power. *Dole*, 483 U.S. at 212. We thus concluded that Congress could endeavor to accomplish the federal objective of regulating the national drinking age by the indirect use of the spending power even though that regulatory authority would otherwise be a matter within state control pursuant to the Twenty-first Amendment.

Our holding in *Dole* did not involve separation-of-powers principles. It concerned only the allocation of power between the Federal Government and the States. Our reasoning that, absent coercion, a sovereign State has both the incentive and the ability to protect its own rights and powers, and therefore may cede such rights and powers, is inapplicable to the issues presented by this case. Here, unlike *Dole*, there is no question about federal power to operate the airports. The question is whether the maintenance of federal control over the airports by means of the Board of Review, which is allegedly a federal instrumentality, is invalid, not because it invades any state power, but because Congress' continued control violates the separation-of-powers principle, the aim of which is to protect not the States but "the whole people from improvident laws." *Chadha*, 462 U.S. at 951. Nothing in our opinion in *Dole* implied that a highway grant to a State could have been conditioned on the State's creating a "Highway Board of Review" composed of Members of Congress. We must therefore consider whether the

---

[16] Petitioners and the United States both place great weight on the fact that the Framers at the Constitutional Convention expressly rejected a constitutional provision that would have prohibited an individual from holding both state and federal office. The Framers apparently were concerned that such a prohibition would limit the pool of talented citizens to one level of government or the other. *See* 1 Max Farrand, Records of the Federal Convention of 1787, pp. 20–21, 217, 386, 389, 428–29 (1911). Neither petitioners nor the United States, however, point to any endorsement by the Framers of offices that are nominally created by the State but for which concurrent federal office is a prerequisite.

powers of the Board of Review may, consistent with the separation of powers, be exercised by an agent of Congress.

V

. . . .

The structure of our Government as conceived by the Framers of our Constitution disperses the federal power among the three branches — the Legislative, the Executive, and the Judicial — placing both substantive and procedural limitations on each. The ultimate purpose of this separation of powers is to protect the liberty and security of the governed. . . .

. . . .

To forestall the danger of encroachment "beyond the legislative sphere," the Constitution imposes two basic and related constraints on the Congress. It may not "invest itself or its Members with either executive power or judicial power." *J.W. Hampton, Jr., & Co. v. United States,* 276 U.S. 394, 406 (1928). And, when it exercises its legislative power, it must follow the "single, finely wrought and exhaustively considered, procedures" specified in Article I. *INS v. Chadha,* 462 U.S. at 951.

The first constraint is illustrated by the Court's holdings in *Springer v. Philippine Islands,* 277 U.S. 189 (1928), and *Bowsher v. Synar,* 478 U.S. 714 (1986). . . .

The second Constraint is illustrated by our decision in *Chadha.* . . .

. . . If the power is executive, the Constitution does not permit an agent of Congress to exercise it. If the power is legislative, Congress must exercise it in conformity with the bicameralism and presentment requirements of Art. I, § 7. . . .

One might argue that the provision for a Board of Review is the kind of practical accommodation between the Legislature and the Executive that should be permitted in a "workable government." Admittedly, Congress imposed its will on the regional authority created by the District of Columbia and the Commonwealth of Virginia by means that are unique and that might prove to be innocuous. However, the statutory scheme challenged today provides a blueprint for extensive expansion of the legislative power beyond its constitutionally confined role. Given the scope of the federal power to dispense benefits to the States in a variety of forms and subject to a host of statutory conditions, Congress could, if this Board of Review were valid, use similar expedients to enable its Members or its agents to retain control, outside the ordinary legislative process, of the activities of state grant recipients charged with executing virtually every aspect of national policy. As James Madison presciently observed, the legislature "can with greater facility, mask under complicated and indirect measures, the encroachments which it makes on the co-ordinate departments." THE FEDERALIST No. 48. Heeding his warning that legislative "power is of an encroaching nature," we conclude that the Board of Review is an impermissible encroachment.[23]

The judgment of the Court of Appeals is affirmed.

JUSTICE WHITE, with whom CHIEF JUSTICE REHNQUIST and JUSTICE MARSHALL join, dissenting.

Today the Court strikes down yet another innovative and otherwise lawful governmental experiment in the name of separation of powers. To reach this result, the

---

[23] Because we invalidate the Board of Review under basic separation-of-power principles, we need not address respondents' claim that Members of Congress serve on the Board in violation of the Incompatibility and Ineligibility Clauses. *See* U.S. Const., Art I, § 6. We also express no opinion on whether the appointment process of the Board of Review contravenes the Appointments Clause, U.S. Const., Art. II, § 2, cl. 2.

majority must strain to bring state enactments within the ambit of a doctrine hitherto applicable only to the Federal Government and strain again to extend the doctrine even though both Congress and the Executive argue for the constitutionality of the arrangement which the Court invalidates. These efforts are untenable because they violate the "cardinal principle that this Court will first ascertain whether a construction of [a] statute is fairly possible by which the [constitutional] question may be avoided." *Ashwander v. TVA*, 297 U.S. 288, 348 (1936) (Brandeis, J., concurring). They are also untenable because the Court's separation-of-powers cases in no way compel the decision the majority reaches.

I

. . . .

A

Both the Airports Authority (Authority) and the Board are clearly creatures of state law. The Authority came into being exclusively by virtue of acts passed by the Commonwealth of Virginia and the District of Columbia. . . .

. . . .

As an initial matter, the Board may not have existed but for Congress, but it does not follow that Congress created the Board or even that Congress' role is a "factor" mandating separation of powers scrutiny. Congressional suggestion does not render subsequent independent state actions federal ones. Aside from the clear statutory language, the majority's conclusion ignores the entire series of voluntary and intervening actions, agreements, and enactments on the part of the Federal Executive, Virginia, the District, and the Authority, without which the Transfer Act would have been a nullity and the Board of Review would not have existed. Congress commonly enacts conditional transfers of federal resources to the States. *See, e.g., Fullilove v. Klutznick*, 448 U.S. 448 (1980); *Lau v. Nichols*, 414 U.S. 563 (1974); *Steward Machine Co. v. Davis*, 301 U.S. 548 (1937). Separation-of-powers doctrine would know few bounds if such transfers compelled its application to the state enactments that result.

. . . .

Considered as a creature of state law, the Board offends no constitutional provision or doctrine. The Court does not assert that congressional membership on a state-created entity, without more, violates the Incompatibility or Ineligibility Clauses. U.S. Const., Art. I, § 6, cl. 2. By their express terms, these provisions prohibit Members of Congress from serving in another *federal* office. They say nothing to bar congressional service in state or state-created offices. To the contrary, the Framers considered and rejected such a bar. 1 MAX FARRAND, RECORDS OF THE FEDERAL CONVENTION OF 1787, pp. 20–21, 217, 386, 428–29 (1966 ed.). . . . The historical practice of the First Congress confirms the Convention's sentiments, insofar as several Members simultaneously sat as state legislators and judges. . . . Constitutional text and history leave no question but that Virginia and the District of Columbia could constitutionally agree to pass reciprocal legislation creating a body to which nonfederal officers would appoint Members of Congress functioning in their individual capacities. No one in this case contends otherwise.

B

The Court's haste to extend separation-of-powers doctrine is even less defensible in light of the federal statute on which it relies. Far from transforming the Board into a federal entity, the Transfer Act confirms the Board's constitutionality inasmuch as that statute is a legitimate exercise of congressional authority under the Property Clause. U.S. Const., Art. IV, § 3, cl. 2. To overlook this fact the Court must once again ignore plain meaning, this time the plain meaning of the Court's controlling precedent regarding Congress' coextensive authority under the Spending Clause.

As the majority acknowledges, in *South Dakota v. Dole*, 483 U.S. 203 (1987), the Court held that Congress could condition a grant of federal funds to a State on the State's raising the drinking age to 21, even assuming that Congress did not have the power to mandate a minimum national drinking age directly. As the majority fails to acknowledge, the Court's holding in no way turned on a State's "incentive and . . . ability to protect its own rights and powers." Rather, the Court stated that Congress could exercise its spending authority so long as the conditional grant of funds did not violate an "independent constitutional bar." *Dole*, 483 U.S. at 209. . . .

Dole states only that Congress may not induce the States to engage in activities that would themselves have been unconstitutional in the absence of the inducement. The decision does not indicate that Congress can act only when its actions implicate "the allocation of power between the Federal Government and the States" as opposed to principles, "the aim of which is to protect not the States but 'the whole people from improvident laws.' " Nor could it. In the context of 42 U.S.C. § 1983, the Court has rejected any broad distinction between constitutional provisions that allocate powers and those that affirm rights. *Dennis v. Higgins*, 498 U.S. 439, 447–48 (1991). The majority's own application of its test to this case illustrates the difficulties in its position. The Court asserts that *Dole* cannot safeguard the Board because separation-of-powers doctrine, ultimately, protects the rights of the people. By this logic, *Dole* itself would have had to come out the other way since the Twenty-first Amendment reinstated state authority over liquor, which in turn strengthened federalism, which in turn theoretically protects the rights of the people no less than separation-of-powers principles. *See* THE FEDERALIST NO. 51 (J. Madison).

There is no question that *Dole*, when faithfully read, places the Board outside the scope of separation-of-powers scrutiny. . . . As noted, no one suggests that Virginia and the District of Columbia could not have created a board of review to which nonfederal officers would appoint Members of Congress had Congress not offered any inducement to do so. The Transfer Act, therefore, did not induce the States to engage in activities that would themselves be unconstitutional. Nor is there any assertion that this case involves the rare circumstance in which "the financial inducement offered by Congress might be so coercive as to pass the point at which pressure turns into compulsion." *Dole*, 483 U.S. at 211. In *Dole*, Congress authorized the Secretary of Transportation to withdraw funding should the States fail to comply with certain conditions. Here, Congress merely indicated that federal control over National and Dulles Airports would continue given a failure to comply with certain conditions. Virginia and the District may sorely have wanted control over the airports for themselves. Placing conditions on a desire, however, does not amount to compulsion. *Dole* therefore requires precisely what the majority denies — the rejection of separation-of-powers doctrine as an "independent bar" against Congress conditioning the lease of federal property in this case.

II

Even assuming that separation-of-powers principles apply, the Court can hold the Board to be unconstitutional only by extending those principles in an unwarranted fashion. The majority contends otherwise, reasoning that the Constitution requires today's result whether the Board exercises executive *or* legislative power. Yet never before has the Court struck down a body on separation-of-powers grounds that neither Congress nor the Executive oppose. . . .

A

Based on its faulty premise that the Board is exercising federal power, the Court first reasons that "[i]f the [Board's] power is executive, the Constitution does not permit an agent of Congress to exercise it." The majority does not, however, rely on the constitutional provisions most directly on point. Under the Incompatibility and Ineligibility Clauses, Members of Congress may not serve in another office that is under the authority of the United States. U.S. Const., Art. I, § 6, cl. 2. If the Board did exercise executive authority that is federal in nature, the Court would have no need to say anything other than that congressional membership on the Board violated these express limitations. The majority's failure is either unaccountable or suggests that it harbors a certain discomfort with its own position that the Board in fact exercises significant federal power. Whichever is the case, the Court instead relies on expanding nontextual principles as articulated in *Bowsher v. Synar*, 478 U.S. 714 (1986). . . . The Court asserts that the Board, again in effect, is controlled by Congress. The analysis the Court has hitherto employed to recognize congressional control, however, show this not to be the case.

. . . .

Our recent case law also compels approval of the Board's composition. The majority makes much of the requirement that appointees to the Board must be members of the enumerated congressional committees. Committee membership, the argument goes, somehow belies the express declaration that Members of Congress are to sit in their individual capacities as representatives of frequent, nationwide travelers. *Mistretta [v. United States*, 488 U.S. 361 (1988)], however, refused to disqualify federal judges, sitting in their individual capacities, from exercising nonjudicial authority simply because they possessed judicial expertise relevant to their posts on the Sentencing Commission. It is difficult, then, to see why Members of Congress, sitting in their individual capacities, should be disqualified from exercising nonlegislative authority because their legislative expertise — as enhanced by their membership on key transportation and finance committees — is relevant to their posts on the Board. . . .

B

The majority alternatively suggests that the Board wields an unconstitutional legislative veto contrary to *INS v. Chadha*, 462 U.S. 919, 952–55 (1983). If the Board's "power is legislative," the Court opines, "Congress must exercise it in conformity with the bicameralism and presentment requirements of Art. I, § 7." The problem with this theory is that if the Board is exercising federal power, it is not legislative. . . .

. . . .

Exercise 6(B):

Consider the following matters with respect to *Metropolitan Washington Airports Authority*:

(1) Does either the majority or the dissent fairly characterize the holding of *South Dakota v. Dole*?

(2) Reconsider Question 6 in Exercise 6(A).

(3) Is there an argument for distinguishing between congressional spending power and power under the Property Clause?

In the context of taxpayer standing cases, the Court has recognized such a distinction, at least as an alternative basis for its decision. *See Valley Forge Christian College v. Americans United for Separation of Church and State*, 454 U.S. 464, 480 (1982) (finding lack of taxpayer standing to challenge transfer of surplus federal property at no cost to a religious school under legislation enacted pursuant to the Property Clause despite precedent authorizing taxpayer standing to challenge federal appropriation of funds that support religion). The dissenting Justices rejected such a distinction. *See id. at* 511–12 (Brennan, J., dissenting) ("It can make no constitutional difference in the case before us whether the donation to the petitioner here was in the form of a cash grant to build a facility . . . or in the nature of a gift of property including a facility already built."); *id.* at 515 (Stevens, J., dissenting) ("[The Court's] decision rests on the premise that the difference between a disposition of funds pursuant to the Spending Clause and a disposition of realty pursuant to the Property Clause is of fundamental jurisprudential significance."). Taxpayer standing is addressed in *Volume 1.*

A FINAL NOTE REGARDING THE SPENDING POWER

In *Pace v. Bogalusa City School Board,* 403 F.3d 272 (5th Cir. 2005) (en banc), the Fifth Circuit determined that Congress validly imposed conditions on federal funds. The judges who disagreed with that conclusion observed:

> [W]ith due regard for precedent, I am compelled to raise the following question: "If not now, and on this showing, when, and on what showing" will federal grants be deemed unconstitutionally coercive? The Rehabilitation Act, pursuant to 29 U.S.C. § 794(a), requires non-consenting States to forfeit all federal funds. For the Louisiana Department of Education, renouncing all federal funds would cut its budget by $804,269,621, or 75%. *Dole* counseled that "in some circumstances the financial inducement offered by Congress might be so coercive as to pass the point at which pressure turns into compulsion." 483 U.S. at 211. To date, the Supreme Court has not found a case that warranted vindication of this principle. Nevertheless, Louisiana and its children would suffer extreme consequences here if the State were to lose massive federal assistance by asserting its constitutional right to sovereign immunity.

Pace, 403 F.3d at 299 n.2 (Jones, J., concurring in part and dissenting in part).

If the dissent fairly characterized the facts in *Pace,* is this a situation where the judiciary should have found the condition to be "coercive"? If not, what circumstances would satisfy that requirement?

CHAPTER 2

THE NATURE OF ENUMERATED COERCIVE POWERS

Chapter One addressed the power of Congress to tax as a way to discourage certain activities and the power to spend funds with attached conditions, so as to provide an incentive for other conduct. To the extent those powers are relatively free from judicial limitations, Congress may have little need for its other powers.

As Chapter One revealed, however, the growth in federal revenue together with the erosion of limits on conditions attached to federal grants are matters of relatively recent development. Throughout much of our history under the Constitution, Congress has relied on other powers to coerce compliance. Before turning attention to the scope of some of the frequently-used coercive powers (in Chapters Three and Four), it may be helpful to consider the nature of the enumerated coercive powers specified in Article I, Section 8. This Chapter addresses two aspects of the coercive powers: (1) whether all such powers are enumerated or, conversely, whether Congress has implied powers, and (2) the application of the Supremacy Clause with respect to congressional enactments.

There are two significant and distinct contexts in which the judiciary is confronted with questions regarding the scope of the coercive powers. First, Congress may enact a law in reliance of one or more of its enumerated powers. A litigant may then *directly* challenge the law as exceeding the constitutional powers under which it was enacted. Second, a litigant may rely upon a State or local law only to have another party assert that such law is invalid by virtue of the Supremacy Clause. U.S. Constitution, Art. VI, ¶ 2. In both contexts, the cases need to overcome the justiciability limitations.

In the second class of cases, two distinct questions are presented. First, if the federal law were valid, would it *preempt* the State or local law? Second, is the federal law valid (or does it exceed the scope of the enumerated power upon which it was based)? In light of the judicial role, which of these two questions should a court address first? Why?

Exercise 7(A):

Review the text of the Constitution and the structure of the government it establishes, as well as materials from the ratification debates and consider:

(1)   Which, if any, of the powers enumerated in Article I, Section 8, are exclusively vested in the central government? Which, if any, may concurrently be exercised by States?

(2)   What, if anything, is excluded from the list of enumerated powers? If you can identify nothing that has been excluded, what purpose is served by the enumeration?

(3)   In addition to the enumerated powers, does Congress also have "implied" powers? If so, what is the limit to such powers?

(4)   How, if at all, does the Tenth Amendment modify your answers to the three previous questions?

THE DRAFTING HISTORY OF THE "NECESSARY AND PROPER" CLAUSE

The draft proposal prepared by the Committee of Detail introduced the first version of the Necessary and Proper Clause: "And to make all laws that shall be necessary and proper for carrying into execution the foregoing powers, and all other powers vested, by this Constitution, in the government of the United States, or in any department or officer thereof."[1] The Convention unanimously adopted the Necessary and Proper Clause as reported by the Committee of Detail.[2] The only debate on the provision was whether expressly to include "and create all offices" in this clause, a proposal which was defeated as superfluous.[3]

The language was surplusage because the phrase "and all other powers vested" authorized Congress to enact such "necessary and proper" laws to implement the structural provisions of Constitution, such as providing for the census and the implied power to authorize appointment of census officials,[4] or to create departments and offices for "the principal Officer in each of the executive Departments" from whom the President may require written reports,[5] or to create offices for the "Ambassadors, other public Ministers and Consuls" that the President is authorized to appoint with the advice and consent of the Senate,[6] or to create offices for non-judicial personnel of the Supreme Court, such as clerks.[7] None of the powers enumerated in Article I, Section 8 expressly authorized these offices yet the power to create such offices is implied elsewhere in the Constitution.

Although the scope of the Necessary and Proper Clause did not draw significant discussion at the Convention, it was a major concern during the ratification debates.

Exercise 7(B):

The examples with respect to the creation of offices suggests that the Necessary and Proper Clause may provide an *implied* power contemplated by other express provisions of the Constitution. Could the clause be read so broadly as to imply powers that the Constitutional Convention discussed but did not expressly incorporate into the final draft? For example, in the absence of an express enumerated power authorizing Congress to charter corporations, could it do so? If Congress could charter corporations, could it charter a central bank? In answering those questions, what weight should be given to the deliberations of the Constitutional Convention?

EXCERPTS OF RATIFICATION DEBATES

In the Pennsylvania Convention that ratified the Constitution, James Wilson (who had attended the Constitutional Convention) was among the leading proponents of ratification. Among other matters, he addressed the scope of legislative authority vested in Congress:

> The gentleman in opposition strongly insists that the general clause at the end of the eighth section [of Article I] gives to Congress a power of legislating

---

[1] 2 MAX FARRAND, THE RECORDS OF THE FEDERAL CONVENTION OF 1787, at 182 (rev. ed. 1966) (Madison's notes of Aug. 6, 1787) (setting forth the entire report of the Committee).

[2] *Id.* at 344–45 (Madison's notes of Aug. 20, 1787).

[3] *Id.*

[4] *See* U.S. Const. art. I, § 2, ¶ 3.

[5] U.S. Const. art II, § 2, ¶ 1.

[6] U.S. Const. art II, § 2, ¶ 2.

[7] U.S. Const. art III, § 1.

generally; but I cannot conceive by what means he will render the words susceptible of that expansion. Can the words, "The Congress shall have power to make all laws which shall be necessary and proper to carry into execution the foregoing powers," be capable of giving them general legislative power? I hope that it is not meant [by the opponents of ratification] to give to Congress merely an illusive show of authority, to deceive themselves or constituents any longer. On the contrary, I trust it is meant that they shall have the power of carrying into effect the laws which they shall make under the powers vested in them by this Constitution.

. . . .

It is urged, as a general objection to this system, that "the powers of Congress are unlimited and undefined, and that they will be the judges, in all cases, of what is necessary and proper for them to do." To bring this subject to your view, I need do no more than point to the words in the Constitution, beginning at [Article I, section 8]. "The Congress," it says, "shall have power," [etcetera]. I need not read over the words, but I leave it to every gentleman to say whether the powers are not as accurately and minutely defined, as can be done on the same subject, in the same language. The old Constitution [i.e., the Articles of Confederation] is as strongly marked on this subject; and even the concluding clause, with which so much fault has been found, gives no more or other powers; nor does it, in any degree, go beyond the particular enumeration; for, when it is said that Congress shall have the power to make all laws which shall be necessary and proper, those words are limited and defined by the following, "for carrying into execution the foregoing powers." It is saying no more than that the powers we have already particularly given, shall be effectually carried into execution.

THE FEDERALIST PAPERS were originally published to influence consideration of the Constitution in the New York ratification convention. In FEDERALIST No. 33, Alexander Hamilton addressed concerns over both the Necessary and Proper Clause and the Supremacy Clause:

The residue of the argument against the provisions in the constitution . . . is ingrafted upon the following clauses; the last clause of the eighth section of the first article of the plan under consideration, authorises the national legislature "to make all laws which shall be *necessary* and *proper,* for carrying into execution *the powers* by that Constitution vested in the government of the United States, or in any department or officer thereof"; and the second clause of the sixth article declares, that "the Constitution and the Laws of the United States made *in pursuance thereof,* and the treaties made by their authority shall be the *supreme law* of the land; anything in the constitution or laws of any State to the contrary notwithstanding."

These two clauses have been the source of much virulent invective and petulant declamation against the proposed constitution, they have been held up to the people, in all the exaggerated colours of misrepresentation, as the pernicious engines by which their local governments were to be destroyed and their liberties exterminated — as the hideous monster whose devouring jaws would spare neither sex nor age, nor high nor low, nor sacred nor profane; and yet strange as it may appear, after all this clamour, to those who may not have happened to contemplate them in the same light, it may be affirmed with perfect confidence, that the constitutional operation of the intended government would be precisely the same, if these clauses were entirely obliterated, as if they were repeated in every article. They are only declaratory of a truth, which would have resulted by necessary and unavoidable implication from the very act of constituting a Federal Government, and vesting it with certain specified powers.

This is so clear a proposition, that moderation itself can scarcely listen to the railings which have been so copiously vented against this part of the plan, without emotions that disturb its equanimity.

What is a power, but the ability or faculty of doing a thing? What is the ability to do a thing but the power of employing the *means* necessary to its execution? What is a LEGISLATIVE power but a power of making LAWS? What are the *means* to execute a LEGISLATIVE power but LAWS? . . . What are the proper means of executing such a [power enumerated] but *necessary* and *proper* laws?

[T]he same process will lead to the same result in relation to all other powers declared in the constitution. And it is *expressly* to execute these powers, that the sweeping clause, as it has been effectually called, authorises the national legislature to pass all *necessary* and *proper* laws. If there is any thing exceptional, it must be sought for in the specific powers, upon which this general declaration is predicated. The declaration itself, though it may be chargeable with tautology or redundancy, is at least perfectly harmless.

. . . .

If the Federal Government should overpass the just bounds of its authority, and make a tyrannical use of its powers; the people whose creature it is must appeal to the standard they have formed, and take such measures to redress the injury done to the constitution, as the exigency may suggest and prudence justify. . . .

[T]he clause which declares the supremacy of the laws of the Union, like the one we have just before considered, only declares a truth, which flows immediately and necessarily from the institution of a Federal Government. It will not, I presume, have escaped observation that it *expressly* confines this supremacy to laws made *pursuant to the Constitution;* which I mention merely as an instance of caution in the Convention; since that limitation would have been to be understood though it had not been expressed.

Though a law therefore for laying a tax for the use of the United States would be supreme in its nature, and could not legally be opposed or controuled; yet a law for abrogating or preventing the collection of a tax laid by the authority of a State (unless upon imports and exports) would not be the supreme law of the land, but an usurpation of power not granted by the constitution. As far as an improper accumulation of taxes on the same object might tend to render the collection difficult or precarious, this would be a mutual inconvenience not arising from a superiority or defect of power on either side, but from an injudicious exercise of power by one or the other, in a manner equally disadvantageous to both. . . .

In FEDERALIST No. 44, James Madison addressed the criticism of the Necessary and Proper Clause:

There are four other possible methods which the Convention might have taken on this subject. . . .

Had the Convention taken the first method of adopting the second article of confederation; it is evident that the new Congress would be continually exposed as their predecessors have been, to the alternative of construing the term *"expressly"* with so much rigour as to disarm the government of all real authority whatever, or with so much latitude as to destroy altogether the force of the restriction. It would be easy to show if it were necessary, that no important power, delegated by the articles of confederation, has been or can be executed by Congress, without recurring more or less to the doctrine of *construction* or *implication*. As the powers delegated under the new system are more extensive, the government which is to administer it would find itself still more distressed with the alternative of betraying the public interest by doing nothing; or of violating the Constitution by exercising powers, indispensably necessary and proper; but at the same time, not *expressly* granted.

Had the convention attempted a positive enumeration of the powers necessary and proper for carrying their other powers into effect; the attempt would have involved a complete digest of laws on every subject to which the Constitution relates; accommodated too not only to the existing state of things, but to all the possible changes which futurity may produce: For in every new application of a general power, the *particular powers*, which are the means of attaining the *object* of the general power, must always vary with that object; and be often properly varied whilst the object remains the same.

Had they attempted to enumerate the particular powers or means, not necessary or proper for carrying the general powers into execution, the task would have been no less chimerical; and would have been liable to this further objection; that every defect in the enumeration, would have been the equivalent to a positive grant of authority. . . .

Had the Constitution been silent on this head, there can be no doubt that all the particular powers, requisite as means of executing the general powers, would have resulted to the government, by unavoidable implication. No axiom is more clearly established in law, or in reason, than that wherever the end is required, the means are authorised; wherever a general power to do a thing is given, every particular power necessary for doing it, is included. Had this last method therefore been pursued by the Convention, every objection now urged against their plan, would remain in all its plausibility . . . .

If it be asked, what is to be the consequence, in case the Congress shall misconstrue this part of the Constitution, and exercise powers not warranted by its true meaning? I answer the same as if they should misconstrue or enlarge any other power vested in them, as if the general power had been reduced to particulars, and any one of these were to be violated; the same in short, as if the State Legislatures should violate their respective constitutional authorities. In the first instance, the success of the usurpation will depend on the executive and judiciary departments, which are to expound and give effect to the legislative acts; and in the last resort a remedy must be obtained from the people, who can by the election of more faithful representatives, annul the acts of the usurpers. The truth is, that this ultimate redress may be more confided in against unconstitutional acts of the federal than of the State Legislatures, for this plain reason, that as every such act of the former, will be an invasion of the rights of the latter, these will be ever ready to mark the innovation, to sound the alarm to the people, and to exert their local influence in effecting a change of federal representatives. . . .

Exercise 7(C):

What explanation did supporters of ratification provide of the Necessary and Proper Clause? Under what circumstances did supporters suggest that it would be appropriate to determine that Congress had implied powers in addition to its enumerated powers?

Under what circumstances could Congress legislate to invalidate a State tax? Under what circumstances would the Constitution itself invalidate a State tax?

CONSTITUTIONAL CONVENTION DEBATES
ON THE POWER TO CHARTER A NATIONAL BANK

On August 18, 1787, James Madison proposed that the enumerated powers of Congress should be expanded to include certain additional matters. Among the proposed additional powers was: "To grant charters of incorporation in cases where the public good may require them, and the authority of a single State may be incompetent."[8] The proposals were referred to the Committee of Detail.[9] In the alternative, Charles Pinckney proposed to provide the power "[t]o grant charters of incorporation."[10]

On September 14, 1787, the Constitutional Convention considered the report of the Committee of Style. Benjamin Franklin proposed to expand the clause authorizing Congress to establish post roads so as to include " 'a power to provide for cutting canals where deemed necessary.' "[11] James Madison suggested that Dr. Franklin's proposed amendment should be expanded and that Congress be vested with "a power 'to grant charters of incorporation where the interest of the U.S. might require & the legislative provisions of individual States may be incompetent.' "[12] Rufus King "thought the power was unnecessary."[13] He explained: "The States will be prejudiced and divided into parties by it — In Philad[elphia] & New York, it will be referred to the establishment of a Bank, which has been a subject of contention in those cities. In other places it will be referred to mercantile monopolies."[14] James Wilson spoke in support of the measure. He "mentioned the importance of facilitating by canals, the communication with the Western Settlements — As to Banks he did not think with Mr. King that the power in that point of view would excite the prejudices & parties apprehended. As to mercantile monopolies they are already included in the power to regulate trade."[15] George Mason sought a vote on the original proposal of Dr. Franklin, "limiting the power to the single case of Canals."[16] Colonel Mason explained that he "was afraid of monopolies of every sort, which he did not think were by any means already implied by the Constitution as supposed by Mr. Wilson."[17] The vote on whether to expand the clause addressing post roads to include the power to establish canals was defeated by a vote of 8 States to 3.[18] The broader measure of permitting Congress to charter corporations "fell of course, as including the power rejected."[19] Three days later the Constitutional Convention adjourned.

Looking back several years later, Abraham Baldwin, who had been a delegate to the Constitutional Convention and later served in the House of Representatives, reported the following incident.

---

[8] Farrand, *supra* note 1, at 325 (Madison's notes); *see id.* at 321 (1911) (Journal of Aug. 18, 1787).

[9] *Id.* at 325 (Madison's notes).

[10] *Id.; see also id.* at 322 (Journal of Aug. 17, 1787).

[11] *Id.* at 615 (Madison's notes).

[12] *Id.*

[13] *Id.*

[14] *Id.* Six of the delegates to the Constitutional Convention had served in the Continental Congress six years earlier that had chartered Bank of North America, including James Madison who had declared the measure unauthorized by the Articles of Confederation. *See* Bray Hammond, BANKS AND POLITICS IN AMERICA FROM THE REVOLUTION TO THE CIVIL WAR 103 (1957).

[15] 2 Max Farrand, *supra* note 1, at 615 (Madison's notes).

[16] *Id.*

[17] *Id.*

[18] *Id.*

[19] *Id.*

When the bank bill was under discussion in the House of Representatives, Ju[stice James] Wilson came in, and was standing by him. Baldwin reminded him of the following fact which passed in the grand convention. Among the enumerated powers given to Congress, was one to erect corporations. It was, on debate, struck out. Several particular powers were then proposed. Among others, Robert Morris proposed to give Congress a power to establish a national bank. Gouverneur Morris opposed it, observing that it was extremely doubtful whether the constitution they were framing could ever be passed at all by the people of America; that to give it its best chance, however, they should make it as palatable as possible, and put nothing into it not very essential, which might raise up enemies; that his colleague (Robert Morris) well knew that 'a bank' was, in their State (Pennsylvania) the very watch-word of party; that *a bank* had been the great bone of contention between the two parties of the State, from the establishment of their constitution, having been erected, put down, and erected again, as either party preponderated; that therefore, to insert this power, would instantly enlist against the whole instrument, the whole of the anti-bank party in Pennsylvania. Whereupon it was rejected, as was every other special power, except that of giving copyrights to authors, and patents to inventors; the general power of incorporating being whittled down to this shred. Wilson agreed to the fact.[20]

THE FIRST CONGRESS

On December 13, 1790, Secretary of the Treasury Alexander Hamilton submitted a report to the House of Representatives favoring legislation to incorporate a national bank. At that time there were at least three significant banks in the United States: the Bank of New York in that city (which opened in 1784 but operated without a charter until 1791), the Bank of Massachusetts in Boston (chartered by the Massachusetts legislature in 1784), and the Bank of North America in Philadelphia.[21]

The Bank of North America originated in a 1781 resolution of the Congress under the Articles of Confederation and "was the first real bank, in the modern sense, on the North American continent."[22] With the end of the Revolutionary War, the central government's stock in the Bank of North America was sold and the central government's debt to the Bank was repaid.[23] The Bank later accepted a new charter for a term of fourteen years from the Commonwealth of Pennsylvania, essentially converting it to a private commercial bank.

In addition to those three banks, the Bank of Maryland, in Baltimore, and seven additional banks were established before the end of 1792.[24]

---

[20] 3 MAX FARRAND, *supra* note 1, at 375–76. Similarly, Thomas Jefferson recorded in 1798 that at the Constitutional Convention "Robert Morris had wished to propose that the Constitution authorize the chartering of a bank and that Gouverneur Morris had urged him not to do so, because the idea was so controversial that its mention would kill the chances of getting the Constitution ratified." BRAY HAMMOND, *supra* note 14, at 104–05.

[21] *See* BRAY HAMMOND, *supra* note 14, at 65–66, 103–04, 114, 144–45, 197.

[22] *Id.* at 50, 144–45.

[23] *See* MURRAY N. ROTHBARD, A HISTORY OF MONEY AND BANKING IN THE UNITED STATES: THE COLONIAL ERA TO WORLD WAR II, 63–64 (2005); *see* BRAY HAMMOND, *supra* note 14, at 53–54, 63.

[24] *See* BRAY HAMMOND, *supra* note 14, at 66–67, 72. For a discussion of the early banks established in New York, see *id.* at 149–64, in Pennsylvania, see *id.* at 164–65, in Massachusetts, see *id.* at 165–66, in Rhode Island, see *id.* at 166–67, and in Maryland, see *id.* at 167–68.

Hamilton's plan expressly provided that the new bank would be guaranteed monopoly status,[25] with Congress granting an exclusive charter to the new bank for a term of twenty years or until final redemption of the national debt. Hamilton's initial report did not address any of the constitutional issues presented by the plan. The Senate passed a bill to incorporate a national bank along the lines proposed by Hamilton. When the matter was transmitted to the House of Representatives for its action, in February 1791, the issue of constitutional authority was raised by Representative James Madison.

A REPORT OF MADISON'S SPEECH
ON THE BILL TO ESTABLISH A NATIONAL BANK
February 2, 1791

[After addressing several policy considerations raised by the Administration's proposal to incorporate a bank of the United States which had already passed in the Senate, James Madison turned his attention to the constitutional issues. He] den[ied] the authority of Congress to pass it. He had entertained this opinion from the date of the Constitution. His impression might, perhaps, be the stronger, because he well recollected that a power to grant charters of incorporation had been proposed in the General Convention and rejected.

Is the power of establishing an incorporated Bank among the powers vested by the Constitution in the Legislature of the United States? That is the question to be examined.

After some general remarks on the limitations of all political power, he took notice of the peculiar manner in which the Federal Government is limited. It is not a general grant; it is a grant of particular powers only, leaving the general mass in other hands. So it had been understood by its friends and its foes, and so it was to be interpreted.

As preliminaries to a right interpretation, he laid down the following rules:

An interpretation that destroys the very characteristic of the Government cannot be just.

Where a meaning is clear, the consequences, whatever they may be, are to be admitted — where doubtful, it is fairly triable by its consequences.

In controverted cases, the meaning of the parties to the instrument, if to be collected by reasonable evidence, is a proper guide.

Contemporary and concurrent expositions are a reasonable evidence of the meaning of the parties.

In admitting or rejecting a constructive authority, not only the degree of its incidentality to an express authority is to be regarded, but the degree of its importance also; since on this will depend the probability or improbability of its being left to construction.

Reviewing the Constitution with an eye to these positions, it was not possible to discover in it the power to incorporate a Bank. The only clauses under which such a power could be pretended, are either:

1. The power to lay and collect taxes to pay the debts, and provide for the common defence and general welfare; or,

---

[25] As Hamilton later explained in his opinion regarding the constitutionality of the bill to incorporate the bank: "The bill proposes in addition, that the government . . . shall permit the bills of the company payable on demand to be receivable in its revenues & stipulates that it shall not grant privileges similar to those which are allowed to this company, to any others."

2. The power to borrow money on the credit of the United States; or

3. The power to pass all laws necessary and proper to carry into execution those powers.

The bill did not come within the first power. It laid no tax to pay the debts, or provide for the general welfare. It laid no tax whatever. It was altogether foreign to the subject.

No argument could be drawn from the terms "common defence and general welfare." The power as to these general purposes was limited to acts laying taxes for them; and the general purposes themselves were limited and explained by the particular enumeration subjoined. To understand these terms in any sense, that would justify the power in question, would give to Congress an unlimited power; would render nugatory the enumeration of particular powers; would supersede all the powers reserved to the State Governments. These terms are copied from the [A]rticles of Confederation; had it ever been pretended that they were to be understood otherwise than as here explained?

It has been said, that "general welfare" meant cases in which a general power might be exercised by Congress, without interfering with the powers of the States; and that the establishment of a National Bank was of this sort. There were, he said, several answers to this novel doctrine.

1. The proposed Bank would interfere, so as indirectly to defeat a State Bank at the same place.

2. It would directly interfere with the rights of the States to prohibit as well as to establish Banks, and the circulation of Bank notes. He mentioned a law in Virginia actually prohibiting the circulation of notes payable to bearer.

3. Interference with the power of the States was no constitutional criterion of the power of Congress. If the power was not given, Congress could not exercise it; if given, they might exercise it, although it should interfere with the laws, or even the Constitution of the States.

4. If Congress could incorporate a Bank merely because the act would leave the States free to establish Banks also, any other incorporations might be made by Congress. They could incorporate companies of manufacturers, or companies for cutting canals, or even religious societies, leaving similar incorporations by the States, like State Banks, to themselves. Congress might even establish religious teachers in every parish, and pay them out of the Treasury of the United States, leaving other teachers unmolested in their functions. These inadmissible consequences condemned the controverted principle.

The case of the Bank established by the former Congress had been cited as a precedent. This was known, he said, to have been the child of necessity. It could never be justified by the regular powers of the [A]rticles of Confederation. Congress betrayed a consciousness of this in recommending to the States to incorporate the Bank also. They did not attempt to protect the Bank notes by penalties against counterfeiters. These were reserved wholly to the authority of the States.

The second clause to be examined is that which empowers Congress to borrow money.

Is this bill to borrow money? It does not borrow a shilling. Is there any fair construction by which the bill can be deemed an exercise of the power to borrow money? The obvious meaning of the power to borrow money, is that of accepting it from, and stipulating payment to those who are able and willing to lend.

To say that the power to borrow involves a power of creating the ability, where there may be the will, to lend, is not only establishing a dangerous principle, as will be immediately shown, but is as forced a construction as to say that it involves the power of compelling the will, where there may be the ability to lend.

The third clause is that which gives the power to pass all laws necessary and proper to execute the specified powers.

Whatever meaning this clause may have, none can be admitted, that would give an unlimited discretion to Congress.

Its meaning must, according to the natural and obvious force of the terms and the context, be limited to means necessary to the end, and incident to the nature of the specified powers.

The clause is in fact merely declaratory of what would have resulted by unavoidable implication, as the appropriate, and, as it were, technical means of executing those powers. In this sense it has been explained by the friends of the Constitution, and ratified by the State Conventions.

The essential characteristic of the Government, as composed of limited and enumerated powers, would be destroyed, if, instead of direct and incidental means, any means could be used, which, in the language of the preamble to the bill, "might be conceived to be conducive to the successful conducting of the finances, or might be conceived to tend to give facility to the obtaining of loans." He urged an attention to the diffuse and ductile terms which had been found requisite to cover the stretch of power contained in the bill. He compared them with the terms necessary and proper, used in the Constitution, and asked whether it was possible to view the two descriptions as synonymous, or the one as a fair and safe commentary on the other.

If, proceeded he, Congress, by virtue of the power to borrow, can create the means of lending, and, in pursuance of these means, can incorporate a Bank, they may do any thing whatever creative of like means.

. . . .

Private capitals are the chief resources for loans to the British Government. Whatever then may be conceived to favor the accumulation of capitals may be done by Congress. They may incorporate manufacturers. They may give monopolies in every branch of domestic industry.

. . . .

The States have, it is allowed on all hands, a concurrent right to lay and collect taxes. This power is secured to them, not by its being expressly reserved, but by its not being ceded by the Constitution. The reasons for the bill cannot be admitted, because they would invalidate that right; why may it not be conceived by Congress, that a uniform and exclusive imposition of taxes, would not less than the proposed Banks, "be conducive to the successful conducting of national finances, and tend to give facility to the obtaining of revenue, for the use of the Government?"

The doctrine of implication is always a tender one. The danger of it has been felt in other Governments. The delicacy was felt in the adoption of our own; the danger may also be felt, if we do not keep close to our chartered authorities.

Mark the reasoning on which the validity of the bill depends! To borrow money is made the end, and the accumulation of capitals implied as the means. The accumulation of capitals is then the end, and a Bank implied as the means. The Bank is then the end, and a charter of incorporation, a monopoly, capital punishments, [etcetera], implied as the means.

If implications, this remote and this multiplied, can be linked together, a chain may be formed that will reach every object of legislation, every object within the whole compass of political economy.

The latitude of interpretation required by the bill is condemned by the rule furnished by the Constitution itself.

Congress have power "to regulate the value of money" yet it is expressly added, not left to be implied, that counterfeiters may be punished.

They have the power "to declare war," to which armies are more incident than incorporated banks to borrowing; yet the power "to raise and support armies" is expressly added; and to this again, the express power "to make rules and regulations for the government of armies;" a like remark is applicable to the powers as to the navy.

The regulation and calling out of the militia are more appertinent to war than the proposed Bank to borrowing; yet the former is not left to construction.

The very power to borrow money is less remote an implication from the power of war, than an incorporated monopoly Bank from the power of borrowing; yet, the power to borrow is not left to implication.

It is not pretended that every insertion or omission in the Constitution is the effect of systematic attention. This is not the character of any human work, particularly the work of a body of men. The examples cited, with others that might be added, sufficiently inculcate, nevertheless, a rule of interpretation very different from that on which the bill rests. They condemn the exercise of any power, particularly a great and important power, which is not evidently and necessarily involved in an express power.

It cannot be denied that the power proposed to be exercised is an important power.

. . . .

The bill gives a power to purchase and hold lands; Congress themselves could not purchase lands within a State "without the consent of its Legislature." How could they delegate a power to others which they did not possess themselves?

. . . .

It involves a monopoly, which affects the equal rights of every citizen.

It leads to a penal regulation, perhaps capital punishments, one of the most solemn acts of sovereign authority.

From this view of the power of incorporation exercised in the bill, it could never be deemed an accessory or subaltern power, to be deduced by implication, as a means of executing another power; it was in its nature a distinct, an independent and substantive prerogative, which not being enumerated in the Constitution, could never have been meant to be included in it, and not being included, could never be rightfully exercised.

He here adverted to a distinction, which he said had not been sufficiently kept in view, between a power necessary and proper for the Government or Union, and a power necessary and proper for executing the enumerated powers. In the latter case, the powers included in the enumerated powers were not expressed, but to be drawn from the nature of each. In the former, the powers composing the Government were expressly enumerated. This constituted the peculiar nature of the Government; no power, therefore, not enumerated could be inferred from the general nature of Government. Had the power of making treaties, for example, been omitted, however necessary it might have been, the defect could only have been lamented, or supplied by an amendment of the Constitution.

But the proposed Bank could not even be called necessary to the Government; at most it could be but convenient. Its uses to the Government could be supplied by keeping the taxes a little in advance; by loans from individuals; by the other Banks, over which the Government would have equal command; nay greater, as it might grant or refuse to these the privilege (a free and irrevocable gift to the proposed Bank) of using their notes in the Federal revenue.

He proceeded next to the contemporary expositions given to the Constitution.

The defence against the charge founded on the want of a bill of rights pre-supposed, he said, that the powers not given were retained; and that those given were not to be extended by remote implications. On any other supposition, the power of Congress to abridge the freedom of the press, or the rights of conscience, [etcetera], could not have been disproved.

The explanations in the State Conventions all turned on the same fundamental principle, and on the principle that the terms necessary and proper gave no additional powers to those enumerated.

[Here he read sundry passages from the Debates of the Pennsylvania, Virginia, and North Carolina Conventions, showing the grounds on which the Constitution had been vindicated by its principal advocates, against a dangerous latitude of its powers, charged on it by its opponents.][26]

. . . .

The explanatory declarations and amendments accompanying the ratifications of the several States formed a striking evidence, wearing the same complexion. He referred those who might doubt on the subject, to the several acts of ratification.

The explanatory amendments proposed by Congress themselves, at least, would be good authority with them; all these renunciations of power proceeded on a rule of construction, excluding the latitude now contended for. These explanations were the more to be respected, as they had not only been proposed by Congress, but ratified by nearly three-fourths of the States. He read several of the articles proposed, remarking particularly on the 11th and 12th; the former, as guarding against a latitude of interpretation; the latter, as excluding every source of power not within the Constitution itself.[27]

With all this evidence of the sense in which the Constitution was understood and adopted, will it not be said, if the bill should pass, that its adoption was brought about by one set of arguments, and that it is now administered under the influence of another set? [A]nd this reproach will have the keener sting, because it is applicable to so many individuals concerned in both the adoption and administration.

In fine, if the power were in the Constitution, the immediate exercise of it cannot be essential; if not there, the exercise of it involves the guilt of usurpation, and establishes a precedent of interpretation leveling all the barriers which limit the powers of the General Government, and protect those of the State Governments. If the point be doubtful only, respect for ourselves, who ought to shun the appearance of precipitancy and ambition; respect for our successors, who ought not lightly to be deprived of the opportunity of exercising the rights of legislation; respect for our constituents, who have had no opportunity of making known their sentiments, and who are themselves to be bound down to the measure for so long a period; all these considerations require that the irrevocable decision should at least be suspended until another session.

---

[26] [*Ed:* This bracketed description of omitted material appears in the record of Madison's speech. It is not attributable to the casebook editor.]

[27] [*Ed:* In this paragraph Madison references the twelve constitutional amendments proposed by the First Congress. Only ten of the twelve were ratified at that time so that his reference to proposals eleven and twelve correspond to the Ninth and Tenth Amendments.]

It appeared on the whole, he concluded, that the power exercised by the bill was condemned by the silence of the Constitution; was condemned by the rule of interpretation arising out of the Constitution; was condemned by its tendency to destroy the main characteristic of the Constitution; was condemned by the expositions of the friends of the Constitution, whilst depending before the public; was condemned by the apparent intention of the parties which ratified the Constitution; was condemned by the explanatory amendment proposed by Congress themselves to the Constitution; and he hoped it would receive its final condemnation by the vote of this House.

Exercise 7(D):

Consider the following matters:

(1)   As indicated in the introductory material of the chapter, the common understanding is that the Framers gave Congress limited and enumerated powers. Does the text of the Constitution support that view? Is there any textual argument that Congress has additional powers beyond those specified in Article I, Section 8?

(a) Would any of the powers enumerated in Article I, Section 8 permit Congress to grant hereditary offices as dukes or barons?

(b) Would any of those powers permit Congress to suspend the writ of habeas corpus?

(c) If the powers enumerated in Article I, Section 8 would not permit Congress to take the actions specified in (a) and (b), why is there any need to prohibit those actions in Article I, Section 9?

(2)   Did the Framers expressly provide Congress with power to establish a national bank? Did they expressly provide Congress with power to charter corporations?

(3)   Did the Framers have any "original intent" as to whether Congress had the power to establish a national bank?

(4)   Assuming that the Framers considered and rejected granting Congress an express power to establish a national bank, what weight, if any, should be given to that determination upon judicial review of legislation chartering a national bank? Why?

(5)   Supporters of the Constitution argued during the ratification debates that no Bill of Rights was necessary because Congress had only limited and enumerated powers which did not include any bases upon which to infringe fundamental rights. They argued, for example, that nothing in Article I, Section 8 authorized Congress to legislate an abridgement of free speech. Moreover, they asserted that a Bill of Rights would be an affirmatively dangerous addition to the Constitution because a declaration protecting free speech, for example, would imply that somewhere in Article I, Section 8, Congress was authorized to enact laws that would abridge free speech. In addition, supporters of ratification of the Constitution without amendment pointed out that any attempt to enumerate fundamental rights in a formal Bill of Rights would imply that rights not included in the enumeration were not protected.

Opponents of the Constitution argued during the ratification debates that Article I, Section 9 was a partial bill of rights which would have been unnecessary if Article I, Section 8 were to be construed as suggested by supporters of the Constitution. In the end, supporters of ratification prevailed only upon the promise that Congress would immediately propose amendments to affirmatively protect fundamental rights to add a second protection against expansive reading of congressional powers. One of the amendments that was included in the Bill of Rights addressed the argument that an enumeration of fundamental rights would be affirmatively dangerous. *See* Amendment IX. Another one of the amendments that was included in the Bill of Rights expressly reinforced the doctrine that Congress was granted only limited and enumerated powers, despite the presence of prohibitions in Article I, Section 9 and in the Bill of Rights. *See* Amendment X.

In light of that history, should the Necessary and Proper Clause be understood as granting Congress implied powers to legislate over matters not enumerated in Article I, Section 8?

(6)   Compare the text of the Tenth Amendment with the text of the second of the Articles of Confederation. Does that comparison change your answer to question 5? Why or why not?

From 1791 to 1819

After considerable debate, the House passed the bill. In response to the constitutional questions raised, President Washington sought legal counsel before deciding whether to sign or veto the bill. Attorney General Edmund Randolph concluded that Congress lacked constitutional authority to incorporate the bank. In further support of that view, Secretary of State Thomas Jefferson submitted a written opinion that the proposed bank was unconstitutional. Among other points, Jefferson observed: "It is known that the very power now proposed *as a means* was rejected as *an end* by the Convention which formed the Constitution." He also reasoned: "the Constitution allows only the means which are *'necessary,'* not those which are merely 'convenient' for effecting the enumerated powers" because the very structure of enumerated and limited powers restrained any implied powers "to those without which the grant of power would be nugatory."

After reviewing the opinions of Randolph and Jefferson, President Washington instructed Hamilton to submit a formal opinion. Hamilton did so on February 23, 1791, concluding that the bank bill was constitutional.

> . . . It is conceded, that implied powers are to be considered as delegated equally with express ones.
>
> Then it follows, that as a power of erecting a corporation may as well be *implied* as any other thing; it may as well be employed as an *instrument* or *means* of carrying into execution any of the specified powers, as any other instrument or mean[s] whatever. The only question must be, in this as in every other case, whether the mean[s] to be employed, or in this instance the corporation to be erected, has a natural relation to any of the acknowledged objects or lawful ends of the government. Thus a corporation may not be erected by congress for superintending the police of the city of Philadelphia because they are not authorised to *regulate* the *police* of that city; but one may be erected in relation to the collection of the taxes, or to the trade with foreign countries, or to the trade between the States, or with the Indian Tribes, because it is the province of the federal government to regulate those objects & because it is incident to a general *sovereign* or *legislative power* to *regulate* a thing, to employ all the means which relate to its regulation to the *best & greatest advantage.*

President Washington asked James Madison to memorialize objections to the bill for use as a veto statement in the event he decided against the measure.[28] Then on the final day permitted, February 25, 1791, the President signed the bill. *See* An Act to Incorporate the Subscribers to the Bank of the United States, ch. X, 1 Stat. 191 (1791) (on DVD-ROM). "[A] substantial number of senators and representatives [were] elected

---

[28] *See* MARK R. KILLENBECK, M'CULLOCH v. MARYLAND: SECURING A NATION 28 (2006); BRAY HAMMOND,, *supra* note 14, at 116.

to the board of the Bank in 1791."[29] Congressional supporters of Hamilton's plan served as Directors of the Bank while simultaneously serving in Congress not only in 1791 but for years thereafter.[30]

If Congress established a governmental agency to perform the functions of a bank, would Members of Congress have been eligible to serve on the board that headed the agency? If your instructor assigned *Volume 2,* consider whether service of Members of Congress as Directors of the Bank (or branches thereof) is consistent with the purposes underlying the incompatibility provisions. Does the incidence of simultaneous service suggest that the Bank was considered a private business (even if federally-chartered) rather than as an instrument of the central government itself?

In 1794, the Senate debated a proposed constitutional amendment that would have declared Congress had no implied power to charter the Bank of the United States. Although that measure did not pass, the debate evidenced continued opposition to the Bank from a substantial minority in the Senate.[31]

In the time from the issuance of the 1791 charter to 1796, eighteen additional banks were established within the United States.[32] In order to mitigate local opposition to the Bank of the United States, Secretary of the Treasury Hamilton opposed the idea of establishing branch offices but the directors of the Bank proceeded to do so,[33] including (in 1792) a branch in Baltimore, Maryland.

After 1796, it was evident that the dispute over the Bank of the United States did not simply follow the divide of the first party system, with Federalists supporting the Bank and Republicans opposing it. President John Adams, himself a Federalist, was displeased with the Bank (and, more broadly, with the powers that had accumulated in the Treasury Department). By the time of the Adams Administration, the Bank's unqualified supporters consisted largely of the so-called "High Federalists" or "Ultra Federalists" led by Alexander Hamilton. On the other hand, President Thomas Jefferson's Secretary of the Treasury, Albert Gallatin, recommended extending the Bank's charter, albeit with significant modifications.[34]

Beginning in 1808, the stockholders of the Bank of the United States petitioned Congress to renew its charter beyond 1811. Several efforts to enact new legislation failed. By 1811, there were over one hundred state banks. In January 1811, Representative Burwell addressed the House and opposed any new legislation on the ground that Congress lacked constitutional authority to incorporate a bank.

> It is my most deliberate conviction the constitution of the country *gives* no authority to Congress to incorporate a bank, and endow the stockholders with chartered immunities, and, even if its dissolution should produce ruin to the merchants, and, what is of equal importance, embarrassment to the Government, they would not be paramount to the sacred obligation of supporting the

---

[29] Mark R. Killenbeck, *supra* note 28, at 34; *see* John Thom Holdsworth & Davis R. Dewey, The First and Second Banks of the United States 34–35, 55, 67 (1910) (published as S. Doc. No. 571, 61st Congress, 2d Sess.).

[30] In the first two elections to the Board of Directors alone, Senators Rufus King (of New York), Samuel Johnson (of North Carolina), Jonathan Mason, Jr. (of Massachusetts), William Bingham (of Pennsylvania), Charles Carroll (of Maryland), and George Cabot (of Massachusetts), were joined in their simultaneous service by Representatives William Smith (of South Carolina), John Laurance (of New York), Jeremiah Wadsworth (of Connecticut), and Fisher Ames (of Massachusetts).

[31] *See* Mark R. Killenbeck, *supra* note 28, at 34–35.

[32] *See* Murray N. Rothbard, *supra* note 23, at 69–70; *see also* Bray Hammond, *supra* note 14, at 144–45 (listing banks chartered from 1781 to 1800).

[33] *See* Mark R. Killenbeck, *supra* note 28, at 32; Bray Hammond, *supra* note 14, at 126.

[34] *See* Mark R. Killenbeck, *supra* note 28, at 43–44.

constitution, though I am persuaded the dreadful evils which have been predicted from the annihilation of the bank, will soon vanish, and that no material shock will be produced by that cause. The construction which the constitution has received by the various persons who have, at different times, administered it, has been rigid or liberal, according to their confidence in the General or State Governments. The unqualified extent given to its general powers, and the inclusion of incidental powers, as flowing from, and belonging to, particular enumerated grants, have constituted the essential points of difference among those who have divided upon the principles of the constitution: this has been the case, not only in the exercise of authority when the right was questioned, but in cases where the right was undeniable, tending, by its operation, to increase the weight of the General Government. In giving to the constitution that rigid construction which sound policy requires, a just regard to the harmony of the States, and the perpetuation of their Union dictates, I cannot find any part of it authorising the exercise of a power, which, from its nature, is obnoxious, its tendency alarming, and its influence in the hands of those who manage its concerns, irresistible. . . . In relation to this particular subject, the proceedings of the convention itself, furnish the plainest evidence, by rejecting the proposition to vest in Congress the right to grant incorporations. I readily admit the motive of deliberative bodies cannot always be known . . . . To my mind it is much more natural to suppose a power to create monopolies had been surrendered to quiet the fears of those who saw in the constitution the germ which would, sooner or later, palsy the vitals of State authority. . . .

. . . .

. . . [A] bank has been improperly considered a *means* of executing some power expressly given to Congress. The nature of incorporations is so clearly a distinct class of political power, that, before they can be converted into means incidental to an object, without the jurisdiction of the General Government, they must be shown to be absolutely *necessary*. . . .

Sir, I am well aware that I can add nothing new upon the constitutional points. This subject was more thoroughly examined in 1791, and more ably elucidated than any since the adoption of the Government. The celebrated speech of Mr. Madison, to which I ascribe my conviction, has been recently presented to us in the newspapers . . . .

Debate in both the Senate and House of Representatives continued for months. After rejection of the bill to renew the charter, the Bank of the United States petitioned for a temporary authority so that it could wind up its business in an orderly manner. Neither house responded favorably to that request.

One matter that hurt the Bank's position was that its Baltimore branch sought to coerce support for a charter extension. "[I]t tightened credit and withdrew funds it had deposited in local banks, provoking a recession in the area."[35] Rather than produce support from local merchants, these actions cost the Bank support among the Maryland delegation to Congress.

Throughout the term of existence of the first Bank of the United States, the question of its constitutionality had not been litigated. The U.S. Supreme Court avoided the constitutional question in *Bank of the United States v. DeVeaux*, 9 U.S. 61 (1809).[36] As

---

[35] *See* MARK R. KILLENBECK, *supra* note 28, at 46.

[36] In *DeVeaux*, the State of Georgia had imposed a tax on the branch of the Bank established at Savannah. When the Bank declined to pay the tax, the State's tax collectors entered the Bank and took possession of

a result, there were no judicial pronouncements on the constitutional issues that divided Congress and President Washington's Cabinet.

In 1814, Congress received a petition to incorporate a new national bank in New York City. The House Committee of Ways and Means disapproved of the plan on the ground of lack of constitutional authority. Several additional efforts to establish a national bank were considered by Congress throughout 1814 and 1815. One bill passed both houses but President James Madison vetoed it and Congress failed to override his veto.

By 1815, the number of state chartered banks had increased to 212 in addition to 35 unincorporated banks.[37] In the absence of a federally-chartered central bank, the nation had waged the War of 1812.

In 1816, Congress enacted a bill to establish a new bank and President Madison approved the bill. *See* An Act to Incorporate the Subscribers to the Bank of the United States, ch. XLIV, 2 Stat. 266 (1816) (on DVD-ROM). This so-called Second Bank of the United States shared three key attributes with its predecessor: it was incorporated by Congress, it was granted "exclusive privileges and benefits" during its term of existence, and it was based in Philadelphia (rather than in the District of Columbia or on other territory as to which Congress held additional powers) with branches located in several States. "Although the United States held one-fifth of the stock and the president appointed five of its twenty-five directors, the Bank was actually a private corporation."[38]

As one historian observed, "[f]rom its inception, the Second Bank launched a spectacular inflation of money and credit" — the predominant factor in a 40.7% increase in money supply in only two years — and "outright fraud" took place, most notably at the branch in Baltimore, Maryland.[39] When the Second Bank refused to accept notes drawn on its own branches, public confidence hit bottom.[40] The Second Bank's efforts to avoid outright collapse produced an economic depression.

Eight States either prohibited branches of banks not chartered by their own legislature or imposed taxes on the operations of such branches.[41]

In January 1819, a congressional investigation reported on substantial misconduct by the Second Bank, particularly by the Baltimore branch, and concluded the Bank had violated its charter.[42] The president of the Second Bank — who had declared

---

$2004. BRAY HAMMOND, *supra* note 14, at 127. The Bank brought suit to recover the sum in federal circuit court. Chief Justice Marshall observed that the Judiciary Act of 1789 did not grant circuit courts a general federal question jurisdiction. MARK R. KILLENBECK, *supra* note 28, at 85. He construed the Act of incorporation as not itself supporting federal question jurisdiction under the circumstances of the case. *Id.* at 85–86. And, for purposes of diversity jurisdiction, the Court held that citizenship of a corporation should be determined by reference to the citizenship of "the individuals who compose the corporation." *Id.* at 92. (Of course, the Court has since departed from that view.) The practical result was that the State of Georgia successfully collected its tax. *See* BRAY HAMMOND, *supra* note 14, at 127.

[37] *See* MURRAY N. ROTHBARD, *supra* note 23, at 73.

[38] MARK R. KILLENBECK, *supra* note 28, at 3; *see* MURRAY N. ROTHBARD, *supra* note 23, at 83; *see also* MARK R. KILLENBECK, *supra* note 28, at 13 (the First Bank, "would actually be a private corporation, albeit one with close government involvement"), 31 (the First Bank "was both a private corporation and dedicated to profit"); JOHN THOM HOLDSWORTH & DAVIS R. DEWEY, *supra* note 29, at 21 ("the bank was to be under private management"). For an explanation of the confusing use of "private" and "public" to describe banking functions, see BRAY HAMMOND, *supra* note 14, at 191–93.

[39] MURRAY N. ROTHBARD, *supra* note 23, at 86–87; *see* MARK R. KILLENBECK, *supra* note 28, at 65–71.

[40] *See* MARK R. KILLENBECK, *supra* note 28, at 67.

[41] *See id.* at 68–69.

[42] *See id.* at 69–71.

bankruptcy shortly before accepting that position — was forced out of office.[43] The successor to the position as president of the Second Bank, Langdon Cheves, observed that when he took over in early 1819, the Bank would not have survived "another month" without a dramatic change and that a "stupendous fraud" had been committed, most dramatically at the Baltimore branch.[44] Cheves later dismissed James McCulloch from his position in the Baltimore branch on the basis that he engaged in frauds in the amount of $1,671,221.87, and concealed frauds of his partners so that "[i]n the office at Baltimore . . . there were near three millions of dollars discounted or appropriated, without any authority, and without any knowledge of the board of the office, or that of the parent bank!"[45]

Several resolutions were introduced into Congress directing the Attorney General to institute litigation to determine that the Second Bank had forfeited its charter or to repeal the charter. Debate on those proposals continued while the Supreme Court heard oral argument in *McCulloch v. Maryland* (excerpted below).

Three days after the nine-day oral argument concluded, Chief Justice Marshall delivered the Court's opinion, suggesting to many that he had prepared at least an outline before the case was submitted for decision.[46]

Exercise 7(E):

How should a federal court have answered the question of whether Congress had authority to establish the first Bank of the United States in 1791? How should a federal court answer the same question with respect to the Second Bank of the United States chartered in 1816?

If Congress had authority to establish the Bank, could it authorize the Bank to establish branches in States that did not consent to its presence? Why or why not?

If Congress had authority to establish the Bank, did it have constitutional authority to declare it exempt from generally-applicable State taxes (such as a property tax or an income tax)? Why or why not? Did Congress, in fact, do so?

Did federal courts have subject matter jurisdiction to resolve these questions? Had the Constitution been amended since *DeVeaux*? Had the statutory authorization for federal court jurisdiction been expanded since *DeVeaux*? Did the legislation establishing the Second Bank differ from the legislation establishing the First Bank in any manner pertinent to this issue?

A NOTE REGARDING PREEMPTION DOCTRINE

In *Hillsborough County v. Automated Medical Laboratories, Inc.*, 471 U.S. 707, 712–13 (1985), the Court summarized its jurisprudence regarding federal preemption of state law.

It is a familiar and well-established principle that the Supremacy Clause, U.S. Const., Art. VI, cl. 2, invalidates state laws that "interfere with, or are contrary to," federal law. *Gibbons v. Ogden*, 22 U.S. 1, 211 (1824) (Marshall, C.J.). Under the Supremacy Clause, federal law may supersede state law in several different ways. First, when acting within constitutional limits, Congress

---

[43] *See id.* at 64, 71.

[44] *See id.* at 159.

[45] *Id.* at 159–61; *see id.* at 90–93. Although the three conspirators were eventually acquitted in 1823, that result in the criminal case "almost certainly reflected a verdict against the Bank itself rather than a judgment that the three had not actually engaged in massive fraud." *Id.* at 186.

[46] *Id.* at 110.

is empowered to pre-empt state law by so stating in express terms. *Jones v. Rath Packing Co.*, 430 U.S. 519, 525 (1977). In the absence of express pre-emptive language, Congress' intent to pre-empt all state law in a particular area may be inferred where the scheme of federal regulation is sufficiently comprehensive to make reasonable the inference that Congress "left no room" for supplementary state regulation. *Rice v. Santa Fe Elevator Corp.*, 331 U.S. 218, 230 (1947). Pre-emption of a whole field also will be inferred where the field is one in which "the federal interest is so dominant that the federal system will be assumed to preclude enforcement of state laws on the same subject." *Id.; see Hines v. Davidowitz*, 312 U.S. 52 (1941).

Even where Congress has not completely displaced state regulation in a specific area, state law is nullified to the extent that it actually conflicts with federal law. Such a conflict arises when "compliance with both federal and state regulations is a physical impossibility," *Florida Lime & Avocado Growers, Inc. v. Paul*, 373 U.S. 132, 142–143 (1963), or when state law "stands as an obstacle to the accomplishment and execution of the full purposes and objectives of Congress," *Hines v. Davidowitz*, 312 U.S. at 67, 61.

We have held repeatedly that state laws can be pre-empted by federal regulations as well as by federal statutes. *See, e.g., Capital Cities Cable, Inc. v. Crisp*, 467 U.S. 691, 699 (1984); *United States v. Shimer*, 367 U.S. 374, 381–383 (1961). Also, for the purposes of the Supremacy Clause, the constitutionality of local ordinances is analyzed in the same way as that of statewide laws. *See, e.g., City of Burbank v. Lockheed Air Terminal, Inc.*, 411 U.S. 624 (1973).

Exercise 8:

Does this description of preemption doctrine help answer whether federal courts should address issues under the Supremacy Clause before or after issues relating to the scope of the enumerated powers?

McCULLOCH v. MARYLAND
17 U.S. 316 (1819)

[The Second Bank of the United States was incorporated by Congress in 1816. The Bank remained controversial and several States were hostile to the establishment of branches within their territory. The Bank established a branch in Baltimore, without any authorization from the State. The Maryland legislature previously had established a Bank of Maryland. Maryland then adopted a tax applicable to "all banks, or branches thereof," operating within its geographical limits that the State legislature had not chartered and sought to impose the tax on the Baltimore branch of the Second Bank of the United States. When the Second Bank of the United States did not pay the tax, Maryland brought suit in state court against James McCulloch, the cashier, for payment of penalties. The state courts held for Maryland, and McCulloch, represented by the United States Attorney General, sought review in the Supreme Court.]

CHIEF JUSTICE MARSHALL delivered the opinion of the Court.

In the case now to be determined, [the plaintiff below], a sovereign state, denies the obligation of a law enacted by the legislature of the Union, and the [defendant below], on his part, contests the validity of an act which has been passed by the legislature of that state. The constitution of our country, in its most interesting and vital parts, is to be considered; the conflicting powers of the government of the Union and of its members, as marked in that constitution, are to be discussed; and an opinion given, which may essentially influence the great operations of the government. . . . On the

Supreme Court of the United States has the constitution of our country devolved this important duty.

[I]

[A]

The first question made in the cause is — has Congress power to incorporate a bank? It has been truly said, that this can scarcely be considered as an open question, entirely unprejudiced by the former proceedings of the nation respecting it. The principle now contested was introduced at a very early period of our history, has been recognised by many successive legislatures, and has been acted upon by the judicial department, in cases of peculiar delicacy, as a law of undoubted obligation.

It will not be denied, that a bold and daring usurpation might be resisted, after an acquiescence still longer and more complete than this. But it is conceived, that a doubtful question, one on which human reason may pause, and the human judgment be suspended, in the decision of which the great principles of liberty are not concerned, but the respective powers of those who are equally the representatives of the people, are to be adjusted; if not put at rest by the practice of the government, ought to receive a considerable impression from that practice. An exposition of the constitution, deliberately established by legislative acts, on the faith of which an immense property has been advanced, ought not to be lightly disregarded.

The power now contested was exercised by the first Congress elected under the present constitution. The bill for incorporating the Bank of the United States did not steal upon an unsuspecting legislature, and pass unobserved. Its principle was completely understood, and was opposed with equal zeal and ability. After being resisted, first, in the fair and open field of debate, and afterwards, in the executive cabinet, with as much persevering talent as any measure has ever experienced, and being supported by arguments which convinced minds as pure and as intelligent as this country can boast, it became a law. The original act was permitted to expire; but a short experience of the embarrassments to which the refusal to revive it exposed the government, convinced those who were most prejudiced against the measure of its necessity, and induced the passage of the present law. It would require no ordinary share of intrepidity, to assert that a measure adopted under these circumstances, was a bold and plain usurpation, to which the constitution gave no countenance. These observations belong to the cause; but they are not made under the impression, that, were the question entirely new, the law would be found irreconcilable with the constitution.

[B]

[1]

In discussing this question, the counsel for the State of Maryland have deemed it of some importance, in the construction of the constitution, to consider that instrument not as emanating from the people, but as the act of sovereign and independent States. The powers of the general government, it has been said, are delegated by the States, who alone are truly sovereign; and must be exercised in subordination to the States, who alone possess supreme dominion. It would be difficult to sustain this proposition. The Convention which framed the constitution was indeed elected by the State legislatures. But the instrument, when it came from their hands, was a mere proposal, without obligation, or pretensions to it. It was reported to the then existing Congress of the United States, with a request that it might "be submitted to a convention of delegates, chosen in each State by the people thereof, under the recommendation of its legislature, for their assent and ratification." This mode of proceeding was adopted; and by the Convention, by Congress, and by the state legislatures, the instrument was submitted to the *people*. They acted upon it in the only manner in which they can act safely, effectively and wisely, on such a subject, by assembling in convention. It is true, they assembled in their several States — and where else should they have assembled? No political dreamer was ever wild enough to think of breaking down the lines which separate the States, and of compounding the American people into one common mass. Of consequence, when they act, they act in their States. But the measures they adopt do not, on that account, cease to be the measures of the people themselves, or become the measures of the State governments.

From these conventions, the constitution derives its whole authority. The government proceeds directly from the people. . . . The assent of the States, in their sovereign capacity, is implied, in calling a convention, and thus submitting that instrument to the people. But the people were at perfect liberty to accept, or to reject it; and their act was final. It required not the affirmance, and could not be negatived, by the state governments. . . .

. . . The government of the Union, then, . . . is, emphatically and truly, a government of the people. In form, and in substance, it emanates from them. Its powers are granted by them, and are to be exercised directly on them, and for their benefit.

[2]

This government is acknowledged by all, to be one of enumerated powers. The principle, that it can exercise only the powers granted to it, would seem too apparent, to have required to be enforced by all those arguments, which its enlightened friends, while it was depending before the people, found it necessary to urge; that principle is now universally admitted. But the question respecting the extent of the powers actually granted, is perpetually arising, and will probably continue to arise, as long as our system shall exist. . . .

If any one proposition could command the universal assent of mankind, we might expect it would be this — that the government of the Union, though limited in its powers, is supreme within its sphere of action. This would seem to result, necessarily, from its nature. It is the government of all; its powers are delegated by all; it represents all, and acts for all. Though any one State may be willing to control its operations, no State is willing to allow others to control them. The nation, on those subjects on which it can act, must necessarily bind its component parts. But this question is not left to mere reason: the people have, in express terms, decided it, by saying, "this constitution, and the laws of the United States, which shall be made in pursuance thereof," "shall be the supreme law of the land," and by requiring that the members of the State legislatures, and the officers of the executive and judicial departments of the States, shall take the oath of fidelity to it. The government of the United States, then, though limited in its powers, is supreme; and its laws, when made in pursuance of the constitution, form the supreme law of the land, "anything in the constitution or laws of any State to the contrary notwithstanding."

[3]

[a]

Among the enumerated powers, we do not find that of establishing a bank or creating a corporation. But there is no phrase in the instrument which, like the articles of confederation, excludes incidental or implied powers; and which requires that everything granted shall be expressly and minutely described. Even the 10th amendment, which was framed for the purpose of quieting the excessive jealousies which had been excited, omits the word "expressly," and declares only, that the powers "not delegated to the United States, nor prohibited to the States, are reserved to the States or to the people;" thus leaving the question, whether the particular power which may become the subject of contest, has been delegated to the one government, or prohibited to the other, to depend on a fair construction of the whole instrument. The men who drew and adopted this amendment had experienced the embarrassments resulting from the insertion of this word in the articles of confederation, and probably omitted it, to avoid those embarrassments. A constitution, to contain an accurate detail of all the subdivisions of which its great powers will admit, and of all the means by which they may be carried into execution, would partake of the prolixity of a legal code, and could scarcely be embraced by the human mind. It would, probably, never be understood by the public. Its nature, therefore, requires, that only its great outlines should be marked, its important objects designated, and the minor ingredients which compose those objects, be deduced from the nature of the objects themselves. That this idea was entertained by the framers of the American constitution, is not only to be inferred from the nature of the instrument, but from the language. Why else were some of the limitations, found in [Article I, Section 9], introduced? It is also, in some degree, warranted by their having omitted to use any restrictive term which might prevent its receiving a fair and just interpretation. In considering this question, then, we must never forget that it is a *constitution* we are expounding.

Although, among the enumerated powers of government, we do not find the word "bank" or "incorporation," we find the great powers, to lay and collect taxes; to borrow money; to regulate commerce; to declare and conduct a war; and to raise and support armies and navies. The sword and the purse, all the external relations, and no inconsiderable portion of the industry of the nation, are entrusted to its government. It can never be pretended, that these vast powers draw after them others of inferior importance, merely because they are inferior. Such an idea can never be advanced. But it may with great reason be contended, that a government, entrusted with such ample powers, on the due execution of which the happiness and prosperity of the nation so vitally depends, must also be entrusted with ample means for their execution. The power being given, it is the interest of the nation to facilitate its execution. It can never be their interest, and cannot be presumed to have been their intention, to clog and embarrass its execution, by withholding the most appropriate means. Throughout this vast republic, from the St. Croix to the Gulf of Mexico, from the Atlantic to the Pacific, revenue is to be collected and expended, armies are to be marched and supported. The exigencies of the nation may require, that the treasure raised in the north should be transported to the south, that raised in the east, conveyed to the west, or that this order should be reversed. Is that construction of the constitution to be preferred, which would render these operations difficult, hazardous, and expensive? Can we adopt that construction (unless the words imperiously require it), which would impute to the framers of that instrument, when granting these powers for the public good, the intention of impeding their exercise, by withholding a choice of means? If, indeed, such be the mandate of the constitution, we have only to obey; but that instrument does not profess to enumerate the means by which the powers it confers may be executed; nor does it prohibit the creation of a corporation, if the existence of such a being be essential, to the beneficial exercise of those powers. It is, then, the subject of fair inquiry, how far such means may be employed.

It is not denied, that the powers given to the government imply the ordinary means of execution. That, for example, of raising revenue, and applying it to national purposes, is admitted to imply the power of conveying money from place to place, as the exigencies of the nation may require, and of employing the usual means of conveyance. But it is denied, that the government has its choice of means; or, that it may employ the most convenient means, if, to employ them, it be necessary to erect a corporation. . . .

The creation of a corporation, it is said, appertains to sovereignty. This is admitted. But to what portion of sovereignty does it appertain? Does it belong to one more than another? In America, the powers of sovereignty are divided between the government of the Union, and those of the States. They are each sovereign, with respect to the objects committed to it, and neither sovereign with respect to the objects committed to the other. . . . [W]e cannot well comprehend the process of reasoning which maintains, that a power appertaining to sovereignty cannot be connected with that vast portion of it which is granted to the general government, so far as it is calculated to subserve the legitimate objects of that government. The power of creating a corporation, though appertaining to sovereignty, is not, like the power of making war, or levying taxes, or of regulating commerce, a great substantive and independent power, which cannot be implied as incidental to other powers, or used as a means of executing them. It is never the end for which other powers are exercised, but a means by which other objects are accomplished. . . . No sufficient reason is, therefore, perceived, why it may not pass as incidental to those powers which are expressly given, if it be a direct mode of executing them.

[b]

But the Constitution of the United States has not left the right of congress to employ the necessary means, for the execution of the powers conferred on the government, to general reasoning. To its enumeration of powers is added, that of making "all laws which shall be necessary and proper, for carrying into execution the foregoing powers, and all other powers vested by this Constitution, in the government of the United States, or in any department thereof." The counsel for the State of Maryland have urged various arguments, to prove that this clause, though in terms, a grant of power, is not so, in effect; but is really restrictive of the general right, which might otherwise be implied, of selecting means for executing the enumerated powers. . . .

. . . .

[T]he argument on which most reliance is placed, is drawn from that peculiar language of this clause. Congress is not empowered by it to make all laws, which may have relation to the powers conferred on the government, but such only as may be *"necessary and proper"* for carrying them into execution. The word *"necessary"* is considered as controlling the whole sentence, and as limiting the right to pass laws for the execution of the granted powers, to such as are indispensable, and without which the power would be nugatory. That it excludes the choice of means, and leaves to Congress, in each case, that only which is most direct and simple.

Is it true, that this is the sense in which the word "necessary" is always used? Does it always import an absolute physical necessity, so strong, that one thing to which another may be termed necessary, cannot exist without that other? We think it does not. If reference be had to its use, in the common affairs of the world, or in approved authors, we find that it frequently imports no more than that one thing is convenient, or useful, or essential to another. To employ the means necessary to an end, is generally understood as employing any means calculated to produce the end, and not as being confined to those single means, without which the end would be entirely unattainable. Such is the character of human language, that no word conveys to the mind, in all situations, one single definite idea; and nothing is more common than to use words in a figurative sense. Almost all compositions contain words, which, taken in their rigorous sense, would convey a meaning different from that which is obviously intended. It is essential to just construction, that many words which import something excessive, should be understood in a more mitigated sense — in that sense which common usage justifies. The word "necessary" is of this description. It has not a fixed character, peculiar to itself. It admits of all degrees of comparison; and is often connected with other words, which increase or diminish the impression the mind receives of the urgency it imports. A thing may be necessary, very necessary, absolutely or indispensably necessary. To no mind would the same idea be conveyed by these several phrases. This comment on the word is well illustrated by the passage cited at the bar, from [Article I, Section 10]. It is, we think, impossible to compare the sentence which prohibits a State from laying "imposts, or duties on imports or exports, except what may be *absolutely* necessary for executing its inspection laws," with that which authorizes Congress "to make all laws which shall be necessary and proper for carrying into execution" the powers of the general government, without feeling a conviction, that the convention understood itself to change materially the meaning of the word "necessary," by prefixing the word "absolutely." This word, then, like others, is used in various senses; and, in its construction, the subject, the context, the intention of the person using them, are all to be taken into view.

. . . It must have been the intention of those who gave these powers, to insure, as far as human prudence could insure, their beneficial execution. This could not be done, by confiding the choice of means to such narrow limits as not to leave it in the power of Congress to adopt any which might be appropriate, and which were conducive to the end. This provision is made in a constitution, intended to endure for ages to come, and consequently, to be adapted to the various *crises* of human affairs. To have prescribed the means by which government should, in all future time, execute its powers, would have been to change, entirely, the character of the instrument, and give it the properties of a legal code. It would have been an unwise attempt to provide, by immutable rules, for exigencies which, if foreseen at all, must have been seen dimly, and which can be best provided for as they occur. . . .

So, with respect to the whole penal code of the United States: whence arises the power to punish, in cases not prescribed by the constitution? All admit, that the government may, legitimately, punish any violation of its laws; and yet, this is not among the enumerated powers of Congress. The right to enforce the observance of law, by punishing its infraction, might be denied, with the more plausibility, because it is expressly given in some cases. Congress is empowered "to provide for the punishment of counterfeiting the securities and current coin of the United States," and "to define and punish piracies and felonies committed on the high seas, and offences against the law of nations." The several powers of Congress may exist, in a very imperfect state, to be sure, but they may exist and be carried into execution, although no punishment should be inflicted, in cases where the right to punish is not expressly given.

. . . .

Take, for example, the power "to establish post offices and post roads." This power is executed, by the single act of making the establishment. But, from this has been inferred the power and duty of carrying the mail along the post road, from one post office to another. And from this implied power, has again been inferred the right to punish those who steal letters from the post office, or rob the mail. It may be said, with some plausibility, that the right to carry the mail, and to punish those who rob it, is not indispensably necessary to the establishment of a post office and post road. This right is indeed essential to the beneficial exercise of the power, but not indispensably necessary to its existence. . . .

. . . .

If this limited construction of the word "necessary" must be abandoned, in order to punish, whence is derived the rule which would reinstate it, when the government would carry its powers into execution, by means not vindictive in their nature? If the word "necessary" means "needful," "requisite," "essential," "conducive to," in order to let in the power of punishment for infraction of the law; why is it not equally comprehensive, when required to authorize the use of means which facilitate the execution of the powers of government, without the infliction of punishment?

In ascertaining the sense in which the word "necessary" is used in this clause of the constitution, we may derive some aid from that with which it is associated. Congress shall have power "to make all laws which shall be necessary and proper to carry into execution" the powers of the government. If the word "necessary" was used in that strict and rigorous sense for which the counsel for the State of Maryland contend, it would be an extraordinary departure from the usual course of the human mind, as exhibited in composition, to add a word, the only possible effect of which is, to qualify that strict and rigorous meaning; to present to the mind the idea of some choice of means of legislation, not strained and compressed within the narrow limits for which gentlemen contend.

But the argument which most conclusively demonstrates the error of the construction contended for by the counsel for the State of Maryland, is founded on the intention of the Convention, as manifested in the whole clause. To waste time and argument in proving that, without it, Congress might carry its powers into execution, would be not much less idle, than to hold a lighted taper to the sun. As little can it be required to prove, that in the absence of this clause, Congress would have some choice of means. That it might employ those which, in its judgment, would most advantageously effect the object to be accomplished. That any means adapted to the end, any means which tended directly to the execution of the constitutional powers of the government, were in themselves constitutional. This clause, as construed by the State of Maryland, would abridge, and almost annihilate, this useful and necessary right of the legislature to select its means. That this could not be intended, is, we should think, had it not been already controverted, too apparent for controversy.

We think so for the following reasons: [First, t]he clause is placed among the powers of Congress, not among the limitations on those powers. [Second, i]ts terms purport to enlarge, not to diminish the powers vested in the government. It purports to be an additional power, not a restriction on those already granted. No reason has been, or can be assigned, for thus concealing an intention to narrow the discretion of the national legislature, under words which purport to enlarge it. The framers of the constitution wished its adoption, and well knew that it would be endangered by its strength, not by its weakness. Had they been capable of using language which would convey to the eye one idea, and, after deep reflection, impress on the mind another, they would rather have disguised the grant of power, than its limitation. If, then, their intention had been, by this clause, to restrain the free use of means which might otherwise have been implied, that intention would have been inserted in another place, and would have been expressed in terms resembling these. "In carrying into execution the foregoing powers, and all others," [etcetera], "no laws shall be passed but such as are necessary and proper." Had the intention been to make this clause restrictive, it would unquestionably have been so in form as well as in effect.

The result of the most careful and attentive consideration bestowed upon this clause is, that if it does not enlarge, it cannot be construed to restrain the powers of Congress, or to impair the right of the legislature to exercise its best judgment in the selection of measures to carry into execution the constitutional powers of the government. If no other motive for its insertion can be suggested, a sufficient one is found in the desire to remove all doubts respecting the right to legislate on that vast mass of incidental powers which must be involved in the constitution, if that instrument be not a splendid bauble.

We admit, as all must admit, that the powers of the government are limited, and that its limits are not to be transcended. But we think the sound construction of the constitution must allow to the national legislature that discretion, with respect to the means by which the powers it confers are to be carried into execution, which will enable that body to perform the high duties assigned to it, in the manner most beneficial to the people. Let the end be legitimate, let it be within the scope of the constitution, and all means which are appropriate, which are plainly adapted to that end, which are not prohibited, but consist with the letter and spirit of the constitution, are constitutional.

. . . .

If a corporation may be employed, indiscriminately with other means, to carry into execution the powers of the government, no particular reason can be assigned for excluding the use of a bank, if required for its fiscal operations. To use one, must be within the discretion of Congress, if it be an appropriate mode of executing the powers of government. That it is a convenient, a useful, and essential instrument in the prosecution of its fiscal operations, is not now a subject of controversy. All those who have been concerned in the administration of our finances, have concurred in representing its importance and necessity; and so strongly have they been felt, that statesmen of the first class, whose previous opinions against it had been confirmed by every circumstance which can fix the human judgment, have yielded those opinions to the exigencies of the nation. Under the confederation, congress, justifying the measure by its necessity, transcended, perhaps, its powers, to obtain the advantage of a bank; and our own legislation attests the universal conviction of the utility of this measure. The time has passed away, when it can be necessary to enter into any discussion, in order to prove the importance of this instrument, as a means to effect the legitimate objects of the government.

But were its necessity less apparent, none can deny its being an appropriate measure; and if it is, the degree of its necessity, as has been very justly observed, is to be discussed in another place. Should Congress, in the execution of its powers, adopt measures which are prohibited by the Constitution; or should Congress, under the pretext of executing its powers, pass laws for the accomplishment of objects not entrusted to the government; it would become the painful duty of this tribunal, should a case requiring such a decision come before it, to say, that such an act was not the law of the land. But where the law is not prohibited, and is really calculated to effect any of the objects entrusted to the government, to undertake here to inquire into the degree of its necessity, would be to pass the line which circumscribes the judicial department, and to tread on legislative ground. This court disclaims all pretensions to such a power.

. . . .

After the most deliberate consideration, it is the unanimous and decided opinion of this Court, that the act to incorporate the Bank of the United States is a law made in pursuance of the Constitution, and is a part of the supreme law of the land.

The branches, proceeding from the same stock, and being conducive to the complete accomplishment of the object, are equally constitutional. . . .

[II]

It being the opinion of the Court, that the act incorporating the Bank is constitutional; and that the power of establishing a branch in the State of Maryland might be properly exercised by the Bank itself, we proceed to inquire —

2. Whether the State of Maryland may, without violating the Constitution, tax that branch? That the power of taxation is one of vital importance; that it is retained by the States; that it is not abridged by the grant of a similar power to the government of the Union; that it is to be concurrently exercised by the two governments — are truths which have never been denied. But such is the paramount character of the Constitution, that its capacity to withdraw any subject from the action of even this power, is admitted. The States are expressly forbidden to lay any duties on imports or exports, except what may be absolutely necessary for executing their inspection laws. If the obligation of this prohibition must be conceded — if it may restrain a State from the exercise of its taxing power on imports and exports — the same paramount character would seem to restrain, as it certainly may restrain, a State from such other exercise of this power, as is in its nature incompatible with, and repugnant to, the constitutional laws of the Union. A law, absolutely repugnant to another, as entirely repeals that other as if express terms of repeal were used.

On this ground the counsel for the Bank place its claim to be exempted from the power of a State to tax its operations. There is no express provision for the case, but the claim has been sustained on a principle which so entirely pervades the Constitution, is so intermixed with the materials which compose it, so interwoven with its web, so blended with its texture, as to be incapable of being separated from it, without rending it into shreds. This great principle is, that the Constitution and the laws made in pursuance thereof are supreme; that they control the Constitution and laws of the respective States, and cannot be controlled by them. From this, which may be almost termed an axiom, other propositions are deduced as corollaries, on the truth or error of which, and on their application to this case, the cause has been supposed to depend. These are, [first], [t]hat a power to create implies a power to preserve; [second], [t]hat a power to destroy, if wielded by a different hand, is hostile to, and incompatible with these powers to create and to preserve; [and, third], [t]hat where this repugnancy exists, that authority which is supreme must control, not yield to that over which it is supreme.

These propositions, as abstract truths, would, perhaps, never be controverted. Their application to this case, however, has been denied . . . .

The power of Congress to create, and of course, to continue, the Bank, was the subject of the preceding part of this opinion; and is no longer to be considered questionable. That the power of taxing it by the States may be exercised so as to destroy it, is too obvious to be denied. But taxation is said to be an absolute power, which acknowledges no other limits than those expressly prescribed in the Constitution, and like sovereign power of every other description, is entrusted to the discretion of those who use it. But the very terms of this argument admit, that the sovereignty of the State, in the article of taxation itself, is subordinate to, and may be controlled by the Constitution of the United States. How far it has been controlled by that instrument, must be a question of construction. In making this construction, no principle, not declared, can be admissible, which would defeat the legitimate operations of a supreme government. It is of the very essence of supremacy, to remove all obstacles to its action within its own sphere, and so to modify every power vested in subordinate governments, as to exempt its own operations from their own influence. . . .

The argument on the part of the State of Maryland, is, not that the States may directly resist a law of Congress, but that they may exercise their acknowledged powers upon it, and that the Constitution leaves them this right, in the confidence that they will not abuse it. . . . The only security against the abuse of this power, is found in the structure of the government itself. In imposing a tax, the legislature acts upon its constituents. This is, in general, a sufficient security against erroneous and oppressive taxation.

The people of a State, therefore, give to their government a right of taxing themselves and their property . . . they prescribe no limits to the exercise of this right, resting confidently on the interest of the legislator, and on the influence of the constituent over their representative, to guard them against its abuse. But the means employed by the government of the Union have no such security, nor is the right of a State to tax them sustained by the same theory. Those means are not given by the people of a particular State, not given by the constituents of the legislature, which claim the right to tax them, but by the people of all the States. They are given by all, for the benefit of all — and upon the theory, should be subjected to that government only which belongs to all.

. . . .

The sovereignty of a State extends to everything which exists by its own authority, or is introduced by its permission; but does it extend to those means which are employed by Congress to carry into execution powers conferred on that body by the people of the United States? We think it demonstrable, that it does not. Those powers are not given by the people of a single State. They are given by the people of the United States, to a government whose laws, made in pursuance of the Constitution, are declared to be supreme. Consequently, the people of a single State cannot confer a sovereignty which will extend over them.

If we measure the power of taxation residing in a State, by the extent of sovereignty which the people of a single State possess, and can confer on its government, we have an intelligible standard, applicable to every case to which the power may be applied. We have a principle which leaves the power of taxing the people and property of a State unimpaired; which leaves to a State the command of all its resources, and which places beyond its reach, all those powers which are conferred by the people of the United States on the government of the Union, and all those means which are given for the purpose of carrying those powers into execution. We have a principle which is safe for the States, and safe for the Union. We are relieved, as we ought to be, from clashing sovereignty; from interfering powers; from a repugnancy between a right in one government to pull down, what there is an acknowledged right in another to build up; from the incompatibility of a right in one government to destroy, what there is a right in another to preserve. We are not driven to the perplexing inquiry, so unfit for the judicial department, what degree of taxation is the legitimate use, and what degree may amount to the abuse of the power. The attempt to use it on the means employed by the government Union, in pursuance of the Constitution, is itself an abuse, because it is the usurpation of a power which the people of a single State cannot give. We find, then, on just theory, a total failure of this original right to tax the means employed by the government of the Union, for the execution of its powers. The right never existed, and the question whether it has been surrendered, cannot arise.

But waiving this theory for the present, let us resume the inquiry, whether this power can be exercised by the respective States, consistently with a fair construction of the Constitution? That the power to tax involves the power to destroy; that the power to destroy may defeat and render useless the power to create; that there is a plain repugnance, in conferring on one government a power to control the constitutional measures of another, which other, with respect to those very measures, is declared to be supreme over that which exerts the control, are propositions not to be denied. But all inconsistencies are to be reconciled by the magic of the word *confidence*. Taxation, it is said, does not necessarily and unavoidably destroy. To carry it to the excess of destruction, would be an abuse, to presume which, would banish that confidence which is essential to all government. But is this a case of confidence? Would the people of any one State trust those of another with a power to control the most insignificant operations of their State government? We know they would not. Why, then, should we suppose, that the people of any one State should be willing to trust those of another with a power to control the operations of a government to which they have confided their most important and most valuable interests? In the legislature of the Union alone, are all represented. The legislature of the Union alone, therefore, can be trusted by the people with the power of controlling measures which concern all, in the confidence that it will not be abused. . . .

. . . If the States may tax one instrument, employed by the government in the execution of its powers, they may tax any and every other instrument. They may tax the mail; they may tax the mint; they may tax patent rights; they may tax the papers of the custom house; they may tax the judicial process; they may tax all the means employed by the government, to an excess which would defeat all the ends of government. This was not intended by the American people. They did not design to make their government dependent on the States.

. . . This is not all. If the controlling power of the States be established; if their supremacy as to taxation be acknowledged; what is to restrain their exercising control in any shape they may please to give it? Their sovereignty is not confined to taxation; that is not the only mode in which it might be displayed. The question is, in truth, a question of supremacy; and if the right of the States to tax the means employed by the general government be conceded, the declaration that the Constitution, and the laws made in pursuance thereof, shall be the supreme law of the land, is empty and unmeaning declamation.

. . . .

It has also been insisted, that, as the power of taxation in the general and State governments is acknowledged to be concurrent, every argument which would sustain the right of the general government to tax banks chartered by the States, will equally sustain the right of the States to tax banks chartered by the general government. But the two cases are not on the same reason. The people of all the States have created the general government, and have conferred upon it the general power of taxation. The people of all the States, and the States themselves, are represented in Congress, and, by their representatives, exercise this power. When they tax the chartered institutions of the States, they tax their constituents; and these taxes must be uniform. But when a State taxes the operations of the government of the United States, it acts upon institutions created, not by their own constituents, but by people over whom they claim no control. It acts upon the measures of a government created by others as well as themselves, for the benefit of others in common with themselves. The difference is that which always exists, and always must exist, between the action of the whole on a part, and the action of a part on the whole — between the laws of a government declared to be supreme, and those of a government which, when in opposition to those laws, is not supreme.

But if the full application of this argument could be admitted, it might bring into question the right of Congress to tax the State banks, and could not prove the right of the States to tax the Bank of the United States.

The Court has bestowed on this subject its most deliberate consideration. The result is a conviction that the States have no power, by taxation or otherwise, to retard, impede, burden, or in any manner control, the operations of the constitutional laws enacted by Congress to carry into execution the powers vested in the general government. This is, we think, the unavoidable consequence of that supremacy which the Constitution has declared. We are unanimously of opinion, that the law passed by the legislature of Maryland, imposing a tax on the Bank of the United States, is unconstitutional and void.

This opinion does not deprive the States of any resources which they originally possessed. It does not extend to a tax paid by the real property of the bank, in common with the other real property within the State, nor to a tax imposed on the interest which the citizens of Maryland may hold in this institution, in common with other property of the same description throughout the State. But this is a tax on the operations of the Bank, and is, consequently, a tax on the operation of an instrument employed by the government of the Union to carry its powers into execution. Such a tax must be unconstitutional.

Exercise 9(A):

Consider the following matters in regard to *McCulloch v. Maryland*:

(1)   Chief Justice Marshall suggested that because the Framers drafted enumerated powers that entrusted to Congress many "great" matters, it should be implied that the Framers intended to confer on Congress a broad choice of means to implement those powers. One might argue, to the contrary, that because the Framers carefully circumscribed legislative powers, it should be implied that the Framers intended not to undo that work by permitting Congress a broad, undefined choice of means. Which of those two approaches best fits the text of Article I, Section 8? Which of those two approaches best fits the ratification debates?

(2)   What argument did Chief Justice Marshall make regarding the placement of the Necessary and Proper Clause in the Constitution?

(3)   Assuming that Congress had constitutional authority to establish a national bank, why does it follow that Maryland had no authority to impose a tax on the bank?

(4)   Assuming Maryland had a state-wide property tax on all land, would the national bank be required to pay the tax on the land on which the physical structure of the Baltimore branch was located?

(5)   Assume that Maryland imposed a tax on all banks operating within its territory, regardless of the source of the bank's charter. Would the national bank be required to pay that tax?

(6)   Assume, instead, that Maryland imposed a tax only upon the "Bank of the United States" and no other. Would that tax be constitutional? Why or why not?

(7)   Was the Maryland tax at issue more like the hypothetical tax in question 5 or the hypothetical tax in question 6? Why?

(8)   The tax imposed by Maryland was relatively minor, falling in the range of 1% or 2%. Should that fact have had greater influence on the Court's analysis? Why or why not?

From 1819 to 1913

The 1819 Supreme Court ruling did not settle the issue of whether the Second Bank of the United States (or any federally-chartered bank) was "necessary". The Bank continued to face political hostility grounded in the fact that most of its investors were foreigners (including substantial investment by the Bank of England), those foreigners earned substantial profits on loans in the United States, and they exercised influence on the national economy. There were additional complaints that the Bank's lending policies were the major source of inflation[47] which, when checked, also became a major source of economic depression.

Opposition to the Second Bank of the United States was one of the unifying themes in the formation of the Democratic Party in the 1820s. Major political figures continued to insist that Congress lacked authority to charter a bank outside the District of Columbia. President Andrew Jackson severely criticized the Bank in 1829 and, in 1831, vetoed a bill to extend its charter. Prior to the 1836 expiration of the Bank's original charter, in 1833, President Jackson ordered federal deposits removed from the Bank and deposited with a number of state banks. By the time set for the expiration of the Bank's original charter, the federal deposits were spread across more than ninety state banks.[48] A decade later, President John Tyler vetoed two bills to charter a national bank, asserting that the measures were unconstitutional.[49]

Not until the Federal Reserve Act, ch. 6, 38 Stat. 251 (1913), did Congress establish a new central bank.[50] Thus the government and economy operated for decades after 1836 (or, in actuality, since 1833) without a central bank. What weight, if any, should be given to that subsequent history in evaluating Chief Justice Marshall's statements regarding whether such an institution was "necessary"? Does the fact that Congress expressly exempted federal reserve banks from certain state and local taxes, *see id.* § 7, 38 Stat. at 258, suggest that if Congress intended to exempt the Second Bank of the United States from state taxes, it would have done so expressly?

Although there was no central bank between the 1830s and until 1914, thousands of state-chartered banks operated. And, in the 1860s, Congress enacted laws permitting those existing banks (and newly organized banks) to obtain federal charters. *See* Act of June 3, 1864, ch. 106, 13 Stat. 99 (the National Bank Act).[51] Does *McCulloch* answer the question of whether Congress could authorize hundreds (or thousands) of companies to obtain federal charters under a single, general statute? Does *McCulloch* answer the question of whether banks that availed themselves of a federal charter under the National Bank Act would be subject to state taxation if the federal statute were silent on the issue?[52]

For an exhaustive account of these matters, see BRAY HAMMOND, BANKS AND POLITICS IN AMERICA FROM THE REVOLUTION TO THE CIVIL WAR (1957). For a more recent and easily accessible account, see RICHARD E. ELLIS, AGGRESSIVE NATIONALISM: *McCULLOCH V. MARYLAND* AND THE FOUNDATION OF FEDERAL AUTHORITY IN THE YOUNG REPUBLIC (2007).

---

[47] *See* MURRAY N. ROTHBARD, *supra* note 23, at 92.

[48] *See* MURRAY N. ROTHBARD, *supra* note 23, at 93.

[49] *See id.* at 178.

[50] It is questionable whether either the First or Second Bank of the United States are properly considered a "central" bank at all. *See* JOHN CHOWN, *Introduction* vi, *in* THOMAS H. GODDARD, A GENERAL HISTORY OF THE MOST PROMINENT BANKS IN EUROPE (1996) (reprinted as part of the 7-volume EARLY ORIGINS OF AMERICAN BANKING) ("The United States had nothing approaching a central bank until the Federal Reserve board was instituted in 1909.").

[51] The 1864 Act repealed legislation for a similar purpose enacted the previous year, the National Currency Act, ch. 58, 12 Stat. 665 (1863) (repealed by National Bank Act § 62, 13 Stat. at 118).

[52] In that regard, note that under the National Bank Act, Congress explicitly addressed the State and local taxes to which chartered banks would be subject. *See* National Bank Act § 41, 13 Stat. at 112.

A FINAL NOTE ON THE "NECESSARY AND PROPER" CLAUSE

In *Printz v. United States,* 521 U.S. 898 (1997), the U.S. Supreme Court held that certain interim provisions of the Brady Handgun Violence Prevention Act, Pub. L. No. 103–159, 107 Stat. 1536, were unconstitutional. The challenged provisions commanded state and local law enforcement officers to conduct background checks and other related tasks with respect to prospective handgun purchasers. The Court relied upon principles of federalism in holding that Congress may not "commandeer" state and local officers to execute the law.

Writing for the Court, Justice Scalia responded to certain arguments raised by the dissenting justices.

> The dissent of course resorts to the last, best hope of those who defend ultra vires congressional action, the Necessary and Proper Clause. It reasons . . . that the power to regulate the sale of handguns under the Commerce Clause, coupled with the power to "make all Laws which shall be necessary and proper for carrying into Execution the foregoing Powers," Art. I, § 8, conclusively establishes the Brady Act's constitutional validity, because the Tenth Amendment imposes no limitations on the exercise of *delegated* powers but merely prohibits the exercise of powers "*not* delegated to the United States." What destroys the dissent's Necessary and Proper Clause argument, however, is not the Tenth Amendment but the Necessary and Proper Clause itself. When a "La[w] . . . for carrying into Execution" the Commerce Clause violates the principles of state sovereignty reflected in the various constitutional provisions we mentioned earlier . . . it is not a "La[w] . . . *proper* for carrying into Execution the Commerce Clause," and is thus, in the words of The Federalist, "merely [an] ac[t] of usurpation" which "deserve[s] to be treated as such." THE FEDERALIST NO. 33, at 204 (A. Hamilton). . . .

> The dissent perceives a simple answer in that portion of Article VI which requires that "all executive and judicial Officers, both of the United States and of the several States, shall be bound by Oath or Affirmation, to support this Constitution," arguing that by virtue of the Supremacy Clause this makes "not only the Constitution, but every law enacted by Congress as well," binding on state officers, including laws requiring state-officer enforcement. . . . The Supremacy Clause, however, makes "Law of the Land" only "Laws of the United States which shall be made in Pursuance [of the Constitution]," Art. VI, cl. 2, so the Supremacy Clause merely brings us back to the question discussed earlier, whether laws conscripting state officers violate state sovereignty and are thus not in accord with the Constitution.

521 U.S. at 923–25.

Exercise 9(B):

If the Court in *McCulloch* had addressed the power of Congress to establish a national bank reading the Necessary and Proper Clause in the same manner as in *Printz,* how would the Court have ruled? Which reading of the Necessary and Proper Clause is more consistent with constitutional text and structure: *McCulloch* or *Printz*? Which reading is more consistent with the views of the Framers?

RESOURCES FOR ADDITIONAL READING
ON THE "NECESSARY AND PROPER CLAUSE"

For an analysis from a textualist perspective, see Gary Lawson & Patricia B. Granger, *The "Proper" Scope of Federal Power: A Jurisdictional Interpretation of the Sweeping Clause*, 43 DUKE L.J. 267 (1993). For an analysis from an originalist perspective, see Randy E. Barnett, *The Original Meaning of the Necessary and Proper Clause*, 6 U. PA. J. CONST. L. 183 (2003).

For an argument that the clause was deliberately intended to be vague so as to grant expansive congressional power, see JOSEPH M. LYNCH, NEGOTIATING THE CONSTITUTION: THE EARLIEST DEBATES OVER ORIGINAL INTENT 25 (1999). For an analysis of the Supreme Court's early interpretations of the meaning of this clause, see David P. Currie, *The Constitution in the Supreme Court: State and Congressional Powers, 1801–1835*, 49 U. CHI. L. REV. 887, 931–34 (1982).

PROVIDENCE BANK v. BILLINGS
29 U.S. 514 (1830)

CHIEF JUSTICE MARSHALL delivered the Opinion of the Court.

This is a writ of error to a judgment entered in the highest court for the state of Rhode Island, in an action of trespass brought by [Providence Bank] against Alpheus Billings and Thomas G. Pittman.

In November 1791 the legislature of Rhode Island granted a charter of incorporation . . . . They are incorporated by the name of the "President, Directors, and Company of the Providence Bank;" and have the ordinary powers which are supposed to be necessary for the usual objects of such associations.

In 1822 the legislature of Rhode Island passed [a statute] . . . in which, among other things, it enacted that there shall be paid, for the use of the state, by each and every bank within the state, except the Bank of the United States, the sum of [one dollar and twenty-five cents] on each and every thousand dollars of capital stock actually paid in.

The Providence Bank, having determined to resist the payment of this tax, brought an action of trespass against the officers by whom a warrant of distress was issued against and served upon the property of the bank, in pursuance of the law. [Billings and Pittman] justify the taking set out in the declaration under the act of assembly imposing the tax; to which plea [the Bank] demurrer[s] that the act is repugnant to the Constitution of the United States, inasmuch as it impairs the obligation of the contract created by their charter of incorporation. Judgment was given . . . in favor of [Billings and Pittman]. . . .

It has been settled that a contract entered into between a State and an individual, is as fully protected by [Article I, Section 10] of the U.S. Constitution, as a contract between two individuals; and it is not denied that a charter incorporation of a bank is a contract. Is this contract impaired by taxing the banks of the state?

This question is to be answered by the charter itself.

[The charter] contains no stipulation promising exemption from taxation. The State, then, has made no express contract which has been impaired by the act of which [Providence Bank] complain[s]. No words have been found in the charter, which, in themselves, would justify the opinion that the power of taxation was in the view of either of the parties; and that an exemption of it was intended, though not expressed. . . . The elaborate and ingenious argument which has been urged amounts, in substance, to this. *The charter authorizes the Bank to employ its capital in banking transactions, for the benefit of the stockholders. It binds the State to permit these transactions for this object. Any law arresting directly the operations of the Bank would violate this obligation, and would come within the prohibition of the Constitution. But, as that cannot be done circuitously which may not be done directly, the charter restrains the State from passing any Act which may indirectly destroy the profits of the Bank. A power to tax the Bank may unquestionably be carried to such an excess as to take all its profits, and still more than its profits for the use of the State; and consequently destroy the institution. Now, whatever may be the rule of expediency, the constitutionality of a measure depends, not upon the degree of its exercise, but on its principle. A power therefore which may in effect destroy the charter, is inconsistent with it; and is impliedly renounced by granting it. Such a power cannot be exercised without impairing the obligation of the contract. When pushed to its extreme point, or exercised in moderation, it is the same power, and is hostile to the rights granted by the charter.* This is substantially the argument for the Bank. [Providence Bank] cite[s] and rel[ies] on several sentiments expressed, on various occasions by this Court, in support of these positions.

The claim of the Providence Bank is certainly of the first impression. The power of taxing moneyed corporations has been frequently exercised; and has never before, so far as is known, been resisted. Its novelty, however, furnished no conclusive argument against it.

That the taxing power is of vital importance; that it is essential to the existence of government; are truths which it cannot be necessary to reaffirm. They are acknowledged and asserted by all. It would seem that the relinquishment of such a power is never to be assumed. We will not say that a State may not relinquish it; . . . that community has a right to insist that its abandonment ought not to be presumed, in a case in which the deliberate purpose of the State to abandon it does not appear.

The plaintiffs would give to this charter the same construction as if it contained a clause exempting the Bank from taxation on its stock in trade. But can it be supposed that such a clause would not enlarge its privileges? They contend that it must be implied; because the power to tax may be wielded as to defeat the purpose for which the charter was granted. . . .

> . . . .

If the power of taxation is inconsistent with the charter, because it may be so exercised as to destroy the object for which the charter is given; it is equally inconsistent with every other charter . . . . If the grant of a power to trade in money to a given amount, implies an exemption of the stock in trade from taxation, because the tax may absorb all the profits; then the grant of any other thing implies the same exemption . . . . Land, for example, has, in many, perhaps in all of the States, been granted by government since the adoption of the Constitution. This grant is a contract, the object of which is that the profits issuing from it shall enure to the benefit of the grantee. Yet the power of taxation may be carried so far as to absorb these profits. Does this impair the obligation of the contract? The idea is rejected by all; and the proposition appears so extravagant, that it is difficult to admit any resemblance in the cases. And yet if the proposition for which [Providence Bank] contend[s] be true, it carries us to this point. That proposition is, that a power which is in itself capable of being exerted to the total destruction of the grant, is inconsistent with the grant; and is therefore impliedly relinquished by the grantor, though the language of the instrument contains no allusion to the subject. If this be an abstract truth, it may be supposed universal. But it is not universal; and therefore its truth cannot be admitted, in these broad terms, in any case. We must look for the exemption in the language of the instrument; and if we do not find it there, it would be going very far to insert it by construction.

The power of legislation, and consequently of taxation, operates on all the persons and property belonging to the body politic. This is an original principle, which has its foundation in society itself. It is granted by all, for the benefit of all. It resides in government as a part of itself, and need not be reserved when property of any description, or the right to use it in any manner, is granted to individuals or corporate bodies. . . . [*McCulloch v. Maryland* and *Osborn v. Bank of the United States*] proceeded on the admission that an incorporated bank, unless its charter shall express the exemption, is no more exempted from taxation, than an unincorporated company would be, carrying on the same business.

. . . .

The reasoning of *McCulloch v. Maryland* has been applied to this case; but the Court itself appears to have provided against this application. Its opinion in that case, as well as in *Osborn v. Bank of the United States,* was founded, expressly, on the supremacy of the laws of Congress, and the necessary consequences of that supremacy to exempt its instruments employed in the execution of its powers, from the operation of any interfering power whatever. . . .

. . . .

The Court was certainly not discussing the question whether a tax imposed by a State on a bank chartered by itself, impaired the obligation of its contract; and these opinions are not conclusive as they would be had they been delivered in such a case: but they show that the question was not considered as doubtful, and that inferences drawn from general expressions pointed to a different subject cannot be correctly drawn.

We have reflected seriously on this case, and are of opinion that the Act of the legislature of Rhode Island, passed in 1822, imposing a duty on . . . bodies corporate within the State, does not impair the obligation of the contract created by the charter granted to the [incorporators of Providence Bank]. It is therefore the opinion of this Court, that there is no error in the judgment of the Supreme Judicial Court for the State of Rhode Island . . . .

Judgment affirmed.

Exercise 10(A):

Reconsider *McCulloch v. Maryland* in light of Chief Justice Marshall's opinion in *Providence Bank v. Billings*:

(1)   If the Court had approached the "power to tax" issue in *McCulloch* in the same manner that it addressed the "power to tax" issue in *Providence Bank,* how would the Court have ruled?

(a)   Should the Court assume that a legislature chartering a corporation intends to immunize the corporation from taxation?

(b)   If, in *Providence Bank,* the absence of an express term exempting the bank from taxation in the state-issued charter was dispositive, should the Court have treated the absence of an express term exempting the bank from taxation in the congressionally-issued charter as dispositive in *McCulloch*?

(c)   If the Court assumes that the power to tax is "of vital importance" so that it may not be assumed to be surrendered, how should constitutional silence on the immunity of federally-chartered corporations from state taxes be viewed?

(2)   Did the Court in *Providence Bank* adequately distinguish *McCulloch*?

PANHANDLE OIL CO. v. STATE OF MISSISSIPPI
EX REL. KNOX
277 U.S. 218 (1928)

Justice Butler delivered the Opinion of the Court.

[A Mississippi statute] provided that "any person engaged in the business of distributor of gasoline . . . shall pay for the privilege of engaging in such business, an excise tax of [four cents] per gallon upon the sale of gasoline," . . . . [Panhandle Oil Company] has been engaged in that business. The State sued to recover taxes claimed on account of sales made by [Panhandle] to the United States for the use of its Coast Guard fleet in service at the Gulf of Mexico and its Veterans' Hospital at Gulfport. . . . [Panhandle] defended on the ground that these statutes, if construed to impose taxes on such sales, are repugnant to the federal Constitution. . . . The [Mississippi] Supreme Court held that the exaction a valid privilege tax measured by the number of gallons sold; that it was not a tax upon instrumentalities of the federal government, and that the United States was not entitled to buy such gasoline without payment of the taxes charged dealers.

The United States is empowered by the Constitution to maintain and operate the fleet and hospital. Article I, Section 8. That authorization and laws enacted pursuant thereto are supreme (Article VI); and, in case of conflict, they control state enactments. The states may not burden or interfere with the exertion of national power or make it a source of revenue to take the funds raised or tax the means used for the performance of federal functions. *McCulloch v. Maryland*, 17 U.S. 316, 425 (1819). . . . The right of the United States to make such purchases is derived from the Constitution. [Panhandle's] right to make such sales to the United States was not given by the State and does not depend upon state laws; it results from the authority of the national government under the Constitution to choose its own means and sources of supply. While Mississippi may impose charges upon [Panhandle] for the privilege of carrying on trade that is subject to the power of the State, it may not lay any tax upon transactions by which the United States secures the things desired for its governmental purposes.

The validity of the taxes claimed is to be determined by the practical effect of enforcement in respect of sales to the government. . . . It is immaterial that the seller and not the purchaser is required to report and make payment to the State. Sale and purchase constitute a transaction by which the tax is measured and on which the burden rests. The amount of money claimed by the State rises and falls precisely as does the quantity of gasoline so secured by the government. It depends immediately upon the number of gallons. The necessary operation of these enactments when so construed is directly to retard, impede, and burden the exertion by the United States of its constitutional powers to operate the fleet and hospital. *McCulloch v. Maryland*, 17 U.S. at 436. To use the number of gallons sold the United States as a measure of the privilege tax is in substance and legal effect to tax the sale. And that is to tax the United States — to exact tribute on its transactions and apply the same to support the State.

The exactions demanded from [Panhandle] infringe its right to have the constitutional independence of the United States in respect of such purchases remain untrammeled. *Osborn v. United States Bank*, 22 U.S. 738, 867 (1824). [Panhandle] is not liable for the taxes claimed.

Judgment reversed.

Justice Holmes, dissenting.

The State of Mississippi . . . imposed upon distributors . . . of gasoline . . . an excise tax of . . . four cents . . . per gallon sold in the State. The Supreme Court of the

State . . . points out that whether the tax is on the privilege [of engaging in business] or on the property it is imposed before the gasoline has left the dealer's hands [it is permissible]. . . . The Supreme Court of the State upheld the tax and pointed out the extreme consequences to which a different decision might lead.

It seems to me that the State Court was right. I should say plainly right, but for the effect of certain *dicta* of Chief Justice Marshall which culminated in or rather were founded upon his often quoted proposition that the power to tax is the power to destroy. In those days it was not recognized as it is today that most of the distinctions of law are distinctions of degree. If the States had any power it was assumed that they had all power, and that the necessary alternative was to deny it altogether. But this Court which so often has defeated the attempt to tax in certain ways can defeat an attempt to discriminate or otherwise go too far without wholly abolishing the power to tax. The power to tax is not the power to destroy while this Court sits. The power to fix rates is the power to destroy if unlimited, but this Court while it endeavors to prevent confiscation does not prevent the fixing of rates. A tax is not an unconstitutional regulation in every case where an absolute prohibition of sales would be one.

To come down more closely to the question before us, when the Government comes into a State to purchase I do not perceive why it should be entitled to stand differently from any other purchaser. It avails itself of the machinery furnished by the State and I do not see why it should not contribute in the same proportion that every other purchaser contributes for the privileges that it uses. . . . The cost of maintaining the State that makes the business possible is just as necessary an element in the cost of production as labor or coal. . . .

. . . I am not aware that the President, the Members of Congress, the Judiciary or, to come nearer to the case in hand, the Coast Guard or the officials of the Veterans' Hospital, because they are instrumentalities of government and cannot function naked and unfed, hitherto having been entitled to have their bills for food and clothing cut down so far as their butchers and tailors have been taxed on their sales; and I had not supposed that the butchers and tailors could omit from their tax returns all receipts from the large class of customers to which I have referred. The question of interference with Government, I repeat, is one of reasonableness and degree and it seems to me that the interference in this case is too remote.

Justice Brandeis and Justice Stone agree with this opinion.

Justice Reynolds, dissenting.

I am unable to think that every man who sells a gallon of gasoline to be used by the United States thereby becomes a federal instrumentality, with the privilege of claiming freedom from taxation by the state. . . .

Justice Stone concurs in these views.

Exercise 10(B):

Reconsider *McCulloch v. Maryland* in light of the dissenting opinion of Justice Holmes in *Panhandle Oil*:

(1)   If the Court had approached the "power to tax" issue in *McCulloch* in the same manner that Justice Holmes addressed the "power to tax" issue in *Panhandle Oil,* how would the Court have ruled?

(2)   Which approach to the "power to tax" best fits the constitutional structure: *McCulloch* or *Providence Bank* or the dissenting opinion of Justice Holmes in *Panhandle Oil Co.*? Which of those cases best reflects the appropriate judicial role?

SOUTH CAROLINA v. BAKER, SECRETARY OF THE TREASURY
485 U.S. 505 (1988)

JUSTICE BRENNAN delivered the opinion of the Court.

[State and local governments (as well as the government of the United States) sell bonds to raise immediate revenue which will be repaid in a specified time with interest. Bonds had been issued in either registered form or in a form payable to the bearer. In Section 310 of a 1982 statute, Congress subjected to the federal income tax the interest paid on unregistered State and local bonds. The State of South Carolina invoked the Supreme Court's original jurisdiction.]

. . . .

South Carolina contends that even if a statute banning state bearer bonds entirely would be constitutional, § 310 unconstitutionally violates the doctrine of intergovernmental tax immunity because it imposes a tax on the interest earned on a state bond. We agree with South Carolina that § 310 is inconsistent with *Pollock v. Farmers' Loan & Trust Co.*, 157 U.S. 429 (1895), which held that any interest earned on a state bond was immune from federal taxation.

. . . The United States cannot convert an unconstitutional tax into a constitutional one simply by making the tax conditional. Whether Congress could have imposed the condition by direct regulation is irrelevant; Congress cannot employ unconstitutional means to reach a constitutional end. Under *Pollock*, a tax on the interest income derived from any state bond was considered a direct tax on the State and thus unconstitutional. 157 U.S. at 585–86. If this constitutional rule still applies, Congress cannot threaten to tax the interest on state bonds that do not conform to congressional dictates. We thus decline to follow a suggestion that would force us to embrace implicitly a proposition of law far more controversial than the current validity of *Pollock*'s ban on taxing state bond interest, and proceed to address whether *Pollock* should be explicitly overruled.

Under the intergovernmental tax immunity jurisprudence prevailing at the time, *Pollock* did not represent a unique immunity limited to income derived from state bonds. Rather, *Pollock* merely represented one application of the more general rule that neither the Federal nor the State Governments could tax income an individual directly derived from *any* contract with another government. . . . Income derived from the same kinds of contracts with the Federal Government were likewise immune from taxation by the States. Cases concerning the tax immunity of income derived from state contracts freely cited principles established in federal tax immunity cases, and vice versa.

This general rule was based on the rationale that any tax on income a party received under a contract with the government was a tax on the contract and thus a tax "on" the government because it burdened the government's power to enter into the contract. . . . Thus, although a tax was collected from an independent private party, the tax was considered to be "on" the government because the tax burden might be passed on to it through the contract. This reasoning was used to define the basic scope of both federal and state tax immunities with respect to all types of government contracts.[11] . . . The commonality of the rationale underlying all these immunities for government contracts was highlighted by *Indian Motorcycle Co. v. United States*, 283 U.S. 570 (1931). In that case, the Court reviewed the then current status of intergovernmental tax immunity

---

[11] The sources of the state and federal immunities are, of course, different: the state immunity arises from the constitutional structure and a concern for protecting state sovereignty whereas the federal immunity arises from the supremacy clause. . . .

doctrine, observing that a tax on interest earned on a state or federal bond was unconstitutional because it would burden the exercise of the government's power to borrow money and that a tax on the salary of a State or Federal Government employee was unconstitutional because it would burden the government's power to obtain the employee's services. *Id.* at 576–78. It then concluded that under the same principle a sales tax imposed on a vendor for a sale to a state agency was unconstitutional because it would burden the sale transaction. *Id.* at 579.

The rationale underlying *Pollock* and the general immunity for government contract income has been thoroughly repudiated by modern intergovernmental immunity caselaw. In *Graves v. New York ex rel. O'Keefe*, 306 U.S. 466 (1939), the Court announced: "The theory . . . that a tax on income is legally or economically a tax on its source, is no longer tenable." *Id.* at 480. . . . The thoroughness with which the Court abandoned the burden theory was demonstrated most emphatically when the Court upheld a state sales tax imposed on a Government contractor even though the financial burden of the tax was entirely passed on, through a cost-plus contract, to the Federal Government. *Alabama v. King & Boozer*, 314 U.S. 1 (1941). . . . *King & Boozer* thus completely foreclosed any claim that the nondiscriminatory imposition of costs on private entities that pass them on to States or the Federal Government unconstitutionally burdens state or federal functions. Subsequent cases have consistently reaffirmed the principle that a nondiscriminatory tax collected from private parties contracting with another government is constitutional even though part or all of the financial burden falls on the other government.

With the rationale for conferring a tax immunity on parties dealing with another government rejected, the government contract immunities recognized under prior doctrine were, one by one, eliminated. . . . The only premodern tax immunity for parties to government contracts that has so far avoided being explicitly overruled is the immunity for recipients of governmental bond interest.[13] That this Court has yet to overrule *Pollock* explicitly, however, is explained not by any distinction between the income derived from government bonds and the income derived from other government contracts, but by the historical fact that Congress has always exempted state bond interest from taxation by statute, beginning with the very first federal income tax statute. Act of Oct. 3, 1913, ch. 16, § II(B), 38 Stat. 168.

In sum, then, under current intergovernmental tax immunity doctrine the States can never tax the United States directly but can tax any private parties with whom it does business, even though the financial burden falls on the United States, as long as the tax does not discriminate against the United States or those with whom it deals. A tax is considered to be directly on the Federal Government only "when the levy falls on the United States itself, or on an agency or instrumentality so closely connected to the Government that the two cannot realistically be viewed as separate entities." *United States v. New Mexico*, 455 U.S. 720, 735 (1982). The rule with respect to state tax immunity is essentially the same, except that at least some nondiscriminatory federal taxes can be collected directly from the States even though a parallel state tax could not be collected directly from the Federal Government.

We thus confirm that subsequent case law has overruled the holding in *Pollock* that state bond interest is immune from a nondiscriminatory federal tax. We see no

---

[13] South Carolina and the Government Finance Officers Association as *amicus curiae* argue that the legislative history of the Sixteenth Amendment, which authorizes Congress to "collect taxes on incomes, from whatever source derived, without apportionment," manifests an intent to freeze into the Constitution the tax immunity for state bond interest that existed in 1913. We disagree. . . . [T]he sole purpose of the Sixteenth Amendment was to remove the apportionment requirement for whichever incomes were otherwise taxable. 45 Cong. Rec. 2245–2246 (1910). Indeed, if the Sixteenth Amendment had frozen into the Constitution all the tax immunities that existed in 1913, then most of modern intergovernmental tax immunity doctrine would be invalid.

constitutional reason for treating persons who receive interest on government bonds differently than persons who receive income from other types of contracts with the government, and no tenable rationale for distinguishing the costs imposed on States by a tax on state bond interest from the costs imposed by a tax on the income from any other state contract. We stated in *Graves* that "as applied to the taxation of salaries of the employees of one government, the purpose of the immunity was not to confer benefits on the employees by relieving them from contributing their share of the financial support of the other government, whose benefits they enjoy, or to give an advantage to a government by enabling it to engage employees at salaries lower than those paid for like services by other employers, public or private." 306 U.S. at 483. Likewise, the owners of state bonds have no constitutional entitlement not to pay taxes on income they earn from state bonds, and States have no constitutional entitlement to issue bonds paying lower interest rates than other issuers.

Indeed, this Court has in effect acknowledged that a holder of a Government bond could constitutionally be taxed on bond interest in *Memphis Bank & Trust Co. v. Garner*, 459 U.S. 392 (1983), which involved a state tax on federal bond interest. . . . [W]e premised our statutory interpretation on the observation that "[o]ur decisions have treated § 742 as principally a restatement of the constitutional rule." 459 U.S. at 397. We then stated: "Where, *as here*, the economic but not the legal incidence of the tax falls upon the Federal Government, such a tax generally does not violate the constitutional immunity if it does not discriminate against holders of federal property or those with whom the Federal Government deals." *Id.* (emphasis added).

[Section] 310 thus clearly imposes no direct tax on the States. The tax is imposed on and collected from bondholders, not States, and any increased administrative costs incurred by States in implementing the registration system are not "taxes" within the meaning of the tax immunity doctrine. . . . Nor does § 310 discriminate against States. The provisions of § 310 seek to assure that *all* publicly offered long-term bonds are issued in registered form, whether issued by state or local governments, the Federal Government, or private corporations. . . .

. . . .

Because . . . a nondiscriminatory federal tax on the interest earned on state bonds does not violate the intergovernmental tax immunity doctrine, we uphold the constitutionality of § 310(b)(1), overrule the exceptions to the Special Master's Report, and approve his recommendation to enter judgment for the defendant.

JUSTICE KENNEDY took no part in the consideration or decision of this case.

[The concurring opinions of Justice Stevens and Justice Scalia, and the opinion of Chief Justice Rehnquist concurring in the judgment, have been omitted.]

JUSTICE O'CONNOR, dissenting.

The Court today overrules a precedent that it has honored for nearly 100 years and expresses a willingness to cancel the constitutional immunity that traditionally has shielded the interest paid on state and local bonds from federal taxation. Henceforth the ability of state and local governments to finance their activities will depend in part on whether Congress voluntarily abstains from tapping this permissible source of additional income tax revenue. I believe that state autonomy is an important factor to be considered in reviewing the National Government's exercise of its enumerated powers. *Garcia v. SAMTA*, 469 U.S. 528, 581 (1985) (O'Connor, J., dissenting). I dissent from the decision to overrule *Pollock v. Farmers' Loan & Trust Co.*, 157 U.S. 429 (1895), and I would invalidate Congress' attempt to regulate the sovereign States by threatening to deprive them of this tax immunity, which would increase their dependence on the National Government.

. . . In my view, the Tenth Amendment and principles of federalism inherent in the Constitution prohibit Congress from taxing or threatening to tax the interest paid on state and municipal bonds. It is also arguable that the States' autonomy is protected from substantial federal incursions by virtue of the Guarantee Clause of the Constitution, Art. IV, § 4.

The Court never expressly considers whether federal taxation of state and local bond interest violates the Constitution. Instead, the majority characterizes the federal tax exemption for state and local bond interest as an aspect of intergovernmental tax immunity, and it describes the decline of the intergovernmental tax immunity doctrine in this century. But constitutional principles do not depend upon the rise or fall of particular legal doctrines. This Court has a continuing responsibility "to oversee the Federal Government's compliance with its duty to respect the legitimate interests of the States." *Garcia*, 469 U.S. at 581 (O'Connor, J., dissenting). In my view, the Court shirks its responsibility because it fails to inquire into the substantial adverse effects on state and local governments that would follow from federal taxation of the interest on state and local bonds.

Long-term debt obligations are an essential source of funding for state and local governments. In 1974, state and local governments issued approximately $23 billion of new municipal bonds; in 1984, they issued $102 billion of new bonds. State and local governments rely heavily on borrowed funds to finance education, road construction, and utilities, among other purposes. As the Court recognizes, States will have to increase the interest rates they pay on bonds by 28–35% if the interest is subject to the federal income tax. Governmental operations will be hindered severely if the cost of capital rises by one-third. If Congress may tax the interest paid on state and local bonds, it may strike at the very heart of state and local government activities.

In the pivotal cases which first set limits to intergovernmental tax immunity, this Court paid close attention to the practical effects of its decisions. The Court limited the government's immunity only after it determined that application of a tax would not substantially affect government operations. Thus in the first case to uphold federal income taxation of revenue earned by a state contractor, this Court observed that "neither government may destroy the other nor curtail in any substantial manner the exercise of its powers." *Metcalf & Eddy v. Mitchell*, 269 U.S. 514, 523–24 (1926). When this Court extended its holding to the case of a state tax on a federal contractor, it expressly noted that the tax "does not interfere in any substantial way with the performance of federal functions." *James v. Dravo Contracting Co.*, 302 U.S. 134, 161 (1937). In upholding the application of the federal income tax to income derived from a state lease, this Court decided that mere theoretical concerns about interference with the functions of government did not justify immunity, but that "[r]egard must be had to substance and direct effects." *Helvering v. Mountain Producers Corp.*, 303 U.S. 376, 386 (1938). . . .

The instant case differs critically from the cases quoted above because the Special Master found that, if the interest on state and local bonds is taxed, the cost of borrowing by state and local governments would rise substantially. This certainly would affect seriously state and local government operations. The majority is unconcerned with this difference because it is satisfied with the formal test of intergovernmental tax immunity that can be distilled from later cases. Under this test, if a tax is not imposed directly on the government, and does not discriminate against the government, then it does not violate intergovernmental tax immunity.

I do not think the Court's bipartite test adequately accommodates the constitutional concerns raised by the prospect of applying the federal income tax to the interest paid on state and local bonds. This Court has a duty to inquire into the devastating effects that such an innovation would have on state and local governments. Although Congress has taken a relatively less burdensome step in subjecting only income from bearer bonds to federal taxation, the erosion of state sovereignty is likely to occur a step at a time. . . .

Federal taxation of state activities is inherently a threat to state sovereignty. As Chief Justice Marshall observed long ago, "the power to tax involves the power to destroy." *McCulloch v. Maryland,* 17 U.S. 316, 431 (1819). Justice Holmes later qualified this principle, observing that "[t]he power to tax is not the power to destroy while this Court sits." *Panhandle Oil Co. v. Mississippi ex rel. Knox,* 277 U.S. 218, 223 (1928) (Holmes, J., dissenting). If this Court is the States' sole protector against the threat of crushing taxation, it must take seriously its responsibility to sit in judgment of federal tax initiatives. I do not think that the Court has lived up to its constitutional role in this case. The Court has failed to enforce the constitutional safeguards of state autonomy and self-sufficiency that may be found in the Tenth Amendment and the Guarantee Clause, as well as in the principles of federalism implicit in the Constitution. I respectfully dissent.

Exercise 10(C):

In light of *South Carolina v. Baker,* consider the following matters:

(1)   Under current constitutional doctrine, what are the limits on the power of a State to subject to its taxing power an officer or agency of the United States, a corporation chartered by the United States, and payments by the United States to its employees or contractors?

(2)   Under current constitutional doctrine, what are the limits on the power of the United States to subject to its taxing power an officer or agency of a State, a corporation chartered by a State, and payments by a State to its employees or contractors?

(3)   Applying the approach of *South Carolina v. Baker* or the cases discussed therein, how would the Court resolve *McCulloch v. Maryland*?

(4)   If your instructor assigned Volume 1, consider whether to the extent the Court in *South Carolina v. Baker* overruled one or more earlier cases, its action was consistent with the principles of *stare decisis* articulated in *Casey.*

(5)   Article IV of the Articles of Confederation expressly addressed governmental immunity from taxation: "no imposition, duties or restrictions shall be laid by any State, on the property of the United States, or either of them." There is no similar provision in the U.S. Constitution. In the absence of any such provision, should the Constitution be understood to limit the taxing powers of the several States with respect to the central government and one another?

(6)   In FEDERALIST No. 33, Alexander Hamilton responded to opponents of ratification who argued that the Supremacy Clause would permit Congress to interfere with the taxing power of the several States. Review that statement and other pertinent statements made during the ratification debates. Is current doctrine consistent with the public understanding at the time of ratification?

CHAPTER 3

CONGRESSIONAL REGULATION OF COMMERCE

Chapter One addressed the power of Congress to provide incentives to encourage or discourage certain conduct. Chapter Two examined the nature of the enumerated coercive powers of Congress. Of the coercive powers enumerated in Article I, Section 8, Congress has made the greatest use of the commerce power. This Chapter considers the scope of that power.

Exercise 11(A):

Before turning attention to judicial precedents and the traditional uses of the Commerce Clause, consider the following matters as they stood in 1791 with the ratification of the Bill of Rights.

(1)   Read Article I, Section 8, Clause 3. What limits, if any, does the plain language impose on the power of Congress to regulate commerce. Stated otherwise, what, if any, "commerce," regardless of the meaning of that term, is excluded from congressional regulation?

(2)   Examine the remainder of the Constitution of 1789 and the Bill of Rights. Do any of the other textual provisions shed additional light on the limits, if any, to the power of Congress to regulate commerce?

(3)   Consider the structure of the government under the Constitution, as amended, in 1791. Do structural considerations suggest any additional limits on the power of Congress to regulate commerce?

(4)   Recall Alexander Hamilton's "Report on Manufactures" (in Chapter 1) presented to the First Congress. In what sense did he use the term "commerce"? What was its implicit meaning? What forms of economic activity, if any, were excluded from his understanding of the term? Consider the material on the DVD-ROM: was Hamilton's usage consistent with usage during the ratification debates?

(5)   Is any part of the power of Congress to regulate commerce exclusive or is it a power exercised concurrently with the States? Stated otherwise, if Congress failed to legislate with respect to a matter within the scope of its power to regulate commerce, would a State have power to do so or not?

(6)   What light, if any, do the early treatises on the meaning of the Constitution (on the DVD-ROM) shed with respect to these questions?

ALEXANDER HAMILTON'S OPINION ON THE CONSTITUTIONALITY OF THE FIRST BANK OF THE UNITED STATES
February 23, 1791

[As noted in Chapter 2, President Washington requested that Secretary of the Treasury Alexander Hamilton prepare a formal opinion responding to the views of the Attorney General and Secretary of State that the proposed Bank was unconstitutional. In his opinion regarding the constitutionality of a congressionally-chartered bank,

Hamilton addressed the scope of power under Article I, section 8, clause 3, as had been described more narrowly in the opinion of Attorney General Edmund Randolph.]

The heads of the power to regulate commerce with foreign nations are stated [by Attorney General Randolph] to be

1. to prohibit them or their commodities from our ports.

2. to impose duties on *them* where none existed before, or to increase existing duties on them.

3. to subject *them* to any species of custom house regulation

4. to grant *them* any exemptions or privileges which policy may suggest.

This enumeration is far more exceptional than either of the former [which purport to identify the scope of permissible exercises of the power to lay and collect taxes, and the power to borrow money]. It omits *every thing* that relates to the *citizens vessels* or *commodities* of the United States. The following palpable omissions occur at once.

1. Of the power to prohibit the exportation of commodities which not only exists at all times, but which in time of war it would be necessary to exercise, particularly with relation to naval and war-like stores.

2. Of the power to prescribe rules concerning the *characteristics & privileges* of an American bottom — how she shall be navigated, as whether by citizens or foreigners, or by a proportion of each.

3. Of the power of regulating the manner of contracting with seamen, the police of ships on their voyages [etcetera] of which the act for the government & regulation of seamen in the merchants service is a specimen.

That the three preceding articles are omissions, will not be doubted. There is a long list of items in addition, which admit of little, if any question; of which a few samples shall be given.

1. The granting of bounties to certain kinds of vessels, & certain species of merchandise. Of this nature is the allowance on dried & pickled fish & salted provisions.

2. The prescribing of rules concerning the *inspection* of commodities to be exported. Though the states individually are competent to this regulation, yet there is no reason, in point of authority at least, why a general system might not be adopted by the United States.

3. The regulation of policies of insurance; of salvage upon goods found at sea, and the disposition of such goods.

4. The regulation of pilots.

5. The regulation of bills of exchange drawn by a merchant of *one state* upon a merchant of *another state*. This last rather belongs to the regulation of trade between the states, but is equally omitted in the specification under that head.

Exercise 11(B):

Does Hamilton's description of the subjects encompassed within the power of Congress to regulate commerce significantly increase the breadth of that power? Does his description here extend to any of the forms of economic activity previously thought to be excluded?

GIBBONS v. OGDEN
22 U.S. 1 (1824)

[To provide an incentive not only for inventions of new devices but also to encourage enterprising individuals to risk the introduction and promotion of new technologies, in England and in many of the States, laws were adopted granting a monopoly for a term of years to those who agreed to undertake such risks. This technique was also employed to encourage investments even in the absence of any technological innovations, such as to encourage the construction of toll bridges, canals, and toll roads. Recall that the central government itself granted a monopoly charter to the first Bank of the United States as an inducement to investors in that enterprise.

Robert Fulton did much to improve the design of steamboats, a promising new invention which seemingly had the potential to replace sailing ships. The State of New York granted Fulton and his investors exclusive rights to navigate the waters of that State "with boats moved by fire or steam," for a certain term of years, on the condition that a specified number of such boats were constructed and put into actual service. Fulton and his investors transferred part of that monopoly concerning routes between New York City and points in New Jersey, including Elizabethtown. Aaron Ogden operated steamboats under an assignment of that authority. Thomas Gibbons operated two competing steamboats from Elizabethtown, New Jersey, to New York City, without any license from Fulton or his assignees.

Ogden sued Gibbons in New York's Court of Chancery. That court enjoined Gibbons from operating his steamboats in the waters of New York without the permission of Ogden. The court rejected Gibbons' argument that a federal license of his boats carried with it authority to disregard the terms of Ogden's exclusive franchise under New York law. The judgment for Ogden was affirmed by the state courts and then appealed to the United States Supreme Court.]

CHIEF JUSTICE MARSHALL delivered the opinion of the Court.

The appellant contends that this decree is erroneous, because the laws which purport to give the exclusive privilege it sustains, are repugnant to the constitution and laws of the United States.

They are said to be repugnant —

[First,] [t]o that clause in the constitution which authorizes Congress to regulate commerce.

[Second,] [t]o that which authorizes Congress to promote the progress of science and useful arts.

. . . .

[I]

The words are, "Congress shall have power to regulate commerce with foreign nations, and among the several States, and with the Indian tribes."

[A]

[1]

The subject to be regulated is commerce; and our constitution being, as was aptly said at the bar, one of enumeration, and not of definition, to ascertain the extent of the power, it becomes necessary to settle the meaning of the word. The counsel for the appellee would limit it to traffic, to buying and selling, or the interchange of commodities, and do not admit that it comprehends navigation. This would restrict a general term, applicable to many objects, to one of its significations. Commerce, undoubtedly, is traffic, but it is something more: it is intercourse. It describes the commercial intercourse between nations, and parts of nations, in all its branches, and is regulated by prescribing rules for carrying on that intercourse. The mind can scarcely conceive a system for regulating commerce between nations, which shall exclude all laws concerning navigation, which shall be silent on the admission of the vessels of the one nation into the ports of the other, and be confined to prescribing rules for the conduct of individuals, in the actual employment of buying and selling, or of barter.

If commerce does not include navigation, the government of the Union has no direct power over that subject, and can make no law prescribing what shall constitute American vessels, or requiring that they shall be navigated by American seamen. Yet this power has been exercised from the commencement of the government, has been exercised with the consent of all, and has been understood by all to be a commercial regulation. All America understands, and has uniformly understood, the word "commerce," to comprehend navigation. It was so understood, and must have been so understood, when the constitution was framed. The power over commerce, including navigation, was one of the primary objects for which the people of America adopted their government, and must have been contemplated in forming it. The convention must have used the word in that sense, because all have understood it in that sense; and the attempt to restrict it comes too late.

If the opinion that "commerce," as the word is used in the constitution, comprehends navigation also, requires any additional confirmation, that additional confirmation is, we think, furnished by the words of the instrument itself.

It is a rule of construction, acknowledged by all, that the exceptions from a power mark its extent; for it would be absurd, as well as useless, to except from a granted power, that which was not granted — that which the words of the grant could not comprehend. If, then, there are in the constitution plain exceptions from the power over navigation, plain inhibitions to the exercise of that power in a particular way, it is a proof that those who made these exceptions, and prescribed these inhibitions, understood the power to which they applied as being granted.

[Article I, Section 9 of the Constitution] declares, that "no preference shall be given, by any regulation of commerce or revenue, to the ports of one State over those of another." This clause cannot be understood as applicable to those laws only which are passed for the purposes of revenue, because it is expressly applied to commercial regulations; and the most obvious preference which can be given to one port over another, in regulating commerce, relates to navigation. But the subsequent part of the sentence is still more explicit. It is, "nor shall vessels bound to or from one State, be obliged to enter, clear, or pay duties, in another." These words have a direct reference to navigation.

The universally acknowledged power of the government to impose embargoes, must also be considered as showing, that all America is united in that construction which comprehends navigation in the word commerce. . . .

. . . .

When Congress imposed that embargo which, for a time, engaged the attention of every man in the United States, the avowed object of the law was, the protection of commerce, and the avoiding of war. By its friends and its enemies it was treated as a commercial, not as a war measure. . . .

The word used in the constitution, then, comprehends, and has been always understood to comprehend, navigation within its meaning; and a power to regulate navigation, is as expressly granted, as if that term had been added to the word "commerce."

[2]

To what commerce does this power extend? The constitution informs us, to commerce "with foreign nations, and among the several States, and with the Indian tribes."

[a]

It has, we believe, been universally admitted, that these words comprehend every species of commercial intercourse between the United States and foreign nations. No sort of trade can be carried on between this country and any other, to which this power does not extend. It has been truly said, that commerce, as the word is used in the constitution, is a unit, every part of which is indicated by the term.

If this be the admitted meaning of the word, in its application to foreign nations, it must carry the same meaning throughout the sentence, and remain a unit, unless there be some plain intelligible cause which alters it.

[b]

The subject to which the power is next applied, is to commerce "among the several States." The word "among" means intermingled with. A thing which is among others, is intermingled with them. Commerce among the States, cannot stop at the external boundary line of each State, but may be introduced into the interior.

It is not intended to say that these words comprehend that commerce, which is completely internal, which is carried on between man and man in a State, or between different parts of the same State, and which does not extend to or affect other States. Such a power would be inconvenient, and is certainly unnecessary.

Comprehensive as the word "among" is, it may very properly be restricted to that commerce which concerns more States than one. The phrase is not one which would probably have been selected to indicate the completely interior traffic of a State, because it is not an apt phrase for that purpose; and the enumeration of the particular classes of commerce, to which the power was to be extended, would not have been made, had the intention been to extend the power to every description. The enumeration presupposes something not enumerated; and that something, if we regard the language or the subject of the sentence, must be the exclusively internal commerce of a State. The genius and character of the whole government seem to be, that its action is to be applied to all the external concerns of the nation, and to those internal concerns which affect the States generally; but not to those which are completely within a particular State, which do not affect other States, and with which it is not necessary to interfere, for the purpose of executing some of the general powers of the government. The completely internal commerce of a State, then, may be considered as reserved for the State itself.

But, in regulating commerce with foreign nations, the power of Congress does not stop at the jurisdictional lines of the several States. It would be a very useless power, if it could not pass those lines. The commerce of the United States with foreign nations, is that of the whole United States. Every district has a right to participate in it. The deep streams which penetrate our country in every direction, pass through the interior of almost every State in the Union, and furnish the means of exercising this right. If Congress has the power to regulate it, that power must be exercised whenever the subject exists. If it exists within the States, if a foreign voyage may commence or terminate at a port within a State, then the power of Congress may be exercised within a State.

The principle is, if possible, still more clear, when applied to commerce "among the several States." They either join each other, in which case they are separated by a mathematical line, or they are remote from each other, in which case other States lie between them. What is commerce "among" them; and how is it to be conducted? Can a trading expedition between two adjoining States, commence and terminate outside of each? And if the trading intercourse be between two States remote from each other, must it not commence in one, terminate in the other, and probably pass through a third? Commerce among the States must, of necessity, be commerce with the States. In the regulation of trade with the Indian tribes, the action of the law, especially when the constitution was made, was chiefly within a State. The power of Congress, then, whatever it may be, must be exercised within the territorial jurisdiction of the several States. The sense of the nation on this subject, is unequivocally manifested by the provisions made in the laws for transporting goods, by land, between Baltimore and Providence, between New York and Philadelphia, and between Philadelphia and Baltimore.

[3]

We are now arrived at the inquiry — What is this power?

[a]

It is the power to regulate; that is, to prescribe the rule by which commerce is to be governed. This power, like all others vested in Congress, is complete in itself, may be exercised to its utmost extent, and acknowledges no limitations, other than are prescribed in the constitution. These are expressed in plain terms, and do not affect the questions which arise in this case, or which have been discussed at the bar. If, as has always been understood, the sovereignty of Congress, though limited to specified objects, is plenary as to those objects, the power over commerce with foreign nations, and among the several States, is vested in Congress as absolutely as it would be in a single government, having in its constitution the same restrictions on the exercise of the power as are found in the constitution of the United States. The wisdom and the discretion of Congress, their identity with the people, and the influence which their constituents possess at elections, are, in this, as in many other instances, as that, for example, of declaring war, the sole restraints on which they have relied, to secure them from its abuse. They are the restraints on which the people must often rely solely, in all representative governments.

The power of Congress, then, comprehends navigation, within the limits of every State in the Union; so far as that navigation may be, in any manner, connected with "commerce with foreign nations, or among the several States, or with the Indian tribes." It may, of consequence, pass the jurisdictional line of New York, and act upon the very waters to which the prohibition now under consideration applies.

[b]

But it has been urged with great earnestness, that, although the power of Congress to regulate commerce with foreign nations, and among the several States, be co-extensive with the subject itself, and have no other limits than are prescribed in the constitution, yet the States may severally exercise the same power, within their respective jurisdictions. In support of this argument, it is said, that they possessed it as an inseparable attribute of sovereignty, before the formation of the constitution, and still retain it, except so far as they have surrendered it by that instrument; that this principle results from the nature of the government, and is secured by the tenth amendment; that an affirmative grant of power is not exclusive, unless in its own nature it be such that the continued exercise of it by the former possessor is inconsistent with the grant, and that this is not of that description.

The appellant, conceding these postulates, except the last, contends, that full power to regulate a particular subject, implies the whole power, and leaves no residuum; that a grant of the whole is incompatible with the existence of a right in another to any part of it.

Both parties have appealed to the constitution, to legislative acts, and judicial decisions; and have drawn arguments from all these sources, to support and illustrate the propositions they respectively maintain.

The grant of the power to lay and collect taxes is, like the power to regulate commerce, made in general terms, and has never been understood to interfere with the exercise of the same power by the States; and hence has been drawn an argument which has been applied to the question under consideration. But the two grants are not, it is conceived, similar in their terms or their nature. Although many of the powers formerly exercised by the States, are transferred to the government of the Union, yet the State governments remain, and constitute a most important part of our system. The power of taxation is indispensable to their existence, and is a power which, in its own nature, is capable of residing in, and being exercised by, different authorities at the same time. We are accustomed to see it placed, for different purposes, in different hands. Taxation is the simple operation of taking small portions from a perpetually accumulating mass, susceptible of almost infinite division; and a power in one to take what is necessary for certain purposes, is not, in its nature, incompatible with a power in another to take what is necessary for other purposes. Congress is authorized to lay and collect taxes, [et cetera] to pay the debts, and provide for the common defence and general welfare of the United States. This does not interfere with the power of the States to tax for the support of their own governments; nor is the exercise of that power by the States, an exercise of any portion of the power that is granted to the United States. In imposing taxes for State purposes, they are not doing what Congress is empowered to do. Congress is not empowered to tax for those purposes which are within the exclusive province of the States. When, then, each government exercises the power of taxation, neither is exercising the power of the other. But, when a State proceeds to regulate commerce with foreign nations, or among the several States, it is exercising the very power that is granted to Congress, and is doing the very thing which Congress is authorized to do. There is no analogy, then, between the power of taxation and the power of regulating commerce.

[c]

In discussing the question, whether this power is still in the States, in the case under consideration, we may dismiss from it the inquiry, whether it is surrendered by the mere grant to Congress, or is retained until Congress shall exercise the power. We may dismiss that inquiry, because it has been exercised, and the regulations which Congress deemed it proper to make, are now in full operation. The sole question is, can a State regulate commerce with foreign nations and among the States, while Congress is regulating it?

The counsel for the respondent answer this question in the affirmative, and rely very much on the restrictions in [Article I, Section 10] as supporting their opinion. They say, very truly, that limitations of a power, furnish a strong argument in favour of the existence of that power . . . .

. . . .

[T]he inspection laws are said to be regulations of commerce, and are certainly recognised in the constitution, as being passed in the exercise of a power remaining in the States.

That inspection laws may have a remote and considerable influence on commerce, will not be denied; but that a power to regulate commerce is the source from which the right to pass them is derived, cannot be admitted. . . . They act upon the subject before it becomes an article of foreign commerce, or of commerce among the States, and prepare it for that purpose. They form a portion of that immense mass of legislation, which embraces every thing within the territory of a State, not surrendered to the general government: all of which can be most advantageously exercised by the States themselves. Inspection laws, quarantine laws, health laws of every description, as well as laws for regulating the internal commerce of a State, and those which respect turnpike roads, ferries, [et cetra], are component parts of this mass.

No direct general power over these objects is granted to Congress; and, consequently, they remain subject to State legislation. If the legislative power of the Union can reach them, it must be for national purposes; it must be where the power is expressly given for a special purpose, or is clearly incidental to some power which is expressly given. [T]he government of the Union, in the exercise of its express powers . . . of regulating commerce with foreign nations and among the States, may use means that may also be employed by a State . . . regulating commerce within the State. If Congress license vessels to sail from one port to another, in the same State, the act is supposed to be, necessarily, incidental to the power expressly granted to Congress, and implies no claim of a direct power to regulate the purely internal commerce of a State . . . .

In our complex system, presenting the rare and difficult scheme of one general government, whose action extends over the whole, but which possesses only certain enumerated powers; and of numerous State governments, which retain and exercise all powers not delegated to the Union, contests respecting power must arise. . . .

. . . .

It has been contended by the counsel for the appellant, that, as the word "to regulate" implies in its nature, full power over the thing to be regulated, it excludes, necessarily, the action of all others that would perform the same operation on the same thing. That regulation is designed for the entire result, applying to those parts which remain as they were, as well as to those which are altered. It produces a uniform whole, which is as much disturbed and deranged by changing what the regulating power designs to leave untouched, as that on which it has operated.

There is great force in this argument, and the Court is not satisfied that it has been refuted.

Since, however, in exercising the power of regulating their own purely internal affairs, whether of trading or police, the States may sometimes enact laws, the validity of which depends on their interfering with, and being contrary to, an act of Congress passed in pursuance of the constitution, the Court will enter upon the inquiry, whether the laws of New York, as expounded by the highest tribunal of that State, have, in their application to this case, come into collision with an act of Congress, and deprived a citizen of a right to which that act entitles him. Should this collision exist, it will be immaterial whether those laws were passed in virtue of a concurrent power "to regulate commerce with foreign nations and among the several States," or, in virtue of a power to regulate their domestic trade and police. In one case and the other, the acts of New York must yield to the law of Congress; and the decision sustaining the privilege they confer, against a right given by a law of the Union, must be erroneous.

[II]

[A]

This opinion has been frequently expressed in this Court, and is founded, as well on the nature of the government as on the words of the constitution. In argument, however, it has been contended, that if a law passed by a State, in the exercise of its acknowledged sovereignty, comes into conflict with a law passed by Congress in pursuance of the constitution, they affect the subject, and each other, like equal opposing powers.

But the framers of our constitution foresaw this state of things, and provided for it, by declaring the supremacy not only of itself, but of the laws made in pursuance of it. The nullity of any act, inconsistent with the constitution, is produced by the declaration, that the constitution is the supreme law. The appropriate application of that part of the clause which confers the same supremacy on laws and treaties, is to such acts of the State Legislatures as do not transcend their powers, but, though enacted in the execution of acknowledged State powers, interfere with, or are contrary to the laws of Congress, made in pursuance of the constitution, or some treaty made under the authority of the United States. In every such case, the act of Congress, or the treaty, is supreme; and the law of the State, though enacted in the exercise of powers not controverted, must yield to it.

[B]

[1]

. . . In the exercise of this power [to regulate commerce], Congress has passed "an act for enrolling or licensing ships or vessels to be employed in the coasting trade and fisheries, and for regulating the same." The counsel for the respondent contend, that this act does not give the right to sail from port to port, but confines itself to regulating a pre-existing right, so far only as to confer certain privileges on enrolled and licensed vessels in its exercise.

It will at once occur, that, when a Legislature attaches certain privileges and exemptions to the exercise of a right over which its control is absolute, the law must imply a power to exercise the right. The privileges are gone, if the right itself be annihilated. It would be contrary to all reason, and to the course of human affairs, to say that a State is unable to strip a vessel of the particular privileges attendant on the exercise of a right, and yet may annul the right itself; that the State of New York cannot prevent an enrolled and licensed vessel, proceeding from . . . New Jersey, to New York, from enjoying, in her course, and on her entrance into port, all the privileges conferred by the act of Congress; but can shut her up in her own port, and prohibit altogether her entering the waters and ports of another State. To the Court it seems very clear, that the whole act on the subject of the coasting trade, according to those principles which govern the construction of statutes, implies, unequivocally, an authority to licensed vessels to carry on the coasting trade.

[2]

But we will proceed briefly to notice those sections [of the Act] which bear more directly on the subject.

The first section declares, that vessels enrolled . . . as described in that act, and having a license in force, as is by the act required, "and no others, shall be deemed ships or vessels of the United States, entitled to the privileges of ships or vessels employed in the coasting trade."

. . . To construe these words otherwise than as entitling the ships or vessels described, to carry on the coasting trade, would be, we think, to disregard the apparent intent of the act.

. . . .

The license must be understood to be what it purports to be, a legislative authority to the steamboat . . . "to be employed in carrying on the coasting trade, for one year from this date."

[a]

. . . The coasting trade is a term well understood. The law has defined it; and all know its meaning perfectly. . . . [I]t cannot, we think, be doubted, that a voyage from New Jersey to New York, is one of those operations.

. . . .

[b]

. . . A coasting vessel employed in the transportation of passengers, is as much a portion of the American marine, as one employed in the transportation of a cargo; and no reason is perceived why such vessel should be withdrawn from the regulating power of that government, which has been thought best fitted for the purpose generally. The provisions of the law respecting native seamen, and respecting ownership, are as applicable to vessels carrying men, as to vessels carrying manufactures; and no reason is perceived why the power over the subject should not be placed in the same hands. The argument urged at the bar, rests on the foundation, that the power of Congress does not extend to navigation, as a branch of commerce, and can only be applied to that subject incidentally and occasionally. But if that foundation be removed, we must show some plain, intelligible distinction, supported by the constitution, or by reason, for discriminating between the power of Congress over vessels employed in navigating the same seas. We can perceive no such distinction.

If we refer to the constitution, the inference to be drawn from it is rather against the distinction. The section which restrains Congress from prohibiting the migration or importation of such persons as any of the States may think proper to admit, until the year 1808, has always been considered as an exception from the power to regulate commerce, and certainly seems to class migration with importation. Migration applies as appropriately to voluntary, as importation does to involuntary, arrivals; and, so far as an exception from a power proves its existence, this section proves that the power to regulate commerce applies equally to the regulation of vessels employed in transporting men, who pass from place to place voluntarily, and to those who pass involuntarily.

If the power reside in Congress, as a portion of the general grant to regulate commerce, then acts applying that power to vessels generally, must be construed as comprehending all vessels. If none appear to be excluded by the language of the act, none can be excluded by construction. Vessels have always been employed to a greater or less extent in the transportation of passengers, and have never been supposed to be, on that account, withdrawn from the control or protection of Congress. Packets which ply along the coast, as well as those which make voyages between Europe and America, consider the transportation of passengers as an important part of their business. Yet it has never been suspected that the general laws of navigation did not apply to them.

. . . .

If, then, it were even true, that [Gibbons' steam ships] were employed exclusively in the conveyance of passengers between New York and New Jersey, it would not follow that this occupation did not constitute a part of the coasting trade of the United States . . . .

. . . .

[c]

This act demonstrates the opinion of Congress, that steam boats may be enrolled and licensed, in common with vessels using sails. They are, of course, entitled to the same privileges, and can no more be restrained from navigating waters, and entering ports which are free to such vessels, than if they were wafted on their voyage by the winds, instead of being propelled by the agency of fire. The one element may be as legitimately used as the other, for every commercial purpose authorized by the laws of the Union; and the act of a State inhibiting the use of either to any vessel having a license under the act of Congress, comes, we think, in direct collision with that act.

[III]

. . . .

Powerful and ingenious minds, taking, as postulates, that the powers expressly granted to the government of the Union, are to be contracted by construction, into the narrowest possible compass, and that the original powers of the States are retained, if any possible construction will retain them, may, by a course of well digested, but refined and metaphysical reasoning, founded on these premises, explain away the constitution of our country, and leave it, a magnificent structure, indeed, to look at, but totally unfit for use. They may so entangle and perplex the understanding, as to obscure principles, which were before thought quite plain, and induce doubts where, if the mind were to pursue its own course, none would be perceived. In such a case, it is peculiarly necessary to recur to safe and fundamental principles to sustain those principles, and, when sustained, to make them the tests of the arguments to be examined.

JUSTICE JOHNSON, concurring.

. . . .

For a century the States had submitted, with murmurs, to the commercial restrictions imposed by the parent State; and now, finding themselves in the unlimited possession of those powers over their own commerce, which they had so long been deprived of, and so earnestly coveted, that selfish principle which, well controlled, is so salutary, and which, unrestricted, is so unjust and tyrannical, guided by inexperience and jealousy, began to show itself in iniquitous laws and impolitic measures, from which grew up a conflict of commercial regulations, destructive to the harmony of the States, and fatal to their commercial interests abroad.

This was the immediate cause, that led to the forming of a convention.

As early as 1778, the subject had been pressed upon the attention of Congress, by a memorial from the State of New Jersey; and in 1781, we find a resolution presented to that body . . . affirming, that "it is indispensably necessary, that the United States, in Congress assembled, should be vested with a right of superintending the commercial regulations of every State, that none may take place that shall be partial or contrary to the common interests." The [1786] resolution of Virginia, appointing her commissioners [to the Philadelphia Convention] expresses their purposes to be, "to take into consideration the trade of the United States, to consider how far an uniform system in their commercial regulations, may be necessary to their common interests and their permanent harmony." And Mr. Madison's resolution, which led to that measure, is introduced with a preamble entirely explicit to this point . . . .

. . . .

There was not a State in the Union, in which there did not, at that time [of ratification of the Constitution], exist a variety of commercial regulations; concerning which it is too much to suppose, that the whole ground covered by those regulations was immediately assumed by actual legislation, under the authority of the Union. . . . By common consent, those laws dropped lifeless from their statute books, for want of the sustaining power, that had been relinquished to Congress.

And the plain and direct import of the words of the grant, is consistent with this general understanding.

The words of the constitution are, "Congress shall have power to regulate commerce with foreign nations, and among the several States, and with the Indian tribes."

It is not material, in my view of the subject, to inquire whether the article *a* or *the* should be prefixed to the word "power." Either, or neither, will produce the same result: if either, it is clear that the article *the* would be the proper one, since the next preceding grant of power is certainly exclusive, to wit: "to borrow money on the credit of the United States." But mere verbal criticism I reject.

My opinion is founded on the application of the words of the grant to the subject of it.

The "power to regulate commerce," here meant to be granted, was that power to regulate commerce which previously existed in the States. But what was that power? The States were, unquestionably, supreme; and each possessed that power over commerce, which is acknowledged to reside in every sovereign State. The definition and limits of that power are to be sought among the features of international law . . . . The law of nations, regarding man as a social animal, pronounces all commerce legitimate in a state of peace, until prohibited by positive law. The power of a sovereign state over commerce, therefore, amounts to nothing more than a power to limit and restrain it at pleasure. And since the power to prescribe the limits to its freedom, necessarily implies the power to determine what shall remain unrestrained, it follows, that the power must be exclusive; it can reside but in one potentate; and hence, the grant of this power carries with it the whole subject, leaving nothing for the State to act upon.

And such has been the practical construction of the act. . . . No statute of the United States, that I know of, was ever passed to permit a commerce, unless in consequence of its having been prohibited by some previous statute.

. . . But another view of the subject leads directly to the same conclusion. Power to regulate *foreign commerce,* is given in the same words, and in the same breath, as it were, with that over the commerce of the States and with the Indian tribes. But the power to regulate *foreign* commerce is necessarily exclusive. The States are unknown to foreign nations; their sovereignty exists only with relation to each other and the general government. Whatever regulations foreign commerce should be subjected to in the ports of the Union, the general government would be held responsible for them; and all other regulations, but those which Congress had imposed, would be regarded by foreign nations as trespasses and violations of national faith and comity.

But the language which grants the power as to one description of commerce, grants it as to all; and, in fact, if ever the exercise of a right, or acquiescence in a construction, could be inferred from contemporaneous and continued assent, it is that of the exclusive effect of this grant.

A right over the subject has never been pretended to in any instance, except as incidental to the exercise of some other unquestionable power.

The present is an instance of the assertion of that kind, as incidental to a municipal power; that of superintending the internal concerns of a State, and particularly of extending protection and patronage, in the shape of a monopoly, to genius and enterprise.

The grant to Livingston and Fulton, interferes with the freedom of intercourse among the States; and on this principle its constitutionality is contested.

When speaking of the power of Congress over navigation, I do not regard it as a power incidental to that of regulating commerce; I consider it as the thing itself; inseparable from it as vital motion is from vital existence.

Commerce, in its simplest signification, means an exchange of goods; but in the advancement of society, labour, transportation, intelligence, care, and various mediums of exchange, become commodities, and enter into commerce; the subject, the vehicle, the agent, and their various operations, become the objects of commercial regulation. Ship building, the carrying trade, and propagation of seamen, are such vital agents of commercial prosperity, that the nation which could not legislate over these subjects, would not possess power to regulate commerce.

. . . .

But, it is almost labouring to prove a self-evident proposition, since the sense of mankind, the practice of the world, the contemporaneous assumption, and continued exercise of the power, and universal acquiescence, have so clearly established the right of Congress over navigation, and the transportation of both men and their goods, as not only incidental to, but actually of the essence of, the power to regulate commerce. . . .

It is impossible, with the views which I entertain of the principle on which the commercial privileges of the people of the United States, among themselves, rests, to concur in the view which this Court takes of the effect of the coasting license in this cause. I do not regard it as the foundation of the right set up in behalf of the appellant. If there was any one object riding over every other in the adoption of the constitution, it was to keep the commercial intercourse among the States free from all invidious and partial restraints. And I cannot overcome the conviction, that if the licensing act was repealed tomorrow, the rights of the appellant to a reversal of the decision complained of, would be as strong as it is under this license. One half the doubts in life arise from the defects of language, and if this instrument had been called an *exemption* instead of a license, it would have given a better idea of its character. Licensing acts, in fact, in legislation, are universally restraining acts; as, for example, acts licensing gaming houses, retailers of spiritous liquors, [et cetera]. The act, in this instance, is distinctly of that character, and forms part of an extensive system, the object of which is to encourage American shipping, and place them on an equal footing with the shipping of other nations. Almost every commercial nation reserves to its own subjects a monopoly of its coasting trade; and a countervailing privilege in favour of American shipping is contemplated, in the whole legislation of the United States on this subject. It is not to give the vessel an American character, that the license is granted; that effect has been correctly attributed to the act of her enrollment. But it is to confer on her American privileges, as contradistinguished from foreign; and to preserve the government from fraud by foreigners, in surreptitiously intruding themselves into the American commercial marine, as well as frauds upon the revenue in the trade coastwise, that this whole system is projected. Many duties and formalities are necessarily imposed upon the American foreign commerce, which would be burdensome in the active coasting trade of the States, and can be dispensed with. A higher rate of tonnage also is imposed, and this license entitles the vessels that take it, to those exemptions, but to nothing more. . . . I consider the license, therefore, as nothing more than what it purports to be, according to the [first] section of this act, conferring on the licensed vessel certain privileges in that trade, not conferred on other vessels; but the abstract right of commercial intercourse, stripped of those privileges, is common to all.

. . . .

But the principal objections to these opinions arise, [first, from] the unavoidable action of some of the municipal powers of the States, upon commercial subjects.

[Second, objections are founded on] passages in the constitution, which are supposed to imply a *concurrent* power in the States in regulating commerce.

It is no objection to the existence of distinct, substantive powers, that, in their application, they bear upon the same subject. The same bale of goods, the same cask of provisions, or the same ship, that may be the subject of commercial regulation, may also be the vehicle of disease. And the health laws that require them to be stopped and ventilated, are no more intended as regulations on commerce, than the laws which permit their importation, are intended to innoculate the community with disease. Their different purposes mark the distinction between the powers brought into action; and while frankly exercised, they can produce no serious collision. As to laws affecting ferries, turnpike roads, and other subjects of the same class, so far from meriting the epithet of commercial regulations, they are, in fact, commercial facilities . . . . Inspection laws are of a more equivocal nature, and it is obvious, that the constitution has viewed that subject with much solicitude. But so far from sustaining an inference in favour of the power of the States over commerce, I cannot but think that the guarded provisions of [Article I, Section 10], on this subject, furnish a strong argument against that inference. It was obvious, that inspection laws must combine municipal with commercial regulations; and, while the power over the subject is yielded to the States, for obvious reasons, an absolute control is given over State legislation on the subject, as far as that legislation may be exercised, so as to affect the commerce of the country. The inferences, to be correctly drawn, from this whole article, appear to me to be altogether in favour of the exclusive grants to Congress of power over commerce, and the reverse of that which the appellee contends for.

This section contains the positive restrictions imposed by the constitution upon State power. The first clause of it, specifies those powers which the States are precluded from exercising, even though the Congress were to permit them. The second, those which the States may exercise with the consent of Congress. And here the sedulous attention to the subject of State exclusion from commercial power, is strongly marked. Not satisfied with the express grant to the United States of the power over commerce, this clause negatives the exercise of that power to the States, as to the only two objects which could ever tempt them to assume the exercise of that power, to wit, the collection of a revenue from imposts and duties on imports and exports; or from a tonnage duty. As to imposts on imports or exports, such a revenue might have been aimed at *directly,* by express legislation, or *indirectly,* in the form of inspection laws; and it became necessary to guard against both. Hence, first, the consent of Congress to such imposts or duties, is made necessary; and as to inspection laws, it is limited to the minimum of expenses. Then, the money so raised shall be paid into the treasury of the United States, or may be sued for, since it is declared to be for their use. And lastly, all such laws may be modified, or repealed, by an act of Congress. It is impossible for a right to be more guarded. . . . But this whole clause, as to these two subjects, appears to have been introduced *ex abundanti cautela,* to remove every temptation to an attempt to interfere with the powers of Congress over commerce, and to show how far Congress might consent to permit the States to exercise that power. Beyond those limits, even by the consent of Congress, they could not exercise it. And thus, we have the whole effect of the clause. The inference which counsel would deduce from it, is neither necessary nor consistent with the general purpose of the clause.

But instances have been insisted on, with much confidence, in argument, in which, by municipal laws, particular regulations respecting their cargoes have been imposed upon shipping in the ports of the United States; and one, in which forfeiture was made the penalty of disobedience.

. . . .

It would be in vain to deny the possibility of a clashing and collision between the measures of the two governments. The line cannot be drawn with sufficient distinctness between the municipal powers of the one, and the commercial powers of the other. In some points they meet and blend so as scarcely to admit of separation. Hitherto the only remedy has been applied which the case admits of; that of a frank and candid co-operation for the general good. Witness the laws of Congress requiring its officers to respect the inspection laws of the States, and to aid in enforcing their health laws; that which surrenders to the States the superintendence of pilotage, and the many laws passed to permit a tonnage duty to be levied for the use of their ports. Other instances could be cited, abundantly to prove that collision must be sought to be produced; and when it does arise, the question must be decided how far the powers of Congress are adequate to put it down. Wherever the powers of the respective governments are frankly exercised, with a distinct view to the ends of such powers, they may act upon the same object, or use the same means, and yet the powers be kept perfectly distinct. A resort to the same means, therefore, is no argument to prove the identity of their respective powers.

Exercise 11(C):

In light of *Gibbons v. Ogden*, consider the following matters:

(1)   As in the *McCulloch* case, *Gibbons v. Ogden* posed two distinct constitutional questions: (a) whether federal law that purports to address an issue is constitutional and, if so, (b) whether the federal law preempts conflicting state law. In the view of the majority, did Congress have constitutional authority to enact the law licensing ships? In the view of the majority, did the federal statute preempt the New York law upon which Ogden relied? On what point did Justice Johnson disagree with the majority?

(2)   In Part I(A)(1) of the opinion, how did the Court define "commerce"? Was that definition broader than previously articulated by Hamilton in either his "Report on Manufactures" or his "Opinion on the Constitutionality of the First Bank of the United States"? Was that definition broader than other contemporaneous usage?

(3)   In Part I(A)(2)(a) of the opinion, the Court asserted that the term "commerce" had the same meaning in the context of trade with foreign nations as in the context of trade with Indian tribes and trade "among the several States." Is there any basis for construing the term differently in any of these three contexts?

(4)   In Part I(A)(2)(b) of the opinion, the Court construed the term "among" to distinguish between matters subject to federal regulation and matters subject to State regulation. What matters inside the boundaries of a single State fall on each side of that line?

(5)   In Part I(A)(3)(a) of the opinion, that Court asserted that the power of Congress is "plenary." In what sense is the commerce power plenary? Did the Court mean that Congress has a general legislative power permitting it to address any subject without judicial interference? If that was the Court's meaning, was that interpretation consistent with the structure of the Constitution? Or, did the Court mean that if a subject properly fell within the scope of an enumerated power — something the judiciary would determine — Congress could exercise the full extent of the enumerated power even if doing so superseded pre-existing state laws? If that was the Court's meaning, was that interpretation consistent with the structure of the Constitution?

(6)   In Part I(A)(3)(b) of the opinion, the Court acknowledged the argument that "States may severally exercise the same power, within their respective jurisdictions." Did the majority confirm or deny that, under the Constitution, States have concurrent power to regulate commerce? Did the Court conclude that States have concurrent power to regulate interstate commerce? Did the Court conclude that States have power to regulate subjects that may incidentally include matters that are within interstate commerce?

(7)   In Part II of the opinion, the Court discussed a federal licensing Act. Was Ogden required to obtain a federal license to continue to operate his steam ships between New Jersey and New York City? Did the fact that Ogden had the right to operate those routes under legislation enacted by New York obviate the need for a federal license? Was it possible for Ogden to comply with *both* federal and state law? If so, what was the source of the conflict?

(8)   In terms of analyzing the conflict, consider the following hypothetical questions:

(a)   If the FCC licensed cable television providers, would such a license in and of itself permit all such providers to disregard any municipal ordinance granting an exclusive franchise to a single provider?

(b)   If the EPA licensed commercial water purification facilities, would such a license in and of itself permit all such facilities to disregard any municipal ordinance establishing a monopoly provider?

(c)   If the U.S. Department of Transportation licensed drivers of long-haul, inter-state, commercial trucks, would such a license in and of itself permit such drivers to disregard local laws regarding the speed limit, toll collection, and/or parking restrictions?

(9)   What did the Court mean by the statement that "Congress is not empowered to tax for those purposes which are within the exclusive province of the States"? Is that position consistent with the Court's decision in *United States v. Butler* and/or *South Dakota v. Dole*?

(10)   Justice Johnson, concurring, asserted that "if the [federal] licensing act was repealed tomorrow" the result of the case would have been the same. How is that possible? In the absence of federal legislation that expressly (or impliedly) prohibited all state-granted monopolies in interstate transportation, on what basis can the exclusive rights granted by New York be held invalid?

(11)   Congress first enacted legislation licensing ships on September 1, 1789 (see DVD-ROM). Prior to that enactment, for example, on July 1, 1789, how should a court have ruled on Ogden's action for an injunction? Why?

(12)   Which of the branches of the central government may employ the commerce power in the view of the majority of the Court? Which of the branches may do so in the view of Justice Johnson?

THE COMMERCE CLAUSE BEFORE THE NEW DEAL

What Is "Commerce"?

The term "commerce" is derived from the Latin for "with merchandise."[1] Dictionaries contemporaneous with the framing of the Constitution defined the term as the "exchange of one thing for another."[2] At the Constitutional Convention, the term

---

[1]   *See United States v. Lopez*, 514 U.S. 549, 586 (1995) (Thomas, J., concurring) (citing 3 Oxford English Dictionary 552 (2d ed. 1989)).

[2]   *See id.* at 585–86 (quoting 1 Samuel Johnson, A Dictionary of the English Language 361 (4th ed. 1773)).

was used interchangeably with "trade."[3] In the ratification debates, the term was similarly understood.[4] Thus, "commerce" was distinguished from agriculture, manufacturing, and industry.[5]

This traditional understanding of the meaning of the term commerce and the consequent limitation on congressional power remained evident at the end of the 1800s and in the early decades of the 1900s. In *Kidd v. Pearson,*[6] the Supreme Court stated: "No distinction is more popular to the common mind, or more clearly expressed in economic and political literature, than that between manufactur[e] and commerce." In *United States v. E.C. Knight Co.,*[7] the Court reaffirmed: "Commerce succeeds to manufacture, and is not a part of it." As recently as 1936, the Court asserted: "Mining brings the subject matter of commerce into existence. Commerce disposes of it."[8]

What Commerce Is Subject to Federal Regulation?

Aside from subjects excluded from the scope of federal regulation because they do not constitute "commerce," the Commerce Clause contains other narrowing words.[9] For example, the Commerce Clause expressly limits congressional authority to that commerce "with foreign Nations, and among the several States, and with the Indian tribes."[10] As Chief Justice Marshall explained: "The enumeration presupposes something not enumerated; and that something, if we regard the language, or the subject of the sentence, must be the exclusively internal commerce of a State."[11] The structure of the Constitution[12] further demonstrates that the Commerce Clause does not extend federal power over all commerce.

Up until 1936, the case law had not yet unleashed the full impact of the "substantial effect" doctrine. Only activities "that affected interstate commerce *directly* were within Congress' power; activities that affected interstate commerce indirectly were beyond

---

[3] For example, Mr. Pinkney proposed that no legislation "for the purpose of regulating the commerce of the U[nited] S[tates] with foreign powers, or among the several States, shall be passed without the assent of two thirds of the members of each House." 2 MAX FARRAND, THE RECORDS OF THE FEDERAL CONVENTION OF 1787, at 449 (rev. ed. 1966) (Madison's notes of Aug. 29, 1787). Speaking in opposition to the proposal, Mr. Randolph "took notice of the argument in favor of giving the power over trade to a majority, drawn from the opportunity foreign powers would have of obstructing retaliating measures, if two third were made requisite."). *Id.* at 449. Later, in discussion of the power to regulate commerce, Roger Sherman and Mr. Langdon spoke of the power "to regulate trade." *Id.* at 639 (Madison's notes of Sept. 15, 1789).

[4] For example, James Madison's discussion of the power "to regulate commerce" also described its subject as the power "to regulate the trade between State and State." FEDERALIST No. 42 (Madison).

[5] *See Lopez* at 587–88, 597 n.6 (Thomas, J., concurring). At the Constitutional Convention, James Madison argued against a supermajority requirement for Congress to enact laws regulating commerce. He explained that the federal power to regulate commerce was unlikely to be abused due to "the provision of 2 branches — by the independence of the Senate, by the negative of the Executive, by the interest of Connecticut & N[ew] Jersey which were agricultural, not commercial States; by the interior interest which was also agricultural in the most commercial States — by the accession of Western States which w[oul]d be altogether agricultural." 2 MAX FARRAND, *supra* note 3, at 449 (Madison's notes of Aug. 29, 1787) (statement of Mr. Madison).

[6] 128 U.S. 1, 20 (1888).

[7] 156 U.S. 1, 12 (1895).

[8] *Carter v. Carter Coal Co.,* 298 U.S. 238, 304 (1936).

[9] *See Lopez,* 514 U.S. at 553 ("limitations on the commerce power are inherent in the very language of the Commerce Clause").

[10] U.S. Const. art. I, § 8, cl. 3.

[11] *Gibbons v. Ogden,* 22 U.S. 1, 194–95 (1824).

[12] "An interpretation of cl. 3 that makes the rest of § 8 superfluous simply cannot be correct." *Lopez,* 514 U.S. at 589 (Thomas, J., concurring).

Congress' reach."[13]

In What Branch Does the Constitution Vest the Power to Regulate Commerce?

Congress enacted the licensing statute at issue in *Gibbons v. Ogden*.[14] Chief Justice Marshall interpreted that statute so as to present a "direct collision" with State law. Under that view of the case, *Gibbons* involved nothing more than a determination that the federal statute was within the scope of congressional power under the Constitution and application of preemption doctrine. In the absence of congressional regulation through enactment of the licensing statute, the State law would have remained in force. This approach squarely places the power to regulate commerce and displace conflicting State law in the hands of Congress.

Justice Johnson wrote separately in *Gibbons* to explain, in his view, the case would be resolved in the same manner even in the absence of the federal licensing statute. Under that view of the case, the Constitution vests exclusive jurisdiction in the federal government to regulate at least certain forms of commerce. Stripped of concurrent jurisdiction over such matters, States would lack constitutional authority to regulate some matters even in the absence of federal legislation. As a result, even if there was no conflict between a State law and federal legislation, the judiciary would remain free to declare that the State law was inconsistent with the Constitution itself. That approach would give the judiciary a significantly greater role in determining what State laws to displace under the so-called "dormant Commerce Clause" or "negative Commerce Clause."

The issue was again presented in *Willson v. Black Bird Creek Marsh Co.*[15] In that case State law authorized the construction of a dam which blocked a navigable creek. A ship licensed under the very same statute at issue in *Gibbons* collided with the dam. Owners of the dam sued the owners of the ship for damages to the dam. Writing for the Court, Chief Justice Marshall observed that the State legislation was concerned with the "value of the property on [the] banks" of the creek and "the health of the inhabitants" of the area — matters traditionally within the general police power of the States. Nonetheless, because the State law blocked a stream used in interstate commerce, the State law would have been invalid if it conflicted "with the powers of the general government." In analyzing whether it did so, the Court concluded:

> If congress had passed any act which bore upon the case; any act in execution of the power to regulate commerce, the object of which was to control state legislation over those small navigable creeks into which the tide flows, and which abound throughout the lower country of the middle and southern states; we should feel not much difficulty in saying that a state law coming in conflict with such act would be void. But congress has passed no such act. The repugnancy of the law of Delaware to the constitution is placed entirely on its repugnancy to the power to regulate commerce with foreign nations and among the several states; a power which has not been so exercised as to affect the question.

> We do not think that the act empowering the Black Bird Creek Marsh Company to place a dam across the creek, can, under all the circumstances of the case, be considered as repugnant to the power to regulate commerce in its dormant state, or as being in conflict with any law passed on the subject. . . .

---

[13] *Lopez*, 514 U.S. at 555 (citing *A.L.A. Schechter Poultry Corp. v. United States*, 295 U.S. 495, 546 (1935)) (emphasis added); *see id.* at 570, 572–73 (Kennedy, J., concurring) (summarizing cases adhering to the direct/indirect distinction from 1895 through 1936); *cf. id.* at 596 (Thomas, J., concurring) ("the case law indicates that the substantial effects test is but an innovation of the 20th century").

[14] 22 U.S. 1 (1824). The statute and a predecessor licensing statute are included on the DVD-ROM.

[15] 27 U.S. 245 (1829).

How can Chief Justice Marshall's interpretation of the federal licensing statute to create a conflict with State law in *Gibbons* be reconciled with his interpretation of the same federal statute to create no conflict with State law in *Willson*? One possible answer is that the State law at issue in *Gibbons* was directly addressed to regulating transportation while the State law at issue in *Willson* was directly addressed to enhancement of property and to the health of individuals, with only a collateral impact on transportation. The fact that *Gibbons* arose in the context of New York harbor (where different States adjoin the waterway) while *Willson* arose in the context of a marsh located entirely within Delaware may provide further support for that view, as well as a basis to distinguish the cases on the ground of whether the commerce appears less likely to be "among the States." Are there other bases to distinguish the cases?

Both *Gibbons* and *Willson* appear to support the view that in the absence of federal legislation, States remain free to legislate in a manner that regulates commerce within their boundaries. Do the cases compel that conclusion? Apart from these judicial precedents, do the structure, text, and shared public understanding of the Constitution support the notion of a "dormant Commerce Clause" enforced by the judiciary? Or, do those sources support the claim of concurrent State power to regulate commerce, subject to preemption by federal legislation?

Not until 1887 did Congress rely upon the Commerce Clause as the basis for a major piece of legislation.[16] For almost an entire century, Congress made only limited use of the commerce power.

Prior to that time the Commerce Clause was predominantly employed by the judiciary under the dormant Commerce Clause doctrine[17] — despite the early precedents casting doubt upon the existence of such an authority — rather than as a source of affirmative legislative authority. As a result, most of the cases addressing the scope of the federal government's power to regulate commerce in the first century under the Constitution were decided in the absence of any implicit congressional definition of commerce. Detailed consideration of the dormant Commerce Clause is beyond the scope of this Volume; by definition it is not an exercise of federal legislative power.

What Doctrinal Changes Were Introduced by the New Deal?

In 1937, the Supreme Court rejected the distinction between "direct" and "indirect" effects on interstate commerce, thereby expanding the scope of federal regulatory power. *See NLRB v. Jones & Laughlin Steel Corp.*, 301 U.S. 1, 36–38 (1937). That shift in doctrine foreshadowed several additional developments reflected in the next two cases.

UNITED STATES v. DARBY
312 U.S. 100 (1941)

JUSTICE STONE delivered the opinion of the Court.

The two principal questions raised by the record in this case are, *first*, whether Congress has constitutional power to prohibit the shipment in interstate commerce of lumber manufactured by employees whose wages are less than a prescribed minimum

---

[16] *See* Interstate Commerce Act of 1887, ch. 104, 24 Stat. 379. The Act established the Interstate Commerce Commission to regulate interstate transportation by railroad.

[17] *See Lopez*, 514 U.S. at 604 (Souter, J., dissenting) ("Congress saw few occasions to exercise [the commerce] power prior to Reconstruction and it was really the passage of the Interstate Commerce Act of 1887 that opened a new age of congressional reliance on the Commerce Clause for authority to exercise general police powers at the national level.") (citing 2 CHARLES WARREN, THE SUPREME COURT IN UNITED STATES HISTORY 729–39 (rev ed. 1935)).

or whose weekly hours of labor at that wage are greater than a prescribed maximum, and, *second,* whether it has power to prohibit the employment of workmen in the production of goods "for interstate commerce" at other than prescribed wages and hours. . . .

Appellee demurred to an indictment found in the district court . . . charging him with violation of . . . the Fair Labor Standards Act of 1938. The district court sustained the demurrer and quashed the indictment. . . .

The Fair Labor Standards Act set up a comprehensive legislative scheme for preventing the shipment in interstate commerce of certain products and commodities produced in the United States under labor conditions as respects wages and hours which fail to conform to standards set up by the Act. Its purpose, as we judicially know from the declaration of policy in § 2(a) of the Act . . . is to exclude from interstate commerce goods produced for the commerce and to prevent their production for interstate commerce, under conditions detrimental to the maintenance of the minimum standards of living necessary for health and general well-being; and to prevent the use of interstate commerce as the means of competition in the distribution of goods so produced, and as the means of spreading and perpetuating such substandard labor conditions among the workers of the several states. . . .

. . . Section 15(1) makes unlawful the shipment in interstate commerce of any goods "in the production of which any employee was employed in violation of section 6 or section 7," which provide, among other things, that during the first year of operation of the Act a minimum wage of 25 cents per hour shall be paid to employees "engaged in [interstate] commerce or in the production of goods for [interstate] commerce," § 6, and that the maximum hours of employment for employees "engaged in commerce or in the production of goods for commerce" without increased compensation for overtime, shall be forty-four hours a week. § 7.

. . . .

The indictment charges that appellee is engaged, in the state of Georgia, in the business of acquiring raw materials, which he manufactures into finished lumber with the intent, when manufactured, to ship it in interstate commerce to customers outside the state, and that he does in fact so ship a large part of the lumber so produced. There are numerous counts charging appellee with the shipment in interstate commerce from Georgia to points outside the state of lumber in the production of which, for interstate commerce, appellee has employed workmen at less than the prescribed minimum wage or more than the prescribed maximum hours without payment to them of any wage for overtime. Other counts charge the employment by appellee of workmen in the production of lumber for interstate commerce at wages of less than 25 cents an hour or for more than the maximum hours per week without payment to them of the prescribed overtime wage. . . .

. . . .

. . . [W]e accept the district court's interpretation of the indictment and confine our decision to the validity and construction of the statute.

. . . .

While manufacture is not of itself interstate commerce the shipment of manufactured goods interstate is such commerce and the prohibition of such shipment by Congress is indubitably a regulation of the commerce. The power to regulate commerce is the power "to prescribe the rule by which commerce is to be governed." *Gibbons v. Ogden,* 22 U.S. 1 (1824). It extends not only to those regulations which aid, foster and protect the commerce, but embraces those which prohibit it. *Lottery Case (Champion v. Ames),* 188 U.S. 321 (1903). It is conceded that the power of Congress to prohibit transportation in interstate commerce includes noxious articles, *id.; Hipolite*

Egg Co. v. United States, 220 U.S. 45 (1911); stolen articles, *Brooks v. United States*, 267 U.S. 432 (1925); kidnapped persons, *Gooch v. United States*, 297 U.S. 124 (1936); and articles such as intoxicating liquor or convict made goods, traffic in which is forbidden or restricted by the laws of the state of destination. *Kentucky Whip & Collar Co. v. Illinois Central R. Co.*, 299 U.S. 334 (1937).

But it is said that the present prohibition falls within the scope of none of these categories; that while the prohibition is nominally a regulation of the commerce its motive or purpose is regulation of wages and hours of persons engaged in manufacture, the control of which has been reserved to the states and upon which Georgia and some of the states of destination have placed no restriction; that the effect of the present statute is not to exclude the prescribed articles from interstate commerce in aid of state regulation as in *Kentucky Whip & Collar Co.*, but instead, under the guise of a regulation of interstate commerce, it undertakes to regulate wages and hours within the state contrary to the policy of the state which has elected to leave them unregulated.

The power of Congress over interstate commerce "is complete in itself, may be exercised to its utmost extent, and acknowledges no limitations, other than are prescribed by the constitution." *Gibbons*, 22 U.S. at 196. That power can neither be enlarged nor diminished by the exercise or non-exercise of state power. *Kentucky Whip & Collar Co.* Congress, following its own conception of public policy concerning the restrictions which may appropriately be imposed on interstate commerce, is free to exclude from the commerce articles whose use in the states for which they are destined it may conceive to be injurious to the public health, morals or welfare, even though the state has not sought to regulate their use. *Ames*, 188 U.S. at 321.

Such regulation is not a forbidden invasion of state power merely because either its motive or its consequence is to restrict the use of articles of commerce within the states of destination; and is not prohibited unless by other Constitutional provisions. It is no objection to the assertion of the power to regulate interstate commerce that its exercise is attended by the same incidents which attend the exercise of the police power of the states. *Seven Cases v. United States*, 239 U.S. 510, 514 (1916).

The motive and purpose of the present regulation are plainly to make effective the Congressional conception of public policy that interstate commerce should not be made the instrument of competition in the distribution of goods produced under substandard labor conditions, which competition is injurious to the commerce and to the states from and to which the commerce flows. The motive and purpose of a regulation of interstate commerce are matters for the legislative judgment upon the exercise of which the Constitution places no restriction and over which the courts are given no control. *McCray v. United States*, 195 U.S. 27 (1904). "The judicial cannot prescribe to the legislative departments of the government limitations upon the exercise of its acknowledged power." *Veazie Bank v. Fenno*, 75 U.S. 533, 548 (1869). Whatever their motive and purpose, regulations of commerce which do not infringe some constitutional prohibition are within the plenary power conferred on Congress by the Commerce Clause. Subject only to that limitation, presently to be considered, we conclude that the prohibition of the shipment interstate of goods produced under the forbidden substandard labor conditions is within the constitutional authority of Congress.

In the more than a century which has elapsed since the decision of *Gibbons v. Ogden*, these principles of constitutional interpretation have been so long and repeatedly recognized by this Court as applicable to the Commerce Clause, that there would be little occasion for repeating them now were it not for the decision of this Court twenty-two years ago in *Hammer v. Dagenhart*, 247 U.S. 251 (1918). In that case it was held by a bare majority of the Court over the powerful and now classic dissent of Justice Holmes setting forth the fundamental issues involved, that Congress was without power to exclude the products of child labor from interstate commerce. The reasoning and conclusion of the Court's opinion there cannot be reconciled with the conclusion which we have reached, that the power of Congress under the Commerce Clause is plenary to exclude any article from interstate commerce subject only to the specific prohibitions of the Constitution.

Hammer v. Dagenhart has not been followed. The distinction on which the decision was rested that Congressional power to prohibit interstate commerce is limited to articles which in themselves have some harmful or deleterious property — a distinction which was novel when made and unsupported by any provision of the Constitution — has long since been abandoned. *Kentucky Whip & Collar Co.* The thesis of the opinion that the motive of the prohibition or its effect to control in some measure the use or production within the states of the article thus excluded from the commerce can operate to deprive the regulation of its constitutional authority has long since ceased to have force. *Ames; Hipolite Egg Co.* And finally we have declared "The authority of the Federal Government over interstate commerce does not differ in extent or character from that retained by the states over intrastate commerce." *United States v. Rock Royal Co-Operative, Inc.*, 307 U.S. 533, 569 (1939).

The conclusion is inescapable that *Hammer v. Dagenhart* was a departure from the principles which have prevailed in the interpretation of the Commerce Clause both before and since the decision and that such vitality, as a precedent, as it then had has long since been exhausted. It should be and now is overruled.

Validity of the wage and hour requirements. Section 15(a)(2) and §§ 6 and 7 require employers to conform to the wage and hour provisions with respect to all employees engaged in the production of goods for interstate commerce. As appellee's employees are not alleged to be "engaged in interstate commerce" the validity of the prohibition turns on the question whether the employment, under other than the prescribed labor standards, of employees engaged in the production of goods for interstate commerce is so related to the commerce and so affects it as to be within the reach of the power of Congress to regulate it.

. . . .

. . . [W]e think the acts alleged in the indictment are within the sweep of the statute. The obvious purpose of the Act was not only to prevent the interstate transportation of the proscribed product, but to stop the initial step toward transportation, production with the purpose of so transporting it. Congress was not unaware that most manufacturing businesses shipping their product in interstate commerce make it in their shops without reference to its ultimate destination and then after manufacture select some of it for shipment interstate and some intrastate according to the daily demands of their business, and that it would be practically impossible, without disrupting manufacturing businesses, to restrict the prohibited kind of production to the particular pieces of lumber, cloth, furniture or the like which later move in interstate rather than intrastate commerce. *Cf. United States v. New York Central R. Co.*, 272 U.S. 457, 464 (1926).

. . . .

There remains the question whether such restriction on the production of goods for commerce is a permissible exercise of the commerce power. The power of Congress over interstate commerce is not confined to the regulation of commerce among the states. It extends to those activities intrastate which so affect interstate commerce or the exercise of the power of Congress over it as to make regulation of them appropriate means to the attainment of a legitimate end, the exercise of the granted power of Congress to regulate interstate commerce. *See McCulloch v. Maryland*, 17 U.S 316, 421 (1819).

. . . .

. . . Congress may . . . by appropriate legislation regulate intrastate activities where they have a substantial effect on interstate commerce. *See Santa Cruz Fruit Packing Co. v. NLRB*, 303 U.S. 453, 466 (1938). A recent example is the National Labor Relations Act for the regulation of employer and employee relations in industries in which strikes, induced by unfair labor practices named in the Act, tend to disturb or obstruct interstate commerce. *See NLRB v. Jones & Laughlin Steel Corp.*, 301 U.S. 1, 38, 40 (1937). But long before the adoption of the National Labor Relations Act, this Court had many times held that the power of Congress to regulate interstate commerce extends to the regulation through legislative action of activities intrastate which have a substantial effect on the commerce or the exercise of the Congressional power over it.

. . . .

Congress, having by the present Act adopted the policy of excluding from interstate commerce all goods produced for the commerce which do not conform to the specified labor standards, it may choose the means reasonably adapted to the attainment of the permitted end, even though they involve control of intrastate activities. Such legislation has often been sustained with respect to powers, other than the commerce power granted to the national government, when the means chosen, although not themselves within the granted power, were nevertheless deemed appropriate aids to the accomplishment of some purpose within an admitted power of the national government. *See Jacob Ruppert, Inc. v. Caffey*, 251 U.S. 264 (1920). . . . A familiar like exercise of power is the regulation of intrastate transactions which are so commingled with or related to interstate commerce that all must be regulated if the interstate commerce is to be effectively controlled. *Shreveport Case*, 234 U.S. 342 (1914). Similarly Congress may require inspection and preventive treatment of all cattle in a disease infected area in order to prevent shipment in interstate commerce of some of the cattle without the treatment. *Thornton v. United States*, 271 U.S. 414 (1926). . . .

. . . The Act is thus directed at the suppression of a method or kind of competition in interstate commerce which it has in effect condemned as "unfair," as the Clayton Act has condemned other "unfair methods of competition" made effective through interstate commerce. *See Van Camp & Sons v. American Can Co.*, 278 U.S. 245 (1929).

The Sherman Act and the National Labor Relations Act are familiar examples of the exertion of the commerce power to prohibit or control activities wholly intrastate because of their effect on interstate commerce. . . .

The means adopted by § 15(a)(2) for the protection of interstate commerce by the suppression of the production of the condemned goods for interstate commerce is so related to the commerce and so affects it as to be within the reach of the commerce power. *See Currin v. Wallace*, 306 U.S. 1 (1939). Congress, to attain its objective in the suppression of nationwide competition in interstate commerce by goods produced under substandard labor conditions, has made no distinction as to the volume or amount of shipments in the commerce or of production for commerce by any particular shipper or producer. It recognized that in present day industry, competition by a small part may affect the whole and that the total effect of the competition of many small producers may be great. The legislation aimed at a whole embraces all its parts. *Cf. NLRB v. Fainblatt*, 306 U.S. 601, 606 (1939).

So far as *Carter v. Carter Coal Co.*, 298 U.S. 238 (1936), is inconsistent with this conclusion, its doctrine is limited in principle by the decisions under the Sherman Act and the National Labor Relations Act, which we have cited and which we follow. . . .

Our conclusion is unaffected by the Tenth Amendment which provides: "The powers not delegated to the United States by the Constitution, nor prohibited by it to the States, are reserved to the States respectively, or to the people." The amendment states but a truism that all is retained which has not been surrendered. There is nothing in the history of its adoption to suggest that it was more than declaratory of the relationship between the national and state governments as it had been established by the Constitution before the amendment or that its purpose was other than to allay fears that the new national government might seek to exercise powers not granted, and that the states might not be able to exercise fully their reserved powers. *See, e.g.,* II ELLIOT'S DEBATES, 123, 131; III *id.* 450, 464, 600; IV *id.* 140, 149; 1 ANNALS OF CONGRESS 432, 761, 767–68; J. STORY, COMMENTARIES ON THE CONSTITUTION §§ 1907–1908.

From the beginning and for many years the amendment has been construed as not depriving the national government of authority to resort to all means for the exercise of a granted power which are appropriate and plainly adapted to the permitted end. *McCulloch v. Maryland,* 17 U.S at 405, 406. Whatever doubts may have arisen of the soundness of that conclusion they have been put at rest by the decisions under the Sherman Act and the National Labor Relations Act which we have cited. *See also Ashwander v. TVA,* 297 U.S. 288, 330–331 (1936).

. . . .

Reversed.

Exercise 12(A):

Consider the following questions in connection with *United States v. Darby*:

(1)   Is the Court's treatment of the commerce power in *Darby* consistent with *Gibbons v. Ogden* and other pre-1900 judicial precedents? If not, in what respect did *Darby* change doctrine?

(2)   Under this case, are there matters that Congress could regulate that were stated to be beyond federal power in *Gibbons v. Ogden* and/or *United States v. Butler*?

(3)   After *Darby*, are there any economic activities that remain beyond the scope of federal legislative authority?

(4)   The Court in *Darby* asserted: "The motive and purpose of a regulation of interstate commerce are matters for the legislative judgment upon the exercise of which the Constitution places no restriction and over which the courts are given no control." Recall that the Court asserted in *McCulloch v. Maryland*: "Let the end be legitimate, let it be within the scope of the constitution, and all means which are appropriate, which are plainly adapted to that end, which are not prohibited, but consist with the letter and spirit of the constitution, are constitutional." Should the *Darby* court have evaluated the statute in light of the legitimacy of "the end" (regulating production) rather than simply considering whether the means selected purported to be a regulation of commerce?

WICKARD, SECRETARY OF AGRICULTURE v. FILBURN
317 U.S. 111 (1942)

JUSTICE JACKSON delivered the opinion of the Court.

The appellee filed his complaint against the Secretary of Agriculture of the United States, three members of the County Agricultural Conservation Committee for Montgomery County, Ohio, and a member of the State Agricultural Conservation Committee for Ohio. He sought to enjoin enforcement against himself of the marketing penalty imposed by the amendment of May 26, 1941, to the Agricultural Adjustment Act of 1938, upon that part of his 1941 wheat crop which was available for marketing in excess of the marketing quota established for his farm. He also sought a declaratory judgment that the wheat marketing quota provisions of the Act as amended and applicable to him were unconstitutional because not sustainable under the Commerce Clause or consistent with the Due Process Clause of the Fifth Amendment.

. . . .

The appellee for many years past has owned and operated a small farm in Montgomery County, Ohio, maintaining a herd of dairy cattle, selling milk, raising poultry, and selling poultry and eggs. It has been his practice to raise a small acreage of winter wheat . . .; to sell a portion of the crop; to feed part to poultry and livestock on the farm, some of which is sold; to use some in making flour for home consumption; and to keep the rest for the following seeding. The intended disposition of the crop here involved has not been expressly stated.

In July of 1940,. . . there were established for the appellee's 1941 crop a wheat acreage allotment of 11.1 acres and a normal yield of 20.1 bushels of wheat an acre. He was given notice of such allotment in July of 1940 before the Fall planting of his 1941 crop of wheat, and again in July of 1941, before it was harvested. He sowed, however, 23 acres, and harvested from his 11.9 acres of excess acreage 239 bushels, which under the terms of the Act as amended on May 26, 1941, constituted farm marketing excess, subject to a penalty of 49 cents a bushel, or $117.11 in all. The appellee has not paid the penalty and he has not postponed or avoided it by storing the excess under regulations of the Secretary of Agriculture, or by delivering it up to the Secretary. The Committee, therefore, refused him a marketing card, which was, under the terms of Regulations promulgated by the Secretary, necessary to protect a buyer from liability to the penalty and upon its protecting lien.

The general scheme of the Agricultural Adjustment Act of 1938 as related to wheat is to control the volume moving in interstate and foreign commerce in order to avoid surpluses and shortages and the consequent abnormally low or high wheat prices and obstructions to commerce. Within prescribed limits and by prescribed standards the Secretary of Agriculture is directed to ascertain and proclaim each year a national acreage allotment for the next crop of wheat, which is then apportioned to the states and their counties, and is eventually broken up into allotments for individual farms. Loans and payments to wheat farmers are authorized in stated circumstances.

. . . .

II

It is urged that under the Commerce Clause of the Constitution, Article I, § 8, clause 3, Congress does not possess the power it has in this instance sought to exercise. The question would merit little consideration since our decision in *United States v. Darby*, 312 U.S. 100 (1941), sustaining the federal power to regulate production of goods for commerce except for the fact that this Act extends federal regulation to production not intended in any part for commerce but wholly for consumption on the farm. The Act includes a definition of "market" and its derivatives so that as related to wheat in addition to its conventional meaning it also means to dispose of "by feeding (in any form) to poultry or livestock which, or the products of which, are sold, bartered, or exchanged, or to be so disposed of." Hence, marketing quotas not only embrace all that may be sold without penalty but also what may be consumed on the premises. Wheat produced on excess acreage is designated as "available for marketing" as so defined, and the penalty is imposed thereon. Penalties do not depend upon whether any part of the wheat either within or without the quota is sold or intended to be sold. The sum of this is that the Federal Government fixes a quota including all that the farmer may harvest for sale or for his own farm needs, and declares that wheat produced on excess acreage may neither be disposed of nor used except upon payment of the penalty, or except it is stored as required by the Act or delivered to the Secretary of Agriculture.

Appellee says that this is a regulation of production and consumption of wheat. Such activities are, he urges, beyond the reach of Congressional power under the Commerce Clause, since they are local in character, and their effects upon interstate commerce are at most "indirect." In answer the Government argues that the statute regulates neither production nor consumption, but only marketing; and, in the alternative, that if the Act does go beyond the regulation of marketing it is sustainable as a "necessary and proper" implementation of the power of Congress over interstate commerce.

The Government's concern lest the Act be held to be a regulation of production or consumption rather than of marketing is attributable to a few dicta and decisions of this Court which might be understood to lay it down that activities such as "production," "manufacturing," and "mining" are strictly "local" and, except in special circumstances which are not present here, cannot be regulated under the commerce power because their effects upon interstate commerce are, as matter of law, only "indirect." Even today, when this power has been held to have great latitude, there is no decision of this Court that such activities may be regulated where no part of the product is intended for interstate commerce or intermingled with the subjects thereof. We believe that a review of the course of decision under the Commerce Clause will make plain, however, that questions of the power of Congress are not to be decided by reference to any formula which would give controlling force to nomenclature such as "production" and "indirect" and foreclose consideration of the actual effects of the activity in question upon interstate commerce.

At the beginning Chief Justice Marshall described the federal commerce power with a breadth never yet exceeded. *Gibbons v. Ogden*, 22 U.S. 1, 194–95 (1824). He made emphatic the embracing and penetrating nature of this power by warning that effective restraints on its exercise must proceed from political rather than from judicial processes. *Id.* at 197.

For nearly a century, however, decisions of this Court under the Commerce Clause dealt rarely with questions of what Congress might do in the exercise of its granted power under the Clause, and almost entirely with the permissibility of state activity which it was claimed discriminated against or burdened interstate commerce. . . . Certain activities such as "production," "manufacturing," and "mining" were occasionally said to be within the province of state governments and beyond the power of Congress under the Commerce Clause.

It was not until 1887 with the enactment of the Interstate Commerce Act, that the interstate commerce power began to exert positive influence in American law and life. The first important federal resort to the commerce power was followed in 1890 by the Sherman Anti-Trust Act and, thereafter, mainly after 1903, by many others. . . .

When it first dealt with this new legislation, the Court adhered to its earlier pronouncements, and allowed but little scope to the power of Congress. *United States v. E.C. Knight Co.*, 156 U.S. 1 (1895).[18] These earlier pronouncements also played an important part in several of the five cases in which this Court later held that Acts of Congress under the Commerce Clause were in excess of its power.[19]

. . . .

Not long after the decision of *United States v. E.C. Knight Co.*, Justice Holmes, in sustaining the exercise of national power over intrastate activity, stated for the Court that "commerce among the States is not a technical legal conception, but a practical one, drawn from the course of business." *Swift & Co. v. United States*, 196 U.S. 375, 398 (1905). It was soon demonstrated that the effects of many kinds of intrastate activity upon interstate commerce were such as to make them a proper subject of federal regulation. In some cases sustaining the exercise of federal power over intrastate

---

[18] [20] *Hopkins v. United States*, 171 U.S. 578 (1898); *Anderson v. United States*, 171 U.S. 604 (1898).

[19] [21] *Employers Liability Cases*, 207 U.S. 463 (1908); *Hammer v. Dagenhart*, 247 U.S. 251 (1918); *Railroad Retirement Bd. v. Alton R. Co.*, 295 U.S. 330 (1935); *A.L.A. Schechter Poultry Corp. v. United States*, 295 U.S. 495 (1935); *Carter v. Carter Coal Co.*, 298 U.S. 238 (1936).

matters the term "direct" was used for the purpose of stating, rather than of reaching, a result; in others it was treated as synonymous with "substantial" or "material"; and in others it was not used at all. Of late its use has been abandoned in cases dealing with questions of federal power under the Commerce Clause.

In the *Shreveport Rate Cases*, 234 U.S. 342 (1914), the Court held that railroad rates of an admittedly intrastate character and fixed by authority of the state might, nevertheless, be revised by the Federal Government because of the economic effects which they had on interstate commerce. The opinion of Justice Hughes found federal intervention constitutionally authorized because of "matters having such a close and substantial relation to interstate traffic that the control is essential or appropriate to the security of that traffic, to the efficiency of the interstate service, and to the maintenance of conditions under which interstate commerce may be conducted upon fair terms and without molestation or hindrance." *Id.* at 351.

The Court's recognition of the relevance of the economic effects in the application of the Commerce Clause, exemplified by this statement, has made the mechanical application of legal formulas no longer feasible. Once an economic measure of the reach of the power granted to Congress in the Commerce Clause is accepted, questions of federal power cannot be decided simply by finding the activity in question to be "production," nor can consideration of its economic effects be foreclosed by calling them "indirect." The present Chief Justice has said in summary of the present state of the law: "The commerce power is not confined in its exercise to the regulation of commerce among the states. It extends to those activities intrastate which so affect interstate commerce, or the exertion of the power of Congress over it, as to make regulation of them appropriate means to the attainment of a legitimate end, the effective execution of the granted power to regulate interstate commerce. . . . The power of Congress over interstate commerce is plenary and complete in itself, may be exercised to its utmost extent, and acknowledges no limitations other than are prescribed in the Constitution. . . . It follows that no form of state activity can constitutionally thwart the regulatory power granted by the commerce clause to Congress. Hence the reach of that power extends to those intrastate activities which in a substantial way interfere with or obstruct the exercise of the granted power." *United States v. Wrightwood Dairy Co.*, 315 U.S. 110, 119 (1942).

Whether the subject of the regulation in question was "production," "consumption," or "marketing" is, therefore, not material for purposes of deciding the question of federal power before us. That an activity is of local character may help in a doubtful case to determine whether Congress intended to reach it. The same consideration might help in determining whether in the absence of Congressional action it would be permissible for the state to exert its power on the subject matter, even though in so doing it to some degree affected interstate commerce. But even if appellee's activity be local and though it may not be regarded as commerce, it may still, whatever its nature, be reached by Congress if it exerts a substantial economic effect on interstate commerce, and this irrespective of whether such effect is what might at some earlier time have been defined as "direct" or "indirect."

. . . .

The wheat industry has been a problem industry for some years. Largely as a result of increased foreign production and import restrictions, annual exports of wheat and flour from the United States during the ten-year period ending in 1940 averaged less than 10 per cent of total production, while during the 1920's they averaged more than 25 per cent. The decline in the export trade has left a large surplus in production which, in connection with an abnormally large supply of wheat and other grains in recent years, caused congestion in a number of markets; tied up railroad cars; and caused elevators in some instances to turn away grains, and railroads to institute embargoes to prevent further congestion.

Many countries . . . have sought to modify the impact of the world market conditions on their own economy. Importing countries have taken measures to stimulate production and self-sufficiency. The four large exporting countries of Argentina, Australia, Canada, and the United States have all undertaken various programs for the relief of growers. Such measures have been designed, in part at least, to protect the domestic price received by producers. Such plans have generally evolved towards control by the central government.

. . . .

The maintenance by government regulation of a price for wheat undoubtedly can be accomplished as effectively by sustaining or increasing the demand as by limiting the supply. The effect of the statute before us is to restrict the amount which may be produced for market and the extent as well to which one may forestall resort to the market by producing to meet his own needs. That appellee's own contribution to the demand for wheat may be trivial by itself is not enough to remove him from the scope of federal regulation where, as here, his contribution, taken together with that of many others similarly situated, is far from trivial. *United States v. Darby*, 312 U.S. 100, 123 (1941); *NLRB v. Fainblatt*, 306 U.S. 601, 606 (1939).

It is well established by decisions of this Court that the power to regulate commerce includes the power to regulate the prices at which commodities in that commerce are dealt in and practices affecting such prices. *Swift & Co. v. United States*, 196 U.S. 375 (1905). One of the primary purposes of the Act in question was to increase the market price of wheat, and to that end to limit the volume thereof that could affect the market. It can hardly be denied that a factor of such volume and variability as home-consumed wheat would have a substantial influence on price and market conditions. This may arise because being in marketable condition such wheat overhangs the market and, if induced by rising prices, tends to flow into the market and check price increases. But if we assume that it is never marketed, it supplies a need of the man who grew it which would otherwise be reflected by purchases in the open market. Home-grown wheat in this sense competes with wheat in commerce. The stimulation of commerce is a use of the regulatory function quite as definitely as prohibitions or restrictions thereon. This record leaves us in no doubt that Congress may properly have considered that wheat consumed on the farm where grown, if wholly outside the scheme of regulation, would have a substantial effect in defeating and obstructing its purpose to stimulate trade therein at increased prices.

It is said, however, that this Act, forcing some farmers into the market to buy what they could provide for themselves, is an unfair promotion of the markets and prices of specializing wheat growers. It is of the essence of regulation that it lays a restraining hand on the self-interest of the regulated and that advantages from the regulation commonly fall to others. The conflicts of economic interest between the regulated and those who advantage by it are wisely left under our system to resolution by the Congress under its more flexible and responsible legislative process. Such conflicts rarely lend themselves to judicial determination. And with the wisdom, workability, or fairness, of the plan of regulation we have nothing to do.

. . . .

Reversed.

Exercise 12(B):

Consider the following matters in connection with the Supreme Court's decision in *Wickard v. Filburn:*

(1) For purposes of defining the scope of federal legislative power, did it matter that Filburn was not primarily a wheat farmer, that he grew wheat to feed his cows and

chickens?

(2) For purposes of defining the scope of federal legislative power, did it matter that a majority of wheat farmers approved the production quotas? Could Congress have imposed the quotas without such a vote?

(3) How did Filburn's production of wheat on his own farm for his own use affect interstate commerce? What was the Court's rationale?

(4) It stretches the imagination to conceive how Filburn's excess production would have had any measurable effect on wheat markets. What new technique did the Court introduce to justify the federal regulation of his production?

(5) What was the meaning of the Court's statement that "effective restraints on" congressional exercise of its power to regulate interstate commerce "must proceed from political rather from judicial processes"? Was the Court saying that the judiciary would not enforce any limits on Congress when legislating under the commerce power? If so, how is that consistent with the Court's self-appointed role as "final arbiter" of the Constitution? May the Court simultaneously insist on judicial review (if not judicial supremacy) and selectively abdicate that role? Assuming the Court could abdicate its role of ensuring Congress remains within constitutional boundaries, should it do so *after* a series of cases in which it overruled precedents defining limits to congressional power?

(6) What limits, if any, remain on federal legislative power after *Wickard*? Is there any measure beyond the reach of Congress under the commerce power?

(7) In *Wickard,* the Court confronted a federal statute designed to support prices for commodities by limiting production. Does federal power to legislate under the Commerce Clause at least require a similar context? That is, must Congress at least be addressing a matter that is predominantly economic or may the commerce power be used to reach other matters that have only an incidental economic effect?

(8) To the extent that *Darby* and/or *Wickard* departed from earlier Supreme Court precedents, do they involve any of the special circumstances that overcome *stare decisis* as stated in *Planned Parenthood v. Casey*, discussed in *Volume 1*?

HEART OF ATLANTA MOTEL, INC. v. UNITED STATES
379 U.S. 241 (1964)

JUSTICE CLARK delivered the opinion of the Court.

This is a declaratory judgment action attacking the constitutionality of Title II of the Civil Rights Act of 1964. In addition to declaratory relief the complaint sought an injunction restraining the enforcement of the Act and damages against appellees based on allegedly resulting injury in the event compliance was required. Appellees counterclaimed for enforcement under § 206(a) of the Act . . . . A three-judge court . . . sustained the validity of the Act and issued a permanent injunction on appellees' counterclaim restraining appellant from continuing to violate the Act . . . . We affirm the judgment.

1. *The Factual Background and Contentions of the Parties*

The case comes here on admissions and stipulated facts. Appellant owns and operates the Heart of Atlanta Motel which has 216 rooms available to transient guests. The motel is located on Courtland Street, two blocks from downtown Peachtree Street. It is readily accessible to interstate highways 75 and 85 and state highways 23 and 41. Appellant solicits patronage from outside the State of Georgia through various national advertising media, including magazines of national circulation; it maintains over 50 billboards and highway signs within the State, soliciting patronage for the motel; it accepts convention trade from outside Georgia and approximately 75% of its registered guests are from out of State. Prior to passage of the Act the motel had followed a practice of refusing to rent rooms to Negroes, and it alleged that it intended to continue to do so. In an effort to perpetuate that policy this suit was filed.

The appellant contends that Congress in passing this Act exceeded its power to regulate commerce under Art. I, § 8, cl. 3, of the Constitution of the United States; [and,] that the Act violates the Fifth Amendment because appellant is deprived of the right to choose its customers and operate its business as it wishes, resulting in a taking of its liberty and property without due process of law and a taking of its property without just compensation . . . .

The appellees counter that the unavailability to Negroes of adequate accommodations interferes significantly with interstate travel, and that Congress, under the Commerce Clause, has power to remove such obstructions and restraints; [and] that the Fifth Amendment does not forbid reasonable regulation and that consequential damage does not constitute a "taking" within the meaning of that amendment . . . .

At the trial the appellant offered no evidence, submitting the case on the pleadings, admissions and stipulation of facts; however, appellees proved the refusal of the motel to accept Negro transients after the passage of the Act. The District Court sustained the constitutionality of the sections of the Act under attack and issued a permanent injunction on the counterclaim of the appellees. It restrained the appellant from "[r]efusing to accept Negroes as guests in the motel by reason of their race or color" and from "[m]aking any distinction whatever upon the basis of race or color in the availability of the goods, services, facilities privileges, advantages or accommodations offered or made available to the guests of the motel, or to the general public, within or upon any of the premises of the Heart of Atlanta Motel, Inc."

2. *The History of the Act*

Congress first evidenced its interest in civil rights legislation in the Civil Rights or Enforcement Act of April 9, 1866. There followed four Acts, with a fifth, the Civil Rights Act of March 1, 1875, culminating the series. In 1883 this Court struck down the public accommodations sections of the 1875 Act in the 1875 Act in the *Civil Rights Cases,* 109 U.S. 3 (1883). No major legislation in this field had been enacted by Congress for 82 years when the Civil Rights Act of 1957 became law. It was followed by the Civil Rights Act of 1960. Three years later, on June 19, 1963, the late President Kennedy called for civil rights legislation in a message to Congress to which he attached a proposed bill. Its stated purpose was

> to promote the general welfare by eliminating discrimination based on race, color, religion, or national origin in . . . public accommodations through the exercise by Congress of the powers conferred upon it . . . to enforce the provisions of the fourteenth and fifteenth amendments, to regulate commerce among the several States, and to make laws necessary and proper to execute the powers conferred upon it by the Constitution.

H.R. Doc. No. 124, 88th Cong., 1st Sess., at 14. Bills were introduced in each House of the Congress, embodying the President's suggestion, one in the Senate being S. 1732 and one in the House, H.R. 7152. However, it was not until July 2, 1964, upon the recommendation of President Johnson, that the Civil Rights Act of 1964, here under attack, was finally passed.

. . . .

The Act as finally adopted was most comprehensive, undertaking to prevent through peaceful and voluntary settlement discrimination in voting, as well as in places of accommodation and public facilities, federally secured programs and in employment.

Since Title II is the only portion under attack here, we confine our consideration to those public accommodation provisions.

3. *Title II of the Act*

This Title is divided into seven sections beginning with § 201(a) which provides that:

All persons shall be entitled to the full and equal enjoyment of the goods, services, facilities, privileges, advantages, and accommodations of any place of public accommodation, as defined in this section, without discrimination or segregation on the ground of race, color, religion, or national origin.

There are listed in § 201(b) four classes of business establishments, each of which "serves the public" and "is a place of public accommodation" within the meaning of § 201(a) "if its operations affect commerce, or if discrimination or segregation by it is supported by State action." . . . [Section 201(c)] declares that "any inn, hotel, motel, or other establishment which provides lodging to transient guests" affects commerce per se.

. . . .

In addition, § 202 affirmatively declares that all persons "shall be entitled to be free, at any establishment or place, from discrimination or segregation of any kind on the ground of race, color, religion, or national origin, if such discrimination or segregation is or purports to be required by any law, statute, ordinance, regulation, rule, or order of a State or any agency or political subdivision thereof."

. . . .

4. *Application of Title II to the Heart of Atlanta Motel*

It is admitted that the operation of the motel brings it within the provisions of § 201(a) of the Act and that appellant refused to provide lodging for transient Negroes because of their race or color and that it intends to continue that policy unless restrained.

The sole question posed is, therefore, the constitutionality of the Civil Rights Act of 1964 as applied to these facts. The legislative history of the Act indicates that Congress based the Act on § 5 and the Equal Protection Clause of the Fourteenth Amendment as well as its power to regulate interstate commerce under Art. I, § 8, cl. 3, of the Constitution.

. . . .

5. *The Civil Rights Cases, 109 U.S. 3 (1883), and their Application*

In light of our ground for decision, it might be well at the outset to discuss the *Civil Rights Cases* which declared provisions of the Civil Rights Act of 1875 unconstitutional. We think that decision inapposite, and without precedential value in determining the constitutionality of the present Act. Unlike Title II of the present legislation, the 1875 Act broadly proscribed discrimination in "inns, public conveyances on land or water, theaters, and other places of public amusement," without limiting the categories of affected businesses to those impinging upon interstate commerce. In contrast, the applicability of Title II is carefully limited to enterprises having a direct and substantial relation to the interstate flow of goods and people, except where state action is involved. Further, the fact that certain kinds of businesses may not in 1875 have been sufficiently involved in interstate commerce to warrant bringing them within the ambit of the commerce power is not necessarily dispositive of the same question today. Our populace had not reached its present mobility, nor were facilities, goods and services circulating as readily in interstate commerce as they are today. Although the principles which we apply today are those first formulated by Chief Justice Marshall in *Gibbons v. Ogden,* 22 U.S. 1 (1824), the conditions of transportation and commerce have changed dramatically, and we must apply those principles to the present state of commerce. The sheer increase in volume of interstate traffic alone would give discriminatory practices which inhibit travel a far larger impact upon the Nation's commerce than such practices had on the economy of another day. Finally, there is language in the *Civil Rights Cases* which indicates that the Court did not fully consider whether the 1875 Act could be sustained as an exercise of the commerce power. Though the Court observed that "no one will contend that the power to pass it was contained in the constitution before the adoption of the last three amendments [Thirteenth, Fourteenth, and Fifteenth]," the Court went on specifically to note that the Act was not "conceived" in terms of the commerce power and expressly pointed out:

> Of course, these remarks [as to the lack of congressional power] do not apply to those cases in which Congress is clothed with direct and plenary powers of legislation over the whole subject, accompanied by an express or implied denial of such power to the States, as in the regulation of commerce with foreign nations, among the several States, and with the Indian tribes . . . . In these cases Congress has power to pass laws for regulating the subjects specified in every detail, and the conduct and transactions of individuals in respect thereof.

109 U.S. at 18. Since the commerce power was not relied on by the Government and was without support in the record it is understandable that the Court narrowed its inquiry and excluded the Commerce Clause as a possible source of power. In any event, it is clear that such a limitation renders the opinion devoid of authority for the proposition that the Commerce Clause gives no power to Congress to regulate discriminatory practices now found substantially to affect interstate commerce. We, therefore, conclude that the *Civil Rights Cases* have no relevance to the basis of decision here where the Act explicitly relies upon the commerce power, and where the record is filled with testimony of obstructions and restraints resulting from the discriminations found to be existing. We now pass to that phase of the case.

6. *The Basis of Congressional Action*

While the Act as adopted carried no congressional findings the record of its passage through each house is replete with evidence of the burdens that discrimination by race or color places upon interstate commerce. *See* Hearings before Senate Comm. on Commerce on S. 1732, 88th Cong., 1st Sess.; S. Rep. No. 872; Hearings before Senate Comm. on the Judiciary on S. 1731, 88th Cong., 1st Sess.; Hearings Before the House Subcomm. No. 5 of the Comm. on the Judiciary on miscellaneous proposals regarding Civil Rights, 88th Cong., 1st Sess., ser. 4; H.R. Rep. No. 914. This testimony included the fact that our people have become increasingly mobile with millions of people of all races traveling from State to State; that Negroes in particular have been the subject of discrimination in transient accommodations, having to travel great distances to secure the same; that often they have been unable to obtain accommodations and have had to call upon friends to put them up overnight; and that these conditions had become so acute as to require the listing of available lodging for Negroes in a special guidebook which was itself "dramatic testimony to the difficulties" Negroes encounter in travel. These exclusionary practices were found to be nationwide, the Under Secretary of Commerce testifying that there is "no question that this discrimination in the North still exists to a large degree" and in the West and Midwest as well. This testimony indicated a qualitative as well as quantitative effect on interstate travel by Negroes. . . . We shall not burden this opinion with further details since the voluminous testimony presents overwhelming evidence that discrimination by hotels and motels impedes interstate travel.

7. *The Power of Congress Over Interstate Travel*

The power of Congress to deal with these obstructions depends on the meaning of the Commerce Clause. Its meaning was first enunciated 140 years ago by the great Chief Justice John Marshall in *Gibbons v. Ogden*, in these words:

> The subject to be regulated is commerce; and . . . to ascertain the extent of the power, it becomes necessary to settle the meaning of the word. The counsel for the appellee would limit it to traffic, to buying and selling, or the interchange of commodities . . . but it is something more: it is intercourse . . . between nations, and parts of nations, in all its branches, and is regulated by prescribing rules for carrying on that intercourse.
>
> . . . .

22 U.S. at 189–190, 193–94, 194–95, 196–97. . . .

That the "intercourse" of which the Chief Justice spoke included the movement of persons through more States than one was settled as early as 1849, in the *Passenger Cases*, 48 U.S. 283 (1849), where Justice McLean stated: "That the transportation of passengers is a part of commerce is not now an open question." *Id.* at 401. Again in 1913 Justice McKenna, speaking for the Court, said: "Commerce among the states, we have said, consists of intercourse and traffic between their citizens, and includes the transportation of persons and property." *Hoke v. United States*, 227 U.S. 308, 320 (1913). . . . Nor does it make any difference whether the transportation is commercial in character. . . .

The same interest in protecting interstate commerce which led Congress to deal with segregation in interstate carriers and the white-slave traffic has prompted it to extend the exercise of its power to gambling, *Lottery Case*, 188 U.S. 321 (1903); to criminal enterprises, *Brooks v. United States*, 267 U.S. 432 (1925); to deceptive practices in the sale of products, *FTC v. Mandel Bros., Inc.*, 359 U.S. 385 (1959); to fraudulent security transactions, *SEC v. Ralston Purina Co.*, 346 U.S. 119 (1953); to misbranding of drugs, *Weeks v. United States*, 245 U.S. 618 (1918); to wages and hours, *United States v. Darby*, 312 U.S. 100 (1941); to members of labor unions, *NLRB v. Jones & Laughlin Steel Corp.*, 301 U.S. 1 (1937); to crop control, *Wickard v. Filburn*, 317 U.S. 111 (1942); to discrimination against shippers, *United States v. Baltimore & Ohio R. Co.*, 333 U.S. 169 (1948); to the protection of small business from injurious price cutting, *Moore v. Mead's Fine Bread Co.*, 348 U.S. 115 (1954); to resale price maintenance, *Hudson Distributors, Inc. v. Eli Lilly & Co.*, 377 U.S. 386 (1964); to professional football, *Radovich v. National Football League*, 352 U.S. 445 (1957); and to racial discrimination by owners and managers of terminal restaurants, *Boynton v. Virginia*, 364 U.S. 454 (1960).

That Congress was legislating against moral wrongs in many of these areas rendered its enactments no less valid. In framing Title II of this Act Congress was also dealing with what it considered a moral problem. . . .

It is said that the operation of the motel here is of a purely local character. But, assuming this to be true, "[i]f it is interstate commerce that feels the pinch, it does not matter how local the operation which applies the squeeze." *United States v. Women's Sportswear Mfrs. Ass'n*, 336 U.S. 460, 464 (1949). . . . As Chief Justice Stone put it in *United States v. Darby*:

> The power of Congress over interstate commerce is not confined to the regulation of commerce among the states. It extends to those activities intrastate which so affect interstate commerce or the exercise of the power of Congress over it as to make regulation of them appropriate means to the attainment of a legitimate end, the exercise of the granted power of Congress to regulate interstate commerce.

312 U.S. 100, 118 (1941) (citing *McCulloch v. Maryland*, 17 U.S. 316, 421 (1819)). Thus the power of Congress to promote interstate commerce also includes the power to regulate the local incidents thereof, including local activities in both the States of origin and destination, which might have a substantial and harmful effect upon that commerce. One need only examine the evidence which we have discussed above to see that Congress may — as it has — prohibit racial discrimination by motels serving travelers, however "local" their operations may appear.

. . . The commerce power invoked here by Congress is a specific and plenary one authorized by the Constitution itself. The only questions are: (1) whether Congress had a rational basis for finding that racial discrimination by motels affected commerce, and (2) if it has such a basis, whether the means it selected to eliminate that evil are reasonable and appropriate. If they are, appellant has no "right" to select its guests as it sees fit, free from governmental regulation.

There is nothing novel about such legislation. Thirty-two States now have it on their books either by statute or executive order and many cities provide such regulation. . . .

. . . .

It is doubtful if in the long run appellant will suffer economic loss as a result of the Act. Experience is to the contrary where discrimination is completely obliterated as to all public accommodations. But whether this be true or not is of no consequence since this Court has specifically held that the fact that a "member of the class which is regulated may suffer economic losses not shared by others . . . has never been a barrier" to such legislation. *Bowles v. Willingham*, 321 U.S. 503, 518 (1944). Likewise in a long line of cases this Court has rejected the claim that the prohibition of racial discrimination in public accommodations interferes with personal liberty. *See District of Columbia v. John R. Thompson Co.*, 346 U.S. 100 (1953), and cases there cited, where we concluded that Congress had delegated law-making power to the District of Columbia "as broad as the police power of a state" which included the power to adopt a "law prohibiting discriminations against Negroes by the owners and managers of restaurants in the District of Columbia." *Id.* at 110. Neither do we find any merit in the claim that the Act is a taking of property without just compensation. The cases are to the contrary. *See Omnia Commercial Co. v. United States*, 261 U.S. 502 (1923).

. . . .

We, therefore, conclude that the action of the Congress in the adoption of the Act as applied here to a motel which concededly serves interstate travelers is within the power granted it by the Commerce Clause of the Constitution, as interpreted by this Court for 140 years. It may be argued that Congress could have pursued other methods to eliminate the obstructions it found in interstate commerce caused by racial discrimination. But this is a matter of policy that rests entirely with the Congress not with the courts. How obstructions in commerce may be removed — what means are to be employed — is within the sound and exclusive discretion of the Congress. It is subject only to one caveat — that the means chosen by it must be reasonably adapted to the end permitted by the Constitution. We cannot say that its choice here was not so adapted. The Constitution requires no more.

Affirmed.

JUSTICE BLACK, concurring.

In the first of these two cases the Heart of Atlanta Motel . . . appeals . . . . In the second case the Acting Attorney General of the United States and a United States Attorney appeal from a judgment of a three-judge United States District Court for the Northern District of Alabama holding that Title II cannot constitutionally be applied to Ollie's Barbecue, a restaurant in Birmingham, Alabama, which serves few if any interstate travelers but which buys a substantial quantity of food which has moved in interstate commerce. It is undisputed that both establishments had and intended to continue a policy against serving Negroes. Both claimed that Congress had exceeded its constitutional powers in attempting to compel them to use their privately owned businesses to serve customers whom they did not want to serve.

. . . .

I

It requires no novel or strained interpretation of the Commerce Clause to sustain Title II as applied in either of these cases. At least since *Gibbons v. Ogden,* 22 U.S. 1, decided in 1824 in an opinion by Chief Justice John Marshall, it has been uniformly accepted that the power of Congress to regulate commerce among the States is plenary, "complete in itself, may be exercised to its utmost extent, and acknowledges no limitations, other than are prescribed in the constitution." *Id.* at 196. Nor is "Commerce" as used in the Commerce Clause to be limited to a narrow, technical concept. It includes not only, as Congress has enumerated in the Act, "travel, trade, traffic, commerce, transportation, or communication," but also all other unitary transactions and activities that take place in more States than one. That some parts or segments of such unitary transactions may take place only in one State cannot, of course, take from Congress its plenary power to regulate them in the national interest. The facilities and instrumentalities used to carry on this commerce, such as railroads, truck lines, ships, rivers, and even highways are also subject to congressional regulation, so far as is necessary to keep interstate traffic upon fair and equal terms. *The Daniel Ball,* 77 U.S. 557 (1870).

Furthermore, it has long been held that the Necessary and Proper Clause, Art. I, § 8, cl. 18, adds to the commerce power of Congress the power to regulate local instrumentalities operating within a single State if their activities burden the flow of commerce among the States. Thus in the *Shreveport Case,* 234 U.S. 342, 353–54 (1914), this Court recognized that Congress could not fully carry out its responsibility to protect interstate commerce were its constitutional power to regulate that commerce to be strictly limited to prescribing the rules for controlling the things actually moving in such commerce or the contracts, transactions, and other activities, immediately concerning them. Regulation of purely intrastate railroad rates is primarily a local problem for state rather than national control. But the *Shreveport Case* sustained the power of Congress under the Commerce Power and the Necessary and Proper Clause to control purely intrastate rates, even though reasonable, where the effect of such rates was found to impose a discrimination injurious to interstate commerce. . . .

. . . .

The restaurant is located in a residential and industrial section of Birmingham, 11 blocks from the nearest interstate highway. Almost all, if not all, its patrons are local people rather than transients. It has seats for about 200 customers and annual gross sales of about $350,000. Most of its sales are of barbecued meat sandwiches and pies. Consequently, the main commodity it purchases is meat, of which during the 12 months before the District Court hearing it bought $69,683 worth (representing 46% of its total expenditures for supplies), which had been shipped into Alabama from outside the State. Plainly, 46% of the goods it sells is a "substantial" portion and amount. Congress concluded that restaurants which purchase a substantial quantity of goods from other States might well burden and disrupt the flow of interstate commerce if allowed to practice racial discrimination, because of the stifling and distorting effect that such discrimination on a wide scale might well have on the sale of goods shipped across state lines. Certainly this belief would not be irrational even had there not been a large body of evidence before the Congress to show the probability of this adverse effect.

The foregoing facts are more than enough, in my judgment, to show that Congress acting within its discretion and judgment has power under the Commerce Clause and the Necessary and Proper Clause to bar racial discrimination in the Heart of Atlanta Motel and Ollie's Barbecue. I recognize that every remote, possible, speculative effect on commerce should not be accepted as an adequate constitutional ground to uproot and throw into the discard all our traditional distinctions between what is purely local, and therefore controlled by state laws, and what affects the national interest and is therefore subject to control by federal laws. I recognize too that some isolated and remote lunchroom which sells only to local people and buys almost all its supplies in the locality may possibly be beyond the reach of the power of Congress to regulate commerce . . . .

Long ago this Court, again speaking through Mr. Chief Justice Marshall, said:

> Let the end be legitimate, let it be within the scope of the constitution, and all means which are appropriate, which are plainly adapted to that end, which are not prohibited, but consist with the letter and spirit of the constitution, are constitutional.

McCulloch v. State of Maryland, 17 U.S. 316, 421 (1819). By this standard Congress acted within its power here. In view of the Commerce Clause it is not possible to deny that the aim of protecting interstate commerce from undue burdens is a legitimate end. In view of the Thirteenth, Fourteenth and Fifteenth Amendments, it is not possible to deny that the aim of protecting Negroes from discrimination is also a legitimate end. The means adopted to achieve these ends are also appropriate, plainly adopted to achieve them and not prohibited by the Constitution but consistent with both its letter and spirit.

. . . .

III

For the foregoing reasons I concur in holding that the anti-racial-discrimination provisions of Title II of the Civil Rights Act of 1964 are valid as applied to this motel and this restaurant. I should add that nothing in the *Civil Rights Cases*, 109 U.S. 3 (1883), which invalidated the Civil Rights Act of 1875, gives the slightest support to the argument that Congress is without power under the Commerce Clause to enact the present legislation, since in the Civil Rights Cases this Court expressly left undecided the validity of such antidiscrimination legislation if rested on the Commerce Clause. *See id.* at 18–19. . . .

JUSTICE DOUGLAS, concurring.

. . . .

Though I join the Court's opinions, I am somewhat reluctant . . . to rest solely on the Commerce Clause. My reluctance is not due to any conviction that Congress lacks the power to regulate commerce in the interests of human rights. It is rather my belief that the right of people to be free of state action that discriminates against them because of race . . ."occupies a more protected position in our constitutional system than does the movement of cattle, fruit, steel and coal across state lines.". . .

Hence I would prefer to rest on the assertion of legislative power contained in § 5 of the Fourteenth Amendment . . . .

A decision based on the Fourteenth Amendment would have a more settling effect, making unnecessary litigation over whether a particular restaurant or inn is within the commerce definitions of the Act or whether a particular customer is an interstate traveler. . . .

. . . .

JUSTICE GOLDBERG, concurring.

I join in the opinions and judgment of the Court, since I agree "that the action of Congress in the adoption of the Act as applied here . . . is within the power granted it by the Commerce Clause of the Constitution, as interpreted by this Court for 140 years."

The primary purpose of the Civil Rights Act of 1964, however, as the Court recognizes, and as I would underscore, is the vindication of human dignity and not mere economics. . . .

. . . The cases cited in the Court's opinions are conclusive that Congress could exercise its powers under the Commerce Clause to accomplish this purpose. As §§ 201(b) and (c) are undoubtedly a valid exercise of the Commerce Clause power for the reasons stated in the opinions of the Court, the Court considers that it is unnecessary to consider whether it is additionally supportable by Congress' exertion of its power under § 5 of the Fourteenth Amendment.

. . . [I]n my view, Congress clearly had authority under both § 5 of the Fourteenth Amendment and the Commerce Clause to enact the Civil Rights Act of 1964.

Exercise 12(C):

Consider the following matters in connection with the Supreme Court's decision in *Heart of Atlanta Motel*:

(1)   In Part 1 of its opinion, the Court observed that the establishment was accessible to Interstate highways and that 75% of its guests were from another State. Were those facts critical to the Court's conclusion? If the establishment had been further removed from the highway and all its clientele were from within the county, would federal regulatory power still reach the establishment? Why or why not?

(2)   In Part 2 of its opinion, the Court noted that in 1883 it held that Congress lacked authority to enact prohibitions regulating discrimination on the basis of race by private owners of public accommodations when Congress sought to do so in 1875. What, if any, additional legislative powers did the Constitution grant Congress in 1964 by amendment subsequent to 1875?

(3)   In Part 3 of its opinion, the Court observed that the Civil Rights Act of 1964 asserted that " 'any inn, hotel, motel, or other establishment which provides lodging to transient guests affect commerce per se." Can Congress deem which activities affect commerce? If Congress does so, what weight should the judiciary give such statements when reviewing the constitutionality of the legislation? In Part 5 of its opinion, did the Court fairly characterize this aspect of the statute? Stated otherwise, if the 1875 Act had been limited to "establishment[s] which provide[] lodging to transient guests" and so excluded "other places of public amusement," would it have been constitutional? Why or why not?

(4)   In Part 5 of its opinion, the Court quoted from its 1883 precedent an assertion that the power of Congress to regulate under the Commerce Clause was an example of a "direct and plenary power[] of legislation over the whole subject, accompanied by an express or implied denial of such power to the States." Is that view of the commerce power consistent with the view of the Court in *Gibbons v. Ogden*? Is it consistent with the view of Justice Johnson in *Gibbons*? If there is an "express or implied denial" of the power for States to regulate commerce, is there a "dormant Commerce Clause"?

(5)   In Part 5 of its opinion, did the Court succeed in distinguishing its precedent in the *Civil Rights Cases*? Why or why not?

(6)   In Part 6 of its opinion, the Court noted that Congress compiled substantial evidence of the relationship between racial discrimination and interstate commerce.

What weight should the Court give to congressional findings and/or congressional investigation respecting whether the subject of its regulation is related to interstate commerce?

(7)   In Part 7 of its opinion, the Court stated that Congress has power under the Commerce Clause to regulate transportation of persons and property, even when the transportation is not "commercial" in character. Does that statement acknowledge any limit to the commerce power?

(8)   In Part 7 of its opinion, the Court asserted that even if an establishment was local in character and operation, Congress could regulate it so as to "promote interstate commerce." Does that statement acknowledge any limit to the commerce power?

(9)   In Part 7 of its opinion, the Court stated that its role in reviewing the legislation enacted under the Commerce Clause was limited to only two inquiries. What are the two inquiries? Do the two inquiries fairly encompass the Court's role in judicial review?

(10)   In Part 7 of its opinion, the Court asserted that its construction of the commerce power was consistent with 140 years of prior precedent. Is that a fair characterization of its earlier cases?

(11)   After the Court's decisions upholding the public accommodation provisions of the Civil Rights Act of 1964, what matters, if any, remain beyond the reach of federal legislation enacted under the commerce power?

(12)   In his concurring opinion, Justice Black made reference to the facts involving application of the Act to Ollie's Barbeque. What additional light, if any, does that information shed on Question 1?

(13)   In light of the Court's determination that Congress had the power under the Commerce Clause to regulate who Ollie's Barbecue chose to serve, what matters, if any, remain beyond the reach of federal legislation enacted under the commerce power?

(14)   In his concurring opinion, Justice Douglas suggested that the Act should be sustained on the basis of Section 5 of the Fourteenth Amendment. What argument, if any, is there that as applied to the specific establishments at issue in the case, the Act could not be upheld under the Equal Protection Clause and/or the power of Congress to enforce the Amendment under Section 5?

THE SOLICITOR GENERAL'S ARGUMENT IN *UNITED STATES v. LOPEZ*

From *Darby* forward, the Supreme Court repeatedly determined that various congressional enactments fell within the scope of the commerce power while continuing to pay at least lip service to the notion that the power was not unlimited. Had the Court explicitly stated otherwise, it would have buried what was left of the concept of a central government of limited and enumerated powers. At oral argument in *United States v. Lopez*, the Solicitor General invited the Court to take that step by repeatedly refusing to concede anything was beyond the scope of congressional power under the Commerce Clause.

Question: Well, let's do exactly that, and ask whether the simple possession of something at or near a school is commerce at all. Is it?

General Days: I think the answer to that is that it is, yes, Your Honor.

Question: I would have thought that it wasn't, and I would have thought that it, moreover, is not interstate.

General Days: Justice O'Connor —

Question: If this is covered, what's left of enumerated powers? . . . What is there that Congress could not do, under this rubric, if you are correct?

General Days: Justice O'Connor, that certainly is a question that one might ask, but this Court has asked that question in a number of other circumstances, and rather than starting from the assumption that something was inherently local, it's looked at the degree to which Congress had a reasonable basis for extending its authority under the commerce power to regulate that particular activity.

Question: But in some of those very cases, General Days, the statement is found that the power is not limitless.

General Days: Well, that is certainly the case, Chief Justice Rehnquist. That's an understanding from the Constitution, but one has to look at where the limitations are that are imposed by the Constitution itself.

Question: Well, what would be — if this case is — Congress can reach under the interstate commerce power, what would be an example of a case which you couldn't reach?

. . . .

Question: Can you tell me, Mr. Days, has there been anything in our recent history in the last 20 years where it appears that Congress made a considered judgment that it could not reach a particular subject?

(Laughter.)

General Days: I don't know whether there's been a conscious effort to do that, but I think as this Court has said in its Tenth Amendment jurisprudence that Congress reflects the will of the people, and it has built into it, and into its operations, a concern about the extent to which its regulations and its legislation would encroach on matters that have been traditionally left to the State.

. . . .

Question: But with reference to the commerce point, realistically, that's where we are. None of us at least can think of anything under our present case law, or at least under your argument, that Congress can't do if it chooses under the Commerce Clause, so if the Federal system must be preserved by someone, and the Commerce Clause is a means by which the Federal structure can be obliterated, and if we have no tools or analytic techniques to make these distinctions, then it follows that the Federal balance is remitted to the political judgment of the Congress.

General Days: Well, I think, Your Honor, in *Garcia* what this Court indicated was that the protection of this balance, insofar as the Tenth Amendment is concerned, really does reside with the political process and in Congress.

Question: I think that's the necessary consequence of the argument that you're making here.

General Days: It's not an argument that I concocted, Justice Kennedy. It's one that I think flows from this Court's decisions, and that one does — as I indicated to Justice O'Connor, one doesn't start the analysis by saying there are things that are clearly local and within local control that Congress cannot reach. The analysis has to be whether one can identify a rational basis for Congress' wanting to extend its commerce power into a particular area.

. . . .

Question: What are the limits, then? . . . How would you describe the check that the Court has?

General Days: Well, I'm perhaps left to repeat myself in some respects. This Court has never said that there are absolute limits to the exercise of the commerce power. It's looked at individual cases and tried to determine, exercising —

Question: What would be a case that would fall outside, other than . . . telling the State, in effect, you serve as federal official for this purpose?

General Days: I don't have —

Question: Don't give away anything here.

(Laughter.)

Question: They might want to do it next —

(Laughter.)

General Days: Your Honor, I —

Question: General Days, could I ask —

General Days: — the court has never looked at this in the abstract. It's not an abstract process. It's been viewed by the Court as an empirical process.

Question: But my point is, Mr. Days, maybe the constitutional system would be better served if we recognize that there are no judicial tools to do this.

UNITED STATES v. LOPEZ
514 U.S. 549 (1995)

CHIEF JUSTICE REHNQUIST delivered the opinion of the Court.

In the Gun-Free School Zones Act of 1990, Congress made it a federal offense "for any individual knowingly to possess a firearm at a place that the individual knows, or has reasonable cause to believe, is a school zone." 18 U.S.C. § 922(q)(1)(A). The Act neither regulates a commercial activity nor contains a requirement that the possession be connected in any way to interstate commerce. We hold that the Act exceeds the authority of Congress "[t]o regulate Commerce . . . among the several states . . . ." U.S. Const., Art. I, § 8, cl. 3.

On March 10, 1992, respondent, who was then a 12th-grade student, arrived at Edison High School in San Antonio, Texas, carrying a concealed .38-caliber handgun and five bullets. . . . He was arrested . . . . The next day, the state charges were dismissed after federal agents charged respondent by complaint with violating the Gun-Free School Zones Act of 1990. 18 U.S.C. § 922(q)(1)(A).

. . . .

On appeal, respondent challenged his conviction based on his claim that § 922(q) exceeded Congress' power to legislate under the Commerce Clause. The Court of Appeals for the Fifth Circuit agreed and reversed respondent's conviction. . . .

We start with first principles. The Constitution creates a Federal Government of enumerated powers. See Art. I, § 8. As James Madison wrote: "The powers delegated by the proposed Constitution to the federal government are few and defined. Those which are to remain in the State governments are numerous and indefinite." The Federalist No. 45. . . . "Just as the separation and independence of the coordinate branches of the Federal Government serve to prevent the accumulation of excessive power in any one branch, a healthy balance of power between the States and the Federal Government will reduce the risk of tyranny and abuse from either front." Gregory v. Ashcroft, 501 U.S. 452, 458 (1991).

. . . The Court, through Chief Justice Marshall, first defined the nature of Congress' commerce power in *Gibbons v. Ogden*, 22 U.S. 1, 189–90 (1824) . . . . The commerce power "is the power to regulate; that is, to prescribe the rule by which commerce is to be governed. This power, like all others vested in congress, is complete in itself, may be exercised to its utmost extent, and acknowledges no limitations other than are prescribed in the constitution." *Id.* at 196. The *Gibbons* Court, however, acknowledged that limitations on the commerce power are inherent in the very language of the Commerce Clause.

> It is not intended to say that these words comprehend that commerce, which is completely internal, which is carried on between man and man in a State, or between different parts of the same State, and which does not extend to or affect other States. Such a power would be inconvenient, and is certainly unnecessary.

> Comprehensive as the word "among" is, it may very properly be restricted to that commerce which concerns more States than one. . . . The enumeration presupposes something not enumerated; and that something, if we regard the language, or the subject of the sentence, must be the exclusively internal commerce of a State.

Id. at 194–94.

For nearly a century thereafter, the Court's Commerce Clause decisions dealt rarely with the extent of Congress' power. . . . Under this line of precedent, the Court held that certain categories of activity such as "production," "manufacturing," and "mining" were . . . beyond the power of Congress under the Commerce Clause. . . .

. . . [Later,] the Court held that, where interstate and intrastate aspects of commerce were so intermingled together that full regulation of interstate commerce required incidental regulation of intrastate commerce, the Commerce Clause authorized such regulation. *See, e.g., Shreveport Rate Cases*, 234 U.S. 342 (1914).

In *A.L.A. Schechter Poultry Corp. v. United States*, 295 U.S. 495, 550 (1935), the Court struck down regulations that fixed the hours and wages of individuals employed by an intrastate business because the activity being regulated related to interstate commerce only indirectly. . . .

Two years later, in the watershed case of *NLRB v. Jones & Laughlin Steel Corp.*, 301 U.S. 1 (1937), the Court upheld the National Labor Relations Act against a Commerce Clause challenge, and in the process, departed from the distinction between "direct" and "indirect" effects on interstate commerce. *Id.* at 36–38. . . .

In *United States v. Darby*, 312 U.S. 100 (1941), the Court upheld the Fair Labor Standards Act. . . .

In *Wickard v. Filburn*, the Court upheld the application of amendments to the Agricultural Adjustment Act of 1938 to the production of homegrown wheat. . . .

Jones & Laughlin Steel, Darby, and *Wickard* ushered in an era of Commerce Clause jurisprudence that greatly expanded the previously defined authority of Congress under that Clause. . . .

But even these modern-era precedents which have expanded congressional power under the Commerce Clause confirm that this power is subject to outer limits. In *Jones & Laughlin Steel*, the Court warned that the scope of the interstate commerce power "must be considered in the light of our dual system of government and may not be extended so as to embrace effects upon interstate commerce so indirect and remote that to embrace them, in view of our complex society, would effectually obliterate the distinction between what is national and what is local and create a completely centralized government." 301 U.S. at 37. . . . Since that time, the Court has heeded that warning and undertaken to decide whether a rational basis existed for concluding that a regulated activity sufficiently affected interstate commerce. . . .

Similarly, in *Maryland v. Wirtz*, 392 U.S. 183 (1968), the Court reaffirmed that "the power to regulate commerce, though broad indeed, has limits" that "[t]he Court has ample power to enforce." *Id.* at 196, overruled on other grounds, *National League of Cities v. Usery*, 426 U.S. 833 (1976), overruled by *Garcia v. SAMTA*, 469 U.S. 528 (1985). . . . [T]he *Wirtz* Court replied that the dissent had misread precedent as "[n]either here nor in *Wickard* has the Court declared that Congress may use a relatively trivial impact on commerce as an excuse for broad general regulation of state or private activities," *id.* at 197 n.27. Rather, "[t]he Court has said only that where a *general regulatory statute bears a substantial relation to commerce*, the *de minimis* character of individual instances arising under the statute is of no consequence." *Id.* (first emphasis added).

Consistent with this structure, we have identified three broad categories of activity that Congress may regulate under its commerce power. First, Congress may regulate the use of the channels of interstate commerce. *See, e.g., Darby*, 312 U.S. at 114; *Heart of Atlanta Motel*, 379 U.S. at 256. . . . Second, Congress is empowered to regulate and protect the instrumentalities of interstate commerce, or persons or things in interstate commerce, even though the threat may come only from intrastate activities. *See, e.g., Shreveport Rate Cases*, 234 U.S. 342 (1914). . . . Finally, Congress' commerce authority includes the power to regulate those activities having a substantial relation to interstate commerce, *Jones & Laughlin Steel*, 301 U.S. at 37, *i.e.*, those activities that substantially affect interstate commerce. *Wirtz*, 392 U.S. at 196 n.27.

Within this final category, admittedly, our case law has not been clear whether an activity must "affect" or "substantially affect" interstate commerce in order to be within Congress' power to regulate it under the Commerce Clause. . . . We conclude, consistent with the great weight of our case law, that the proper test requires an analysis of whether the regulated activity "substantially affects" interstate commerce.

We now turn to consider the power of Congress, in the light of this framework, to enact § 922(q). The first two categories of authority may be quickly disposed of: § 922(q) is not a regulation on the use of the channels of interstate commerce, nor is it an attempt to prohibit the interstate transportation of a commodity through the channels of commerce; nor can § 922(q) be justified as a regulation by which Congress has sought to protect an instrumentality of interstate commerce or a thing in interstate commerce. Thus, if § 922(q) is to be sustained, it must be under the third category as a regulation of an activity that substantially affects interstate commerce.

First, we have upheld a wide variety of congressional Acts regulating intrastate economic activity where we have concluded that the activity substantially affected interstate commerce. Examples include the regulation of intrastate coal mining, intrastate extortionate credit transactions, restaurants utilizing substantial interstate supplies, inns and hotels catering to interstate guests, and production and consumption of homegrown wheat. . . . Where economic activity substantially affects interstate commerce, legislation regulating that activity will be sustained.

Even *Wickard*, which is perhaps the most far reaching example of Commerce Clause authority over intrastate activity, involved economic activity in a way that the possession of a gun in a school zone does not. . . . The Court said, in an opinion sustaining the application of the Act to Filburn's activity: "One of the primary purposes of the Act in question was to increase the market price of wheat and to that end to limit the volume thereof that could affect the market. It can hardly be denied that a factor of such volume and variability as home-consumed wheat would have a substantial influence on price and market conditions. . . ." 317 U.S. at 128.

Section 922(q) is a criminal statute that by its terms has nothing to do with "commerce" or any sort of economic enterprise, however broadly one might define those terms.[3] Section 922(q) is not an essential part of a larger regulation of economic activity, in which the regulatory scheme could be undercut unless the intrastate activity were regulated. It cannot, therefore, be sustained under our cases upholding regulations of activities that arise out of or are connected with a commercial transaction, which viewed in the aggregate, substantially affects interstate commerce.

Second, § 922(q) contains no jurisdictional element which would ensure, through case-by-case inquiry, that the firearm possession in question affects interstate commerce. For example, in *United States v. Bass*, 404 U.S. 336 (1971), the Court interpreted former 18 U.S.C. § 1202(a), which made it a crime for a felon to "receiv[e], posses[s], or transpor[t] in commerce or affecting commerce . . . any firearm." 404 U.S. at 337. The Court interpreted the possession component of § 1202(a) to require an additional nexus to interstate commerce both because the statute was ambiguous and because "unless Congress conveys its purpose clearly, it will not be deemed to have significantly changed the federal-state balance." *Id.* at 349. . . . Unlike the statute in *Bass*, § 922(q) has no express jurisdictional element which might limit its reach to a discrete set of firearm possessions that additionally have an explicit connection with or effect on interstate commerce.

Although as part of our independent evaluation of constitutionality under the Commerce Clause we of course consider legislative findings, and indeed even congressional committee findings, regarding effect on interstate commerce,. . . the Government concedes that "[n]either the statute nor its legislative history contain[s] express congressional findings regarding the effects upon interstate commerce of gun possession in a school zone." Brief for United States 5–6. We agree with the Government that Congress normally is not required to make formal findings as to the substantial burdens that an activity has on interstate commerce. . . . But to the extent that congressional findings would enable us to evaluate the legislative judgment that the activity in question substantially affected interstate commerce, even though no such substantial effect was visible to the naked eye, they are lacking here.

The Government argues that Congress has accumulated institutional expertise regarding the regulation of firearms through previous enactments. . . . [I]mportation of previous findings to justify § 922(q) is especially inappropriate here because the "prior federal enactments or Congressional findings [do not] speak to the subject matter of section 922(q) or its relationship to interstate commerce. Indeed, section 922(q) plows thoroughly new ground and represents a sharp break with the long-standing pattern of federal firearms legislation."

The Government's essential contention, *in fine*, is that we may determine here that § 922(q) is valid because possession of a firearm in a local school zone does indeed substantially affect interstate commerce. Brief for United States 17. The Government argues that possession of a firearm in a school zone may result in violent crime and that violent crime can be expected to affect the functioning of the national economy in two ways. First, the costs of violent crime are substantial, and, through the mechanism of insurance, those costs are spread throughout the population. Second, violent crime reduces the willingness of individuals to travel to areas within the country that are perceived to be unsafe. *Cf. Heart of Atlanta Motel*, 379 U.S. at 253. The Government also argues that the presence of guns in schools poses a substantial threat to the educational process by threatening the learning environment. A handicapped educational process, in turn, will result in a less productive citizenry. That, in turn, would have an adverse effect on the Nation's economic well-being. As a result, the Government argues that Congress

---

[3] Under our federal system, the "States possess primary authority for defining and enforcing the criminal law." *Brecht v. Abrahamson*, 507 U.S. 619, 635 (1993). . . .

could rationally have concluded that § 922(q) substantially affects interstate commerce.

We pause to consider the implications of the Government's arguments. The Government admits, under its "costs of crime" reasoning, that Congress could regulate not only all violent crime, but all activities that might lead to violent crime, regardless of how tenuously they relate to interstate commerce. Similarly, under the Government's "national productivity" reasoning, Congress could regulate any activity that it found was related to the economic productivity of individual citizens: family law (including marriage, divorce, and child custody), for example. Under the theories that the Government presents in support of § 922(q), it is difficult to perceive any limitation on federal power, even in areas such as criminal law enforcement or education where States historically have been sovereign. Thus, if we were to accept the Government's arguments, we are hard pressed to posit any activity by an individual that Congress is without power to regulate.

Although Justice Breyer argues that acceptance of the Government's rationales would not authorize a general federal police power, he is unable to identify any activity that the States may regulate but Congress may not. . . .

. . . .

Admittedly, a determination whether an intrastate activity is commercial or noncommercial may in some cases result in legal uncertainty. But, so long as Congress' authority is limited to those powers enumerated in the Constitution, and so long as those enumerated powers are interpreted as having judicially enforceable outer limits, congressional legislation under the Commerce Clause always will engender "legal uncertainty." . . . The Constitution mandates this uncertainty by withholding from Congress a plenary police power that would authorize enactment of every type of legislation. See Art. I, § 8. Congress has operated within this framework of legal uncertainty ever since this Court determined that it was the Judiciary's duty "to say what the law is." Marbury v. Madison, 5 U.S. 137, 177 (1803) (Marshall, C.J.). Any possible benefit from eliminating this "legal uncertainty" would be at the expense of the Constitution's system of enumerated powers.

. . . .

. . . The possession of a gun in a local school zone is in no sense an economic activity that might, through repetition elsewhere, substantially affect any sort of interstate commerce. Respondent was a local student at a local school; there is no indication that he had recently moved in interstate commerce, and there is no requirement that his possession of the firearm have any concrete tie to interstate commerce.

To uphold the Government's contentions here, we would have to pile inference upon inference in a manner that would bid fair to convert congressional authority under the Commerce Clause to a general police power of the sort retained by the States. Admittedly, some of our prior cases have taken long steps down that road, giving great deference to congressional action. The broad language in these opinions has suggested the possibility of additional expansion, but we decline here to proceed any further. To do so would require us to conclude that the Constitution's enumeration of powers does not presuppose something not enumerated, cf. Gibbons v. Ogden, 22 U.S. at 195, and that there never will be a distinction between what is truly national and what is truly local, cf. Jones & Laughlin Steel, at 301 U.S. at 30. This we are unwilling to do.

For the foregoing reasons the judgment of the Court of Appeals is Affirmed.

JUSTICE KENNEDY, with whom JUSTICE O'CONNOR joins, concurring.

. . . .

The history of our Commerce Clause decisions contains at least two lessons of relevance to this case. The first, as stated at the outset, is the imprecision of content-based boundaries used without more to define the limits of the Commerce Clause. The second, related to the first but of even greater consequence, is that the Court as an institution and the legal system as a whole have an immense stake in the stability of our Commerce Clause jurisprudence as it has evolved to this point. *Stare decisis* operates with great force in counseling us not to call in question the essential principles now in place respecting the congressional power to regulate transactions of a commercial nature. That fundamental restraint on our power forecloses us from reverting to an understanding of commerce that would serve only an 18th-century economy, dependent then upon production and trading practices that had changed but little over the preceding centuries; it also mandates against returning to the time when congressional authority to regulate undoubted commercial activities was limited by judicial determination that those matters had an insufficient connection to an interstate system. Congress can regulate in the commercial sphere on the assumption that we have a single market and a unified purpose to build a stable national economy.

. . . It does not follow, however, that in every instance the Court lacks the authority and responsibility to review congressional attempts to alter the federal balance. This case requires us to consider our place in the design of the Government and to appreciate the significance of federalism in the whole structure of the Constitution.

Of the various structural elements in the Constitution, separation of powers, checks and balances, judicial review, and federalism, only concerning the last does there seem to be much uncertainty respecting the existence, and the content, of standards that allow the Judiciary to play a significant role in maintaining the design contemplated by the Framers. . . .

There is irony in this, because of the four structural elements in the Constitution just mentioned, federalism was the unique contribution of the Framers to political science and political theory. Though on the surface the idea may seem counterintuitive, it was the insight of the Framers that freedom was enhanced by the creation of two governments, not one. "In the compound republic of America, the power surrendered by the people is first divided between two distinct governments, and then the portion allotted to each subdivided among distinct and separate departments. Hence a double security arises to the rights of the people. The different governments will control each other, at the same time that each will be controlled by itself." The Federalist No. 51 (J. Madison). . . .

The theory that two governments accord more liberty than one requires for its realization two distinct and discernable lines of political accountability: one between the citizens and the Federal Government; the second between the citizens and the States. If, as Madison expected, the Federal and State Governments are to control each other and hold each other in check by competing for the affections of the people, those citizens must have some means of knowing which of the two governments to hold accountable for failure to perform a given function. . . . Were the Federal Government to take over the regulation of entire areas of traditional state concern, areas having nothing to do with the regulation of commercial activities, the boundaries between the spheres of federal and state authority would blur and political responsibility would become illusory. . . .

To be sure, one conclusion that could be drawn from The Federalist Papers is that the balance between national and state power is entrusted in its entirety to the political process. . . .

For these reasons, it would be mistaken and mischievous for the political branches to forget that the sworn obligation to preserve and protect the Constitution in maintaining the federal balance is their own in the first and primary instance. . . .

At the same time, the absence of structural mechanisms to require those officials to undertake this principled task, and the momentary political convenience often attendant upon their failure to do so, argue against a complete renunciation of the judicial role.

Although it is the obligation of all officers of the Government to respect the constitutional design, the federal balance is too essential a part of our constitutional structure and plays too vital a role in securing freedom for us to admit inability to intervene when one or the other level of Government has tipped the scales too far.

. . . .

The statute before us upsets the federal balance to a degree that renders it an unconstitutional assertion of the commerce power, and our intervention is required. As the Chief Justice explains, unlike the earlier cases to come before the Court here neither the actors nor their conduct has a commercial character, and neither the purposes nor the design of the statute has an evident commercial nexus. The statute makes the simple possession of a gun within 1,000 feet of the grounds of the school a criminal offense. In a sense any conduct in this interdependent world of ours has an ultimate commercial origin or consequence, but we have not yet said the commerce power may reach so far. If Congress attempts that extension, then at the least we must inquire whether the exercise of national power seeks to intrude upon an area of traditional state concern.

An interference of these dimensions occurs here, for it is well established that education is a traditional concern of the states. . . .

. . . .

If a State or municipality determines that harsh criminal sanctions are necessary and wise to deter students from carrying guns on school premises, the reserved powers of the States are sufficient to enact those measures. Indeed, over 40 States already have criminal laws outlawing the possession of firearms on or near school grounds. . . .

. . . .

. . . Absent a stronger connection or identification with commercial concerns that are central to the Commerce Clause, that interference contradicts the federal balance the Framers designed and that this Court is obliged to enforce.

For these reasons, I join in the opinion and judgment of the Court.

JUSTICE THOMAS, concurring.

. . . Although I join the majority, I write separately to observe that our case law has drifted far from the original understanding of the Commerce Clause. In a future case, we ought to temper our Commerce Clause jurisprudence in a manner that both makes sense of our more recent case law and is more faithful to the original understanding of that Clause.

We have said that Congress may regulate not only "Commerce . . . among the several States," U.S. Const., Art. I, § 8, cl. 3, but also anything that has a "substantial effect" on such commerce. This test, if taken to its logical extreme, would give Congress a "police power" over all aspects of American life. Unfortunately, we have never come to grips with this implication of our substantial effects formula. Although we have supposedly applied the substantial effects test for the past 60 years, we *always* have rejected readings of the Commerce Clause and the scope of federal power that would permit Congress to exercise a police power; our cases are quite clear that there are real limits to federal power. *See New York v. United States,* 505 U.S. 144, 155 (1992) ("[N]o one disputes the proposition that '[t]he Constitution created a Federal Government of limited powers' ") . . . .

. . . .

In an appropriate case, I believe that we must further reconsider our "substantial effects" test with an eye toward constructing a standard that reflects the text and history of the Commerce Clause without totally rejecting our more recent Commerce Clause jurisprudence.

. . . .

I

At the time the original Constitution was ratified, "commerce" consisted of selling, buying, and bartering, as well as transporting for these purposes. *See* 1 S. JOHNSON, A DICTIONARY OF THE ENGLISH LANGUAGE 361 (4th ed. 1773) (defining commerce as "Intercour[s]e; exchange of one thing for another; interchange of any thing; trade; traffick"); N. BAILEY, AN UNIVERSAL ETYMOLOGICAL ENGLISH DICTIONARY (26th ed. 1789) ("trade or traffic"); T. SHERIDAN, A COMPLETE DICTIONARY OF THE ENGLISH LANGUAGE (6th ed. 1796) ("Exchange of one thing for another; trade; traffick"). . . . In fact, when Federalists and Anti-Federalists discussed the Commerce Clause during the ratification period, they often used trade (in its selling/bartering sense) and commerce interchangeably. *See* The Federalist No. 4 (J. Jay) (asserting that countries will cultivate our friendship when our "trade" is prudently regulated by the Federal Government); *id.*, No. 7 (A. Hamilton) (discussing "competitions of commerce" between States resulting from state "regulations of trade"); *id.*, No. 40 (J. Madison) (asserting that it was an "acknowledged object of the Convention . . . that the regulation of trade should be submitted to the general government") . . . .

As one would expect, the term "commerce" was used in contradistinction to productive activities such as manufacturing and agriculture. . . .

Moreover, interjecting a modern sense of commerce into the Constitution generates significant textual and structural problems. For example, one cannot replace "commerce" with a different type of enterprise, such as manufacturing. When a manufacturer produces a car, assembly cannot take place "with a foreign nation" or "with the Indian Tribes." Parts may come from different States or other nations and hence may have been in the flow of commerce at one time, but manufacturing takes place at a discrete site. Agriculture and manufacturing involve the production of goods; commerce encompasses traffic in such articles.

The Port Preference Clause also suggests that the term "commerce" denoted sale and/or transport rather than business generally. . . .

The Constitution not only uses the word "commerce" in a narrower sense than our case law might suggest, it also does not support the proposition that Congress has authority over all activities that "substantially affect" interstate commerce. The Commerce Clause[2] does not state that Congress may "regulate matters that substantially affect commerce with foreign Nations, and among the several states, and with the Indian Tribes." In contrast, the Constitution itself temporarily prohibited amendments that would "affect" Congress' lack of authority to prohibit or restrict the slave trade or to enact unproportioned direct taxation. Art. V. Clearly, the Framers could have drafted a Constitution that contained a "substantially affects interstate commerce" Clause had that been their objective.

In addition to its powers under the Commerce Clause, Congress has the authority to enact such laws as are "necessary and proper" to carry into execution its powers to regulate commerce among the several States. U.S. Const., Art. I, § 8, cl. 18. But on this

---

[2] Even to speak of "the Commerce Clause" perhaps obscures the actual scope of that Clause. As an original matter, Congress did not have authority to regulate all commerce; Congress could only "regulate Commerce with the foreign Nations, and among the several States, and with the Indian Tribes." U.S. Const., Art. I, § 8, cl. 3. Although the precise line between interstate/foreign commerce and purely intrastate commerce was hard to draw, the Court attempted to adhere to such a line for the first 150 years of our Nation.

Court's understanding of congressional power under these two Clauses, many of Congress' other enumerated powers under Art. I, § 8, are wholly superfluous. After all, if Congress may regulate all matters that substantially affect commerce, there is no need for the Constitution to specify that Congress may enact bankruptcy laws, cl. 4, or coin money and fix the standard of weights and measures, cl. 5, or punish counterfeiters of United States coin and securities, cl. 6. . . . Indeed, if Congress could regulate matters that substantially affect interstate commerce, there would have been no need to specify that Congress can regulate international trade and commerce with the Indians. As the Framers surely understood, these other branches of trade substantially affect interstate commerce.

Put simply, much if not all of Art. I, § 8 (including portions of the Commerce Clause itself), would be surplusage if Congress had been given authority over matters that substantially affect interstate commerce. An interpretation of cl. 3 that makes the rest of § 8 superfluous simply cannot be correct. Yet this Court's Commerce Clause jurisprudence has endorsed just such an interpretation: the power we have accorded Congress has swallowed Art. I, § 8.[3]

Our construction of the scope of congressional authority has the additional problem of coming close to turning the Tenth Amendment on its head. Our case law could be read to reserve to the United States all powers not expressly *prohibited* by the Constitution. Taken together, these fundamental textual problems should, at the very least, convince us that the "substantial effects" test should be reexamined.

II

The exchanges during the ratification campaign reveal the relatively limited reach of the Commerce Clause and of federal power generally. The Founding Fathers confirmed that most areas of life (even many matters that would have substantial affects on commerce) would remain outside the reach of the Federal Government. Such affairs would continue to be under the exclusive control of the States.

Early Americans understood that commerce, manufacturing, and agriculture, while distinct activities, were intimately related and dependent on each other — that each "substantially affected" the others. . . .

Yet, despite being well aware that agriculture, manufacturing, and other matters substantially affected commerce, the founding generation did not cede authority over all these activities to Congress. . . .

The comments of Hamilton and others about federal power reflected the well-known truth that the new Government would have only the limited and enumerated powers found in the Constitution. . . .

Where the Constitution was meant to grant federal authority over an activity substantially affecting interstate commerce, the Constitution contains an enumerated power over that particular activity. Indeed, the Framers knew that many of the other enumerated powers in § 8 dealt with matters that substantially affected interstate commerce. . . .

In short, the Founding Fathers were well aware of what the principal dissent calls " 'economic . . . realities.' ". . . . Even though the boundary between commerce and other matters may ignore "economic reality" and thus seem arbitrary or artificial to

---

[3] . . . Congress has plenary power over the District of Columbia and the territories. *See* U.S. Const., Art. I, § 8, cl. 17, and Art. IV, § 3, cl. 2. The grant of comprehensive legislative power over certain areas of the Nation, when read in conjunction with the rest of the Constitution, further confirms that Congress was not ceded plenary authority over the *whole* Nation.

some, we must nevertheless respect a constitutional line that does not grant Congress power over all that substantially affects interstate commerce.

III

If the principal dissent's understanding of our early case law were correct, there might be some reason to doubt this view of the original understanding of the Constitution. According to that dissent, Chief Justice Marshall's opinion in *Gibbons v. Ogden* established that Congress may control all local activities that "significantly affect interstate commerce." And, "with the exception of one wrong turn subsequently corrected," this has been the "traditiona[l] method of interpreting the Commerce Clause.". . .

In my view, the dissent is wrong about the holding and reasoning of *Gibbons*. Because this error leads the dissent to characterize the first 150 years of this Court's case law as a "wrong turn," I feel compelled to put the last 50 years in proper perspective. . . .

A

. . . .

There is a much better interpretation of the "affect[s]" language [in *Gibbons*]: Because the Court had earlier noted that the commerce power did not extend to wholly intrastate commerce, the Court was acknowledging that although the line between intrastate and interstate/foreign commerce would be difficult to draw, federal authority could not be construed to cover purely intrastate commerce. Commerce that did not affect another State could *never* be said to be commerce "among the several States."

But even if one were to adopt the dissent's reading, the "affect[s]" language, at most, permits Congress to regulate only intrastate *commerce* that substantially affects interstate and foreign commerce. There is no reason to believe that Chief Justice Marshall was asserting that Congress could regulate *all* activities that affect interstate commerce.

. . . The [*Gibbons*] Court was *not* saying that whatever Congress believes is a national matter becomes an object of federal control. The matters of national concern are enumerated in the Constitution . . . .

B

I am aware of no cases prior to the New Deal that characterized the power flowing from the Commerce Clause as sweepingly as does our substantial effects test. My review of the case law indicates that the substantial effects test is but an innovation of the 20th century.

. . . .

. . . From the time of the ratification of the Constitution to the mid-1930's, it was widely understood that the Constitution granted Congress only limited powers, notwithstanding the Commerce Clause. . . .

IV

Apart from its recent vintage and its corresponding lack of any grounding in the original understanding of the Constitution, the substantial effects test suffers from the further flaw that it appears to grant Congress a police power over the Nation. When asked at oral argument if there were *any* limits to the Commerce Clause, the

Government was at a loss for words. Likewise the principle dissent insists that there are limits, but it cannot muster even one example. . . .

The substantial effects test suffers from this flaw, in part, because of its "aggregation principle." Under so-called "class of activities" statutes, Congress can regulate whole categories of activities that are not themselves either "interstate" or "commerce." In applying the effects test, we ask whether the class of activities *as a whole* substantially affects interstate commerce, not whether any specific activity within the class has such affects when considered in isolation.

The aggregation principle is clever, but has no stopping point. Suppose all would agree that gun possession within 1,000 feet of a school does not substantially affect commerce, but that possession of weapons generally (knives, brass knuckles, nunchakus, etc.) does. Under our substantial effects doctrine, even though Congress cannot single out gun possession, it can prohibit weapon possession generally. But one *always* can draw the circle broadly enough to cover an activity that, when taken in isolation, would not have substantial effects on commerce. . . .

V

. . . .

At an appropriate juncture, I think we must modify our Commerce Clause jurisprudence. Today, it is easy enough to say that the Clause certainly does not empower Congress to ban gun possession within 1,000 feet of a school.

JUSTICE STEVENS, dissenting.

. . . .

Guns are both articles of commerce and articles that can be used to restrain commerce. Their possession is the consequence, either directly or indirectly, of commercial activity. In my judgment, Congress' power to regulate commerce in firearms includes the power to prohibit possession of guns at any location because of their potentially harmful use . . . .

JUSTICE SOUTER, dissenting.

In reviewing congressional legislation under the Commerce Clause, we defer to what is often a merely implicit congressional judgment that its regulation addresses a subject substantially affecting interstate commerce "if there is any rational basis for such a finding." *Hodel v. Virginia Surface Mining & Reclamation Assn., Inc.,* 452 U.S. 264, 276 (1981). If that congressional determination is within the realm of reason, "the only remaining question for judicial inquiry is whether 'the means chosen by Congress [are] reasonably adapted to the end permitted by the Constitution.' " *Id.*

The practice of deferring to rationally based legislative judgments "is a paradigm of judicial restraint." *FCC v. Beach Communications, Inc.,* 508 U.S. 307, 314 (1993). In judicial review under the Commerce Clause, it reflects our respect for the institutional competence of Congress on a subject expressly assigned to it by the Constitution and our appreciation of the legitimacy that comes from Congress's political accountability in dealing with matters open to a wide range of possible choices. *See id.* at 313–16.

. . . .

I

. . . [T]he period from the turn of the century to 1937 is better noted for a series of cases applying highly formalistic notions of "commerce" to invalidate federal social and economic legislation . . . .

These restrictive views of commerce subject to congressional power complemented the Court's activism in limiting the enforceable scope of state economic regulation. It is most familiar history that during this same period the Court routinely invalidated state social and economic legislation under an expansive conception of Fourteenth Amendment substantive due process. . . . [Doctrine in these two areas rested on different bases], but under each conception of judicial review the Court's character for the first third of the century showed itself in exacting judicial scrutiny of a legislature's choice of economic ends and of the legislative means selected to reach them.

It was not merely coincidental, then, that sea changes in the Court's conceptions of its authority under the Due Process and Commerce Clauses occurred virtually together, in 1937 . . . .

. . . [W]ith the challenge to congressional Commerce Clause authority to prohibit racial discrimination in places of public accommodation . . . the Court simply made explicit what the earlier cases had implied: "where we find that the legislators, in light of the facts and testimony before them, have a rational basis for finding a chosen regulatory scheme necessary to the protection of commerce, our investigation is at an end . . . ."

II

There is today, however, a backward glance at both the old pitfalls, as the Court treats deference under the rationality rule as subject to gradation according to the commercial or noncommercial nature of the immediate subject of the challenged regulation. The distinction between what is patently commercial and what is not looks much like the old distinction between what directly affects commerce and what only touches it indirectly. . . . Thus, it seems fair to ask whether the step taken by the Court today does anything but portend a return to the untenable jurisprudence from which the Court extricated itself almost 60 years ago. The answer is not reassuring. . . .

Further glosses on rationality review, moreover, may be in the offing. Although this case turns on commercial character, the Court gestures toward two other considerations that it might sometime entertain in applying rational basis scrutiny (apart from a statutory obligation to supply independent proof of a jurisdictional element): does the congressional statute deal with subjects of traditional state regulation, and does the statute contain explicit factual findings supporting the otherwise implicit determination that the regulated activity substantially affects interstate commerce? Once again, any appeal these considerations may have depends on ignoring the painful lessons learned in 1937, for neither of the Court's suggestions would square with rational basis scrutiny.

A

The Court observes that the Gun-Free School Zones Act operates in two areas traditionally subject to legislation by the States, education and enforcement of criminal law. The suggestion is either that a connection between commerce and these subjects is remote, or that the commerce power is simply weaker when it touches subjects on which the States have historically been the primary legislators. Neither suggestion is tenable. . . . The commerce power, we have often observed, is plenary. *Hodel,* 452 U.S. at 276; *Gibbons v. Ogden,* 22 U.S. 1, 196–97 (1824). . . .

. . . .

B

. . . .

The question for the courts, as all agree, is not whether as a predicate to legislation Congress in fact found that a particular activity substantially affects interstate commerce. The legislation implies such a finding, and there is no reason to entertain claims that Congress acted ultra vires intentionally. Nor is the question whether Congress was correct in so finding. The only question is whether the legislative judgment is within the realm of reason. . . . Congressional findings do not, however, directly address the question of reasonableness; they tell us what Congress actually has found, not what it could rationally find. If, indeed, the Court were to make the existence of explicit congressional findings dispositive in some close or difficult cases something other than rationality review would be afoot. . . .

. . . .

JUSTICE BREYER, with whom JUSTICE STEVENS, JUSTICE SOUTER, and JUSTICE GINSBURG join, dissenting.

. . . In my view, the statute falls well within the scope of the commerce power as this Court has understood that power over the last half century.

I

In reaching this conclusion, I apply three basic principles of Commerce Clause interpretation. First, the power to "regulate Commerce . . . among the several States," U.S. Const., Art. I, § 8, cl. 3, encompasses the power to regulate local activities insofar as they significantly affect interstate commerce. *See, e.g. Gibbons v. Ogden*, 22 U.S. 1, 194–95 (1824) (Marshall, C.J.); *Wickard v. Filburn*, 317 U.S. 111, 125 (1942). As the majority points out, the Court, in describing how much of an effect the Clause requires, sometimes has used the word "substantial" and sometimes has not. . . . And, as the majority also recognizes in quoting Justice Cardozo, the question of degree (how *much* effect) requires an estimate of the "size" of the effect that no verbal formulation can capture with precision. I use the word "significant" because the word "substantial" implies a somewhat narrower power than recent precedent suggests. . . . But to speak of "substantial effect" rather than "significant effect" would make no difference in this case.

Second, in determining whether a local activity will likely have a significant effect upon interstate commerce, a court must consider, not the effect of an individual act (a single instance of gun possession), but rather the cumulative effect of all similar instances (*i.e.*, the effect of all guns possessed in or near schools). *See Wickard*, 317 U.S. at 127–28. . . .

Third, the Constitution requires us to judge the connection between a regulated activity and interstate commerce, not directly, but at one remove. Courts must give Congress a degree of leeway in determining the existence of a significant factual connection between the regulated activity and interstate commerce — both because the Constitution delegates the commerce power directly to Congress and because the determination requires an empirical judgment of a kind that a legislature is more likely than a court to make with accuracy. The traditional words "rational basis" capture this leeway. Thus, the specific question before us, as the Court recognizes, is not whether the "regulated activity sufficiently affected interstate commerce," but, rather, whether Congress could have had *"a rational basis"* for so concluding.

I recognize that we must judge this matter independently. "[S]imply because Congress may conclude that a particular activity substantially affects interstate commerce does not necessarily make it so.". . .

. . . .

II

Applying these principles to the case at hand, we must ask whether Congress could have had a *rational basis* for finding a significant (or substantial) connection between gun-related school violence and interstate commerce. . . . As long as one views the commerce connection, not as a "technical legal conception," but as "a practical one," *Swift & Co. v. United States*, 196 U.S. 375, 398 (1905) (Holmes, J.), the answer to this question must be yes. Numerous reports and studies — generated both inside and outside government — make clear that Congress could reasonably have found the empirical connection that its law, implicitly or explicitly, asserts. . . .

For one thing, reports, hearings, and other readily available literature make clear that the problem of guns in and around schools is widespread and extremely serious. . . . [S]everal hundred thousand schoolchildren are victims of violent crimes in or near their schools. . . . And, they report that this widespread violence in schools throughout the Nation significantly interferes with the quality of education in those schools. . . . Based on reports such as these, Congress obviously could have thought that guns and learning are mutually exclusive. . . . Congress could therefore have found a substantial educational problem — teachers unable to teach, students unable to learn — and concluded that guns near schools contribute substantially to the size and scope of that problem.

Having found that guns in schools significantly undermine the quality of education in our Nation's classrooms, Congress could also have found, given the effect of education upon interstate and foreign commerce, that gun-related violence in and around schools is a commercial, as well as a human, problem. Education, although far more than a matter of economics, has long been inextricably intertwined with the Nation's economy. . . . Scholars estimate that nearly a quarter of America's economic growth in the early years of this century is traceable directly to increased schooling . . . .

In recent years the link between secondary education and business has strengthened, becoming both more direct and more important. Scholars on the subject report that technological changes and innovations in management techniques have altered the nature of the workplace so that more jobs now demand greater educational skills. . . .

Increasing global competition also has made primary and secondary education economically more important. . . .

Finally, there is evidence that, today more than ever, many firms base their location decisions upon the presence, or absence, of a work force with a basic education. . . .

The economic links I have just sketched seem fairly obvious. Why then is it not equally obvious, in light of those links, that a widespread, serious, and substantial physical threat to teaching and learning also substantially threatens the commerce to which that teaching and learning is inextricably tied? That is to say, guns in the hands of six percent of inner-city high school students and gun-related violence throughout a city's schools must threaten the trade and commerce that those schools support. The only question, then, is whether the latter threat is (to use the majority's terminology) "substantial." The evidence of (1) the *extent* of the gun-related violence problem, (2) the *extent* of the resulting negative effects on classroom learning, and (3) the *extent* of the consequent negative commercial effects, when taken together, indicate a threat to trade and commerce that is "substantial." At the very least, Congress could rationally have concluded that the links are "substantial."

Specifically, Congress could have found that gun-related violence near the classroom poses a serious economic threat (1) to consequently inadequately educated workers who must endure low paying jobs, and (2) to communities and businesses that might (in today's "information society") otherwise gain, from a well-educated work force, an important commercial advantage, of a kind that location near a railhead or harbor provided in the past. Congress might also have found these threats to be no different in kind from other threats that this Court has found within the commerce power, such as the threat that loan sharking poses to the "funds" of "numerous localities," *Perez v. United States*, 402 U.S., at 157, and that unfair labor practices pose to instrumentalities of commerce, *see* Consolidated Edison Co. v. NLRB, 305 U.S. 197, 221-222. . . . The violence-related facts, the educational facts, and the economic facts, taken together, make this conclusion rational. And, because under our case law the sufficiency of the constitutionally necessary Commerce Clause link between a crime of violence and interstate commerce turns simply upon size or degree, those same facts make the statute constitutional.

To hold this statute constitutional is not to "obliterate" the "distinction between what is national and what is local;" nor is it to hold that the Commerce Clause permits the Federal Government to "regulate any activity that it found was related to the economic productivity of individual citizens," to regulate "marriage, divorce, and child custody," or to regulate any and all aspects of education. First, this statute is aimed at curbing a particularly acute threat to the educational process — the possession (and use) of life-threatening firearms in, or near, the classroom. . . . Second, the immediacy of the connection between education and the national economic well-being is documented by scholars and accepted by society at large in a way and to a degree that may not hold true for other social institutions. . . .

In sum, a holding that the particular statute before us falls within the commerce power would not expand the scope of that Clause. Rather, it simply would apply pre-existing law to changing economic circumstances. *See Heart of Atlanta Motel, Inc. v. United States*, 379 U.S. 241, 251 (1964). It would recognize that, in today's economic world, gun-related violence near the classroom makes a significant difference to our economic, as well as our social, well-being. . . .

III

The majority's holding — that § 922 falls outside the scope of the Commerce Clause — creates three serious legal problems. First, the majority's holding runs contrary to modern Supreme Court cases that have upheld congressional actions despite connections to interstate or foreign commerce that are less significant than the effect of school violence. In *Perez v. United States*, the Court held that the Commerce Clause authorized a federal statute that makes it a crime to engage in loan sharking ("[e]xtortionate credit transactions") at a local level. . . . Presumably, Congress reasoned that threatening or using force, say with a gun on a street corner, to collect a debt occurs sufficiently often so that the activity (by helping organized crime) affects commerce among the States. But, why then cannot Congress also reason that the threat or use of force — the frequent consequence of possessing a gun — in or near a school occurs sufficiently often so that such activity (by inhibiting basic education) affects commerce among the States? The negative impact upon the national economy of an inability to teach basic skills seems no smaller (nor less significant) than that of organized crime.

In *Katzenbach v. McClung*, 379 U.S. 294 (1964), this Court upheld, as within the commerce power, a statute prohibiting racial discrimination at local restaurants . . . in part because that discrimination affected purchases of food and restaurant supplies from other States. . . . In *Daniel v. Paul*, 395 U.S. 298 (1969), this Court found an effect on commerce caused by an amusement park located several miles down a country road in the middle of Alabama — because some customers (the Court assumed), some food, 15 paddle-boats, and a juke box had come from out of state. . . .

In *Wickard v. Filburn,* 317 U.S. 111 (1942), this Court sustained the application of the Agricultural Adjustment Act of 1938 to wheat that Filburn grew and consumed on his own local farm . . . .

The second legal problem the Court creates comes from its apparent belief that it can reconcile its holding with earlier cases by making a critical distinction between "commercial" and noncommercial "transaction[s]." That is to say, the Court believes the Constitution would distinguish between two local activities, each of which has an identical effect upon interstate commerce, if one, but not the other, is "commercial" in nature. As a general matter, this approach fails to heed this Court's earlier warning not to turn "questions of the power of Congress" upon "formula[s]" that would give "controlling force to nomenclature such as 'production' and 'indirect' and foreclose consideration of the actual effects of the activity in question upon interstate commerce." *Wickard,* 317 U.S. at 120. . . . Although the majority today attempts to categorize *Perez, McClung,* and *Wickard* as involving intrastate "economic activity," the Courts that decided each of those cases did not focus upon the economic nature of the activity regulated. Rather, they focused upon whether that activity *affected* interstate or foreign commerce. . . .

. . . .

. . . In 1990, the year Congress enacted the statute before us, primary and secondary schools spent $230 billion — that is, nearly a quarter of a trillion dollars — which accounts for a significant portion of our $5.5 trillion gross domestic product for that year. The business of schooling requires expenditure of these funds . . . .

The third legal problem created by the Court's holding is that it threatens legal uncertainty in an area of law that, until this case, seemed reasonably well settled. Congress has enacted many statutes (more than 100 sections of the United States Code), including criminal statutes (at least 25 sections), that use words "affecting commerce" to define their scope . . . and other statutes that contain no jurisdictional language at all . . . .

IV

. . . [Upholding this statute] would interpret the [Commerce] Clause as this Court has traditionally interpreted it, with the exception of one wrong turn subsequently corrected. *See Gibbons v. Ogden,* 22 U.S. at 195 (holding that the commerce power extends "to all the external concerns of the nation, and to those internal concerns which affect the States generally") . . . . Upholding this legislation would do no more than simply recognize that Congress had a "rational basis" for finding a significant connection between guns in or near school and (through their effect on education) the interstate and foreign commerce they threaten. For these reasons, I would reverse the judgment of the Court of Appeals. Respectfully, I dissent.

Exercise 13:

After reviewing the opinions in *Lopez,* consider the following matters.

(1) What purpose, if any, did the Court assert was served by limiting the power of the federal government relative to the power of the States?

(2) What are the three categories of power to legislate under the Commerce Clause that the Court summarizes from its prior decisions? Do those three categories encompass all prior exercises of the commerce power that we have considered? Did the separate opinions in concurrence and/or dissent suggest that the commerce power is broader than those three categories?

(3)   Which of the three categories was at issue in *Lopez*? Is there any argument that another category would be applicable to the statute at issue? Why or why not?

(4)   The majority asserted that the statute at issue in *Lopez* had "nothing to do with 'commerce' or any sort of economic enterprise." Do you agree?

(5)   The majority asserted that the statute at issue in *Lopez* had no "jurisdictional element." What language in the statute would constitute such a jurisdictional element? Would the presence of such language, without any other change, have rendered the statute constitutional? Why or why not?

(6)   The majority asserted that the statute at issue in *Lopez* was not accompanied by congressional findings. How did the majority's treatment of that issue compare with *Heart of Atlanta Motel*? Would the presence of such findings, without any other change, have rendered the statute constitutional? Why or why not?

(7)   Consider the arguments articulated by the federal government in support of the statute at issue in *Lopez*. If the Court had adopted either the "costs of crime" reasoning or the "national productivity" reasoning, would there have been any basis to prevent Congress from regulating under the commerce clause any of the following matters: marriage, divorce, child custody, local criminal law enforcement, or education?

(8)   In seeking to uphold the statute at issue in *Lopez,* counsel for the federal government refused to identify any matter that would be outside the scope of federal regulation under the commerce clause. What difference should the failure to identify a limiting principle play in adjudicating cases?

(9)   How did the separate opinion authored by Justice Kennedy differ from the approach of the majority?

(10)   How did the separate opinion authored by Justice Thomas differ from the approach of the majority?

(11)   Justice Stevens observed that guns are "articles of commerce." Under existing precedents, was that a sufficient basis to permit federal regulation of possession of guns under the commerce power? Why or why not?

(12)   Justice Souter asserted that it would be improper for the judiciary to "review for congressional wisdom" a statute purportedly based on the commerce power. Would that view leave any judicial role to evaluate the constitutionality of the *substance* of legislation once Congress invoked the commerce power? Justice Souter also asserted that it would be improper for the judiciary to "review for deliberateness" a statute purportedly based on the commerce power. Would that view leave any judicial role to evaluate the *procedure* (or process) of legislation — aside from bicameralism and presentment — once Congress invoked the commerce power? If Justice Souter eschewed judicial review of substance and procedure, did he envision any role for the Court in ensuring that Congress did not exceed its constitutional powers? If not, is there any reason to distinguish between the commerce power and any other provision of the Constitution in terms of the appropriateness of judicial review? How is it consistent to assert judicial review (if not judicial supremacy in constitutional interpretation) and to leave to Congress to define for itself the scope of its power to regulate commerce?

(13)   Justice Breyer began his dissenting opinion with a three-step argument. With which, if any, of those three propositions did a majority of the Court disagree? Did the majority reject the view that Congress has the power to regulate local activities that significantly affect interstate commerce? Did the majority reject the view that in determining what activities significantly affect interstate commerce, Congress may aggregate the impact of all similar local activities by all parties? Did the majority reject the view that a congressional determination that particular local activities significantly

affect interstate commerce must be upheld if there was a "rational basis" for Congress to reach the conclusion?

(14)   Is it possible to agree with each of Justice Breyer's three steps but still reach the same judgment as the majority? Why or why not?

(15)   Justice Breyer identified three concerns with the approach of the majority. He asserted that the Court's ruling "runs contrary to modern Supreme Court cases" and that, in so breaking with precedent, the Court "threatens legal uncertainty." Assuming, for purposes of discussion, that the majority did break with precedent, how much weight should be given to *stare decisis* in such matters?

(a)   *If* the Supreme Court had departed from both constitutional text and a historical understanding of the scope of the commerce power shared by the Framers (and for more than fifty years following ratification), would a return to a view of the commerce power grounded in text and history justify overturning Supreme Court precedent?

(b)   Does the degree of reliance on the Court's interpretation of the Constitution provide a basis for the Court to decline from "correcting" a mistake? For example, should it matter whether Congress enacted many statutes premised on the misinterpretation? Should it matter more or less if the reliance is by private parties rather than coordinate branches of government? For example, should it matter that individuals and business enterprises arranged their affairs taking into account judicial precedent?

(16)   **In advance of class,** draft a revised version of 18 U.S.C. § 922(q) that would survive judicial review after *Lopez.*

THE IMPACT OF *LOPEZ*

A. *Does* Lopez *represent a lone example of the post-New Deal Supreme Court finding Congress exceeded its commerce power?*

In *United States v. Morrison,* 529 U.S. 598 (2000), the Court reaffirmed *Lopez,* and held that the civil remedy provision of the Violence Against Women Act of 1994 (VAWA) exceeded congressional power under the Commerce Clause.

Applying the three-part framework of the commerce power jurisprudence outlined in *Lopez,* the Court concluded that, as in *Lopez* itself, Congress relied only on the branch applicable to "substantial effects" on interstate commerce. In analyzing the scope of federal power under the "substantial effects" test, the Court distilled four factors from *Lopez:* (1) the economic nature of the activity to be regulated; (2) the presence of an express jurisdictional element requiring case-by-case judicial determination; (3) congressional findings documenting the affect on interstate commerce of the regulated activity; and (4) the "attenuated" link between interstate commerce and the regulated activity — a connection stronger than either the "cost of crime" rationale or the "national productivity" rationale. All four factors were absent in *Lopez.* In *Morrison,* the first two factors were absent. In enacting VAWA, however, Congress held hearings, generated a substantial legislative history with respect to gender-motivated violence, and included express findings.

The *Morrison* Court discounted the congressional findings because of the rationale on which they relied. VAWA found there was an affect on interstate commerce:

by deterring potential victims from traveling interstate, from engaging in employment in interstate business, and from transacting with business, and in places involved in interstate commerce; . . . by diminishing national productivity, increasing medical and other costs, and decreasing the supply of and the demand for interstate products.

Because Congress seemingly relied on the general "cost of crime" and "national productivity" rationales rejected in *Lopez*, the Court determined that, again, the link was too attenuated and that findings based on such a link were inapposite. The Court observed that the legislative history and findings were directed to illustrating the problem of gender-motivated violence rather than illustrating how that violence had a "substantial effect" on interstate commerce. Only very generalized links could be drawn between the violence and interstate commerce and, in *Lopez*, the Court had already required some link with a limiting principle. VAWA seemingly offered no limiting principle.

> We accordingly reject the argument that Congress may regulate noneco-nomic, violent criminal conduct based solely on that conduct's aggregate effect on interstate commerce. The Constitution requires a distinction between what is truly national and what is truly local. . . . In recognizing this fact we preserve one of the few principles that has been consistent since the Clause was adopted. The regulation and punishment of intrastate violence that is not directed at the instrumentalities, channels, or goods involved in interstate commerce has always been the province of the States. Indeed, we can think of no better example of the police power, which the Founders denied the National Govern-ment and reposed in the States, than the suppression of violent crime and vindication of its victims.

As in *Lopez*, Justice Thomas presented a concurring opinion suggesting a broader reconsideration of Commerce Clause doctrine. As in *Lopez*, Justices Stevens, Souter, Ginsburg, and Breyer, dissented.

B. *What further consequences follow from recognizing limits to the commerce power?*

In *Jones v. United States*, 529 U.S. 848 (2000), Justice Ginsburg, writing for the Court construed a federal arson statute to be inapplicable to the facts presented. Although three Justices joined in concurring opinions, no one dissented.

The criminal statute at issue literally extended to "property used in interstate or foreign commerce or in any activity affecting interstate or foreign commerce." The Court determined that the statute did not apply to an owner-occupied residence even though the residence received from out-of-state a supply of natural gas, was collateral for a mortgage loan with an institution from out-of-state, and both the owner and mortgage lender interests were insured by a company from out-of-state. In reaching that result, the Court relied, in part, on the canon of constitutional avoidance in statutory interpretation.

The Court thus avoided an interpretation of the statute that would have required resolution of whether Congress could regulate under its commerce power every building that received utilities from out-of-state, or all property that served as collateral for a loan from out-of-state, or all persons and things insured by an out-of-state company. In this respect, the acknowledgment of limits to the commerce power casts a shadow through the process of statutory interpretation. As with the non-delegation doctrine, the Court does not need to declare a statute unconstitutional for the constitutional limit to be felt.

Other, more-recent cases illustrate the continued use of the doctrine of constitutional avoidance with respect to the commerce power. For example, in *Solid Waste Agency of Northern Cook County v. United States Army Corps of Engineers*, 531 U.S. 159 (2001)

(*SWANCC*), the same 5-4 majority of the Court as in *Lopez* avoided addressing the scope of the commerce power by construing the term "navigable waters" in the federal Clean Water Act so as not to "confer federal authority over an abandoned sand and gravel pit in northern Illinois which provides habitat for migratory birds." *Id.* at 162.

In *Rapanos v. United States*, 547 U.S. 715 (2006), a four-Justice plurality would have construed the Clean Water Act to not apply to a parcel of "land with sometimes-saturated soil conditions" where the "nearest body of navigable water was 11 to 20 miles away" and thereby avoid addressing a "theory of jurisdiction that presses the envelope of constitutional validity." Justice Kennedy, who provided the fifth vote for the judgment, determined that the lower courts failed to apply the appropriate statutory standard established by *SWANCC* and so supported a remand without relying upon the canon of constitutional avoidance. Nonetheless, the result in *Rapanos*, like the result (and reasoning) in *SWANCC*, relied upon statutory interpretation as a means to avoid deciding the scope of the commerce power.

C. Is the Court likely to extend Lopez and Morrison to the extent of reconsidering other Commerce Clause doctrine?

In *Gonzales v. Raich*, 545 U.S. 1 (2005), the Court reviewed a determination of the U.S. Court of Appeals for the Ninth Circuit that the federal Controlled Substances Act exceeded the scope of the commerce power as applied to intrastate cultivation and possession of cannabis for personal medical use pursuant to a prescription authorized by California's Compassionate Use Act. The case arose after federal agents seized and destroyed all six of Monson's cannabis plants. The case presented a vehicle for the Court to extend *Lopez* and *Morrison* with an express overruling of *Wickard v. Filburn*. Or, the Court could have affirmed the Ninth Circuit and distinguished *Wickard* on the basis that there was a legitimate national market for wheat but no lawful market for cannabis,[23] or on the basis that Filburn operated a commercial farming operation while Monson did not sell any of her production,[24] or on several other bases.[25] The Court took neither approach. Instead, the Court reversed relying upon the authority of *Wickard*.

The Court distinguished *Lopez* and *Morrison* as challenges to statutory provisions that allegedly were beyond the scope of the commerce power in their entirety; that is, they were facial challenges to the statutes at issue. In *Raich*, by contrast, the parties conceded that the statute was generally valid but contended that it was invalid as applied to their unusual circumstances. The Court reaffirmed its prior precedents that

> [w]hen Congress decides that the " 'total incidence' " of a practice poses a threat to a national market, it may regulate the entire class. *See Perez v. United States*, 402 U.S. 146, 154–55 (1971) (quoting *Westfall v. United States*, 274 U.S. 256, 259 (1927) (" '[W]hen it is necessary in order to prevent an evil to make the law embrace more than the precise thing to be prevented it may do so' ")). In this vein, we have reiterated that when " 'a general regulatory statute bears a substantial relation to commerce, the *de minimis* character of individual instances arising under that statute is of no consequence.' " *E.g.*, *Lopez*, 514 U.S. at 558 (emphasis deleted) (quoting *Maryland v. Wirtz*, 392 U.S. 183, 196 n.27 (1968)).

---

[23] In a footnote, the Court explicitly rejected that distinction as "of no constitutional import" because precedents establish that the "power to regulate commerce includes the power to prohibit commerce in a particular commodity." *See Raich*, 545 U.S. at 19 n.29.

[24] The Court noted that *Wickard* had considered Filburn's excess wheat production as a separate matter from his commercial farming operations. *See Raich*, 545 U.S. at 20 & n 30.

[25] The Court observed that while "factually accurate" the distinctions did "not diminish the precedential force of this Court's reasoning [in *Wickard*]." *See Raich*, 545 U.S. at 20.

Stated otherwise, "[w]here the class of activities is regulated and that class is within the reach of the federal power, the courts have no power 'to excise, as trivial, individual instances' of the class." *Id.* at 23 (quoting *Perez,* 402 U.S. at 154). As a second basis for distinguishing *Lopez* and *Morrison,* the Court noted that those cases involved statutes directed to activity that had nothing to do with commerce or any sort of economic enterprise. *Id.* at 23–25. In contrast, the Court observed that there is an established and lucrative interstate market for cannabis.

The dissent maintained that the result in *Raich* was inconsistent with *Lopez* and *Morrison.*

> [T]he Court announces a rule that gives Congress a perverse incentive to legislate broadly pursuant to the Commerce Clause — nestling questionable assertions of its authority into comprehensive regulatory schemes — rather than with precision. That rule and the result it produces in this case are irreconcilable with our decisions in *Lopez* and *Morrison.*

545 U.S. at 43 (O'Connor, J., dissenting); *see also id.* at 57–58 (Thomas, J., dissenting) ("Respondents . . . use marijuana that has never been bought or sold, that has never crossed state lines, and that has had no demonstrable effect on the national market for marijuana. If Congress can regulate this under the Commerce Clause, then it can regulate virtually anything — and the Federal Government is no longer one of limited and enumerated powers.").

The problem, as viewed by the dissent, was to find a proper level of generalization at which to evaluate legislation.

> The hard work for courts, then, is to identify objective markers for confining the analysis in Commerce Clause cases. Here, respondents challenge the constitutionality of the CSA as applied to them and those similarly situated. I agree with the Court that we must look beyond respondents' own activities. Otherwise, individual litigants could always exempt themselves from Commerce Clause regulation merely by pointing to the obvious — that their personal activities do not have a substantial effect on interstate commerce. The task is to identify a mode of analysis that allows Congress to regulate more than nothing (by declining to reduce each case to its litigants) and less than everything (by declining to let Congress set the terms of analysis). The analysis may not be the same in every case, for it depends on the regulatory scheme at issue and the federalism concerns implicated. *See generally Lopez,* 514 U.S. at 567; *id.* at 579 (Kennedy, J., concurring).

Raich, 545 U.S. at 47–48 (O'Connor, J., dissenting); *see also id.* at 68 (Thomas, J., dissenting) ("By defining the class at a high level of generality (as the intrastate manufacture and possession of marijuana), the majority overlooks that individuals authorized by state law to manufacture and possess medical marijuana exert no demonstrable effect on the interstate drug market").

Does *Raich* suggest that the Court is unlikely to build on *Lopez* and *Morrison?*

CHAPTER 4

LEGISLATIVE ENFORCEMENT OF THE FOURTEENTH AMENDMENT

Chapter One addressed the power of Congress to provide incentives to encourage or discourage certain conduct. Chapter Two examined the nature of the enumerated coercive powers of Congress and the scope of implied powers. Chapter Three then examined the most often employed of the coercive powers of Article I, Section 8: the Commerce Clause.

By subsequent Amendment, the Constitution conveys other powers to Congress beyond those specified in Article I, Section 8. Together with the Thirteenth and Fifteenth Amendments, the Fourteenth Amendment was adopted during the Reconstruction Era to address certain problems that resulted from the history of slavery, including problems of race relations.

Aside from the expansion of revenue-raising capacity (and the resulting ability to expend funds with attached conditions) flowing from the Sixteenth Amendment's authorization of the federal income tax, no other Amendment has provided a greater range of new powers than the Fourteenth Amendment. The scope of those powers are the subject of this Chapter.

Exercise 14(A):

Read the Thirteenth, Fourteenth, and Fifteenth Amendments.

(1) In what respect do these Amendments modify the structure of the government established by the Constitution of 1789?

(2) What new individual rights, if any, do those Amendments provide?

(3) What new powers, if any, do those Amendments give Congress? Stated otherwise, what, if anything, could Congress do after adoption of those Amendments that it could not have accomplished under its previously-granted powers?

(a) If *United States v. Sanchez* accurately describes the power of Congress to regulate matters through taxes, could Congress accomplish the same ends with "disincentives" as it could with its enforcement power under Section Five of the Fourteenth Amendment?

(b) If *South Dakota v. Dole* accurately describes the power of Congress to accomplish ends by placing conditions on federal spending, could Congress accomplish the same ends with "incentives" as it could with its enforcement power under Section Five of the Fourteenth Amendment?

(c) If *Heart of Atlanta Motel, Inc. v. United States* accurately describes the power of Congress to regulate matters under the Commerce Clause, could Congress accomplish the same ends under that clause as it could with its enforcement power under Section Five of the Fourteenth Amendment?

KATZENBACH v. MORGAN
384 U.S. 641 (1966)

JUSTICE BRENNAN delivered the opinion of the Court.

These cases concern the constitutionality of § 4(e) of the Voting Rights Act of 1965. That law, in the respects pertinent in these cases, provides that no person who has successfully completed the sixth primary grade in a public school, or in a private school accredited by, the Commonwealth of Puerto Rico in which the language of instruction was other than English shall be denied the right to vote in any election because of his inability to read or write English. Appellees, registered voters in New York City, brought this suit to challenge the constitutionality of § 4(e) insofar as it *pro tanto* prohibits the enforcement of the election laws of New York requiring an ability to read and write English as a condition of voting. . . . Upon cross motions for summary judgment, [the three-judge district] court, one judge dissenting, granted the declaratory and injunctive relief sought. The court held that in enacting § 4(e) Congress exceeded the powers granted to it by the Constitution and therefore usurped powers reserved to the States by the Tenth Amendment. . . . We reverse. We hold that, in the application challenged in these cases, § 4(e) is a proper exercise of the powers granted to Congress by § 5 of the Fourteenth Amendment and that by force of the Supremacy Clause, Article VI, the New York English literacy requirement cannot be enforced to the extent that it is inconsistent with § 4(e).

Under the distribution of powers effected by the Constitution, the States establish qualifications for voting for state officers, and the qualifications established by the States for voting for members of the most numerous branch of the state legislature also determine who may vote for United States Representatives and Senators, Art. I, § 2; Seventeenth Amendment. But, of course, the States have no power to grant or withhold the franchise on conditions that are forbidden by the Fourteenth Amendment, or any other provisions of the Constitution. Such exercises of state power are no more immune to the limitations of the Fourteenth Amendment than any other state action. The Equal Protection Clause itself has been held to forbid some state laws that restrict the right to vote.

The Attorney General of the State of New York argues that an exercise of congressional power under § 5 of the Fourteenth Amendment that prohibits the enforcement of a state law can only be sustained if the judicial branch determines that the state law is prohibited by the provisions of the Amendment that Congress sought to enforce. More specifically, he urges that § 4(e) cannot be sustained as appropriate legislation to enforce the Equal Protection Clause unless the judiciary decides — even with the guidance of congressional judgment — that the application of the English literacy requirement prohibited by § 4(e) is forbidden by the Equal Protection Clause itself. We disagree. Neither the language nor history of § 5 support such a construction. As we said with regard to § 5 in *Ex parte Virginia*, 100 U.S. 339, 345 (1879), "It is the power of Congress which has been enlarged. Congress is authorized to *enforce* the prohibitions by appropriate legislation. Some legislation is contemplated to make the amendments fully effective." A construction of § 5 that would require a judicial determination that the enforcement of the state law precluded by Congress violated the Amendment, as a condition of sustaining the congressional enactment, would depreciate both congressional resourcefulness and congressional responsibility for implementing the Amendment. It would confine the legislative power in this context to the insignificant role of abrogating only those state laws that the judicial branch was prepared to adjudge unconstitutional, or merely informing the judgment of the judiciary by particularizing the "majestic generalities" of § 1 of the Amendment. *See Fay v. New York*, 332 U.S. 261, 282–84 (1947).

Thus our task in this case is not to determine whether the New York English literacy requirement as applied to deny the right to vote to a person who successfully completed the sixth grade in a Puerto Rican school violates the Equal Protection Clause. Accordingly, our decision in *Lassiter v. Northampton Election Bd.*, 360 U.S. 45 (1959), sustaining the North Carolina English literacy requirement as not in all circumstances prohibited by the first sections of the Fourteenth and Fifteenth Amendments, is inapposite. *Lassiter* did not present the question before us here: Without regard to whether the judiciary would find that the Equal Protection Clause itself nullifies New York's English literacy requirement as so applied, could Congress prohibit the enforcement of the state law by legislating under § 5 of the Fourteenth Amendment? In answering this question, our task is limited to determining whether such legislation is, as required by § 5, appropriate legislation to enforce the Equal Protection Clause.

By including § 5 the draftsmen sought to grant to Congress, by a specific provision applicable to the Fourteenth Amendment, the same broad powers expressed in the Necessary and Proper Clause, Art. I, § 8, cl. 18.[9] The classic formulation of the reach of those powers was established by Chief Justice Marshall in *McCulloch v. Maryland*, 17 U.S. 316, 421 (1819):

> Let the end be legitimate, let it be within the scope of the constitution, and all means which are appropriate, which are plainly adapted to that end, which are not prohibited, but consist with the letter and spirit of the constitution, are constitutional.

Ex parte Virginia, 100 U.S. at 345–46, decided 12 years after the adoption of the Fourteenth Amendment, held that the congressional power under § 5 had the same broad scope. . . . Section 2 of the Fifteenth Amendment grants Congress a similar power to enforce by "appropriate legislation" the provisions of that amendment; and we recently held in *South Carolina v. Katzenbach*, 383 U.S. 301, 326 (1966), that "[t]he basic test to be applied in a case involving § 2 of the Fifteenth Amendment is the same as in all cases concerning the express powers of Congress with relation to the reserved powers of the States." That test was identified as the one formulated in *McCulloch v. Maryland*. Thus the *McCulloch v. Maryland* standard is the measure of what constitutes "appropriate legislation" under § 5 of the Fourteenth Amendment. Correctly viewed, § 5 is a positive grant of legislative power authorizing Congress to exercise its discretion in determining whether and what legislation is needed to secure the guarantees of the Fourteenth Amendment.

We therefore proceed to the consideration whether § 4(e) is "appropriate legislation" to enforce the Equal Protection Clause, that is, under the *McCulloch v. Maryland* standard, whether § 4(e) may be regarded as an enactment to enforce the Equal Protection Clause, whether it is "plainly adapted to that end" and whether it is not prohibited by but is consistent with "the letter and spirit of the constitution."[10]

---

[9] In fact, earlier drafts of the proposed Amendment employed the "necessary and proper" terminology to describe the scope of congressional power under the Amendment. *See* tenBroek, The Anti-Slavery Origins of the Fourteenth Amendment 187–90 (1951). The substitution of the "appropriate legislation" formula was never thought to have the effect of diminishing the scope of this congressional power. *See, e.g.*, Cong. Globe, 42nd Cong., 1st Sess., App. 83 (Rep. Bingham, a principal draftsman of the Amendment and earlier proposals).

[10] Contrary to the suggestion of the dissent, § 5 does not grant Congress power to exercise discretion in the other direction and to enact "statutes so as in effect to dilute equal protection and due process decisions of this Court." We emphasize that Congress' power under § 5 is limited to adopting measures to enforce the guarantees of the Amendment; § 5 grants Congress no power to restrict, abrogate, or dilute these guarantees. Thus, for example, an enactment authorizing the States to establish racially segregated systems of education would not be — as required by § 5 — a measure "to enforce" the Equal Protection Clause since that clause of its own force prohibits such state laws.

There can be no doubt that § 4(e) may be regarded as an enactment to enforce the Equal Protection Clause. Congress explicitly declared that it enacted § 4(e) "to secure the rights under the fourteenth amendment of persons educated in American-flag schools in which the predominant classroom language was other than English." The persons referred to include those who have migrated from the Commonwealth of Puerto Rico to New York and who have been denied the right to vote because of their inability to read and write English, and the Fourteenth Amendment rights referred to include those emanating from the Equal Protection Clause. More specifically, § 4(e) may be viewed as a measure to secure for the Puerto Rican community residing in New York non-discriminatory treatment by government — both in the imposition of voting qualifications and the provision or administration of governmental services, such as public schools, public housing and law enforcement.

Section 4(e) may be readily seen as "plainly adapted" to furthering these aims of the Equal Protection Clause. The practical effect of § 4(e) is to prohibit New York from denying the right to vote to large segments of its Puerto Rican community. Congress has thus prohibited the State from denying to that community the right that is "preservative of all rights." *Yick Wo v. Hopkins*, 118 U.S. 356, 370 (1886). This enhanced political power will be helpful in gaining non-discriminatory treatment in public services for the entire Puerto Rican community. Section 4(e) thereby enables the Puerto Rican minority better to obtain "perfect equality of civil rights and the equal protection of the laws." It was well within congressional authority to say that this need of the Puerto Rican minority for the vote warranted federal intrusion upon any state interests served by the English literacy requirement. It was for Congress, as the branch that made the judgment, to assess and weigh the various conflicting considerations — the risk or pervasiveness of the discrimination in governmental services, the effectiveness of eliminating the state restriction on the right to vote as a means of dealing with the evil, the adequacy or availability of alternative remedies, and the nature and significance of the state interests that would be affected by the nullification of the English literacy requirement as applied to residents who have successfully completed the sixth grade in a Puerto Rican school. It is not for us to review the congressional resolution of those factors. It is enough that we be able to perceive a basis upon which the Congress might resolve the conflict as it did. There plainly was such a basis to support § 4(e) in the application in question in this case. Any contrary conclusion would require us to be blind to realities familiar to the legislators.

The result is no different if we confine our inquiry to the question whether § 4(e) was merely legislation aimed at the elimination of an invidious discrimination in establishing voter qualification. We are told New York's English literacy requirement originated in the desire to provide an incentive for non-English speaking immigrants to learn the English language and in order to ensure the intelligent exercise of the franchise. Yet Congress might well have questioned, in light of the many exemptions provided, and some evidence suggesting that prejudice played a prominent role in the enactment of the requirement, whether these were actually the interests being served. Congress might have also questioned whether denial of a right deemed so precious and fundamental in our society was a necessary or appropriate means of encouraging persons to learn English, or of furthering the goal of an intelligent exercise of the franchise. Finally, Congress might well have concluded that as a means of furthering the intelligent exercise of the franchise, an ability to read and understand Spanish is as effective as ability to read English for those to whom Spanish-language newspapers and Spanish-language radio and television programs are available to inform them of election issues and governmental affairs. Since Congress undertook to legislate so as to preclude the enforcement of the state law, and did so in the context of a general appraisal of the literacy requirements for voting, to which it brought a specially informed legislative competence, it was Congress' prerogative to weigh these competing considerations. Here again, it is enough that we perceive a basis upon which Congress might predicate a judgment that the application of New York's English literacy requirement to deny the right to vote to a person with a sixth grade education in Puerto Rican schools in which the language of instruction was other than English constituted an invidious discrimination in violation of the Equal Protection Clause.

There remains the question whether the congressional remedies adopted in § 4(e) constitute means which are not prohibited by, but are consistent "with the letter and spirit of the constitution." The only respect in which appellees contend that § 4(e) fails in this regard is that the section itself works an invidious discrimination in violation of the Fifth Amendment by prohibiting the enforcement of the English literacy requirement only for those educated in American-flag schools (schools located within United States jurisdiction) in which the language of instruction was other than English, and not for those educated in schools beyond the territorial limits of the United States in which the language of instruction was also other than English. This is not a complaint that Congress, in enacting § 4(e), has unconstitutionally denied or diluted anyone's right to vote but rather that Congress violated the Constitution by not extending the relief effected in § 4(e) to those educated in non-American-flag schools. We need not pause to determine whether appellees have a sufficient personal interest to have § 4(e) invalidated on this ground, since the argument in our view, falls on the merits.

Section 4(e) does not restrict or deny the franchise but in effect extends the franchise to persons who otherwise would be denied it by state law. . . . We need only decide whether the challenged limitation on the relief effected in § 4(e) was permissible. In deciding that question, the principle that calls for the closest scrutiny of distinctions in laws *denying* fundamental rights . . . is inapplicable; for the distinction challenged by appellees is presented only as a limitation on a reform measure aimed at eliminating an existing barrier to the exercise of the franchise. Rather, in deciding the constitutional propriety of the limitations in such a reform measure we are guided by the familiar principles that a "statute is not invalid under the Constitution because it might have gone farther than it did," *Roschen v. Ward*, 279 U.S. 337, 339 (1929), that a legislature need not "strike at all evils at the same time," *Semler v. Dental Examiners*, 294 U.S. 608, 610 (1935), and that "reform may take one step at a time, addressing itself to the phase of the problem which seems most acute to the legislative mind," *Williamson v. Lee Optical Co.*, 348 U.S. 483, 489 (1955).

Guided by these principles, we are satisfied that appellees' challenge to this limitation in § 4(e) is without merit. . . .

We therefore conclude that § 4(e), in the application challenged in this case, is appropriate legislation to enforce the Equal Protection Clause and that the judgment of the District Court must be and hereby is reversed.

[The concurring opinion of Justice Douglas has been omitted.]

JUSTICE HARLAN, with whom JUSTICE STEWART joins, dissenting.

Worthy as its purposes may be thought by many, I do not see how § 4(e) . . . can be sustained except at the sacrifice of fundamentals in the American constitutional system — the separation between the legislative and judicial function and the boundaries between federal and state political authority . . . .

I

. . . .

Any analysis of this problem must begin with the established rule of law that the franchise is essentially a matter of state concern, *Minor v. Happersett*, 88 U.S. 162 (1874); *Lassiter v. Northampton Election Bd.*, 360 U.S. 45, 52 (1959), subject only to the overriding requirements of various federal constitutional provisions dealing with the franchise, *e.g.*, the Fifteenth, Seventeenth, Nineteenth, and Twenty-fourth Amendments, and, as more recently decided, to the general principles of the Fourteenth Amendment. *Reynolds v. Sims*, 377 U.S. 533 (1963); *Carrington v. Rash*, 380 U.S. 89 (1965).

. . . .

In 1959, *Lassiter v. Northampton Election Bd.*, this Court dealt with substantially the same question and resolved it unanimously in favor of the legitimacy of a state literacy qualification. There a North Carolina English literacy test was challenged. We held that there was a "wide scope" for State qualifications of this sort. 360 U.S. at 51. . . .

I believe the same interests recounted in *Lassiter* indubitably point toward upholding the rationality of the New York voting test. . . .

Although to be sure there is a difference between a totally illiterate person and one who is literate in a foreign tongue, I do not believe that this added factor vitiates the constitutionality of the New York statute. . . . New York may justifiably want its voters to be able to understand candidates directly, rather than through possibly imprecise translations or summaries reported in a limited number of Spanish news media. . . . Relevant too is the fact that the New York English test is not complex, that it is fairly administered, and New York maintains free adult education classes which appellant and members of her class are encouraged to attend. . . . I would uphold the validity of the New York statute, unless the federal statute prevents that result, the question to which I now turn.

II

. . . .

The pivotal question in this instance is what effect the added factor of a congressional enactment has on the straight equal protection argument dealt with above. The Court declares that since § 5 of the Fourteenth Amendment gives to the Congress power to "enforce" the prohibitions of the Amendment by "appropriate" legislation, the test for judicial review of any congressional determination in this area is simply one of rationality; that is, in effect, was Congress acting rationally in declaring that New York's statute is irrational? . . . I believe the Court has confused the issue of how much enforcement power Congress possesses under § 5 with the distinct issue of what questions are appropriate for congressional determination and what questions are essentially judicial in nature.

When recognized state violations of federal constitutional standards have occurred, Congress is of course empowered by § 5 to take appropriate remedial measures to redress and prevent the wrongs. But it is a judicial question whether the condition with which Congress has thus sought to deal is in truth an infringement of the Constitution, something that is the necessary prerequisite to bringing the § 5 power into play at all. Thus, in *Ex parte Virginia*, 100 U.S. 339 (1879), involving a federal statute making it a federal crime to disqualify anyone from jury service because of race, the Court first held as a matter of constitutional law that "the Fourteenth Amendment secures, among other civil rights, to colored men, when charged with criminal offences against a State, an impartial jury trial, by jurors indifferently selected or chosen without discrimination against such jurors because of their color." *Id.* at 345. Only then did the Court hold that to enforce this prohibition upon state discrimination, Congress could enact a criminal statute of the type under consideration. . . .

A more recent Fifteenth Amendment case also serves to illustrate this distinction. In *South Carolina v. Katzenbach*, 383 U.S. 301 (1966), decided earlier this Term, we held certain remedial sections of the Voting Rights Act of 1965 constitutional under the

Fifteenth Amendment, which is directed against deprivations of the right to vote on account of race. In enacting those sections of the Voting Rights Act the Congress made a detailed investigation of various state practices that had been used to deprive Negroes of the franchise. *See* 383 U.S. at 308–15. In passing upon the remedial provisions, we reviewed first the "voluminous legislative history" as well as judicial precedents supporting the basic congressional finding that the clear commands of the Fifteenth Amendment had been infringed by various state subterfuges. *See* 383 U.S. at 309, 329–30, 333–34. Given the existence of the evil, we held the remedial steps taken by the legislature under the Enforcement Clause of the Fifteenth Amendment to be a justifiable exercise of congressional initiative.

Section 4(e), however, presents a significantly different type of congressional enactment. The question here is not whether the statute is appropriate remedial legislation to cure an established violation of a constitutional command, but whether there has in fact been an infringement of that constitutional command, that is, whether a particular state practice or, as here, a statute is so arbitrary or irrational as to offend the command of the Equal Protection Clause of the Fourteenth Amendment. That question is one for the judicial branch ultimately to determine. Were the rule otherwise, Congress would be able to qualify this Court's constitutional decisions under the Fourteenth and Fifteenth Amendments, let alone those under other provisions of the Constitution, by resorting to congressional power under the Necessary and Proper Clause. In view of this Court's holding in *Lassiter*, 360 U.S. 45, that an English literacy test is a permissible exercise of state supervision over its franchise, I do not think it is open to Congress to limit the effect of that decision as it has undertaken to do by § 4(e). In effect the Court reads § 5 of the Fourteenth Amendment as giving Congress the power to define the *substantive* scope of the Amendment. If that indeed be the true reach of § 5, then I do not see why Congress should not be able as well to exercise its § 5 "discretion" by enacting statutes so as in effect to dilute equal protection and due process decisions of this Court. In all such cases there is room for reasonable men to differ as to whether or not a denial of equal protection or due process has occurred, and the final decision is one of judgment. Until today this judgment has always been one for the judiciary to resolve.

I do not mean to suggest in what has been said that a legislative judgment of the type incorporated in § 4(e) is without any force whatsoever. Decisions on questions of equal protection and due process are based not on abstract logic, but on empirical foundations. To the extent "legislative facts" are relevant to a judicial determination, Congress is well equipped to investigate them, and such determinations are of course entitled to due respect. In *South Carolina v. Katzenbach*, 383 U.S. 301, such legislative findings were made to show that racial discrimination in voting was actually occurring. Similarly, in *Heart of Atlanta Motel, Inc. v. United States*, 379 U.S. 241 (1964), and *Katzenbach v. McClung*, 379 U.S. 294 (1964), this Court upheld Title II of the Civil Rights Act of 1964 under the Commerce Clause. There again the congressional determination that racial discrimination in a clearly defined group of public accommodations did effectively impede interstate commerce was based on "voluminous testimony," 379 U.S. at 253, which had been put before the Congress and in the context of which it passed remedial legislation.

But no such factual data provide a legislative record supporting § 4(e) . . . . There is simply no legislative record supporting such hypothesized discrimination of the sort we have hitherto insisted upon when congressional power is brought to bear on constitutionally reserved state concerns. *See Heart of Atlanta Motel*, 379 U.S. 241; *South Carolina v. Katzenbach*, 383 U.S. 301.

Thus, we have here not a matter of giving deference to a congressional estimate, based on its determination of legislative facts, bearing upon the validity *vel non* of a statute, but rather what can at most be called a legislative announcement that Congress believes a state law to entail an unconstitutional deprivation of equal protection. Although this kind of declaration is of course entitled to the most respectful consideration, coming as it does from a concurrent branch and one that is knowledgeable in matters of popular political participation, I do not believe it lessens our responsibility to decide the fundamental issue of whether in fact the state enactment violates federal constitutional rights.

. . . [I]t should be recognized that while the Fourteenth Amendment is a "brooding omnipresence" over all state legislation, the substantive matters which it touches are all within the primary legislative competence of the States. Federal authority, legislative no less than judicial, does not intrude unless there has been a denial by state action of Fourteenth Amendment limitations, in this instance a denial of equal protection. At least in the area of primary state concern a state statute that passes constitutional muster under the judicial standard of rationality should not be permitted to be set at naught by a mere contrary congressional pronouncement unsupported by a legislative record justifying that conclusion.

. . . .

I would affirm the judgments in each of these cases.

Exercise 14(B):

Consider the following matters in connection with *Katzenbach v. Morgan*:

(1)   How did the Constitution of 1789 address the qualifications for voters in federal elections? How did it do so with respect to State elections?

(2)   Under the Constitution *prior* to the Civil War Amendments — that is the Thirteenth, Fourteenth, and Fifteenth Amendments — is there some power that Congress may have relied upon as the basis for the Voting Rights Act of 1965?

(3)   Did the Civil War Amendments contain any other provision that, at least arguably, could have supported the Voting Rights Act of 1965?

(4)   New York argued that § 4(e) of the Voting Rights Act exceeded the power granted to Congress under Section 5 of the Fourteenth Amendment. The Supreme Court had previously held, in *Lassiter v. Northampton County Board of Elections*, 360 U.S. 45 (1959), that a State could impose an English literacy requirement as a condition of voting, without violating the U.S. Constitution. Nonetheless, Congress prohibited the application of certain English literacy requirements in a statute that purported to "enforce" the Equal Protection Clause. Was Congress free to simply disagree with the Court's view of whether the Constitution prohibited English literacy requirements as a condition of voting? If so, does the Supreme Court remain the "final arbiter" of the Constitution?

(5)   The majority asserted that Section Five was designed to serve a purpose parallel to the Necessary and Proper Clause. Is that analogy sound?

(6)   If one accepts the view that Congress is not bound in exercising its Section Five power only to "enforce" the substantive provisions of the Fourteenth Amendment as they are construed by the judiciary, is there any logic to prohibiting Congress from legislating to "enforce" its view of the Fourteenth Amendment even when its view would provide less protection to certain groups or fundamental rights than the view of the judiciary?

(7)   Assume that under Section Five Congress could mandate affirmative action — say, for the benefit of African Americans — in situations where the judiciary would not impose an affirmative action plan as a remedy in a specific case. If the Supreme Court would uphold that exercise of Section Five, is there any principle that would prohibit

Congress from forbidding the imposition of affirmative action plans — say, from concern for "reverse discrimination" — in situations where the judiciary would otherwise impose an affirmative action plan as a remedy in a specific case? Why or why not?

(8)   The majority referenced the right at issue as the "right that is 'preservative of all rights.'" Did it make a difference that voting rights were at issue?

(9)   In dissent, Justice Harlan asserted that "the necessary prerequisite to bringing the [Section 5] power into play" is "whether the condition with which Congress . . . sought to deal is in truth an infringement of the Constitution" which, in turn, is a question "essentially judicial in nature." Is that description of the Section Five power more consistent with the Court's construction of the respective roles of Congress and the judiciary with respect to Article I powers?

(10)   Four years after *Katzenbach v. Morgan*, the Court held that Congress lacked authority under Section Five of the Fourteenth Amendment to establish a minimum voting age of twenty-one years in State elections. That decision in *Oregon v. Mitchell*, 400 U.S. 112 (1970), prompted adoption of the Twenty-Sixth Amendment (proposed by Congress on March 23, 1971, and ratified within 107 days). If Congress could rely upon Section Five to preempt State laws requiring English literacy tests for participation in State elections, why could Congress not rely upon Section Five to preempt State laws requiring individuals to attain age 21 to participate in State elections?

SEMINOLE TRIBE OF FLORIDA v. FLORIDA
517 U.S. 44 (1996)

CHIEF JUSTICE REHNQUIST delivered the Opinion of the Court.

The Indian Gaming Regulatory Act provides that an Indian tribe may conduct certain gaming activities only in conformance with a valid compact between the tribe and the State in which the gaming activities are located. 25 U.S.C. § 2710(d)(1)(C). The Act, passed by Congress under the Indian Commerce Clause, U.S. Const., Art. I, § 8, cl. 3, imposes upon the States a duty to negotiate in good faith with an Indian tribe toward the formation of a compact, § 2710(d)(3)(A), and authorizes a tribe to bring suit in federal court against a State in order to compel performance of that duty, § 2710(d)(7). We hold that notwithstanding Congress' clear intent to abrogate the States' sovereign immunity, the Indian Commerce Clause does not grant Congress that power, and therefore § 2710(d)(7) cannot grant jurisdiction over a State that does not consent to be sued. We further hold that the doctrine of *Ex parte Young*, 209 U.S. 123 (1908), may not be used to enforce § 2710(d)(3) against a state official.

I

Congress passed the Indian Gaming Regulatory Act in 1988 in order to provide a statutory basis for the operation and regulation of gaming by Indian tribes. *See* 25 U.S.C. § 2702. The Act divides gaming on Indian lands into three classes — I, II, and III — and provides a different regulatory scheme for each class. Class III gaming — the type with which we are here concerned — is defined as "all forms of gaming that are not class I gaming or class II gaming," § 2703(8), and includes such things as slot machines, casino games, banking card games, dog racing, and lotteries. It is the most heavily regulated of the three classes. The Act provides that class III gaming is lawful only where it is: (1) authorized by an ordinance or resolution that (a) is adopted by the governing body of the Indian tribe, (b) satisfies certain statutorily prescribed requirements, and (c) is approved by the National Indian Gaming Commission; (2) located in a State that permits such gaming for any purpose by any person, organization, or entity; and (3) "conducted in conformance with a Tribal-State compact entered into by the Indian tribe and the State under paragraph (3) that is in effect." § 2710(d)(1).

The "paragraph (3)" to which the last prerequisite of § 2710(d)(1) refers is § 2710(d)(3), which describes the permissible scope of a Tribal-State compact, *see* § 2710(d)(3)(C), and provides that the compact is effective "only when notice of approval by the Secretary [of the Interior] of such compact has been published by the Secretary in the Federal Register," § 2710(d)(3)(B). More significant for our purposes, however, is that § 2710(d)(3) describes the process by which a State and an Indian tribe begin negotiations toward a Tribal-State compact:

> (A) Any Indian tribe having jurisdiction over the Indian lands upon which a class III gaming activity is being conducted, or is to be conducted, shall request the State in which such lands are located to enter into negotiations for the purpose of entering into a Tribal-State compact governing the conduct of gaming activities. Upon receiving such a request, the State shall negotiate with the Indian tribe in good faith to enter into such a compact.

The State's obligation to "negotiate with the Indian tribe in good faith" is made judicially enforceable by §§ 2710(d)(7)(A)(i) and (B)(i):

> (A) The United States district courts shall have jurisdiction over —

> (i) any cause of action initiated by an Indian tribe arising from the failure of a State to enter into negotiations with the Indian tribe for the purpose of entering into a Tribal-State compact under paragraph (3) or to conduct such negotiations in good faith. . .

Sections 2710(d)(7)(B)(ii)–(vii) describe an elaborate remedial scheme designed to ensure the formation of a Tribal-State compact. A tribe that brings an action under § 2710(d)(7)(A)(i) must show that no Tribal-State compact has been entered and that the State failed to respond in good faith to the tribe's request to negotiate; at that point, the burden then shifts to the State to prove that it did in fact negotiate in good faith. § 2710(d)(7)(B)(ii). If the district court concludes that the State has failed to negotiate in good faith toward the formation of a Tribal-State compact, then it "shall order the State and Indian Tribe to conclude such a compact within a 60-day period." § 2710(d)(7)(B)(iii). If no compact has been concluded 60 days after the court's order, then "the Indian tribe and the State shall each submit to a mediator appointed by the court a proposed compact that represents their last best offer for a compact." § 2710(d)(7)(B)(iv). The mediator chooses from between the two proposed compacts the one "which best comports with the terms of [the Act] and any other applicable Federal law and with the findings and order of the court," *id.*, and submits it to the State and the Indian tribe, § 2710(d)(7)(B)(v). If the State consents to the proposed compact within 60 days of its submission by the mediator, then the proposed compact is "treated as a Tribal-State compact entered into under paragraph (3)." § 2710(d)(7)(B)(vi). If, however, the State does not consent within that 60-day period, then the Act provides that the mediator "shall notify the Secretary [of the Interior]" and that the Secretary "shall prescribe . . . procedures . . . under which class III gaming may be conducted on the Indian lands over which the Indian tribe has jurisdiction." § 2710(d)(7)(B)(vii).

In September 1991, the Seminole Tribe of Florida, petitioner, sued the State of Florida and its Governor, Lawton Chiles, respondents. Invoking jurisdiction under 25 U.S.C. § 2710(d)(7)(A), as well as 28 U.S.C. §§ 1331 and 1362, petitioner alleged that respondents had "refused to enter into any negotiation for inclusion of [certain gaming activities] in a tribal-state compact," thereby violating the "requirement of good faith negotiation" contained in § 2710(d)(3). Respondents moved to dismiss the complaint, arguing that the suit violated the State's sovereign immunity from suit in federal court.

The District Court denied respondents' motion and respondents took an interlocutory appeal of that decision.

The Court of Appeals for the Eleventh Circuit reversed the decision of the District Court, holding that the Eleventh Amendment barred petitioner's suit against respondents. The court agreed with the District Court that Congress in § 2710(d)(7) intended to abrogate the States' sovereign immunity, and also agreed that the Act had been passed pursuant to Congress' power under the Indian Commerce Clause, U.S. Const., Art. I, § 8, cl. 3. The court disagreed with the District Court, however, that the Indian Commerce Clause grants Congress the power to abrogate a State's Eleventh Amendment immunity from suit, and concluded therefore that it had no jurisdiction over petitioner's suit against Florida. The court further held that *Ex parte Young*, 209 U.S. 123 (1908), does not permit an Indian tribe to force good-faith negotiations by suing the Governor of a State. Finding that it lacked subject-matter jurisdiction, the Eleventh Circuit remanded to the District Court with directions to dismiss petitioner's suit.

. . . [W]e granted certiorari in order to consider two questions: (1) Does the Eleventh Amendment prevent Congress from authorizing suits by Indian tribes against States for prospective injunctive relief to enforce legislation enacted pursuant to the Indian Commerce Clause?; and (2) Does the doctrine of *Ex parte Young* permit suits against a State's Governor for prospective injunctive relief to enforce the good-faith bargaining requirement of the Act? We answer the first question in the affirmative, the second in the negative, and we therefore affirm the Eleventh Circuit's dismissal of petitioner's suit.

The Eleventh Amendment provides:

> The Judicial power of the United States shall not be construed to extend to any suit in law or equity, commenced or prosecuted against one of the United States by Citizens of another State, or by Citizens or Subjects of any Foreign State.

Although the text of the Amendment would appear to restrict only the Article III diversity jurisdiction of the federal courts, "we have understood the Eleventh Amendment to stand not so much for what it says, but for the presupposition . . . which it confirms." *Blatchford v. Native Village of Noatak*, 501 U.S. 775, 779 (1991). That presupposition, first observed over a century ago in *Hans v. Louisiana*, 134 U.S. 1 (1890), has two parts: first, that each State is a sovereign entity in our federal system; and second, that " '[i]t is inherent in the nature of sovereignty not to be amenable to the suit of an individual without its consent,' " *id.* at 13 (emphasis deleted), *quoting* THE FEDERALIST NO. 81 (A. Hamilton). . . . For over a century we have reaffirmed that federal jurisdiction over suits against unconsenting States "was not contemplated by the Constitution when establishing the judicial power of the United States." *Hans*, 134 U.S. at 15.

Here, petitioner has sued the State of Florida and it is undisputed that Florida has not consented to the suit. *See Blatchford*, 501 U.S. at 782 (States by entering into the Constitution did not consent to suit by Indian tribes). Petitioner nevertheless contends that its suit is not barred by state sovereign immunity. First, it argues that Congress through the Act abrogated the States' sovereign immunity. Alternatively, petitioner maintains that its suit against the Governor may go forward under *Ex parte Young*. We consider each of those arguments in turn.

II

Petitioner argues that Congress through the Act abrogated the States' immunity from suit. In order to determine whether Congress has abrogated the States' sovereign immunity, we ask two questions: first, whether Congress has "unequivocally expresse[d] its intent to abrogate the immunity," *Green v. Mansour*, 474 U.S. 64, 68 (1985); and second, whether Congress has acted "pursuant to a valid exercise of power," *id.*

A

Congress' intent to abrogate the States' immunity from suit must be obvious from "a clear legislative statement." *Blatchford*, 501 U.S. at 786. This rule arises from a recognition of the important role played by the Eleventh Amendment and the broader principles that it reflects. *See Atascadero State Hospital v. Scanlon*, 473 U.S. 234, 238–39 (1985). In *Atascadero*, we held that "[a] general authorization for suit in federal court is not the kind of unequivocal statutory language sufficient to abrogate the Eleventh Amendment." 473 U.S. at 246; *see also Blatchford*, 501 U.S. at 786 n.4 ("The fact that Congress grants jurisdiction to hear a claim does not suffice to show Congress has abrogated all defenses to that claim") (emphases deleted). Rather, as we said in *Dellmuth v. Muth*, 491 U.S. 223 (1989):

. . . .

Here, we agree with the parties, with the Eleventh Circuit in the decision below and with virtually every other court that has confronted the question that Congress has in § 2710(d)(7) provided an "unmistakably clear" statement of its intent to abrogate. . . .

B

. . . [W]e turn now to consider whether the Act was passed "pursuant to a valid exercise of power." *Green v. Mansour*, 474 U.S. at 68. Before we address that question here, however, we think it necessary first to define the scope of our inquiry.

Petitioner suggests that one consideration weighing in favor of finding the power to abrogate here is that the Act authorizes only prospective injunctive relief rather than retroactive monetary relief. But we have often made it clear that the relief sought by a plaintiff suing a State is irrelevant to the question whether the suit is barred by the Eleventh Amendment. *See, e.g., Cory v. White*, 457 U.S. 85, 90 (1982) ("It would be a novel proposition indeed that the Eleventh Amendment does not bar a suit to enjoin the State itself simply because no money judgment is sought"). We think it follows *a fortiori* from this proposition that the type of relief sought is irrelevant to whether Congress has power to abrogate States' immunity. The Eleventh Amendment does not exist solely in order to "preven[t] federal-court judgments that must be paid out of a State's treasury," *Hess v. Port Authority Trans-Hudson Corporation*, 513 U.S. 30, 48 (1994); it also serves to avoid "the indignity of subjecting a State to the coercive process of judicial tribunals at the instance of private parties," *Puerto Rico Aqueduct and Sewer Authority*, 506 U.S. 139, 146 (1993).

. . . .

Thus our inquiry into whether Congress has the power to abrogate unilaterally the States' immunity from suit is narrowly focused on one question: Was the Act in question passed pursuant to a constitutional provision granting Congress the power to abrogate? *See, e.g., Fitzpatrick v. Bitzer*, 427 U.S. 445, 452–56 (1976). Previously, in conducting that inquiry, we have found authority to abrogate under only two provisions of the Constitution. In *Fitzpatrick*, we recognized that the Fourteenth Amendment, by expanding federal power at the expense of state autonomy, had fundamentally altered the balance of state and federal power struck by the Constitution. *Id.* at 455. We noted that § 1 of the Fourteenth Amendment contained prohibitions expressly directed at the States and that § 5 of the Amendment expressly provided that "The Congress shall have power to enforce, by appropriate legislation, the provisions of this article." *See id.* at 453.

We held that through the Fourteenth Amendment, federal power extended to intrude upon the province of the Eleventh Amendment and therefore that § 5 of the Fourteenth Amendment allowed Congress to abrogate the immunity from suit guaranteed by that Amendment.

In only one other case has congressional abrogation of the States' Eleventh Amendment immunity been upheld. In *Pennsylvania v. Union Gas Co.*, 491 U.S. 1 (1989), a plurality of the Court found that the Interstate Commerce Clause, Art. I, § 8, cl. 3, granted Congress the power to abrogate state sovereign immunity, stating that the power to regulate interstate commerce would be "incomplete without the authority to render States liable in damages." 491 U.S. at 19–20. Justice White added the fifth vote necessary to the result in that case, but wrote separately in order to express that he "[did] not agree with much of [the plurality's] reasoning." *Id.* at 57 (opinion concurring in judgment in part and dissenting in part).

In arguing that Congress through the Act abrogated the States' sovereign immunity, petitioner does not challenge the Eleventh Circuit's conclusion that the Act was passed pursuant to neither the Fourteenth Amendment nor the Interstate Commerce Clause. Instead, accepting the lower court's conclusion that the Act was passed pursuant to Congress' power under the Indian Commerce Clause, petitioner now asks us to consider whether that Clause grants Congress the power to abrogate the States' sovereign immunity.

Petitioner begins with the plurality decision in *Union Gas* and contends that "[t]here is no principled basis for finding that congressional power under the Indian Commerce Clause is less than that conferred by the Interstate Commerce Clause." Noting that the *Union Gas* plurality found the power to abrogate from the "plenary" character of the grant of authority over interstate commerce, petitioner emphasizes that the Interstate Commerce Clause leaves the States with some power to regulate, *see, e.g., West Lynn Creamery, Inc. v. Healy*, 512 U.S. 186 (1994), whereas the Indian Commerce Clause makes "Indian relations . . . the exclusive province of federal law." *County of Oneida v. Oneida Indian Nation*, 470 U.S. 226, 234 (1985). Contending that the Indian Commerce Clause vests the Federal Government with "the duty of protect[ing]" the tribes from "local ill feeling" and "the people of the States," petitioner argues that the abrogation power is necessary "to protect the tribes from state action denying federally guaranteed rights."

Respondents dispute petitioner's analogy between the Indian Commerce Clause and the Interstate Commerce Clause. They note that we have recognized that "the Interstate Commerce and Indian Commerce Clauses have very different applications," and from that they argue that the two provisions are "wholly dissimilar." Respondents contend that the Interstate Commerce Clause grants the power of abrogation only because Congress' authority to regulate interstate commerce would be "incomplete" without that "necessary" power. The Indian Commerce Clause is distinguishable, respondents contend, because it gives Congress complete authority over the Indian tribes. Therefore, the abrogation power is not "necessary" to Congress' exercise of its power under the Indian Commerce Clause.

Both parties make their arguments from the plurality decision in *Union Gas*, and we, too, begin there. We think it clear that Justice Brennan's opinion finds Congress' power to abrogate under the Interstate Commerce Clause from the States' cession of their sovereignty when they gave Congress plenary power to regulate interstate commerce. *See Union Gas*, 491 U.S. at 17 ("The important point . . . is that the provision both expands federal power and contracts state power"). Respondents' focus elsewhere is misplaced. While the plurality decision states that Congress' power under the Interstate Commerce Clause would be incomplete without the power to abrogate, that statement is made solely in order to emphasize the broad scope of Congress' authority over interstate commerce. *Id.* at 19–20. Moreover, respondents' rationale would mean that where Congress has less authority, and the States have more, Congress' means for exercising that power must be greater. We read the plurality opinion to provide just the opposite. Indeed, it was in those circumstances where Congress exercised complete authority that Justice Brennan thought the power to abrogate most necessary. *Id.* at 20 ("Since the States may not legislate at all in [the aforementioned] situations, a conclusion that Congress may not create a cause of action for money damages against the States would mean that no one could do so. And in many situations, it is only money damages that will carry out Congress' legitimate objectives under the Commerce Clause").

Following the rationale of the *Union Gas* plurality, our inquiry is limited to determining whether the Indian Commerce Clause, like the Interstate Commerce Clause, is a grant of authority to the Federal Government at the expense of the States. The answer to that question is obvious. If anything, the Indian Commerce Clause accomplishes a greater transfer of power from the States to the Federal Government than does the Interstate Commerce Clause. This is clear enough from the fact that the States still exercise some authority over interstate trade but have been divested of virtually all authority over Indian commerce and Indian tribes. Under the rationale of *Union Gas,* if the States' partial cession of authority over a particular area includes cession of the immunity from suit, then their virtually total cession of authority over a different area must also include cession of the immunity from suit. *See id.* at 42. . . .

Respondents argue, however, that we need not conclude that the Indian Commerce Clause grants the power to abrogate the States' sovereign immunity. Instead, they contend that if we find the rationale of the *Union Gas* plurality to extend to the Indian Commerce Clause, then " *Union Gas* should be reconsidered and overruled." Generally, the principle of *stare decisis,* and the interests that it serves, *viz.,* "the evenhanded, predictable, and consistent development of legal principles, . . . reliance on judicial decisions, and . . . the actual and perceived integrity of the judicial process," *Payne v. Tennessee,* 501 U.S. 808, 827 (1991), counsel strongly against reconsideration of our precedent. Nevertheless, we always have treated *stare decisis* as a "principle of policy," *Helvering v. Hallock,* 309 U.S. 106, 119 (1940), and not as an "nexorable command," *Payne,* 501 U.S. at 828. "[W]hen governing decisions are unworkable or are badly reasoned, 'this Court has never felt constrained to follow precedent.' " *Id.* at 827. Our willingness to reconsider our earlier decisions has been "particularly true in constitutional cases, because in such cases 'correction through legislative action is practically impossible.' " *Payne,* 501 U.S. at 828.

The Court in *Union Gas* reached a result without an expressed rationale agreed upon by a majority of the Court. We have already seen that Justice Brennan's opinion received the support of only three other Justices. Of the other five, Justice White, who provided the fifth vote for the result, wrote separately in order to indicate his disagreement with the plurality's rationale and four Justices joined together in a dissent that rejected the plurality's rationale. Since it was issued, *Union Gas* has created confusion among the lower courts that have sought to understand and apply the deeply fractured decision. *See, e.g., Chavez v. Arte Publico Press,* 59 F.3d 539, 543–45 (5th Cir. 1995) ("Justice White's concurrence must be taken on its face to disavow" the plurality's theory); *Seminole Tribe of Florida v. Florida,* 11 F.3d 1016, 1027 (11th Cir. 1994) (Justice White's "vague concurrence renders the continuing validity of *Union Gas* in doubt").

The plurality's rationale also deviated sharply from our established federalism jurisprudence and essentially eviscerated our decision in *Hans. See Union Gas,* 491 U.S. at 36 ("If *Hans* means only that federal-question suits for money damages against the States cannot be brought in federal court unless Congress clearly says so, it means nothing at all") (Scalia, J., dissenting). It was well established in 1989 when *Union Gas* was decided that the Eleventh Amendment stood for the constitutional principle that state sovereign immunity limited the federal courts' jurisdiction under Article III. The text of the Amendment itself is clear enough on this point: "The Judicial power of the United States shall not be construed to extend to any suit . . . ." And our decisions since *Hans* had been equally clear that the Eleventh Amendment reflects "the fundamental principle of sovereign immunity [that] limits the grant of judicial authority in Art. III," *Pennhurst State School and Hospital v. Halderman*, 465 U.S. 89, 97–98 (1984).

Never before the decision in *Union Gas* had we suggested that the bounds of Article III could be expanded by Congress operating pursuant to any constitutional provision other than the Fourteenth Amendment. Indeed, it had seemed fundamental that Congress could not expand the jurisdiction of the federal courts beyond the bounds of Article III. *Marbury v. Madison*, 5 U.S. 137 (1803). The plurality's citation of prior decisions for support was based upon what we believe to be a misreading of precedent. *See Union Gas*, 491 U.S. at 40–41 (Scalia, J., dissenting). The plurality claimed support for its decision from a case holding the unremarkable, and completely unrelated, proposition that the States may waive their sovereign immunity and cited as precedent propositions that had been merely assumed for the sake of argument in earlier cases.

The plurality's extended reliance upon our decision in *Fitzpatrick v. Bitzer*, 427 U.S. 445 (1976), that Congress could under the Fourteenth Amendment abrogate the States' sovereign immunity was also, we believe, misplaced. *Fitzpatrick* was based upon a rationale wholly inapplicable to the Interstate Commerce Clause, *viz.*, that the Fourteenth Amendment, adopted well after the adoption of the Eleventh Amendment and the ratification of the Constitution, operated to alter the pre-existing balance between state and federal power achieved by Article III and the Eleventh Amendment. *Id.* at 454. As the dissent in *Union Gas* made clear, *Fitzpatrick* cannot be read to justify "limitation of the principle embodied in the Eleventh Amendment through appeal to antecedent provisions of the Constitution."

Reconsidering the decision in *Union Gas*, we conclude that none of the policies underlying *stare decisis* require our continuing adherence to its holding. The decision has, since its issuance, been of questionable precedential value, largely because a majority of the Court expressly disagreed with the rationale of the plurality. *See Nichols v. United States*, 511 U.S. 738, 746 (1994) (the "degree of confusion following a splintered decision . . . is itself a reason for reexamining that decision"). The case involved the interpretation of the Constitution and therefore may be altered only by constitutional amendment or revision by this Court. Finally, both the result in *Union Gas* and the plurality's rationale depart from our established understanding of the Eleventh Amendment and undermine the accepted function of Article III. We feel bound to conclude that *Union Gas* was wrongly decided and that it should be, and now is, overruled.

The dissent makes no effort to defend the decision in *Union Gas*, but nonetheless would find congressional power to abrogate in this case. Contending that our decision is a novel extension of the Eleventh Amendment, the dissent chides us for "attend[ing]" to *dicta*. We adhere in this case, however, not to mere *obiter dicta*, but rather to the well-established rationale upon which the Court based the results of its earlier decisions. When an opinion issues for the Court, it is not only the result but also those portions of the opinion necessary to that result by which we are bound. *Cf. Burnham v. Superior Court*, 495 U.S. 604, 613 (1990) (exclusive basis of a judgment is not *dicta*) (plurality); *County of Allegheny v. American Civil Liberties Union*, 492 U.S. 573, 668 (1989) ("As a general rule, the principle of *stare decisis* directs us to adhere not only to the holdings of our prior cases, but also to their explications of the governing rules of law") (Kennedy, J., concurring and dissenting); *Sheet Metal Workers v. EEOC*, 478 U.S. 421, 490 (1986) ("Although technically *dicta*, . . . an important part of the Court's rationale for the result that it reache[s] . . . is entitled to greater weight") (O'Connor, J., concurring). For over a century, we have grounded our decisions in the oft-repeated understanding of state sovereign immunity as an essential part of the Eleventh Amendment. In

Principality of Monaco v. Mississippi, 292 U.S. 313 (1934), the Court held that the Eleventh Amendment barred a suit brought against a State by a foreign state. Chief Justice Hughes wrote for a unanimous Court:

. . . .

> Manifestly, we cannot rest with a mere literal application of the words of [Article III § 2], or assume that the letter of the Eleventh Amendment exhausts the restrictions upon suits against non-consenting States. Behind the words of the constitutional provisions are postulates which limit and control. There is the essential postulate that the controversies, as contemplated, shall be found to be of a justiciable character. There is also the postulate that States of the Union, still possessing attributes of sovereignty, shall be immune from suits, without their consent, save where there has been a "surrender of this immunity in the plan of the convention."

Id. at 321–23.

. . . .

The dissent mischaracterizes the *Hans* opinion. That decision found its roots not solely in the common law of England, but in the much more fundamental " 'jurisprudence in all civilized nations.' " *Hans*, 134 U.S. at 17, *quoting Beers v. Arkansas*, 61 U.S. 527, 529 (1858); *see also* THE FEDERALIST No. 81 (A. Hamilton) (sovereign immunity "is the general sense and the general practice of mankind"). The dissent's proposition that the common law of England, where adopted by the States, was open to change by the Legislature is wholly unexceptionable and largely beside the point: that common law provided the substantive rules of law rather than jurisdiction. *Cf. Monaco*, 292 U.S. at 323 (state sovereign immunity, like the requirement that there be a "justiciable" controversy, is a constitutionally grounded limit on federal jurisdiction). It also is noteworthy that the principle of state sovereign immunity stands distinct from other principles of the common law in that only the former prompted a specific constitutional amendment.

Hans — with a much closer vantage point than the dissent — recognized that the decision in *Chisholm* was contrary to the well-understood meaning of the Constitution. The dissent's conclusion that the decision in *Chisholm* was "reasonable" certainly would have struck the Framers of the Eleventh Amendment as quite odd: That decision created "such a shock of surprise that the Eleventh Amendment was at once proposed and adopted." *Monaco*, 292 U.S. at 325. The dissent's lengthy analysis of the text of the Eleventh Amendment is directed at a straw man — we long have recognized that blind reliance upon the text of the Eleventh Amendment is " 'to strain the Constitution and the law to a construction never imagined or dreamed of.' " *Monaco*, 292 U.S. at 326, *quoting Hans*, 134 U.S. at 15. The text dealt in terms only with the problem presented by the decision in *Chisholm;* in light of the fact that the federal courts did not have federal question jurisdiction at the time the Amendment was passed (and would not have it until 1875), it seems unlikely that much thought was given to the prospect of federal-question jurisdiction over the States.

. . . .

III

Petitioner argues that we may exercise jurisdiction over its suit to enforce § 2710(d)(3) against the Governor notwithstanding the jurisdictional bar of the Eleventh Amendment. Petitioner notes that since our decision in *Ex parte Young*, 209 U.S. 123 (1908), we often have found federal jurisdiction over a suit against a state official when that suit seeks only prospective injunctive relief in order to "end a continuing violation of federal law." *Green v. Mansour,* 474 U.S. at 68. The situation presented here, however, is sufficiently different from that giving rise to the traditional *Ex parte Young* action so as to preclude the availability of that doctrine.

Here, the "continuing violation of federal law" alleged by petitioner is the Governor's failure to bring the State into compliance with § 2710(d)(3). But the duty to negotiate imposed upon the State by that statutory provision does not stand alone. Rather, as we have seen, Congress passed § 2710(d)(3) in conjunction with the carefully crafted and intricate remedial scheme set forth in § 2710(d)(7).

Where Congress has created a remedial scheme for the enforcement of a particular federal right, we have, in suits against federal officers, refused to supplement that scheme with one created by the judiciary. *Schweiker v. Chilicky,* 487 U.S. 412, 423 (1988) ("When the design of a Government program suggests that Congress has provided what it considers adequate remedial mechanisms for constitutional violations that may occur in the course of its administration, we have not created additional . . . remedies"). Here, of course, the question is not whether a remedy should be created, but instead is whether the Eleventh Amendment bar should be lifted, as it was in *Ex parte Young,* in order to allow a suit against a state officer. Nevertheless, we think that the same general principle applies: Therefore, where Congress has prescribed a detailed remedial scheme for the enforcement against a State of a statutorily created right, a court should hesitate before casting aside those limitations and permitting an action against a state officer based upon *Ex parte Young.*

. . . [A]n action brought against a state official under *Ex parte Young* would expose that official to the full remedial powers of a federal court, including, presumably, contempt sanctions. If § 2710(d)(3) could be enforced in a suit under *Ex parte Young,* § 2710(d)(7) would have been superfluous; it is difficult to see why an Indian tribe would suffer through the intricate scheme of § 2710(d)(7) when more complete and more immediate relief would be available under *Ex parte Young.*

Here, of course, we have found that Congress does not have authority under the Constitution to make the State suable in federal court under § 2710(d)(7). Nevertheless, the fact that Congress chose to impose upon the State a liability that is significantly more limited than would be the liability imposed upon the state officer under *Ex parte Young* strongly indicates that Congress had no wish to create the latter under § 2710(d)(3). Nor are we free to rewrite the statutory scheme in order to approximate what we think Congress might have wanted had it known that § 2710(d)(7) was beyond its authority. If that effort is to be made, it should be made by Congress, and not by the federal courts. We hold that *Ex parte Young* is inapplicable to petitioner's suit against the Governor of Florida, and therefore that suit is barred by the Eleventh Amendment and must be dismissed for a lack of jurisdiction.

IV

The Eleventh Amendment prohibits Congress from making the State of Florida capable of being sued in federal court. The narrow exception to the Eleventh Amendment provided by the *Ex parte Young* doctrine cannot be used to enforce § 2710(d)(3) because Congress enacted a remedial scheme, § 2710(d)(7), specifically designed for the enforcement of that right. The Eleventh Circuit's dismissal of petitioner's suit is hereby affirmed.

It is so ordered.

JUSTICE STEVENS, dissenting.

. . . .

The importance of the majority's decision to overrule the Court's holding in *Pennsylvania v. Union Gas Co.* cannot be overstated. The majority's opinion does not simply preclude Congress from establishing the rather curious statutory scheme under which Indian tribes may seek the aid of a federal court to secure a State's good-faith negotiations over gaming regulations. Rather, it prevents Congress from providing a federal forum for a broad range of actions against States, from those sounding in copyright and patent law, to those concerning bankruptcy, environmental law, and the regulation of our vast national economy.

There may be room for debate over whether, in light of the Eleventh Amendment, Congress has the power to ensure that such a cause of action may be enforced in federal court by a citizen of another State or a foreign citizen. There can be no serious debate, however, over whether Congress has the power to ensure that such a cause of action may be brought by a citizen of the State being sued. Congress' authority in that regard is clear.

As Justice Souter has convincingly demonstrated, the Court's contrary conclusion is profoundly misguided. Despite the thoroughness of his analysis, supported by sound reason, history, precedent, and strikingly uniform scholarly commentary, the shocking character of the majority's affront to a coequal branch of our Government merits additional comment.

I

. . . .

The language of Article III certainly gives no indication that such an implicit [jurisdictional] bar exists. That provision's text specifically provides for federal-court jurisdiction over all cases arising under federal law. Moreover, as I have explained, Justice Iredell's dissent argued that it was the Judiciary Act of 1789, not Article III, that prevented the federal courts from entertaining Chisholm's diversity action against Georgia. Therefore, Justice Iredell's analysis at least suggests that it was by no means a fixed view at the time of the founding that Article III prevented Congress from rendering States suable in federal court by their own citizens. In sum, little more than speculation justifies the conclusion that the Eleventh Amendment's express but partial limitation on the scope of Article III reveals that an implicit but more general one was already in place.

II

. . . .

Hans does not hold, however, that the Eleventh Amendment, or any other constitutional provision, precludes federal courts from entertaining actions brought by citizens against their own States in the face of contrary congressional direction. As I have explained before, *see Pennsylvania v. Union Gas Co.*, 491 U.S. 1, 25–26 (Stevens, J., concurring), and as Justice Souter effectively demonstrates, *Hans* instead reflects, at the most, this Court's conclusion that, as a matter of federal common law, federal courts should decline to entertain suits against unconsenting States. Because *Hans* did not announce a constitutionally mandated jurisdictional bar, one need not overrule *Hans*, or even question its reasoning, in order to conclude that Congress may direct the federal courts to reject sovereign immunity in those suits not mentioned by the Eleventh Amendment. Instead, one need only follow it.

. . . .

Given the nature of the cause of action involved in *Hans*, as well as the terms of the underlying jurisdictional statute, the Court's decision to apply the common law doctrine of sovereign immunity in that case clearly should not control the outcome here. The reasons that may support a federal court's hesitancy to construe a judicially crafted constitutional remedy narrowly out of respect for a State's sovereignty do not bear on whether Congress may preclude a State's invocation of such a defense when it expressly establishes a federal remedy for the violation of a federal right.

. . . .

III

. . . .

The Court's holdings in *Fitzpatrick v. Bitzer*, 427 U.S. 445 (1976), and *Pennsylvania v. Union Gas Co.*, 491 U.S. 1 (1989), do unquestionably establish, however, that Congress has the power to deny the States and their officials the right to rely on the nonconstitutional defense of sovereign immunity in an action brought by one of their own citizens. As the opinions in the latter case demonstrate, there can be legitimate disagreement about whether Congress intended a particular statute to authorize litigation against a State. Nevertheless, the Court there squarely held that the Commerce Clause was an adequate source of authority for such a private remedy. In a rather novel rejection of the doctrine of *stare decisis*, the Court today demeans that holding by repeatedly describing it as a "plurality decision" because Justice White did not deem it necessary to set forth the reasons for his vote. As Justice Souter's opinion today demonstrates, the arguments in support of Justice White's position are so patent and so powerful that his actual vote should be accorded full respect. Indeed, far more significant than the "plurality" character of the three opinions supporting the holding in *Union Gas* is the fact that the issue confronted today has been squarely addressed by a total of 13 Justices, 8 of whom cast their votes with the so-called "plurality."

The fundamental error that continues to lead the Court astray is its failure to acknowledge that its modern embodiment of the ancient doctrine of sovereign immunity "has absolutely nothing to do with the limit on judicial power contained in the Eleventh Amendment." *Id.* at 25 (Stevens, J., concurring). It rests rather on concerns of federalism and comity that merit respect but are nevertheless, in cases such as the one before us, subordinate to the plenary power of Congress.

IV

. . . .

While I am persuaded that there is no justification for permanently enshrining the judge-made law of sovereign immunity, I recognize that federalism concerns — and even the interest in protecting the solvency of the States that was at work in *Chisholm* and *Hans* — may well justify a grant of immunity from federal litigation in certain classes of cases. Such a grant, however, should be the product of a reasoned decision by the policymaking branch of our Government. For this Court to conclude that timeworn shibboleths iterated and reiterated by judges should take precedence over the deliberations of the Congress of the United States is simply irresponsible.

. . . .

For these reasons, as well as those set forth in Justice Souter's opinion, I respectfully dissent.

JUSTICE SOUTER, with whom JUSTICE GINSBURG and JUSTICE BREYER join, dissenting.

In holding the State of Florida immune to suit under the Indian Gaming Regulatory Act, the Court today holds for the first time since the founding of the Republic that Congress has no authority to subject a State to the jurisdiction of a federal court at the behest of an individual asserting a federal right. [T]he Court invokes the Eleventh Amendment as authority for this proposition . . . . [W]e have two Eleventh Amendments, the one ratified in 1795, the other (so-called) invented by the Court nearly a century later in *Hans v. Louisiana*, 134 U.S. 1 (1890). . . .

. . . .

It is useful to separate three questions: (1) whether the States enjoyed sovereign immunity if sued in their own courts in the period prior to ratification of the National Constitution; (2) if so, whether after ratification the States were entitled to claim some such immunity when sued in a federal court exercising jurisdiction either because the suit was between a State and a nonstate litigant who was not its citizen, or because the issue in the case raised a federal question; and (3) whether any state sovereign immunity recognized in federal court may be abrogated by Congress.

The answer to the first question is not clear, although some of the Framers assumed that States did enjoy immunity in their own courts. The second question was not debated at the time of ratification, except as to citizen-state diversity jurisdiction; there was no unanimity, but in due course the Court in *Chisholm v. Georgia* answered that a state defendant enjoyed no such immunity. As to federal-question jurisdiction, state sovereign immunity seems not to have been debated prior to ratification, the silence probably showing a general understanding at the time that the States would have no immunity in such cases.

. . . The *Hans* Court erroneously assumed that a State could plead sovereign immunity against a noncitizen suing under federal-question jurisdiction, and for that reason held that a State must enjoy the same protection in a suit by one of its citizens. The error of *Hans*'s reasoning is underscored by its clear inconsistency with the Founders' hostility to the implicit reception of common-law doctrine as federal law, and with the Founders' conception of sovereign power as divided between the States and the National Government for the sake of very practical objectives.

The Court's answer today to the third question is likewise at odds with the Founders' view that common law, when it was received into the new American legal system, was always subject to legislative amendment. In ignoring the reasons for this pervasive understanding at the time of the ratification, and in holding that a nontextual common-law rule limits a clear grant of congressional power under Article I, the Court follows a course that has brought it to grief before in our history, and promises to do so again.

Beyond this third question that elicits today's holding, there is one further issue. To reach the Court's result, it must not only hold the *Hans* doctrine to be outside the reach of Congress, but must also displace the doctrine of *Ex parte Young* that an officer of the government may be ordered prospectively to follow federal law, in cases in which the government may not itself be sued directly. None of its reasons for displacing *Young*'s jurisdictional doctrine withstand scrutiny.

. . . .

. . . [T]he 1787 Constitution might have addressed state sovereign immunity by eliminating whatever sovereign immunity the States previously had, as to any matter subject to federal law or jurisdiction; by recognizing an analogue to the old immunity in the new context of federal jurisdiction, but subject to abrogation as to any matter within that jurisdiction; or by enshrining a doctrine of inviolable state sovereign immunity in the text, thereby giving it constitutional protection in the new federal jurisdiction.

. . . The 1787 draft in fact said nothing on the subject, and it was this very silence that occasioned some, though apparently not widespread, dispute among the Framers and others over whether ratification of the Constitution would preclude a State sued in federal court from asserting sovereign immunity as it could have done on any matter of nonfederal law litigated in its own courts.

. . . .

The history and structure of the Eleventh Amendment convincingly show that it reaches only to suits subject to federal jurisdiction exclusively under the Citizen-State Diversity Clauses. In precisely tracking the language in Article III providing for citizen-state diversity jurisdiction, the text of the Amendment does, after all, suggest to common sense that only the Diversity Clauses are being addressed. If the Framers had meant the Amendment to bar federal-question suits as well, they could not only have made their intentions clearer very easily, but could simply have adopted the first post-*Chisholm* proposal, introduced in the House of Representatives by Theodore Sedgwick of Massachusetts on instructions from the Legislature of that Commonwealth. Its provisions would have had exactly that expansive effect:

> [N]o state shall be liable to be made a party defendant, in any of the judicial courts, established, or which shall be established under the authority of the United States, at the suit of any person or persons, whether a citizen or citizens, or a foreigner or foreigners, or of any body politic or corporate, whether within or without the United States.

Gazette of the United States 303 (Feb. 20, 1793).

With its references to suits by citizens as well as non-citizens, the Sedgwick amendment would necessarily have been applied beyond the Diversity Clauses, and for a reason that would have been wholly obvious to the people of the time. Sedgwick sought such a broad amendment because many of the States, including his own, owed debts subject to collection under the Treaty of Paris. Suits to collect such debts would "arise under" that Treaty and thus be subject to federal-question jurisdiction under Article III. Such a suit, indeed, was then already pending against Massachusetts, having been brought in this Court by Christopher Vassall, an erstwhile Bostonian whose move to England on the eve of revolutionary hostilities had presented his former neighbors with the irresistible temptation to confiscate his vacant mansion. 5 DOCUMENTARY HISTORY OF THE SUPREME COURT OF THE UNITED STATES, 1789–1800, pp. 352–449 (M. Marcus ed.1994).

Congress took no action on Sedgwick's proposal, however, and the Amendment as ultimately adopted two years later could hardly have been meant to limit federal-question jurisdiction, or it would never have left the States open to federal-question suits by their own citizens. To be sure, the majority of state creditors were not citizens, but nothing in the Treaty would have prevented foreign creditors from selling their debt instruments (thereby assigning their claims) to citizens of the debtor State. If the Framers of the Eleventh Amendment had meant it to immunize States from federal-question suits like those that might be brought to enforce the Treaty of Paris, they would surely have drafted the Amendment differently.

It should accordingly come as no surprise that the weightiest commentary following the Amendment's adoption described it simply as constricting the scope of the Citizen-State Diversity Clauses. In *Cohens v. Virginia*, 19 U.S. 264 (1821), for instance, Chief Justice Marshall, writing for the Court, emphasized that the Amendment had no effect on federal courts' jurisdiction grounded on the "arising under" provision of Article III and concluded that "a case arising under the constitution or laws of the United States, is cognizable in the Courts of the Union, whoever may be the parties to that case." *Id.* at 383. The point of the Eleventh Amendment, according to *Cohens*, was to bar jurisdiction in suits at common law by Revolutionary War debt creditors, not "to strip the government of the means of protecting, by the instrumentality of its courts, the constitution and laws from active violation." *Id.* at 407.

The treatment of the Amendment in *Osborn v. Bank of United States*, 22 U.S. 738 (1824), was to the same effect. The Amendment was held there to be no bar to an action against the State seeking the return of an unconstitutional tax. "The eleventh amendment of the constitution has exempted a State from the suits of citizens of other States, or aliens," Marshall stated, omitting any reference to cases that arise under the Constitution or federal law. *Id.* at 847.

The good sense of this early construction of the Amendment as affecting the diversity jurisdiction and no more has the further virtue of making sense of this Court's repeated exercise of appellate jurisdiction in federal-question suits brought against States in their own courts by out-of-staters. Exercising appellate jurisdiction in these cases would have been patent error if the Eleventh Amendment limited federal-question jurisdiction, for the Amendment's unconditional language ("shall not be construed") makes no distinction between trial and appellate jurisdiction.

. . . .

In sum, reading the Eleventh Amendment solely as a limit on citizen-state diversity jurisdiction has the virtue of coherence with this Court's practice, with the views of John Marshall, with the history of the Amendment's drafting, and with its allusive language. Today's majority does not appear to disagree, at least insofar as the constitutional text is concerned; the Court concedes, after all, that "the text of the Amendment would appear to restrict only the Article III diversity jurisdiction of the federal courts."

. . . .

The majority does not dispute the point that *Hans v. Louisiana*, 134 U.S. 1 (1890), had no occasion to decide whether Congress could abrogate a State's immunity from federal-question suits. The Court insists, however, that the negative answer to that question that it finds in *Hans* and subsequent opinions is not "mere *obiter dicta*, but rather . . . the well-established rationale upon which the Court based the results of its earlier decisions." The exact rationale to which the majority refers, unfortunately, is not easy to discern. The Court's opinion says, immediately after its discussion of *stare decisis*, that "[f]or over a century, we have grounded our decisions in the oft-repeated understanding of state sovereign immunity as an essential part of the Eleventh Amendment." This cannot be the "rationale," though, because this Court has repeatedly acknowledged that the Eleventh Amendment standing alone cannot bar a federal-question suit against a State brought by a state citizen. *See, e.g., Edelman v. Jordan*, 415 U.S. 651, 662 (1974) (acknowledging that "the Amendment by its terms does not bar suits against a State by its own citizens"). Indeed, as I have noted, Justice Bradley's opinion in *Hans* conceded that Hans might successfully have pursued his claim "if there were no other reason or ground [other than the Amendment itself] for abating his suit." 134 U.S. at 10. The *Hans* Court, rather, held the suit barred by a nonconstitutional common-law immunity. *See id.* at 11.

. . . .

Three critical errors in *Hans* weigh against constitutionalizing its holding as the majority does today. The first we have already seen: the *Hans* Court misread the Eleventh Amendment. It also misunderstood the conditions under which common-law doctrines were received or rejected at the time of the founding, and it fundamentally mistook the very nature of sovereignty in the young Republic that was supposed to entail a State's immunity to federal-question jurisdiction in a federal court. While I would not, as a matter of *stare decisis*, overrule *Hans* today, an understanding of its failings on these points will show how the Court today simply compounds already serious error in taking *Hans* the further step of investing its rule with constitutional inviolability against the considered judgment of Congress to abrogate it.

. . . .

There is and could be no dispute that the doctrine of sovereign immunity that *Hans* purported to apply had its origins in the "familiar doctrine of the common law," *The Siren*, 74 U.S. 152, 153 (1869), "derived from the laws and practices of our English ancestors," *United States v. Lee*, 106 U.S. 196 (1882). Although statutes came to affect its importance in the succeeding centuries, the doctrine was never reduced to codification, and Americans took their understanding of immunity doctrine from Blackstone, *see* 3 WILLIAM BLACKSTONE, COMMENTARIES ON THE LAWS OF ENGLAND, ch. 17 (1768). Here, as in the mother country, it remained a common-law rule.

This fact of the doctrine's common-law status in the period covering the founding and the later adoption of the Eleventh Amendment should have raised a warning flag to the *Hans* Court and it should do the same for the Court today. For although the Court has persistently assumed that the common law's presence in the minds of the early Framers must have functioned as a limitation on their understanding of the new Nation's constitutional powers, this turns out not to be so at all. One of the characteristics of the founding generation, on the contrary, was its joinder of an appreciation of its immediate and powerful common-law heritage with caution in settling that inheritance on the political systems of the new Republic. It is not that the Framers failed to see themselves to be children of the common law; as one of their contemporaries put it, "[w]e live in the midst of the common law, we inhale it at every breath, imbibe it at every pore . . . [and] cannot learn another system of laws without learning at the same time another language." PETER S. DU PONCEAU, A DISSERTATION ON THE NATURE AND EXTENT OF JURISDICTION OF COURTS OF THE UNITED STATES 91 (1824). But still it is clear that the adoption of English common law in America was not taken for granted, and that the exact manner and extent of the common law's reception were subject to careful consideration by courts and legislatures in each of the new States. An examination of the States' experience with common-law reception will shed light on subsequent theory and practice at the national level, and demonstrate that our history is entirely at odds with *Hans*'s resort to a common-law principle to limit the Constitution's contrary text.

. . . .

This American reluctance to import English common law wholesale into the New World is traceable to the early colonial period. One scholar of that time has written that "[t]he process which we may call the reception of the English common law by the colonies was not so simple as the legal theory would lead us to assume. While their general legal conceptions were conditioned by, and their terminology derived from, the common law, the early colonists were far from applying it as a technical system, they often ignored it or denied its subsidiary force, and they consciously departed from many of its most essential principles." P. REINSCH, ENGLISH COMMON LAW IN THE EARLY AMERICAN COLONIES 58 (1899). For a variety of reasons, including the absence of trained lawyers and judges, the dearth of law books, the religious and ideological commitments of the early settlers, and the novel conditions of the New World, the colonists turned to a variety of other sources in addition to principles of common law.

It is true that, with the development of colonial society and the increasing sophistication of the colonial bar, English common law gained increasing acceptance in colonial practice. *See id.* at 7–8. But even in the late colonial period, Americans insisted that "the whole body of the common law . . . was not transplanted, but only so much as was applicable to the colonists in their new relations and conditions. Much of the common law related to matters which were purely local, which existed under the English political organization, or was based upon the triple relation of king, lords and commons, or those peculiar social conditions, habits and customs which have no counterpart in the New World. Such portions of the common law, not being applicable to the new conditions of the colonists, were never recognised as part of their jurisprudence."

The result was that "the increasing influx of common-law principles by no means obliterated the indigenous systems which had developed during the colonial era and that there existed important differences in law in action on the two sides of the Atlantic."

. . . .

The consequence of this anti-English hostility and awareness of changed circumstances was that the independent States continued the colonists' practice of adopting only so much of the common law as they thought applicable to their local conditions. . . .

Given the refusal to entertain any wholesale reception of common law, given the failure of the new Constitution to make any provision for adoption of common law as such, and given the protests already quoted that no general reception had occurred, the *Hans* Court and the Court today cannot reasonably argue that something like the old immunity doctrine somehow slipped in as a tacit but enforceable background principle. The evidence is even more specific, however, that there was no pervasive understanding that sovereign immunity had limited federal-question jurisdiction.

As I have already noted briefly, the Framers and their contemporaries did not agree about the place of common-law state sovereign immunity even as to federal jurisdiction resting on the Citizen-State Diversity Clauses. . . .

. . . .

Hamilton says that a State is "not . . . amenable to the suit of an individual without its consent . . . [u]nless . . . there is a surrender of this immunity in the plan of the convention." THE FEDERALIST NO. 81, at 548–49. He immediately adds, however, that "[t]he circumstances which are necessary to produce an alienation of state sovereignty, were discussed in considering the article of taxation, and need not be repeated here." *Id.* at 549. The reference is to THE FEDERALIST NO. 32, also by Hamilton, which has this to say about the alienation of state sovereignty:

> [A]s the plan of the Convention aims only at a partial Union or consolidation, the State Governments would clearly retain all the rights of sovereignty which they before had and which were not by that act *exclusively* delegated to the United States. This exclusive delegation or rather this alienation of State sovereignty would only exist in three cases; where the Constitution in express terms granted an exclusive authority to the Union; where it granted in one instance an authority to the Union and in another prohibited the States from exercising the like authority; and where it granted an authority to the Union, to which a similar authority in the States would be absolutely and totally *contradictory* and *repugnant*. I use these terms to distinguish this last case from another which might appear to resemble it; but which would in fact be essentially different; I mean where the exercise of a concurrent jurisdiction might be productive of occasional interferences in the *policy* of any branch of administration, but would not imply any direct contradiction or repugnancy in point of constitutional authority.

Id. at 200 (emphasis in original).

The first embarrassment Hamilton's discussion creates for the majority turns on the fact that the power to regulate commerce with Indian tribes has been interpreted as making "Indian relations . . . the exclusive province of federal law." *County of Oneida v. Oneida Indian Nation,* 470 U.S. 226, 234 (1985). We have accordingly recognized that "[s]tate laws generally are not applicable to tribal Indians on an Indian reservation except where Congress has expressly provided that State laws shall apply." *McClanahan v. Arizona State Tax Comm'n,* 411 U.S. 164, 170–71 (1973). We have specifically held, moreover, that the States have no power to regulate gambling on Indian lands. *California v. Cabazon Band of Mission Indians,* 480 U.S. 202, 221–22 (1987). In sum, since the States have no sovereignty in the regulation of commerce with the tribes, on Hamilton's view there is no source of sovereign immunity to assert in a suit based on congressional regulation of that commerce. If Hamilton is good authority, the majority of the Court today is wrong.

. . . .

In sum, either the majority reads Hamilton as I do, to say nothing about sovereignty or immunity in such a case, or it will have to read him to say something about it that bars any state immunity claim. That is the dilemma of the majority's reliance on Hamilton's THE FEDERALIST No. 81, with its reference to No. 32. Either way, he is no authority for the Court's position.

Thus, the Court's attempt to convert isolated statements by the Framers into answers to questions not before them is fundamentally misguided. The Court's difficulty is far more fundamental, however, than inconsistency with a particular quotation, for the Court's position runs afoul of the general theory of sovereignty that gave shape to the Framers' enterprise. An enquiry into the development of that concept demonstrates that American political thought had so revolutionized the concept of sovereignty itself that calling for the immunity of a State as against the jurisdiction of the national courts would have been sheer illogic.

. . . .

Today's majority discounts this concern. Without citing a single source to the contrary, the Court dismisses the historical evidence regarding the Framers' vision of the relationship between national and state sovereignty, and reassures us that "the Nation survived for nearly two centuries without the question of the existence of [the abrogation] power ever being presented to this Court." But we are concerned here not with the survival of the Nation but the opportunity of its citizens to enforce federal rights in a way that Congress provides. The absence of any general federal-question statute for nearly a century following ratification of Article III (with a brief exception in 1800) hardly counts against the importance of that jurisdiction either in the Framers' conception or in current reality; likewise, the fact that Congress has not often seen fit to use its power of abrogation (outside the Fourteenth Amendment context, at least) does not compel a conclusion that the power is not important to the federal scheme. In the end, is it plausible to contend that the plan of the convention was meant to leave the National Government without any way to render individuals capable of enforcing their federal rights directly against an intransigent State?

. . . .

History confirms the wisdom of Madison's abhorrence of constitutionalizing common-law rules to place them beyond the reach of congressional amendment. The Framers feared judicial power over substantive policy and the ossification of law that would result from transforming common law into constitutional law, and their fears have been borne out every time the Court has ignored Madison's counsel on subjects that we generally group under economic and social policy. It is, in fact, remarkable that as we near the end of this century the Court should choose to open a new constitutional chapter in confining legislative judgments on these matters by resort to textually unwarranted common-law rules, for it was just this practice in the century's early decades that brought this Court to the nadir of competence that we identify with *Lochner v. New York*, 198 U.S. 45 (1905).

It was the defining characteristic of the *Lochner* era, and its characteristic vice, that the Court treated the common-law background (in those days, common-law property rights and contractual autonomy) as paramount, while regarding congressional legislation to abrogate the common law on these economic matters as constitutionally suspect. *See, e.g., Adkins v. Children's Hospital*, 261 U.S. 525, 557 (1923) (finding abrogation of common-law freedom to contract for any wage an unconstitutional "compulsory exaction"). . . .

The majority today, indeed, seems to be going *Lochner* one better. When the Court has previously constrained the express Article I powers by resort to common-law or background principles, it has done so at least in an ostensible effort to give content to some other written provision of the Constitution, like the Due Process Clause, the very object of which is to limit the exercise of governmental power. *See, e.g., Adair v. United States*, 208 U.S. 161 (1908). Some textual argument, at least, could be made that the Court was doing no more than defining one provision that happened to be at odds with another. Today, however, the Court is not struggling to fulfill a responsibility to reconcile two arguably conflicting and Delphic constitutional provisions, nor is it struggling with any Delphic text at all. For even the Court concedes that the Constitution's grant to Congress of plenary power over relations with Indian tribes at the expense of any state claim to the contrary is unmistakably clear, and this case does not even arguably implicate a textual trump to the grant of federal-question jurisdiction.

. . . .

There is, finally, a response to the Court's rejection of *Young* that ought to go without saying. Our longstanding practice is to read ambiguous statutes to avoid constitutional infirmity, *Edward J. DeBartolo Corp. v. Florida Gulf Coast Building & Constr. Trades Council*, 485 U.S. 568, 575 (1988) (" 'every reasonable construction must be resorted to, in order to save a statute from unconstitutionality' ") (quoting *Hooper v. California*, 155 U.S. 648, 657 (1895)). This practice alone (without any need for a clear statement to displace *Young*) would be enough to require *Young*'s application. So, too, would the application of another rule, requiring courts to choose any reasonable construction of a statute that would eliminate the need to confront a contested constitutional issue (in this case, the place of state sovereign immunity in federal-question cases and the status of *Union Gas*). *NLRB v. Catholic Bishop of Chicago*, 440 U.S. 490, 500–01 (1979). Construing the statute to harmonize with *Young*, as it readily does, would have saved an Act of Congress and rendered a discussion on constitutional grounds wholly unnecessary. This case should be decided on this basis alone.

. . . .

. . . Because neither text, precedent, nor history supports the majority's abdication of our responsibility to exercise the jurisdiction entrusted to us in Article III, I would reverse the judgment of the Court of Appeals.

Exercise 15:

In connection with *Seminole Tribe*, consider the following questions:

(1)   What was the two-part test the Court used to determine whether Congress constitutionally abrogated a State's immunity from suit in federal court by a private individual?

(2)   Is the first part of the two-part test one of procedure or substance?

(3)   With respect to the second part of the two-part test, what grant of legislative power did the Court unanimously agree satisfied the test?

(4)   Is there any principled basis to distinguish between the power identified in question 3 and Article I powers?

(5)   Other than congressional abrogation of Eleventh Amendment immunity, what alternative means are available for judicial enforcement of obligations of federal law against States? Eleventh Amendment doctrine is introduced in *Volume 1*.

(a)   Are there any plaintiffs who may sue a State in federal court without regard for Eleventh Amendment immunity or a State's sovereign immunity?

(b)   Are there any governmental defendants who may be sued in federal court by private individuals without regard for Eleventh Amendment immunity or a State's sovereign immunity?

(c)   Are there judicial fora that may consider cases brought by private plaintiffs directly against a State without regard for the Eleventh Amendment?

(d)   If the Eleventh Amendment protects only *unconsenting* States, when Congress lacks power to abrogate Eleventh Amendment immunity does Congress retain the power to induce such consent? How?

(6)   What factors did the majority identify as the basis for overruling *Pennsylvania v. Union Gas Co.*? If your instructor assigned *Volume 1*, consider how those factors compare with the reasons articulated in *Planned Parenthood v. Casey*. Compared to other cases we have explored in which the Court overruled a prior decision (including express overrulings as in *Darby* and *Wickard* as well as silent overrulings as in *Dole*) which situation presented the stronger example for appropriately overruling precedent?

(7)   The majority asserted that *Marbury v. Madison* established that — at least under the Constitution of 1789 — Congress lacked authority to "expand the jurisdiction of the federal courts beyond the bounds of Article III." If your instructor assigned *Volume 1*, reconsider *Marbury*. Do you agree with that reading of *Marbury v. Madison*? If you accept that reading of *Marbury*, must the question of sovereign immunity turn on construction of Article III rather than on whether Congress legislated under Article I?

(8)   In 1989, when the Supreme Court decided *Pennsylvania v. Union Gas Company*, was there any existing precedent on whether the Eleventh Amendment applied to cases arising under federal law rather than applying only to cases within diversity jurisdiction? To the extent there were any such precedents, how, if at all, are they distinguishable?

(9)   In dissent, Justice Stevens asserted that in *Chisholm v. Georgia*, "Justice Iredell — whose dissent provided the blueprint for the Eleventh Amendment — assumed that Congress had" the power to subject unconsenting States to suit in federal court by private individuals, but that with respect to sovereign immunity, "Justice Iredell believed that the expansive text of Article III did not *prevent Congress from imposing* this common-law limitation on federal-court jurisdiction." If your instructor assigned *Volume 1*, consider whether Justice Stevens fairly characterized the views of Justice Iredell. To the extent Justice Iredell did assume any such congressional power, was that a concession that the issue could be resolved by simple legislation? Or, was Justice Iredell employing a means of avoiding a constitutional question — *see Ashwander v. TVA* from *Volume 1* — without endorsing the majority's reading of the Constitution or characterizing the nature of sovereign immunity as merely a common law doctrine? If you accept the former view of Justice Iredell's opinion (the view proposed by Justice Stevens), was a constitutional amendment required rather than a mere change to the Judiciary Act of 1789?

(10)   In dissent, Justice Souter asserted that "the Court today holds for the first time since the founding of the Republic that Congress has no authority to subject a State to the jurisdiction of a federal court at the behest of an individual asserting a federal right." Is it true that there was no existing precedent contrary to Justice Souter's views?

(11)   In dissent, Justice Souter asserted that three analytically distinct questions are presented regarding the immunity of States. With respect to his first question — whether States enjoyed sovereign immunity before ratification of the Constitution — Justice Souter asserted that the answer "is not clear." If your instructor assigned *Volume 1*, consider whether a majority of the Court in *Chisholm v. Georgia* found that

States enjoyed sovereign immunity in their own courts prior to ratification of the Constitution.

(12)   In dissent, Justice Souter asserted with respect to his second question — "whether after ratification the States were entitled to claim some such immunity when sued in a federal court" — that the issue "was not debated at the time of the ratification." Is that true? If your instructor assigned *Volume 1*, recall that in *Brutus XIII*, for example, the author wrote:

> I conceive the clause [of Article III] which extends the power of the judicial to controversies arising between a state and citizens of another state, improper in itself, and will, in its exercise, prove most pernicious and destructive.
>
> It is improper, because it subjects a state to answer in a court of law, to the suit of an individual. This is humiliating and degrading to a government, and, what I believe, the supreme authority of no state ever submitted to.
>
> The states are now subject to no such actions. . . .

The specific context of the objection was a suit to enforce the debt obligations of a State by an individual who held a note from the issuing State but was a citizen of a different State. In FEDERALIST No. 81 (on DVD-ROM), Hamilton replied:

> It is inherent in the nature of sovereignty, not to be amenable to the suit of an individual *without its consent*. This is the general sense and the general practice of mankind; and the exemption, as one of the attributes of sovereignty, is now enjoyed by the government of every state in the union. Unless, therefore, there is a surrender of this immunity in the plan of the convention, it will remain with the states, and the danger intimated must be merely ideal. . . . [T]here is no colour to present that the state governments, would by the adoption of that plan, be divested of the privilege of paying their own debts in their own way. . . . They confer no right of action independent of the sovereign will.

Do the terms of the exchange support the view that the objection to Article III was limited to diversity jurisdiction alone, or was the objection to subjecting an unconsenting State to suit in federal court by individuals? To the extent that the objection was to suit by individuals, does it apply equally to suits by individuals based upon federal question jurisdiction?

(13)   In dissent, Justice Souter asserted with respect to his third question — "whether any state sovereign immunity recognized in federal court may be abrogated by Congress" — that it was decided contrary to the views of the Framers that "legislative amendment" could overcome such immunity. Is that true?

Do the terms of the exchange between Brutus and Hamilton support the view that the objection to Article III was limited to a self-executing constitutional rule subjecting an unconsenting State to suit by individuals alone, or was the objection to any federal authority to subject an unconsenting State to suit in federal court by individuals? To the extent that the objection was to any federal authority to subject an unconsenting State to suit in federal court by individuals, does it apply equally to a congressional power to "abrogate" State immunity from such suits? In *Brutus XIII*, the author wrote:

> It may be said that the apprehension that the judicial power will operate in this manner is merely visionary, for that the legislature will never pass laws that will work these effects. Or if they were disposed to do it, they cannot provide for levying an execution on a state . . . .
>
> To this I would reply, if this is a power which will not or cannot be executed, it was useless and unwise to grant it to the judicial. For what purpose is a power given which it is imprudent or impossible to exercise? If it be improper for a government to exercise a power, it is improper they should be vested with it.

And it is unwise to authorise a government to do what they cannot effect.

And in the second part of *Brutus XIV*, the author concluded:

> The just way of investigating any power given to a government, is to examine its operation supposing it to be put into exercise. If upon enquiry, it appears that the power, if exercised, would be prejudicial, it ought not to be given. For to answer objections made to a power given to a government, by saying it will never be exercised, is really admitting that the power ought not to be exercised, and therefore ought not to be granted.

Did Brutus anticipate the distinction suggested by the plurality in *Pennsylvania v. Union Gas Company*, which was endorsed by the dissent in *Seminole Tribe*?

Recall that Hamilton, in FEDERALIST NO. 80, responded, in part, by observing that if some applications of the judicial power specified in Article III were problematic, "the national legislature will have ample authority to make such *exceptions* and to prescribe such regulations as will be calculated to obviate or remove those inconveniences."

Did Hamilton's reference to the power of Congress to make exceptions to Article III jurisdiction imply that, if there was constitutional authority to subject unconsenting States to suit in federal court by individuals, that authority derived directly from Article III alone?

(14)   In dissent, Justice Souter asserted that the Eleventh Amendment should be construed more narrowly than the view adopted by the majority because Congress did not act on a broadly-worded alternative proposal. Assuming Congress acted deliberately and affirmatively rejected the proposal quoted by Justice Souter in preference for the text of the Eleventh Amendment, why would Congress do so? Are the only differences between the proposal and the adopted text pertinent to (a) whether actions arising under federal law are also barred and (b) whether Congress may "abrogate" immunity (if the differences are even material to those questions)? Or, would the quoted proposal sweep more broadly than the Eleventh Amendment as construed by the majority in *Seminole Tribe*?

(15)   In dissent, Justice Souter asserted that the view of the Eleventh Amendment followed by the majority is illogical. "If it is indeed true that private suits against States [are] not permitted under Article III . . . then it is hard to see how a State's sovereign immunity may be waived any more than it may be abrogated by Congress." Can the two positions be reconciled?

(16)   In dissent, Justice Souter asserted that by the time of the Constitutional Convention "American political thought had so revolutionized the concept of sovereignty itself that calling for the immunity of a State as against the jurisdiction of the national courts would have been sheer illogic." Is that the same argument asserted by the majority in *Chisholm v. Georgia*? Did the calls for impeachment that followed the decision and the swift adoption of the Eleventh Amendment reflect a contrary understanding?

(17)   In dissent, Justice Souter asserted that the Framers shared a "general concern with curbing abuses by state governments." Did the Framers perceive the potential for abuses in the state governments alone or were they equally concerned with all governmental power? Accepting, for sake of discussion, such a "general concern," Justice Souter asserted that it "would be amazing if the scheme of delegated powers embodied in the Constitution had left the National Government powerless to render the States judicially accountable for violations of federal rights." Does the majority's opinion do so?

(18)   What limitation, if any, would Justice Souter recognize on the power of Congress to abrogate Eleventh Amendment immunity?

(19) Recall that the federal statute at issue in *Seminole Tribe* was enacted in 1988, prior to the Supreme Court's decision in *Pennsylvania v. Union Gas Company*. The congressional effort to "abrogate" State immunity thus cannot be seen as a response to that decision. Why would Congress believe that it could abrogate immunity in advance of Supreme Court authority addressing the question? In answering that question, recall the status of the Supreme Court's Commerce Clause jurisprudence at the time — prior to its decisions in *United States v. Lopez* and *United States v. Morrison* — as well as its jurisprudence regarding any federalism limitations on the exercise of that power — shortly after the Supreme Court's decision in *South Dakota v. Dole*, but prior to *New York v. United States* and *Printz v. United States*.

CITY OF BOERNE v. FLORES
521 U.S. 507 (1997)

JUSTICE KENNEDY delivered the opinion of the Court.

A decision by local zoning authorities to deny a church a building permit was challenged under the Religious Freedom Restoration Act of 1993 (RFRA or Act), 107 Stat. 1488, 42 U.S.C. § 2000bb *et seq*. The case calls into question the authority of Congress to enact RFRA. We conclude the statute exceeds Congress' power.

I

[St. Peter Catholic Church in Boerne, Texas, could no longer serve its growing parish. It sought to expand its building. Boerne adopted an ordinance that required all construction on historic buildings be approved by the city council. Based on that ordinance, Boerne denied the requested construction permit. The church brought suit relying on the RFRA and Boerne challenged RFRA's constitutionality.]

II

Congress enacted RFRA in direct response to the Court's decision in *Employment Division, Department of Human Resources of Oregon v. Smith*, 494 U.S. 872 (1990). There we considered a Free Exercise Clause claim brought by members of the Native American Church who were denied unemployment benefits when they lost their jobs because they had used peyote. Their practice was to ingest peyote for sacramental purposes, and they challenged an Oregon statute of general applicability which made use of the drug criminal. In evaluating the claim, we declined to apply the balancing test set forth in *Sherbert v. Verner*, 374 U.S. 398 (1963), under which we would have asked whether Oregon's prohibition substantially burdened a religious practice and, if it did, whether the burden was justified by a compelling government interest. We stated:

> [G]overnment's ability to enforce generally applicable prohibitions of socially harmful conduct . . . cannot depend on measuring the effects of a governmental action on a religious objector's spiritual development. To make an individual's obligation to obey such a law contingent upon the law's coincidence with his religious beliefs, except where the State's interest is "compelling" . . . contradicts both constitutional tradition and common sense.

494 U.S. at 885 (internal quotation marks and citations omitted). The application of the *Sherbert* test, the *Smith* decision explained, would have produced an anomaly in the law, a constitutional right to ignore neutral laws of general applicability. The anomaly would have been accentuated, the Court reasoned, by the difficulty of determining whether a particular practice was central to an individual's religion. We explained, moreover, that it "is not within the judicial ken to question the centrality of particular beliefs or practices to a faith, or the validity of particular litigants' interpretations of those

creeds."494 U.S. at 887 (internal quotation marks and citation omitted).

The only instances where a neutral, generally applicable law had failed to pass constitutional muster, the *Smith* Court noted, were cases in which other constitutional protections were at stake. *Id.* at 881–82. In *Wisconsin v. Yoder,* 406 U.S. 205 (1972), for example, we invalidated Wisconsin's mandatory school-attendance law as applied to Amish parents who refused on religious grounds to send their children to school. That case implicated not only the right to the free exercise of religion but also the right of parents to control their children's education.

The *Smith* decision acknowledged the Court had employed the *Sherbert* test in considering free exercise challenges to state unemployment compensation rules on three occasions where the balance had tipped in favor of the individual. Those cases, the Court explained, stand for "the proposition that where the State has in place a system of individual exemptions, it may not refuse to extend that system to cases of religious hardship without compelling reason." 494 U.S. at 884 (internal quotation marks omitted). By contrast, where a general prohibition, such as Oregon's, is at issue, "the sounder approach, and the approach in accord with the vast majority of our precedents, is to hold the test inapplicable to [free exercise] challenges." *Id.* at 885. *Smith* held that neutral, generally applicable laws may be applied to religious practices even when not supported by a compelling governmental interest.

Four Members of the Court disagreed. . . .

These points of constitutional interpretation were debated by Members of Congress in hearings and floor debates. Many criticized the Court's reasoning, and this disagreement resulted in the passage of RFRA. . . .

RFRA prohibits "[g]overnment" from "substantially burden[ing]" a person's exercise of religion even if the burden results from a rule of general applicability unless the government can demonstrate the burden "(1) is in furtherance of a compelling governmental interest; and (2) is the least restrictive means of furthering that compelling governmental interest." § 2000bb-1. The Act's mandate applies to . . . "the United States," as well as to any "State, or . . . subdivision of a State." § 2000bb-2(1). The Act's universal coverage is confirmed in § 2000bb-3(a), under which RFRA "applies to all Federal and State law, and the implementation of that law, whether statutory or otherwise, and whether adopted before or after [RFRA's enactment]." In accordance with RFRA's usage of the term, we shall use "state law" to include local and municipal ordinances.

III

A

. . . .

Congress relied on its Fourteenth Amendment enforcement power in enacting the most far-reaching and substantial of RFRA's provisions, those which impose its requirements on the States. . . . The parties disagree over whether RFRA is a proper exercise of Congress' § 5 power "to enforce" by "appropriate legislation" the constitutional guarantee that no State shall deprive any person of "life, liberty, or property, without due process of law," nor deny any person "equal protection of the laws."

In defense of the Act, [the church] contends . . . that RFRA is permissible enforcement legislation. Congress, it is said, is only protecting by legislation one of the liberties guaranteed by the Fourteenth Amendment's Due Process Clause, the free exercise of religion, beyond what is necessary under *Smith*. It is said the congressional decision to dispense with proof of deliberate or overt discrimination and instead concentrate on a law's effects accords with the settled understanding that § 5 includes the power to enact legislation designed to prevent, as well as remedy, constitutional violations. It is further contended that Congress' § 5 power is not limited to remedial or preventative legislation.

All must acknowledge that § 5 is "a positive grant of legislative power" to Congress. *Katzenbach v. Morgan*, 384 U.S. 641, 651 (1966). . . . Legislation which deters or remedies constitutional violations can fall within the sweep of Congress' enforcement power even if in the process it prohibits conduct which is not itself unconstitutional and intrudes into "legislative spheres of autonomy previously reserved to the States." *Fitzpatrick v. Bitzer*, 427 U.S. 445, 455 (1976). For example, the Court upheld a suspension of literacy tests and similar voting requirements under Congress' parallel power to enforce the provisions of the Fifteenth Amendment as a measure to combat racial discrimination in voting, *South Carolina v. Katzenbach*, 383 U.S. 301, 308 (1966), despite the facial constitutionality of the tests under *Lassiter v. Northampton County Bd. of Elections*, 360 U.S. 45 (1959). . . .

It is also true, however, that "[a]s broad as the congressional enforcement power is, it is not unlimited." *Oregon v. Mitchell*, 400 U.S. 112, 128 (1970) (opinion of Black, J.). In assessing the breadth of § 5's enforcement power, we begin with its text. Congress has been given the power "to enforce" the "provisions of this article." We agree with [the church], of course, that Congress can enact legislation under § 5 enforcing the constitutional right to the free exercise of religion. The "provisions of this article," to which § 5 refers, include the Due Process Clause of the Fourteenth Amendment. Congress' power to enforce the Free Exercise Clause follows from our holding in *Cantwell v. Connecticut*, 310 U.S. 296, 303 (1940), that the "fundamental concept of liberty embodied in [the Fourteenth Amendment's Due Process Clause] embraces the liberties guaranteed by the First Amendment". . . .

Congress' power under § 5, however, extends only to "enforc[ing]" the provisions of the Fourteenth Amendment. The Court has described this power as "remedial." *South Carolina v. Katzenbach*, 383 U.S. at 326. The design of the Amendment and the text of § 5 are inconsistent with the suggestion that Congress has the power to decree the substance of the Fourteenth Amendment's restrictions on the States. Legislation which alters the meaning of the Free Exercise Clause cannot be said to be enforcing the Clause. Congress does not enforce a constitutional right by changing what the right is. It has been given the power "to enforce," not the power to determine what constitutes a constitutional violation. Were it not so, what Congress would be enforcing would no longer be, in any meaningful sense, the "provisions of [the Fourteenth Amendment]."

While the line between measures that remedy or prevent unconstitutional actions and measures that make a substantive change in the governing law is not easy to discern, and Congress must have wide latitude in determining where it lies, the distinction exists and must be observed. There must be a congruence and proportionality between the injury to be prevented or remedied and the means adopted to that end. Lacking such a connection, legislation may become substantive in operation and effect. History and our case law support drawing the distinction, one apparent from the text of the Amendment.

1

The Fourteenth Amendment's history confirms the remedial, rather than substantive, nature of the Enforcement Clause. The Joint Committee on Reconstruction of the 39th Congress began drafting what would become the Fourteenth Amendment in January 1866. The objections to the Committee's first draft of the Amendment, and the rejection of the draft, have a direct bearing on the central issue of defining Congress' enforcement power. In February, Republican Representative John Bingham of Ohio reported the following draft Amendment to the House of Representatives on behalf of the Joint Committee:

> The Congress shall have the power to make all laws which shall be necessary and proper to secure to the citizens of each State all privileges and immunities of citizens in the several States, and to all persons in the several States equal protection in the rights of life, liberty, and property.

Cong. Globe, 39th Cong., 1st Sess., 1034 (1866).

The proposal encountered immediate opposition, which continued through three days of debate. Members of Congress from across the political spectrum criticized the Amendment, and the criticisms had a common theme: The proposed Amendment gave Congress too much legislative power at the expense of the existing constitutional structure. . . . Democrats and conservative Republicans argued that the proposed Amendment would give Congress a power to intrude into traditional areas of state responsibility, a power inconsistent with the federal design central to the Constitution. Typifying these views, Republican Representative Robert Hale of New York labeled the Amendment "an utter departure from every principle ever dreamed of by the men who framed our Constitution," *id.* at 1063, and warned that under it "all State legislation, in its codes of civil and criminal jurisprudence and procedure . . . may be overridden, may be repealed or abolished, and the law of Congress established instead." *Id.* Senator William Stewart of Nevada likewise stated the Amendment would permit "Congress to legislate fully upon all subjects affecting life, liberty, and property," such that "there would not be much left for the State Legislatures," and would thereby "work an entire change in our form of government." *Id.* at 1082. . . .

As a result of these objections having been expressed from so many different quarters, the House voted to table the proposal until April. . . . The congressional action was seen as marking the defeat of the proposal. . . . The measure was defeated "chiefly because so many members of the legal profession s[aw] in [it] . . . a dangerous centralization of power," *The Nation*, Mar. 8, 1866, p. 291, and "many leading Republicans of th[e] House [of Representatives] would not consent to so radical a change in the Constitution." Cong. Globe, 42nd Cong., 1st Sess., at App. 151 (statement of Rep. Garfield). The Amendment in its early form was not again considered. Instead, the Joint Committee began drafting a new article of Amendment, which it reported to Congress on April 30, 1866.

Section 1 of the new draft Amendment imposed self-executing limits on the States. Section 5 prescribed that "[t]he Congress shall have the power to enforce, by appropriate legislation, the provisions of this article." Under the revised Amendment, Congress' power was no longer plenary but remedial. Congress was granted the power to make substantive constitutional prohibitions against the States effective. Representative Bingham said the new draft would give Congress "the power . . . to protect by national law the privileges and immunities of all the citizens of the Republic . . . whenever the same shall be abridged or denied by the unconstitutional acts of any State." Cong. Globe, 39th Cong., 1st Sess. at 2542. Representative Stevens described the new draft amendment as "allow[ing] Congress to correct the unjust legislation of the States." *Id.* at 2459. . . . The revised Amendment proposal did not raise the concerns expressed earlier regarding broad congressional power to prescribe uniform national laws with respect to life, liberty, and property. . . . After revisions not relevant here, the new measure passed both Houses and was ratified in July 1868 as the Fourteenth Amendment.

The significance of the defeat of the Bingham proposal was apparent even then. During the debates over the Ku Klux Klan Act only a few years after the Amendment's ratification, Representative James Garfield argued there were limits on Congress' enforcement power, saying "unless we ignore both the history and the language of these clauses we cannot, by any reasonable interpretation, give to [§ 5] . . . the force and effect of the rejected [Bingham] clause." Cong. Globe, 42d Cong., 1st Sess., at App. 151; *see also id.* at 115–16 (statement of Rep. Farnsworth). Scholars of successive generations have agreed with this assessment. . . .

The design of the Fourteenth Amendment has proved significant also in maintaining the traditional separation of powers between Congress and the Judiciary. The first eight Amendments to the Constitution set forth self-executing prohibitions on governmental action, and this Court has had primary authority to interpret those prohibitions. The Bingham draft, some thought, departed from that tradition by vesting in Congress primary power to interpret and elaborate on the meaning of the new Amendment through legislation. Under it, "Congress, and not the courts, was to judge whether or not any of the privileges or immunities were not secured to citizens in the several States." HORACE E. FLACK, THE ADOPTION OF THE FOURTEENTH AMENDMENT 64 (1908). While this separation-of-powers aspect did not occasion the widespread resistance which was caused by the proposal's threat to the federal balance, it nonetheless attracted the attention of various members. . . . As enacted, the Fourteenth Amendment confers substantive rights against the States which, like the provisions of the Bill of Rights, are self-executing. . . . The power to interpret the Constitution in a case or controversy remains in the Judiciary.

2

The remedial power and preventive nature of Congress' enforcement power, and the limitation inherent in the power, were confirmed in our earliest cases on the Fourteenth Amendment. In the *Civil Rights Cases*, 109 U.S. 3 (1883), the Court invalidated sections of the Civil Rights Act of 1875 which prescribed criminal penalties for denying to any person "the full enjoyment of" public accommodations and conveyances, on the grounds that it exceeded Congress' power by seeking to regulate private conduct. The Enforcement Clause, the Court said, did not authorize Congress to pass "general legislation upon the rights of the citizen, but corrective legislation, that is, such as may be necessary and proper for counteracting such laws as the States may adopt or enforce, and which, by the amendment, they are prohibited from making or enforcing . . . ." *Id.* at 13–14. The power to "legislate generally upon" life, liberty, and property, as opposed to the "power to provide modes of redress" against offensive state action, was "repugnant" to the Constitution. *Id.* at 15. . . . Although the specific holdings of these early cases might have been superseded or modified . . . their treatment of Congress' § 5 power as corrective or preventive, not definitional, has not been questioned.

Recent cases have continued to revolve around the question whether § 5 legislation can be considered remedial. In *South Carolina v. Katzenbach,* 383 U.S. at 308, we emphasized that "[t]he constitutional propriety of [legislation adopted under the Enforcement Clause] must be judged with reference to the historical experience . . . it reflects." 383 U.S. at 308. There we upheld various provisions of the Voting Rights Act of 1965, finding them to be "remedies aimed at areas where voting discrimination has been most flagrant," *id.* at 315, and necessary to "banish the blight of racial discrimination in voting, which has infected the electoral process in parts of our country for nearly a century," *id.* at 308. We noted evidence in the record reflecting the subsisting and pervasive discriminatory — and therefore unconstitutional — use of literacy tests. *Id.* at 333–34. The Act's new remedies, which used the administrative resources of the Federal Government, included the suspension of both literacy tests and, pending federal review, all new voting regulations in covered jurisdictions, as well as the assignment of federal examiners to list qualified applicants enabling those listed to vote. The new, unprecedented remedies were deemed necessary given the ineffectiveness of the existing voting rights laws, *see id.* at 313–15, and the slow, costly character of case-by-case litigation, *id.* at 328.

. . . .

3

Any suggestion that Congress has a substantive, non-remedial power under the Fourteenth Amendment is not supported by our case law. In *Oregon v. Mitchell*, 400 U.S. at 112, a majority of the Court concluded Congress had exceeded its enforcement powers by enacting legislation lowering the minimum age of voters from 21 to 18 in state and local elections. The five members of the Court who reached this conclusion explained that the legislation intruded into an area reserved by the Constitution to the States. *See id.* at 125 . . . . Four of these five were explicit in rejecting the position that § 5 endowed Congress with the power to establish the meaning of constitutional provisions. . . . Justice Black's rejection of this position might be inferred from his disagreement with Congress' interpretation of the Equal Protection Clause. *See id.* at 125.

There is language in our opinion in *Katzenbach v. Morgan*, 384 U.S. 641 (1966), which could be interpreted as acknowledging a power in Congress to enact legislation that expands the rights contained in § 1 of the Fourteenth Amendment. This is not a necessary interpretation, however, or even the best one. In *Morgan*, the Court considered the constitutionality of § 4(e) of the Voting Rights Act of 1965, which provided that no person who had successfully completed the sixth primary grade in a public school in, or a private school accredited by, the Commonwealth of Puerto Rico in which the language of instruction was other than English could be denied the right to vote because of an inability to read or write English. New York's Constitution, on the other hand, required voters to be able to read and write English. The Court provided two related rationales for its conclusion that § 4(e) could "be viewed as a measure to secure for the Puerto Rican community residing in New York undiscriminatory treatment by the government." *Id.* at 652. Under the first rationale, Congress could prohibit New York from denying the right to vote to large segments of its Puerto Rican community, in order to give the Puerto Ricans "enhanced political power" that would be "helpful in gaining nondiscriminatory treatment in public services for the entire Puerto Rican community." *Id.* Section 4(e) thus could be justified as a remedial measure to deal with "discrimination in governmental services." *Id.* at 653. The second rationale, an alternative holding, did not address discrimination in the provision of public services but "discrimination in establishing voter qualifications." *Id.* at 654. The Court perceived a factual basis on which Congress could have concluded that New York's literacy requirement "constituted an invidious discrimination in violation of the Equal Protection Clause." *Id.* at 656. Both rationales for upholding § 4(e) rested on unconstitutional discrimination by New York and Congress' reasonable attempt to combat it. As Justice Stewart explained in *Oregon v. Mitchell*, 400 U.S. at 296, interpreting *Morgan* to give Congress the power to interpret the Constitution "would require an enormous extension of that decision's rationale."

If Congress could define its own powers by altering the Fourteenth Amendment's meaning, no longer would the Constitution be "superior paramount law, unchangeable by ordinary means." It would be "on a level with ordinary legislative acts and, like other acts . . . alterable when the legislature shall please to alter it." *Marbury v. Madison*, 5 U.S. at 177. Under this approach, it is difficult to conceive of a principle that would limit congressional power. . . . Shifting legislative majorities could change the Constitution and effectively circumvent the difficult and detailed amendment process contained in Article V.

We now turn to consider whether RFRA can be considered enforcement legislation under § 5 of the Fourteenth Amendment.

B

Respondent contends that RFRA is a proper exercise of Congress' remedial or preventative power. The Act, it is said, is a reasonable means of protecting the free exercise of religion as defined by *Smith*. It prevents and remedies laws which are enacted with the unconstitutional object of targeting religious beliefs and practices. *See Church of Lukumi Babalu Aye, Inc. v. Hialeah*, 508 U.S. 520, 533 (1993) ("[A] law targeting religious beliefs as such is never permissible"). To avoid the difficulty of proving such violations, it is said, Congress can simply invalidate any law which imposes a substantial burden on a religious practice unless it is justified by a compelling interest and is the least restrictive means of accomplishing that interest. If Congress can prohibit laws with discriminatory effects in order to prevent racial discrimination in violation of the Equal Protection Clause . . . then it can do the same, respondent argues, to promote religious liberty.

While preventative rules are sometimes appropriate remedial measures, there must be a congruence between the means used and the ends to be achieved. The appropriateness of remedial measures must be considered in light of the evil presented. *See South Carolina v. Katzenbach*, 383 U.S. at 308. Strong measures appropriate to address one harm may be an unwarranted response to another, lesser one. *Id.* at 334.

A comparison between RFRA and the Voting Rights Act is instructive. In contrast to the record which confronted Congress and the Judiciary in the voting rights cases, RFRA's legislative record lacks examples of modern instances of generally applicable laws passed because of religious bigotry. The history of persecution in this country detailed in the hearings mentions no episodes occurring in the past 40 years. . . . The absence of more recent episodes stems from the fact that, as one witness testified, "deliberate persecution is not the usual problem in this country." . . . Rather, the emphasis of the hearings was on laws of general applicability which place incidental burdens on religion. Much of the discussion centered upon anecdotal evidence of autopsies performed on Jewish individuals and Hmong immigrants in violation of their religious beliefs. . . . It is difficult to maintain that they are examples of legislation enacted or enforced due to animus or hostility to the burdened religious practices or that they indicate some widespread pattern of religious discrimination in this country. Congress' concern was with the incidental burdens imposed, not the object or purpose of the legislation. . . . This lack of support in the legislative record, however, is not RFRA's most serious shortcoming. Judicial deference, in most cases, is based not on the state of the legislative record Congress compiles but "on due regard for the decision of the body constitutionally appointed to decide." *Oregon v. Mitchell*, 400 U.S. at 207 (opinion of Harlan, J.). As a general matter, it is for Congress to determine the method by which it will reach a decision.

Regardless of the state of the legislative record, RFRA cannot be considered remedial, preventative legislation, if those terms are to have any meaning. RFRA is so out of proportion to a supposed remedial or preventative object that it cannot be understood as responsive to, or designed to prevent, unconstitutional behavior. It appears, instead, to attempt a substantive change in constitutional protections. Preventative measures prohibiting certain types of laws may be appropriate when there is reason to believe that many of the laws affected by the congressional enactment have a significant likelihood of being unconstitutional. . . . Remedial legislation under § 5 "should be adapted to the mischief and wrong which the [Fourteenth] [A]mendment was intended to provide against." *Civil Rights Cases*, 109 U.S. at 13.

RFRA is not so confined. Sweeping coverage ensures its intrusion at every level of government, displacing laws and prohibiting official actions of almost every description and regardless of subject matter. RFRA's restrictions apply to every agency and official of the Federal, State, and local Governments. 42 U.S.C. § 2000bb-2(1). RFRA applies to all federal and state law, statutory or otherwise, whether adopted before or after its enactment. § 2000bb-3(a). RFRA has no termination date or termination mechanism. Any law is subject to challenge at any time by any individual who alleges a substantial burden on his or her free exercise of religion.

The reach and scope of RFRA distinguish it from other measures passed under Congress' enforcement power, even in the area of voting rights. In *South Carolina v. Katzenbach*, the challenged provisions were confined to those regions of the country where voting discrimination had been most flagrant, *see* 383 U.S. at 315, and affected a discrete class of state laws, *i.e.*, state voting laws. Furthermore, to ensure that the reach of the Voting Rights Act was limited to those cases in which constitutional violations were most likely (in order to reduce the possibility of overbreadth), the coverage under the Act would terminate "at the behest of States and political subdivisions in which the danger of substantial voting discrimination has not materialized during the preceding five years." *Id.* at 331. The provisions restricting and banning literacy tests, upheld in *Katzenbach v. Morgan*, 384 U.S. 641 (1966), and *Oregon v. Mitchell*, 400 U.S. 112 (1970), attacked a particular type of voting qualification, one with a long history as a "notorious means to deny and abridge voting rights on racial grounds." *South Carolina v. Katzenbach*, 383 U.S. at 355 (Black, J., concurring and dissenting). In *City of Rome v. United States*, 446 U.S. 156 (1980), the Court rejected a challenge to the constitutionality of a Voting Rights Act provision which required certain jurisdictions to submit changes in electoral practices to the Department of Justice for preimplemantation review. The requirement was placed only on jurisdictions with a history of intentional racial discrimination in voting. *Id.* at 177. Like the provisions at issue in *South Carolina v. Katzenbach*, this provision permitted a covered jurisdiction to avoid preclearance requirements under certain conditions and, moreover, lapsed in seven years. This is not to say, of course, that § 5 legislation requires termination dates, geographic restrictions, or egregious predicates. Where, however, a congressional enactment pervasively prohibits constitutional state action in an effort to remedy or to prevent unconstitutional state action, limitations of this kind tend to ensure Congress' means are proportionate to ends legitimate under § 5.

The stringent test RFRA demands of state laws reflects a lack of proportionality or congruence between the means adopted and the legitimate end to be achieved. If an objector can show a substantial burden on his free exercise, the State must demonstrate a compelling governmental interest and show that the law is the least restrictive means of furthering its interest. Claims that a law substantially burdens someone's exercise of religion will often be difficult to contest. . . . Requiring a State to demonstrate a compelling interest and show that it has adopted the least restrictive means of achieving that interest is the most demanding test known to constitutional law. If " 'compelling interest' really means what it says . . ., many laws will not meet the test. . . . [The test] would open the prospect of constitutionally required religious exemptions from civic obligations of almost every conceivable kind." *Smith*, 494 U.S. at 888. Laws valid under *Smith* would fall under RFRA without regard to whether they had the object of stifling or punishing free exercise. We make these observations not to reargue the position of the majority in *Smith* but to illustrate the substantive alteration of its holding attempted by the RFRA. Even assuming RFRA would be interpreted in effect to mandate some lesser test, say, one equivalent to intermediate scrutiny, the statute nevertheless would require searching judicial scrutiny of state law with the attendant likelihood of invalidation. This is a considerable congressional intrusion into the States' traditional prerogatives and general authority to regulate for the health and welfare of their citizens.

The substantial costs RFRA exacts, both in practical terms of imposing a heavy litigation burden on the States and in terms of curtailing their traditional general regulatory power, far exceed any pattern or practice of unconstitutional conduct under the Free Exercise Clause as interpreted in *Smith*. Simply put, RFRA is not designed to identify and counteract state laws likely to be unconstitutional because of their treatment of religion. In most cases, the state laws to which RFRA applies are not ones which will have been motivated by religious bigotry. If a state law disproportionately burdened a particular class of religious observers, this circumstance might be evidence of an impermissible legislative motive. RFRA's substantial-burden test, however, is not even a discriminatory-effects or disparate-impact test. It is a reality of the modern regulatory state that numerous state laws, such as the zoning regulations at issue here, impose a substantial burden on a large class of individuals. When the exercise of religion has been burdened in an incidental way by a law of general application, it does not follow that the persons affected have been burdened anymore than other citizens, let alone burdened because of their religious beliefs. In addition, the Act imposes in every case a least restrictive means requirement — a requirement that was not used in the pre-*Smith* jurisprudence RFRA purported to codify — which also indicates that the legislation is broader than is appropriate if the goal is to prevent and remedy constitutional violations.

When Congress acts within its sphere of power and responsibilities, it has not just the right but the duty to make its own informed judgment on the meaning and force of the Constitution. This has been clear from the early days of the Republic. In 1789, when a Member of the House of Representatives objected to a debate on the constitutionality of legislation based on the theory that "it would be officious" to consider the constitutionality of a measure that did not affect the House, James Madison explained that "it is incontrovertibly of as much importance to this branch of the Government as to any other, that the constitution should be preserved entire. It is our duty." 1 Annals of Congress 500 (1789). Were it otherwise, we would not afford Congress the presumption of validity its enactments now enjoy.

Our national experience teaches that the Constitution is preserved best when each part of the Government respects both the Constitution and the proper actions and determinations of the other branches. . . . When the political branches of the Government act against the background of a judicial interpretation of the Constitution already issued, it must be understood that in later cases and controversies the Court will treat its precedents with the respect due them under settled principles, including *stare decisis,* and contrary expectations must be disappointed. RFRA was designed to control cases and controversies, such as the one before us; but as the provisions of the federal statute here involved are beyond congressional authority, it is this Court's precedent, not RFRA, which must control.

It is for Congress in the first instance to "determin[e] whether and what legislation is needed to secure the guarantees of the Fourteenth Amendment," and its conclusions are entitled to much deference. *Katzenbach v. Morgan,* 384 U.S. at 651. Congress' discretion is not unlimited, however, and the courts retain the power, as they have since *Marbury v. Madison,* to determine if Congress has exceeded its authority under the Constitution. Broad as the power of Congress is under the Enforcement Clause of the Fourteenth Amendment, RFRA contradicts vital principles necessary to maintain separation of powers and the federal balance. The judgment of the Court of Appeals sustaining the Act's constitutionality is reversed.

JUSTICE STEVENS, concurring.

In my opinion, the Religious Freedom Restoration Act . . . is a "law respecting an establishment of religion" that violates the First Amendment to the Constitution. . . .

JUSTICE SCALIA, with whom JUSTICE STEVENS joins, concurring in part.

I write to respond briefly to the claim of Justice O'Connor's dissent . . . that historical materials support a result contrary to the one reached in *Employment Div., Dept. of Human Resources of Ore. v. Smith,* 494 U.S. 872 (1990). . . .

. . . .

JUSTICE O'CONNOR, with whom JUSTICE BREYER joins except as to the first paragraph of Part I, dissenting.

I dissent from the Court's disposition of this case. . . . I remain of the view that *Smith* was wrongly decided, and I would use this case to reexamine the Court's holding there. . . .

I

I agree with much of the reasoning set forth in Part III-A of the Court's opinion. Indeed, if I agreed with the Court's standard in *Smith*, I would join the opinion. As the Court's careful and thorough historical analysis shows, Congress lacks the "power to decree the *substance* of the Fourteenth Amendment's restrictions on the States." Rather, its power under § 5 of the Fourteenth Amendment extends only to *enforcing* the Amendment's provisions. In short, Congress lacks the ability independently to define or expand the scope of constitutional rights by statute. . . . [W]hen it enacts legislation in furtherance of its delegated powers, Congress must make its judgments consistent with this Court's exposition of the Constitution and with the limits placed on its legislative authority by provisions such as the Fourteenth Amendment.

. . . .

Stare decisis concerns should not prevent us from revisiting our holding in *Smith*. " '[S]tare decisis* is a principle of policy and not a mechanical formula of adherence to the latest decision, however recent and questionable, when such adherence involves collision with a prior doctrine more embracing in its scope, intrinsically sounder, and verified by experience.' " *Adarand Constructors, Inc. v. Pena*, 515 U.S. 200, 231 (1995). . . .

. . . .

JUSTICE SOUTER, dissenting.

. . . For the reasons stated in my opinion in *Church of Lukumi Babalu Aye, Inc. v. Hialeah*, 508 U.S. 520, 564–77 (1993) (opinion concurring in part and concurring in judgment), I have serious doubts about the precedential value of the *Smith* rule and its entitlement to adherence. . . .

JUSTICE BREYER, dissenting.

. . . I do not, however, find it necessary to consider the question whether, assuming *Smith* is correct, § 5 of the Fourteenth Amendment would authorize Congress to enact the legislation before us. Thus, while I agree with some of the views expressed in the first paragraph of Part I of Justice O'Connor's dissent, I do not necessarily agree with all of them. I therefore join Justice O'Connor's dissent, with the exception of the first paragraph of Part I.

Exercise 16:

Consider the following matters in connection with *City of Boerne*:

(1)   After the Supreme Court decided *United States v. Lopez* in 1995, it became significantly more important to identify the scope of other legislative powers. When, in 1996, the Court in *Seminole Tribe* interpreted the power of Congress to "abrogate" Eleventh Amendment immunity as limited to constitutional grants of legislative power adopted subsequent to the Eleventh Amendment, the scope of legislative power under Section 5 of the Fourteenth Amendment became even more important. In light of those then-recent developments, in 1997, the Court's decision in *City of Boerne* had immediate implications for *both* the power of Congress to address substantive issues *and* the range of remedies available to Congress to enforce its substantive policies. As a consequence,

it is very important to identify the bases for the Court's decision. What issues in the case were dispositive?

(2)   The First Amendment prohibits Congress from making laws "prohibiting the free exercise" of religion. In 1940, the Supreme Court held that the Due Process Clause of the Fourteenth Amendment served to "incorporate" that individual right as a limitation on the power of States as well. Most obviously, the Free Exercise Clause prohibits government from enacting laws with the intent of burdening specific religions. Thus, for example, it would be problematic for a city to bar a specific religious group from establishing a place of worship within its limits while permitting other religious groups to freely do so. Does the Free Exercise Clause do more than simply prohibit such laws that intentionally discriminate against a particular religion? A series of cases presented the question whether government was required to make an exception to a law that, on its face, did not discriminate against religion but which, in practice, imposed a burden on religious exercise. For example, assume that a town or county (or, during Prohibition, the entire nation) adopted the public policy that alcohol was a social harm. In order to implement that policy, assume the government enacted a law criminalizing, anywhere within its territory, the purchase, sale, consumption, or possession of any "alcoholic beverage or spirit." It seems extremely unlikely that any such law would have been adopted with the purpose of burdening any particular religious group. Nonetheless, the law literally criminalizes the serving of wine in religious ceremonies, such as communion. Does the Free Exercise Clause require an exception to an otherwise blanket prohibition on consumption of alcohol? In a series of cases — including *Sherbert v. Verner* (1963) and *Wisconsin v. Yoder* (1972) — the Court held that at least sometimes even a broadly applicable law adopted for a purpose having nothing to do with religion would have to permit an exception for religious practices. When the rule of those cases applied, government was required to identify a "compelling governmental interest" to support the law and to demonstrate that the law adopted "was narrowly tailored to achieve" that end. One way to "narrowly tailor" a law would be to expressly make exceptions for religious activity that was incidentally burdened. So, our hypothetical law against consumption of alcohol may well have been written with an express exception for alcohol used in religious ceremonies. With such an exception, the law would be much more likely to be upheld than if it had to satisfy the stringent compelling interest standard.

In 1990, the Supreme Court decided a case in which the law at issue did not make any express exception from its general terms for burdens incidentally imposed on religion. In *Department of Human Resources of Oregon v. Smith,* the Court held that the approach of *Sherbert* only applied when some additional constitutional interest was at stake co-joined with the Free Exercise Clause claim. (The majority asserted that a careful reading of its precedents confirmed that limit.) When the Free Exercise Clause interest stood alone, however, government was not required to make exceptions to a generally applicable law that had been adopted without the intent of discriminating against religion. Under that approach, our hypothetical law against consumption of alcohol may well have been constitutional even if it permitted no exception for communion or other religious uses.

Congress responded to the *Smith* decision by enacting RFRA which would have required government (federal, State, and local) to apply the compelling governmental interest test to all laws which arguably placed an indirect burden on religion regardless of whether any additional constitutional interest was at stake.

When Congress legislated, in 1993, which pre-dated the Supreme Court's decision in *United States v. Lopez*, could Congress have relied upon its power to regulate commerce as a basis for RFRA? What problems, if any, would you anticipate if Congress had acted on that basis?

Is there any other federal legislative power that Congress may have more reliably invoked as a basis for RFRA?

(3)   Did *either* the City of Boerne's enactment of its historic preservation ordinance *or* the denial of a building permit for alteration of a historic church violate the Free Exercise Clause as construed in *Smith*?

(4)   Was it the position of the majority that, under Section 5 of the Fourteenth Amendment, Congress was authorized only to prohibit matters that violate the substantive terms of the Fourteenth Amendment? Was it the position of the majority that, under Section 5 of the Fourteenth Amendment, even if Congress would otherwise be authorized to legislate, its authority must yield when the legislation would intrude into traditional areas of State concern?

(5)   Is the text of the Fourteenth Amendment consistent with congressional power to define the meaning of that Amendment's substantive limitations on State action? Why or why not?

(6)   Is the drafting history of the Fourteenth Amendment consistent with congressional power to define the meaning of that Amendment's substantive limitations on State action? Why or why not?

(7)   Would construction of the Fourteenth Amendment to grant Congress power to define the meaning of that Amendment's substantive limitations on State action be consistent with the structure of government created by the Constitution as a whole? Why or why not?

(8)   Would construction of the Fourteenth Amendment to grant Congress power to define the meaning of that Amendment's substantive limitations on State action be consistent with nearly-contemporaneous congressional construction of its power? Why or why not? Should that matter?

(9)   Would construction of the Fourteenth Amendment to grant Congress power to define the meaning of that Amendment's substantive limitations on State action be consistent with the Supreme Court's precedents? Why or why not?

(10)   What test did the majority formulate to distinguish proper exercises of power under Section 5?

(11)   Was the test articulated by the majority consistent with the outcome in *Katzenbach v. Morgan*?

(12)   **In advance of class**, redraft RFRA as an exercise of Section Five power consistent with the test applied by the majority.

THE SYNERGIES OF *SEMINOLE TRIBE, CITY OF BOERNE,* AND *LOPEZ*

A. *The Scope of Seminole Tribe*

Three years after the *Seminole Tribe* decision, the Supreme Court reaffirmed that ruling in a trilogy of cases decided by the same 5-4 split.

In *Florida Prepaid Postsecondary Education Expense Board v. College Savings Bank*, 527 U.S. 627 (1999), the Court held that neither the Commerce Clause nor the Patent Clause authorized Congress to abrogate State immunity in federal court for suits alleging patent infringement. The Court further held that under Section Five of the Fourteenth Amendment, Congress lacked the power to authorize such actions as a means to ensure due process for the property reflected in the patent. This ruling precluded Congress from circumventing *Seminole Tribe* by recharacterizing exercises of Article I powers as interests subject to protection under the Due Process Clause.

The Court rejected the argument that a "uniform remedy" under which States were placed "on the same footing" as private parties was sufficient to justify abrogation.

In *College Savings Bank v. Florida Prepaid Postsecondary Education Expense Board,* 527 U.S. 666 (1999), the Court held that the State's participation in the market for prepaid education did not constitute waiver of the State's immunity, and that Congress did not validly abrogate the State's immunity by the Trademark Remedy Clarification Act. This ruling limited the power of Court to infer a "waiver" where Congress could not directly, under *Seminole Tribe,* abrogate immunity.

In *Alden v. Maine,* 527 U.S. 706 (1999), the Court held that Congress lacked power to strip States of immunity in the courts of their own State where Congress similarly lacked power to strip States of Eleventh Amendment immunity. The statute there at issue was the federal Fair Labor Standards Act. This ruling prevented Congress from circumventing *Seminole Tribe* by subjecting States to suit on federal causes of action in State court.

Then, in *Federal Maritime Commission v. South Carolina State Ports Authority,* 535 U.S. 743 (2002), the Court held that a federal agency lacked authority to adjudicate a case by a private company brought against a State where the Eleventh Amendment would bar suit in an Article III court. The Court aligned along the same 5-4 split. This ruling foreclosed another possible means of circumventing *Seminole Tribe.*

In her final Term on the Court, Justice O'Connor joined with the four dissenting Justices to craft an exception to the broad language of *Seminole Tribe* in *Central Virginia Community College v. Katz,* 546 U.S. 356 (2006). The issue presented was whether a bankruptcy trustee could bring suit against a State to recover the debtor's preferential transfer of assets to the State. The Court held that the Bankruptcy Clause, Art. I, § 8, cl. 4, not only authorized federal legislation but contemplated the States' surrender of immunity in bankruptcy proceedings, justified, in part, by the *in rem* nature of most bankruptcy matters. The five-Justice majority expressly stressed the unique history of the bankruptcy power in reaching this conclusion.

B. *The Implication of City of Boerne for Seminole Tribe*

At the same time that the Court issued a series of rulings regarding the scope of *Seminole Tribe,* the Court decided a series of cases illustrating the combined consequences of *Seminole Tribe* and *City of Boerne.*

As noted above, in *Florida Prepaid,* 527 U.S. 627 (1999), the Court applied the congruence and proportionality test of *City of Boerne* to preclude recharacterization of legislation designed to protect intellectual property into a Due Process Clause claim. The consequence of doing so was that the statute did not fit within the limited scope of situations where *Seminole Tribe* acknowledged Congress could abrogate state immunity.

In *Kimel v. Florida Board of Regents,* 528 U.S. 62 (2000), the Court addressed a suit for money damages brought by employees against their State-government employer under the Age Discrimination in Employment Act (ADEA). The Court had previously held that the ADEA was an exercise of the commerce power. After *Seminole Tribe,* that constitutional basis for the legislation did not authorize abrogation of Eleventh Amendment immunity. The Court thus considered whether the ADEA also could be upheld under Section Five of the Fourteenth Amendment. Applying *City of Boerne,* the Court found that the ADEA lacked congruence and proportionality to any pattern of unconstitutional age discrimination by States and local governments. As such, Congress' effort failed to abrogate immunity. Part IV of the Court's opinion addressing these issues was decided by the same 5-4 majority as in *Seminole Tribe.*

In *Board of Trustees of the University of Alabama v. Garrett,* 531 U.S. 356 (2001), the Court evaluated a claim under Title I of the Americans with Disabilities Act (ADA), the portion of the ADA addressing discrimination in employment. State employees sued their employer for money damages. The Court reiterated that under its Article I powers, Congress could not abrogate Eleventh Amendment immunity (relying upon *Seminole Tribe*) and proceeded to consider whether the ADA was a valid exercise of Section Five of the Fourteenth Amendment. The Court had previously held that the class of disabled individuals did not benefit from any special protection under the Equal Protection Clause. Although the legislative record included material regarding discrimination by States and local government on the basis of disability, the Court observed that virtually all such evidence addressed the provision of governmental services rather than governmental employment. 531 U.S. at 371 n.7. Finding no pattern of unconstitutional discrimination in employment by States on the basis of disability, the same 5-Justice majority as in *Seminole Tribe* concluded that Title I of the ADA lacked congruence and proportionality under *City of Boerne*. The purported abrogation of State immunity was declared invalid. In a footnote, the Court reserved judgment on whether portions of the ADA directed to the provision of governmental services (such as Title II) could be upheld under Section Five. *See* 531 U.S. at 360 n.1.

In *Nevada Department of Human Resources v. Hibbs*, 538 U.S. 721 (2003), the Court considered a suit for money damages brought by employees against their State-government employer under the federal Family and Medical Leave Act (FMLA). The Court upheld the abrogation of Eleventh Amendment immunity (consistent with *Seminole Tribe*), distinguishing the gender-based discrimination that served as the premise of the FLRA from the age discrimination at issue in the ADEA and the disability-based discrimination at issue in the ADA, both of which the Court had previously rejected as classifications subject to special scrutiny under the Equal Protection Clause. The Court had previously determined that gender was an appropriate classification for greater protection under the Equal Protection Clause. Observing that Congress considered significant evidence of a long and extensive history of gender-based discrimination in the administration of leave benefits by State employers, the Court concluded that the FLRA was a congruent and proportional response (under *City of Boerne*). Chief Justice Rehnquist and Justice O'Connor joined with the four dissenting Justices in *Seminole Tribe* to produce this result.

The following Term, in *Tennessee v. Lane*, 541 U.S. 509 (2004), the Court addressed the issue left open in *Garrett* and upheld abrogation of Eleventh Amendment immunity under Title II of the ADA. Justice O'Connor joined with the four dissenting Justices in *Seminole Tribe*. The Court held that Title II — which addressed discrimination in the provision of public services — was supported by adequate legislative findings of discrimination against the disabled in terms of physical accessibility that the legislation was congruent and proportional under Section Five. The case involved the accessibility of courthouses to two wheelchair-bound individuals: a criminal defendant and a court reporter. The Court observed that, in such a setting, fundamental rights were at issue, including the right of access to the courts, to a meaningful opportunity to be heard, and to confront accusing witnesses. The Court limited its holding to that context:

> Whatever might be said about Title II's other applications, the question presented in this case is . . . whether Congress had the power under § 5 to enforce the constitutional right of access to the courts. Because we find that Title II unquestionably is valid § 5 legislation as it applies to the class of cases implicating the accessibility of judicial services, we need go no further.

Id. at 530–31. Thus, the Court held that Title II was a congruent and proportional response to the discrimination.

Together, *Hibbs* and *Tennessee v. Lane* illustrate that Congress retains significant power under Section Five even within the boundary marked by *City of Boerne*.

C. *The Combined Impact of Lopez and City of Boerne*

In *United States v. Morrison*, 529 U.S. 598 (2000), by the same 5-4 majority, the Court not only held that the federal civil remedy in the Violence Against Women Act (VAWA) exceeded the scope of the commerce power (relying upon *Lopez*) but that it also could not be justified under Section Five of the Fourteenth Amendment (relying upon *City of Boerne*). The result in that case depended upon the limitations of congressional power articulated in both *Lopez* and *City of Boerne*. The absence of *either* limitation would have permitted Congress to enact the provision at issue. (But, with respect to actions brought against States, only if VAWA were upheld under Section Five would it qualify for abrogation of immunity under *Seminole Tribe*.)

As this long list of cases since 1999 illustrates, the law in this area has had little time to settle. The sharp division on the Court producing results by slim margins adds to the problem of discerning the nuances of current doctrine. The retirement of Justice O'Connor and the death of Chief Justice Rehnquist add to the potential confusion.

TABLE OF CASES

[References are to pages]

[References are to pages]

FEDERAL CONSTITUTIONAL LAW

[References are to pages.]

A

ADA (See AMERICANS WITH DISABILITY ACT (ADA))

ADEA (See AGE DISCRIMINATION IN EMPLOYMENT ACT (ADEA))

AGE DISCRIMINATION IN EMPLOYMENT ACT (ADEA)
Fourteenth Amendment Section 5, validity under . . . 226

AGRICULTURE
Agricultural Adjustment Act of 1933, constitutionality of processing taxes under . . . 53-62
Commerce regulation and government's right to exert quotas on agriculture products . . . 148-152
Taxation of farm products . . . 53-62

AIRPORTS
Separation of Powers issue and transfer of federally owned and operated airports to local control . . . 73-80

ALCOHOL
Drinking age, conditioning award of federal highway spending funds on adoption of minimum . . . 67-71
Prohibition against manufacture, sale or transportation of intoxicating liquors . . . 13
Repeal of Amendment XVIII prohibiting manufacture, sale or transportation of intoxicating liquor . . . 14

AMERICANS WITH DISABILITY ACT (ADA)
Sovereign immunity under Eleventh Amendment, abrogation of . . . 226-227

ASSEMBLY, FREEDOM OF
Bill of Rights . . . 9

ATTORNEYS
Bill of Rights, right to counsel . . . 9

B

BAIL
Bill of Rights, prohibition against imposition of excessive bail or fines . . . 9

BANKS AND BANKING
Chartering national bank
    Congressional authority . . . 101-113
    Constitutional convention debates on . . . 88-100
First Bank of the United States, Alexander Hamilton's opinion on constitutionality of . . . 125-126
Taxation
    Exemption from state tax levied on bank's real assets . . . 115-117
    National banks chartered in state . . . 100-112

BILL OF RIGHTS
Generally . . . 9
Arms, right to keep and bear . . . 9
Assembly, freedom of . . . 9
Counsel, right to . . . 9
Cruel and unusual punishment, prohibition against . . . 9
Double jeopardy, prohibition against . . . 9
Due process . . . 9
Excessive bail or fines, prohibition against imposition of . . . 9
Grand jury, requirement of indictment by . . . 9
Income tax, levy of . . . 12
Jury trial . . . 9
Petition, freedom to . . . 9
Protection under . . . 9-16
Reconstruction Amendments . . . 11-12
Religion, freedom of . . . 9
Search and seizure, prohibition against unreasonable . . . 9
Self-incrimination, prohibition against, . . . 9
Senate, composition of . . . 12
Slavery, abolishment under Amendment XIII . . . 11
Soldier, quartering in house . . . 9
Speech, freedom of . . . 9
Speedy trial . . . 9
States, reservation of powers to . . . 9
Text . . . 9

BONDS
Taxation immunity doctrine and federal taxation of interest earned on state bonds, intergovernmental . . . 120-124

C

CIVIL RIGHTS ACT OF 1964
Interstate Commerce clause as basis for enacting . . . 153-161

CLEAN WATER ACT
Commerce power, exceeding scope of . . . 183

COMMERCE REGULATION
Generally . . . 125-184
Agriculture products, government's right to exert quotas on . . . 148-152
Civil Rights Act of 1964 enactment based on . . . 153-161
Clean Water Act exceeding scope of commerce power . . . 183
Commerce defined . . . 129-130; 140-141
Controlled Substances Act exceeding scope of commerce power . . . 183
Dormant Commerce Clause . . . 142-143
Fair Labor Standards Act, Supreme Court upholding validity of . . . 143-148

[References are to pages.]

[References are to pages.]

[References are to pages.]

[References are to pages.]